Brown, Fraser & Associates

Sweeter than Honey: Harnessing the Power of Entertainment, Second Edition

ISBN 978-0-9860495-5-2

This title is also available as an Amazon e-book

Library of Congress Cataloging-in-Publication Data

Brown, William J.

Sweeter than Honey: Harnessing the Power of Entertainment, Second Edition

---

Cover Design: *William J. Brown*

Cover Photography: William J. Brown

Printed in the United States of America

Table of Contents

Sweeter than Honey Index & Copyright Information

Dedication

Dedicated to my parents, William G. Brown and Elizabeth A. Brown, who have given me a great heritage by encouraging me to ask questions, to seek knowledge, to value people and their experiences, to enjoy entertainment, and to discover how we learn.

Preface

In the first edition of *Sweeter than Honey* published seven years ago, I sought to do something unique, so I made it an interactive eBook with many dozens of web links. Many people requested a hard copy edition of the book, but I made it exclusively online and interactive. I subsequently discovered many of my fellow academics and many graduate students still like hard copies of books and are not fond of reading books electronically. Now, seven years later, I have taken out the web links and I am publishing a traditional paperback print version and eBook version.

I noted in the preface of the first edition that during the last three decades of the twentieth century, academic scholars and media pundits produced a plethora of studies and commentaries on the harmful effects of entertainment media. We have learned that film can prop up dictatorships, television can present a dangerous world that encourages aggressive behavior and violence, internet pornography can foster the objectification and abuse of women and video games can produce social isolation. While all the negative influences of the mass media attracted research dollars and news headlines, the positive influences of media have been under-studied and under-reported. That trend continues into the 21st century. Despite all of the harmful influences of entertainment, stories about the powerful influence of entertainment for good are not difficult to find. Yet, many of these stories remain either unknown or underappreciated.

You will read some of these stories in this book. Its purpose is to help you to understand why entertainment is the most powerful educator of today, and how it can be harnessed for our good. You will learn how entertainment is increasing literacy, helping communities and families to plan their growth, reducing high-risk sexual behavior and HIV/AIDS, raising the status of women, promoting cancer prevention, reinforcing social equality, improving he environment, and helping to raise the quality of life throughout the world. Although the findings and principles presented in this book are based on social science theory and research, the fascinating experiences and anecdotes from many different countries provide a more nuanced picture of how entertainment is changing the world, providing a powerful medicine to society. Indeed, entertainment can be sweeter than honey.

William J. Brown
Chesapeake, Virginia
October 22, 2020

Acknowledgments

There are so many people to thank who encouraged me during this book writing journey. In my first edition, I had voluminous materials on entertainment-education from my more than 25 years of research and teaching on this subject. These materials included books, academic articles, academic book chapters, dissertations, masters theses, newspaper articles, web articles, videotapes, DVDs, games, comics, and hundreds of examples of dramas and stories used to promote social change through radio programs, television programs, short films, feature films, and drama programs available through websites. The task seemed overwhelming and my initial two-year goal turned into a five-year writing project. The finish line seemed to be constantly moving as my 10K race turned into a marathon. There are many people to thank.

First, there is my wife Nancy and my daughters and their husbands, Natalie and Aaron and Heidi and John, who are a constant joy and support to me. Nancy has lived and breathed the concepts and practices of entertainment-education with me throughout the world. Next, my friends Terry Lindvall and Ben Fraser constantly encouraged me to write this book. Terry helped me to brainstorm possible titles and Ben collaborated with me on entertainment-education research in many countries. Both Terry and Ben's scholarship address important aspects of using entertainment for social change. All three of us loved the concept of sweeter than honey. Ben's recently published book, *Hide & Seek: The Sacred Arts of Indirect Communication,* explains many of the philosophical foundations of indirect communication, and much entertainment-education is indirect. His book should be considered as a companion book to *Sweeter than Honey*; or this book is a companion book to his work.

In addition to Dr. Lindvall and Dr. Fraser, there are a mighty (or motley) group of colleagues who share breakfast on Wednesday mornings for fellowship and prayer for many years. When COVID-19 hit this year, we moved our group to Friday mornings online. During our meetings, we share our ideas, praise the good ones and mock the bad ones, and discuss writing projects. The ebb and flow of this group has involved many different people over many years, but the regulars have been a great blessing to me, including Terry, Ben, Dr. Dennis Bounds, Dr. Gil Elvgren, Professor John Lawing, and Professor Andrew Quicke; and this year Dr. Harry Sova, Dr. George Selig, Dr. Michael Graves, and Professor James Duane have been joining us, with an occasional visit from Dr. David Clark, the founding Dean of our School of Communication and the Arts at Regent University.

This book slowly blossomed as a direct result of the exceptional work of my friends, colleagues and mentors that have collaborated with me on scholarly writings and projects and whose work I have drawn much from. These include my mentors at the University of Southern California, Dr. Everett M. Rogers, the former Walter H. Annenberg Professor of

Communication at the Annenberg School for Communication, and Dr. Michael J. Cody, another great scholar recognized by USC for his exceptional mentoring of graduate students. Michael directed my doctoral dissertation on India's first long-running television soap opera designed to promote social change. My dissertation research was only possible through the generous spirit of my friend and colleague, Dr. Arvind Singhal, who was willing to collaborate on research of the same television program in his home nation of India. Dr. Singhal and Dr. Rogers published one of the first books and the most widely cited book on entertainment-education in 1999. I have drawn numerous examples from Arvind's work and he has been a continual personal and professional source of inspiration to me.

Dr. Martine Bouman, another wonderful friend and colleague, contributed much to enabling me to write this book. Through her facilitation of my Fulbright work in the Netherlands at the Center for Media and Health in Gouda, I have been able to learn about the practical collaboration that is needed between media professionals and communication scholars to produce effective entertainment media for social change. Martine and Peter Fokker have been the most gracious hosts who made Nancy and I feel so much at home during our many visits to the Netherlands to collaborate on entertainment-education activities and they facilitated my first Fulbright visiting scholar award.

I also want to thank Dr. Asbjorn Simonnes, who arranged my second Fulbright visiting award to Norway to lecture on entertainment-education and to collaborate on the beginnings of a project on the contributions of Hans Nielsen Hauge to the transformation of Norway. Asbjorn and his wife, Inger Tove, were amazing hosts and gave Nancy and I many wonderful memories as we travelled to several different cities in western Norway.

I also want to thank the administration at Regent University, including my current and past deans, for supporting my academic work and travels. I especially thank my administrative assistants during the past 20 years, especially Suzanne Morton, Diane Clark, and Margie Ackerman, for their invaluable service.

Thanks to the film directing and producing skills of Dr. Lorene Wales and Kenny Jackson, the scriptwriting skills of Gil Elvgren and Steve Silvester, funding from the U.S. Department of Defense and the Newington Cropsey Foundation, the executive producing skills of Terry Lindvall, the research skills of Ben Fraser, and the leadership of Dr. Steven Kiruswa, a Member of Parliament in Tanzania, I have been directly involved in multiple award-winning entertainment-education film projects in the U.S. and Africa. I thank all those who worked with us on these projects.

Finally, I thank my students, especially the ones that have worked with me on entertainment-education projects and doctoral dissertations. As you will see through my liberal citations of your dissertations, I have learned much from all of you and have enjoyed the journeys we have taken to learn more about how to harness the power of entertainment for good.

Introduction

So, he said to them, "Out of the eater came something to eat, and out of the strong came something sweet." Now for three days they could not explain the riddle. So the men of the city said to him on the seventh day before the sun went down, "What is sweeter than honey? And what is stronger than a lion?"

... Judges 14: 14, 18

When Sampson posed this riddle to the men of Timnah in the land of Philistine more than 3000 years ago, he was not trying to become the first Alex Trebek. Long before television and the popular game show Jeopardy, entertainment was used as a means of attracting the attention of people, providing information, and serving as an educational forum. Sampson's riddle effectively set the agenda for what would be discussed in the community of Timnah, offering a reward of thirty changes of clothes to whoever could solve the riddle. The intellectual puzzle, much like the modern television game show, provided a means for engaging a community.

Distinguished media scholar Neil Postman, author of 21 books and former professor at New York University, was asked a few years before his death about the educational influence of commercial television. He responded, "All television programs educate, even television commercials." Much like the parables Jesus told to teach the kingdom of God, sophisticated advertising agencies spend billions of dollars constructing parables to sell us every kind of product imaginable, convincing us that buying the right mouthwash is the immediate solution to fixing an unsuccessful romance, buying the right shampoo will launch a successful acting career, using the mail services will ensure the success of a home business, and wearing the right tennis shoe will enable us to achieve the dream of becoming a wealthy professional athlete.

There is no doubt that effective commercials are entertaining. There is also no doubt that entertaining commercials educate us in a way that persuades us to part with something of great value, our money. If entertainment persuades and educates, then why not use the power of entertainment to promote the values, beliefs, and cultural symbols that will create the kind of society we want? That question is being answered throughout the world by an explosion of entertainment media and programs that are designed to both educate and influence hundreds of millions of people.

What is sweeter than honey? It is a metaphor for describing how entertainment media and the arts can function as a beneficial educational influence in society. Entertainment media products, for many good reasons, have been ridiculed by academics, vilified by moral educators, and attacked by the very public that consume them. Like the Titanic barreling full throttle toward the iceberg of moral incoherence, we have commissioned our entertainment industry to apply the best technology to enhance our pleasure, but have invested very little into charting the waters of moral values, moral character, and moral culture. Although the public has complained for decades about individual television programs, such protests are likened to complaints about a dinner entree on the Titanic. The entertainment industry needs society's assistance in carefully charting its direction if it is to avoid its demise as a constructive moral force in society.

Moral responsibility is not a tasty medicine. It is inconsistent with our desires for the forbidden fruits of greed, lust, and the pride of life. Being reminded that supreme selfishness violates the humanity and happiness of others is like taking a spoonful of castor oil, a nauseating medicine of the twentieth century. Our multi-billion-dollar pharmaceutical companies have solved this problem. As Dick Van Dyke and Julie Andrews sang in *Mary Poppins*, "Just a spoonful of sugar helps the medicine go down in the most delightful way." If our culture cannot survive without a strong sense of moral responsibility and if entertainment media are powerful moral educators of today, then why not at least make the moral medicine we have to take taste good by sweetening it with enjoyable entertainment quality?

What is stronger than a lion? The second part of the answer to Sampson's riddle also serves as a metaphor for entertainment. The lion rules the animal kingdom in which it lives. Its social influence on all other animals is unmistakable. Likewise, entertainment dominates the social lives of people throughout the world. We cannot escape its influence. Entertainment is the most powerful social force in our culture.

Rather than seeing entertainment as an inevitably poor moral educator and source of mindless distraction, we need to see it as a valuable public and private resource that can enrich our lives by contributing to a more just, more responsible, and more caring society. Before we discard the idea that entertainment can never promote a serious discussion of moral behavior and its consequences, we need to historically assess the evidence. Has entertainment effectively contributed to moral education in the past? Have countries other than the United States had any success with the use of entertainment media to address moral and ethical issues; and in doing so, improve the quality of life? Are there examples today of how entertainment media can serve as powerful sources of learning that benefit society? This book will address each of these questions and will demonstrate why Pooh Bear goes after the honey even though the honey comes with the bees, representing the unpleasant circumstances of life. Will an audience that knows the medicine of moral education and learning is mixed with the sweetness of entertainment still consume the entertainment-education morsel? Like Edwin's weakness for Turkish taffy in Lewis' *The Lion, the Witch and the Wardrobe*, I think the answer to this question is "yes" and will explain why this is the case. Entertainment is central to our lives now and will be central to our lives for a long time to come. The more we learn how to use it for good, the better our lives will be.

Chapter 1
The Ubiquitous World of Entertainment

Early one nearly morning nearly two decades ago, my 17-year-old daughter woke up to her radio alarm tuned in to her favorite radio station. She listened to a couple of songs while in the bathroom getting herself ready to face the world, before grabbing her cell phone to check her voice mail to see what messages might have been left on her phone the previous evening after she turned it off. After coming downstairs to get herself some breakfast in the kitchen, she put a music CD in our CD player in the living room to play some of her morning music. After leaving the house, she drove to school, flicking through 4-5 different radio stations searching for some songs she liked. During her second bell in history class, her teacher showed a video about World War II. During lunch break, she went to the library to use the Internet to check the reviews of a recent film. Her last class was theater, where she watched several scenes from the 1998 film, "Shakespeare in Love." She also sent a text message to her friend about going to the movies with her in the evening.

On her way home from school, she listened to two of her favorite CDs, skipping around to specific songs she wanted to hear. Within minutes after returning home, she found the remote control to the downstairs television and turned it on to channel 67 – VH1. After watching a couple music videos while snacking on tortilla chips, she also checked out 15-20 other stations to see what was on, settling on a rerun of *Friends* on TBS.

Before the episode was finished, her best friend called her on her cell to see if she had checked the times for the film, *The Morning After*. She told her they could go together to the 7:30 showing at the Loews' multiplex. She finished Friends and ate dinner with us. She finally had a meaningful conversation without the use of media as she ate dinner with my wife and I and our younger daughter, although we did receive two calls from telemarketers during that time.

After dinner, our daughter went to the movie she had checked out earlier on the Internet and then stopped by a coffee house on the way home with her friend to listen to a couple of bands. She returned home at 11:00 p.m., just in time to make curfew on a school night. After briefly checking in with us for a five-minute conversation, she promptly logged onto her email account on the computer, answered some emails, and down-loaded two photographs and one song sent to her by friends. She finally went to bed at 11:45 p.m., having accumulated the following: total time learning from a teacher at school: 2 hours 27 minutes, total time interacting with parents: 46 minutes, total time consuming media or interacting with others through mediated communication: 6 hours and 52 minutes. This was all before Instagram, Facebook, YouTube and Twitter.

This description was a typical weekday in the life of my oldest daughter in 2002. Her younger sister experienced much of the same immersion into new communication technology. Now both daughters have their own children who will soon be entering their teenage years, and, due to their own experiences, they are seeking to help their children limit their complete immersion into a completely social mediated world. Our daughters didn't have to deal with social media; but their children will need to manage it or completely be overwhelmed by it. Many of you with teenage daughters and sons know that I am not exaggerating. Our children kept this intense media interactivity before the popularity of social networking sites, before YouTube, before Twitter, before iPhones and Samsung Galaxy, and before web blogs and podcasts became popular. Likewise, my oldest grandchildren's mediated lifestyle in the near future, with their mobile phone video cameras with 24/7 text messaging and access to hundreds of millions of websites, pictures, videos, social media posts, podcasts, video games, and so much more, will completely immerse them in a mediated world dominated by entertainment.

My wife and I, although we have learned to be proficient in using new communication technologies along with millions of other baby boomers, grew up in a world where entertainment consumption was a conscious activity, not like breathing air. For Generations Z, Y, and Millennials, those born in the mid to late 1980s through to the first decade of the 20th century, using media technologies for entertainment purposes requires little forethought – it is interwoven with all other activities throughout one's waking hours. Consider that in my opening example, both my daughters interacted with media more than with their teachers and parents combined. That is still the experience of most teenagers in the United States. Media are not just part of the landscape of their lives; they are the center of life. We live in an ocean of mediated reality that we learn to negotiate day to day.

In an average day, our children are exposed to thousands of advertisements and thousands of message appeals, telling them how to look, what to wear, what to drive, what to eat, what to drink, what to watch, and what music to listen to when you want to relax. More specifically, young people today are told what is expected of them on a first or second date, how they should think about sex, what they should believe about historical events, and how to interact with their parents. It's troublesome to think that television and film productions teach children how they should interact with their parents, siblings, and friends.

Even more disconcerting, is to know that by the end of each day, impressionable teenage daughters and sons throughout the world will have been bombarded by sexual images, graphic song lyrics, violent visual scenes, and highly politicized news, blurring fact and fiction, real people and fictional characters, news stories and reality television programs. Unfortunately, they will consume most of these visual images without adequate time to assess them critically. They will not think carefully about mimicking anorexic looking female models, which have been banned in some countries like Israel[i]; or that such models in product advertising communicate that approval from the opposite sex comes as a result of being thin. They will not have time to process the provocative clothing advertised and modeled by the new celebrity sensations who will take the place of Britney Spears, Christiana Aguilera, J-Lo, and Beyonce in the new music videos that will be produced. They will not have the knowledge to understand exactly how the producers of the reality show they watch manipulate the environment to make the religious participant look stupid. Neither will they be able to perceive that the underlying message of the music video they had watched that day was that their parents will never be able to understand them; or that their parents only want to limit their freedoms.

My two daughters are not atypical in their media consumption, a consumption that exposes them to hundreds of competing positive and negative social influences every day. Not including cell phone use, the five activities that take up the most time in the lives of the average American besides sleeping (6.1 hours) and working (6.6 hours) are: watching television (3 hours), using the Internet on a home computer (2.4 hours), listening to the radio (1.7 hours) and reading books (1.5 hours).[1] Since there are not enough hours on the day to consume all this media, most Americans are multi-tasking and consuming multiple forms of media at the same time, especially teenagers. If every teenager had the time and skills to analyze the messages they were exposed to, they would be astounded. Most of the messages they consume are not flattering to them and regard them as not very intelligent. Other messages will be affirming, promoting healthy thoughts, important values, and positive self-esteem. Most media consumers are only partially aware of the messages to which they are exposed daily. People consume entertainment as a natural part of everyday life that does not require much thought. Media scholars Todd Gitlin,[2] Neal Gabler,[3] and more recently James Potter[4] document the prolific growth of entertainment media worldwide; which immerses much of the world in a continuous stream of sounds, images, and text that form our collective worldviews, beliefs, and behavior. Although people are strategic in their media use, unwanted exposure to media messages is a continual occurrence.

Global expansion of media

Media have expanded at an unprecedented rate during the past couple of decades. By 2010, there were more than one billion television viewers in China and another billion viewers in India. The U.S., Russia and Great Britain add another 660 million viewers. In addition to the

---

i Reynolds, Emma. "Underweight Models BANNED in Israel to Fight Anorexia: New law Forces Women in Ads to Stay Healthy." *Daily Mail.* Accessed Sept. 7, 2020. https://www.dailymail.co.uk/news/article-2256025/Underweight-models-BANNED-Israel-fight-anorexia-New-law-forces-women-ads-stay-healthy-faked-images-identified-too.html

phenomenal growth in the world's two most populous nations, television audiences are growing the most in heavily populated developing countries like Indonesia, Pakistan and Nigeria. While television is expanding its reach, so is the Internet. The U.S had more than 186 million Internet users by the end of 2004, and India had more than 37 million users. In 2005, there were more than 300 million people using the Internet as many cell phone users in China as the population of the U.S. By the end of 2010, the number of internet users surpassed two billion people and is rapidly increasing.[5] Now, in 2020, media consumers around the world spend an average of 7.5 hours per day with media.[ii] American consumers tend to average more time than the world average, as Americans spend around 369 minutes per day consuming traditional media along with 363 minutes using digital media.[iii] The number of Internet and cell phone users will continue to grow rapidly until they rival the use of radio and television.

Media saturation is especially impacting the younger generation. In a Kaiser Family Foundation study of children and media use a decade ago, children ages 8-19 daily spent 4.5 hours per watching television, 2.5 hours consuming music, 1.5 hours on the computer, and more than one hour playing video games, in addition to other media activities like watching movies and reading books and magazines.[6] This totals an amazing cumulative 10 hours and 45 minutes of media consumption every day, an increase in more than two hours of media consumption since the previous study sponsored by the Kaiser Foundation in 2004.[7] Of course, to squeeze in that much media consumption in a 24-hour period, 29 percent of children's media consumption is multi-tasking, often while doing homework.[8]

The same media consumption growth experienced by children in the United States is taking place throughout the world, particularly with the growth of the Internet. Radio and television programs, movies, video games, music videos and virtually every form of media and artistic presentation can be accessed on the Internet. Connectivity to the Internet is a standard service in most office settings, providing employees with free access to the Internet. The proliferation of smart phones, tablets, and versatile laptop computers is expanding access to the Internet rapidly throughout the world. Even among the poorest of those living in the U.S. without personal computers at home and who do not have jobs can still gain internet access through public libraries and internet cafes. Even traditional office service centers such as Kinkos in the U.S. now offer internet access. Cities such as Santa Monica, California, Tokyo, and London have provided public computers linked to the Internet to provide internet access to the homeless.[iv] These kinds of public access points

---

ii Watson, Amy. "Media Use – Statistics and Facts." *Statista.* Accessed September 7, 2020. https://www.statista.com/topics/1536/media-use/

iii Ibid.

will increase in years to come, until the Internet will be available within easy walking distance from everyone's home, even if they live in public parks or in the street.

In the U.S., 84% of 8-18-year-olds had home Internet access in 2009, including one-third of those with access in their bedrooms.[9] Yet, the digital revolution was only beginning at that time. Those who can afford cell phones are now able to access the Internet anywhere their cell phone can get service. Each day more and more people link to the Internet through their cell phones. More than two-thirds of American children have cell phones and they view television programs 41 percent of the time through digital technology other than live TV.[10] Cellular companies want their customers to use their phones more; therefore, they will provide future systems that make it easy access to read your email on your cell phone display. Email will also be more than text as it becomes easier to record and input visual and audio information. Since cell phones already have cameras that can record still and moving pictures, very soon, standard cell phone features will include the ability to send person to person audio-visual messages that are stored and recalled like audio messages are today. In addition, real time conversations with full audio-visual interactivity, already available, will become common and affordable; enabling you to see the person you are talking to on your cell phone display. These technological innovations are already available but have not been widely diffused due to costs for increased bandwidth capacities. Once these capacities were expanded and made affordable, videoconferencing with multiple people on your cell phone has become a common practice. The video game industry is also booming. By 2009, about 4 out of every 10 U.S. households own a video game system, according to a report from the Cable & Telecommunications Association for Marketing.[11] Today, 59% of Americans play video games and 51% of households own two consoles on average.[v]

Popularity of online gaming also is rising, with 34 percent of American children and teens who use the Internet reporting that they visited a virtual world at least once a month in 2008, a percentage that is expected to rise to 42 percent in 2009.[12] The dramatic changes in the communication landscape enabled by such interconnectivity will be truly amazing to us. More time is now spent by American children playing video games through handheld players than through video game consoles.[13]

We have only begun to envision how a worldwide integrated communication network will affect our personal, social and professional lives. Nicholas Negroponte discussed some of

---

iv Haines, Gavin. "Homeless People to Receive Free Smartphones to Help them Stay Connected. *Positive News.* Retrieved Sept. 7, 2020. https://www.positive.news/society/homeless-people-to-receive-free-smartphones-to-help-them-stay-connected/

v Luke, Thomas. 59% of Americans Play Video Games, 51% of Households Own Two Consoles on Average, Report Finds. *Dual Shockers* Accessed Set. 7, 2020. https://www.dualshockers.com/59-of-americans-play-video-games-51-of-households-own-two-consoles-on-average-report-finds/

these changes in his in his book, *Being Digital*,[14] but his insights are only the beginning of what we will experience soon. Much of the discussion has centered on information. However, what we haven't discussed nearly enough is the proliferation of entertainment worldwide throughout this digital network. If we think we are inundated with entertainment now, just wait until we are fully immersed in a worldwide digital communication network. We'll be watching television programs and movies from all over the world, subtitled or translated with exceptional dubbing techniques, any time we want from any digital display, whether than be our HDTV sets, computer monitors, cell phones, or PDAs.

You may wonder how this would work. Services like Netflix have expanded from their embryonic stage and now allow their users to develop the applications of their products. We can simply tell our personal computers, tablets, smart phones or other hand-held electronic devices to find the entertainment programs we want by searching the digital libraries of the world. Once they find what we want, they can retrieve and store our requests and let us know the costs associated with each item found. For example, on a Thursday I might think about watching some movies over the weekend. Suppose I decide to watch World War II movies. I can direct my PC to find the World War II movies available worldwide, to then select the ten most popular movies based on sales and viewing data, and then to download for me reviews in English of those ten films. On Thursday evening, after a relaxing dinner, I can read the reviews and select the films that I wanted to see. I can then instruct my computer to find websites where I could purchase a weekend rental of the film for the best price, and then download those films electronically onto my computer to be accessed later for viewing. My computer can also arrange payment for the rentals using my personal credit card information and prior authorization. Friday after work, the three films I selected, say an American, Russian, and Japanese film, can be available for viewing on my widescreen digital television monitor. Thus, six hours of weekend entertainment can be arranged on my PC or smart phone in about five minutes.

Compare that to what we had to do before Netflix. I had to drive 3 or 4 miles to a Blockbuster or Hollywood Video (places where they used to rent videos for you Net Geners), go through the aisles, find the three films I wanted, wait in line to pay for them, and then drive back home. That whole process took me about 30 minutes, and I had a very small selection of product as compared to what I would have on the world wide web. By ordering a film electronically I will have saved 30 minutes and gas money and obtained a better entertainment experience for probably less money than I am paying now to rent videos. Many of you are too young to remember Blockbuster. This is just one simple example of how access to entertainment is going to expand in the years to come. The ease of accessing visual media will also improve dramatically, as demonstrated by Microsoft's Office Labs vision 2019.[15]

A Digital Revolution for Entertainment or Education?

For too long we have created a false dichotomy between entertainment and education. This division was partially due to the establishment of public broadcasting, like the broadcast network PBS, which we traditionally thought of as "educational television," and commercial networks, which we commonly thought of as "commercial television." Public television was supposed to be educational and of course, expected to be boring; while commercial television was supposed to be exciting, and of course, mindless. Hence the nickname "boob tube" became popular when commercial television exploded during the 1950s and 1960s. The news and information stations were considered informative; the commercial stations were regarded as entertainment.

The oversimplification of the differences between educational and commercial broadcasting was brought to light by the tremendous success of *Sesame Street*, an educational television program that was created out of a government-funded program of research and educational development called the Children's Television Workshop. From its debut on November 10, 1969, Sesame Street[vi] was an entertaining television program designed to educate young children. It was never intended to be pedantic or boring or merely "instructional." The research used to build a theoretical framework for Sesame Street revealed that children learn best when they are fully engaged in learning, not just cognitively but also emotionally. Sesame Street became one of the most successful television programs in history, not merely because of its educational value, but also because it was highly entertaining, making the learning process fun for children.

Adults are not that much different. We also learn best when we are entertained. Just think about all the classes you have taken in your lifetime. What do you remember about all the content you learned in social studies, history, English literature, math, science and so forth? If you attend religious services of any kind, think about all the sermons or homilies you have heard. How many can you recall? If you're like me, you probably don't remember many lectures or sermons. Now think about all the movies and television programs you have seen. How many scenes or lines can you recall? Even the most highly educated among us will probably be embarrassed doing this exercise, because most people remember a lot more entertainment programming than anything else. People can sing the theme songs to entertainment programs 40 to 50 years after they have been off the air; baby boomers feel free to test yourselves with the theme song to *Gilligan's Island*.[vii]

In a similar manner, you will find that the lectures and sermons that you do remember were likely highly entertaining and often included powerful stories. Stories, by their very

---

vi "Sesame Street" Debuts. Accessed September 7, 2020. https://www.history.com/this-day-in-history/sesame-street-debuts

vii Go to https://www.youtube.com/watch?v=yfSLuEj99d0

nature and structure, include dramatic content that keeps us engaged. Good stories, in short, are highly entertaining. It is no coincidence that great communicators are engaging and captivate people's attention. There are strategic reasons why Jesus did most of his teaching by telling great stories (parables) and by doing dramatic demonstrations (miracles). They enhanced learning. If you happen to see the movie *Dead Poet's Society*, you will likely recall a scene when Robin Williams, who plays a university professor, jumps on top of a desk during a lecture. Everyone in class remembered that lecture.[viii] Robin Williams has a communication style that scholars call "impression leaving." That is why so many of his film performances are easy to remember.

In the same way, we remember more and learn best when the educational content is delivered in an entertaining way. Think about some of the most popular educational programs that have been broadcast on television such as *Crocodile Hunter, Bill Nye the Science Guy,* and survivalist Bear Grylls' *Man vs. Wild*; they are highly entertaining yet they have much to teach. Vice-versa, some of the most successful entertainment programs like ER and the CSI series are very educational. It was on some of Steve Irwin's most dangerous adventures when viewers learned the most about wildlife.[ix] Many young people under age 25 learn their news from Comedy Central, *The Tonight Show* and *Late Night with David Letterman* in addition to traditional news programs.[17] The late Johnny Carson, the master of news entertainment, read the newspaper every day to create 5-10 jokes based on his simple commentary of the humor associated with real life situations.

Notice that many political candidates now openly campaign on entertainment programs like *The Tonight Show*, *Late Night*, and *MTV*.[16] These are the venues where political perceptions and beliefs are formed. Michael Moore's 2004 film, *Fahrenheit 451*, would not have created such a political stir for presenting President Bush as a warmonger if it wasn't for the fact that millions of people believed the film was an accurate portrayal of the President. When filmmaker Oliver Stone produced *JFK*, it was not the first time that a conspiracy theorist had presented all kinds of theories about who assassinated President John F. Kennedy. What is spectacular of today's entertainment is that many people believed the film was fact rather than fiction. Many more young people will see Oliver Stone's epic film, *Alexander*, than will read history books about the real life of Alexander the Great. Even fiction stories like Dan Brown's *DaVinci Code* can bamboozle media consumers into confusing historical events with fictional stories.[x] Today's powerful forms of entertainment

---

viii Go to https://www.youtube.com/watch?v=w8fu-hq3S7A

[ix] Go to https://www.youtube.com/watch?v=d0qealfPeDM

[x] Go to http://www.historyversusthedavincicode.com/

blur the lines between reality and fantasy, between information and speculation, and between education and entertainment.

Blending Entertainment and Education

Clearly, the false dichotomy between entertainment and education; that is, the idea that consuming media and the arts for entertainment or consuming them for learning are different processes with different outcomes, is not valid. The popularity of entertainment media and growth of entertainment programming content has pushed out traditional educational programs, even in countries where media were introduced as primarily educational tools to promote national development. For example, when television was introduced in India in 1959, it was regarded as an educational medium to advance the government's development goals. Although the Indian government today still produces educational television programming, by the 1990s, entertainment programming had become the dominant content of Indian television, which is now commercialized nationwide.

The information revolution in India also is taking place in many developing nations.[18] Entertainment media are now a dominant form of social influence throughout the world, rivaling traditional influence structures such as the family, the church, mosque, synagogue or temple, or other religious, educational, and community organizations.[19] Therefore, it has been in the interest of national governments to help meet people's educational, health, and development needs by blending entertainment and education.

In summary, it is not difficult to recognize that entertainment and education are inseparable. We learn through entertainment and good education engages both the mind and the emotions. If a speaker, university professor, newscaster, pastor, politician or teacher is boring, we will lose interest and will not learn very much from that person. If he or she is exciting, attractive, and captivating, we will more likely be influenced by the messages they communicate. In the next chapter we will contemplate the qualities of entertainment that make it a powerful source of persuasive influence that can both reinforce and change our attitudes, beliefs and behavior.

Questions for Discussion

1. How much total media do you consume on average each day? Compare yourself with two or three of your friends or classmates.
2. Does media consumption now control your life, or do you control it? Consider whether or not you always pick up your cell phone when it rings or pings, like Pavlov's dogs salivated each time the dinner bell rung.
3. Has media consumption eroded the amount of time you spend directly when others, face-to-face? Consider the last time you spent directly talking to someone more than an hour (not through media technology).
4. How much do you allow entertainment media to formulate your beliefs on what you think is true? Consider how tightly you hold on to beliefs about individuals and groups of people you have never personally met or spent time with.

Chapter 2
The Persuasive Power of Entertainment

I am always amused to hear television industry executives defend themselves against the charge that much of the television content that their media networks broadcast promotes sexual irresponsibility and violence. Most people realize the foolishness of the common defense that "it's just entertainment" or "we only show what is already taking place in society." Why are such arguments an illogical excuse for the moral messages of television programs? They are illogical because the entire entertainment industry is based on advertising. In the case of commercial television, programs only stay on the air if they sell products. Thus, television commercials are a powerful form of social influence. They persuade us to part with our hard-earned dollars and purchase products – many that we don't need. If entertaining ads only entertained, then why are they so effective?

Hundreds of studies are published in academic journals every year documenting the effectiveness of various types of advertising strategies. Why would a company spend more than five million dollars for a 30-second commercial during the Superbowl? Only because some very smart people know that a good advertisement, even that expensive, can pay off by inducing increased sales. In short, television ads are persuasive. They can change the way we think about our needs, wants and desires. They can even create needs that we don't even know we have. Thousands of products have been created throughout the world based on creating unfelt needs.

Consider one powerful industry built on this principle of creating perceived need – the multi-billion-dollar cosmetics industry. Before the age of television, the sale of cosmetics in the United States was only a small fraction of what it is today. Toothpaste, mouthwash, and hair styling gel were available, as were several basic items like blush, lipstick, and perfume, but not much variety or volume was sold. Many cosmetic products were viewed as luxuries rather than necessities.[1] In the age of radio, the most common form of electronic mass media, it was difficult to sell beauty. Television, particularly color television, changed the industry dramatically. The industry could employ attractive models to visually demonstrate the transformational power of cosmetics. Although multi-colored print advertisements also employed models, the addition of facial movements and sound greatly accentuated the persuasive influence of a model on a potential consumer. An audience member could emotionally identify with a model in a way that did not occur with static print advertisements. After all, live models talking to you were real people that created a sense of intimacy, not just pictures of people on a newspaper or magazine page.

Suddenly, a whole new range of products could be sold on television. Not only could companies model new cosmetic products through television, but they could also show how people respond to a person using a cosmetic product. A print or radio ad could not show that same kind of interaction. Suddenly men needed to shave with "new advanced razors" to get a "close shave" if they wanted to be attractive; and women needed to use new luxurious shaving creams if they wanted to remove "unattractive hair." A simple industry like "hair removal" went from a relatively unimportant personal preference to a collective social norm that rapidly expanded the practice. In much of Europe, the Middle East, South Asia, and many other regions of the world, sporting facial hair for men is the cultural norm; and women are not expected to regularly shave their arms and legs. Hair removal is a manufactured industry in the sense that it is a manufactured need, a social preference, not a necessity.

The reverse is also true – hair addition is culturally determined. Hair loss in men has not been much of a serious concern for most of man's history. Of course, the Europeans popularized the wearing of wigs by men in positions of authority. The idea of transplanting hair, however, would have seemed ridiculous even 150 years ago. With advertising, however, we can create the perception that balding is unattractive and therefore should be remedied. Again, this persuasion was difficult to achieve before the age of television; but not now. The hair growing, hair transplanting industry has grown tremendously. I know an entrepreneur who has become wealthy through his hair-transplanting and hair removal business. It is a very lucrative business since there are millions of people who either want more hair or less hair. Having hair and not having hair are completely cosmetic characteristics of a person. Yet, Americans spend billions of dollars each year growing and removing hair, depending upon our felt needs. Speaking from the position of someone who shaves every morning but who once enjoyed a full beard, I am forced to spend increasing amounts of money every year to keep this practice. Have you noticed how the cost of razor blades and shaving cream seems to consistently increase year after year? When I began shaving several decades ago, I used a single razor blade. Now I use a Gillette Fusion razor with five blades which is much more expensive! I was using a quadrapro razor when I wrote the first edition of this book but the ads convinced me that I need 5 blades. The hair removal industry has us right where they want us – dependent on their products in order to satisfy manipulated social norms.

Since advertising through media is such an important form of social influence, so powerful that it can actually change our behavior by convincing us to part with our money, can any intellectually honest person claim that the mass media doesn't influence other types of beliefs and behavior? The obvious answer to this question is "No!" The idea that a television sitcom is "just entertainment" or a "rap music video" only entertains but doesn't teach certain us certain beliefs or promote certain behavior is ludicrous and intellectually indefensible. The notion that we don't need to think about the content of entertainment and its effects on us is completely irresponsible, both to academics and to non-academics. Common sense tells us that entertainment is one of the most powerful forms of social influence today. The important question is not whether entertainment influences us or not, but rather, "how does it influence us?" The answer to that question is much of the focus of this book. We need to understand the mechanisms or processes through which entertainment works and its characteristics in order to understand why it is a powerful source of social influence.

Characteristics of Entertainment Media

Very few people have the time to think actively about the characteristics of entertainment that make it such a powerful force. This is quite understandable since we are immersed in it daily. Just as fish, according to the Disney animated character *Nemo*, spend little time thinking about the water, people spend little time contemplating the entertainment environment in which they live.

There are many reasons why entertainment is such a powerful force in society, especially in today's media saturated world. I review nine reasons that I refer to as the "nine p's of entertainment." These characteristics have been noted by a number of communication scholars and give entertainment its enormous persuasive influence. Entertainment is perennial, pervasive, popular, personal, pleasurable, persuasive, passionate, profitable, and practical.

First, entertainment is a perennial form of communication. It was present thousands of years ago, it is here today, and it will continue to flourish in the future. People throughout the world, irrespective of culture, language, socio-political identity, religious affiliation, or class, like to be entertained. The earliest forms of communication discovered by archeologists show that entertainment has always had a central place in virtually every culture. Some people groups had more time to create and consume entertainment than others, depending upon how much time they needed to meet basic needs of food, clothing and shelter. Yet even the most primitive cultures had their forms of public amusement. Public holidays, seasonal gatherings, and special events all carry important components of entertainment culture.

Second, entertainment is pervasive, expanding in all countries through various forms of media and performing arts. Even in the most remote regions of the world, the mountain villages of the Himalayas in Nepal, the remote jungle enclaves of the Amazon River Basin, the wind-swept deserts of Sudan, or the ice houses of Antarctica, you can watch the Tour de France or CNN News or the World Cup, or even reruns of Baywatch. I remember several decades ago hiking through the hills of the Golden Triangle where Thailand, Laos and Burma come together, traveling from village to village where there is no running water or electricity. I was shocked on one arduous hike through the jungle to hear what sounded to me like Rod Stewart singing, "I love you more than I can say." Sure enough, on the small trail crossing our path were three young local men walking through the jungle with a battery-powered boom box playing Rod Stewart. The sound quality was pretty good too.

There is virtually no place you can go on the planet to escape the reach of entertainment media. Even astronauts on the space stations have access to entertainment media on earth.

Entertainment also is universally popular. Good entertainment attracts people like honey attracts Pooh Bear. If you look at the highest rated radio and television programs throughout the world, you will find that they are highly entertaining. It's the programs with the highest entertainment value that get exported all over the world. The world's multi-billion-dollar film industry thrives on the most popular films. In the U.S., many of the feature films gross more revenue overseas than in the U.S. Three of highest-grossing films of all-time, *Titanic*, *The Lord of the Rings: The Return of the King*, and *Pirates of the Caribbean: Dead Man's Chest*, which all grossed more than one billion dollars worldwide, earned more than 60 percent of their box office revenues overseas.[2] Media consumers throughout the world watch movies every week because people seek out good entertainment. Audiences flock to see dramatic plays not primarily to learn, or to be morally stimulated, but to be amused. The whole world of sports, which creates the most attended public gatherings in the world, is a world of entertainment. From the hanging gardens of Babylon to the Roman coliseums to the modern-day Olympic stadiums, entertainment through sports remains one of the most enduring and most popular forms of social activities.

Entertainment messages also can be very personal, speaking to us in a way that no one else could do. Programs can present educational content in a more intimate manner than is often presented in real life situations where taboo communication is avoided. For example, while a personal friend might be hesitant to discuss various family planning options with a friend who needs guidance, a character in a television soap opera can more openly communicate such personalized information. Issues that may be difficult to discuss interpersonally such as the abuse of children, contraception, HIV/AIDS, illiteracy, drug and alcohol use, spousal abuse, depression and suicide can be more openly addressed through media characters on entertainment programs. Entertainment creates the social atmosphere to more openly discuss important issues that we may be reluctant to face or that are considered taboo.

Entertainment is pleasurable; it represents play and can provide "release" or "escape." In the fast pace of life in many technologically advanced countries, entertainment helps people to reduce stress and release pent up emotions through catharsis. It also can cause laughter which has positive physical benefits. Now that the world population has shifted from a majority living in rural areas to a majority living in urban areas, adding a great deal of stress to people's lives, the demand for play, release and escape through entertainment is even more pronounced.

One of the primary reasons why entertainment is powerful is because it can be very persuasive, moving audiences to adopt specific attitudes, beliefs and behaviors. Prosocial entertainment can persuade people to adopt more healthy lifestyles, reduce relationship conflicts, give financially to help victims of disasters, and do other things to benefit their own lives and their community. Involvement with entertaining media personalities we are exposed to on a regular basis can also persuade us to change unhealthy behaviors such as alcohol abuse, drinking and driving, tobacco use, illegal drug use, unhealthy food consumption, and other destructive practices.

Entertainment programs can be passionate; they can stir strong audience emotions about a social issue or educational need. For example, the treatment of the topic of AIDS in a television soap opera is not just communicating "five million dead and 50 million HIV-infected," but the suffering of Jonathan, who is dying of AIDS, who is married to Rolinda, and whose suffering is also causing their families to suffer. The ability to communicate passion can have a strong emotional effect on entertainment consumers.

Entertainment programs earn high audience ratings, are more attractive to commercial sponsors, and are usually profitable. The profit potential of entertainment creates a continue pool of funding from investors who want to make money through their ownership of entertainment products. Thus, entertainment productions have a much easier time attracting sponsors than other types of media and creative arts.

Finally, the ninth "p" of entertainment is that it is practical. People learn from entertainment; therefore, it is the most practical means of carrying educational-development messages. Large audiences can be reached at reasonable costs per person with prosocial media campaigns. Many countries are now capitalizing on the practical feasibility of creating and implementing entertainment-education programs through a variety of media and arts.

In summary, these nine characteristics of entertainment make it one of the most powerful forms of popular culture.[3] It seems counter-intuitive not to think of the learning potential of entertainment, given its unique qualities. Unfortunately, much of the scholarly focus on media effects has been on negative aspects of entertainment rather than on its powerful potential to teach and shape beliefs and behavior. There is likely no more powerful means of learning today than through entertainment.

How we use Entertainment Media

During the past eight decades, communication scholars have been seeking to understand how people use mass media. Up until the Second World War, the dominant thinking was that people were more passive consumers of media. This led to common colloquial phrases previously noted such as "coach potatoes," a reference to those who laid inactively on the coach and watched television; or "the boob tube," which strongly implies that people disengage their brain while watching television. The view of media consumers as passive processors of information changed during the 1970s and 1980s, when media scholars began to approach the audience as active consumers of media who make strategic decisions about their media consumption.

Today, most media scholars view audiences as active participants in the media consumption process. People actively engage media messages and want to receive certain benefits through their media consumption. Our general use of media is not simply to pass time or because we have a habit of turning on the television. Rather, we consume media purposefully with certain outcomes in mind. Scholars who study the strategic use of media refer to their scholarship as the "uses and gratifications" approach to mass media.

Uses and gratifications has been a popular theoretical perspective that has guided a great number of audience studies for many decades. The approach assumes that when individuals selectively seek media content, they are seeking to fulfill their pre-determined goals and satisfy their perceived needs. Individual predispositions, social and environmental factors, are all important variables that influence media consumption. Some of the seminal scholars who developed this approach, including Jay Blumler,[4] Elihu Katz,[5] Michael Gurevitch,[6] Dennis McQuail,[7] Karl Rosengren,[8] Alan Rubin,[9] and Sven Windahl,[10] have generated a number of important studies. These scholars have reviewed the history, summarized scholarship and articulated prominent criticisms associated with this theoretical perspective.

Although the predictive quality of the uses and gratifications approach has been limited, the research it has generated provides a beneficial way to explore why people use certain mediums like television, particular genres of media programming and even individual programs. Swanson suggested it is a valuable perspective for exploring the relationship between specific media content, including drama, and how audiences interpret it.[11] Alan Rubin identified relaxation, companionship, habit, passing time, entertainment, social interaction, information, arousal and escape as common motives for (or gratifications derived from) viewing television. He was able to group these motivations for watching television into two basic types of television viewers: (1) "ritualized" viewers who habitually use it for time consumption, relaxation, companionship and entertainment, and (2) more goal-oriented "instrumental" viewers who use it for information.[12] James Lull stressed the importance of considering a variety of "structural" and "relational" social uses of television.[13]

The relationship between religion and television viewing has been explored to some extent by Robert Abelman and Stewart Hoover[14] and Daniel Stout and Juddith Buddenbaum;[15] however, empirical studies which examine religious or spiritual television viewing factors from an audience uses and gratifications perspective have been rare. Buddenbaum[16] found that viewers of religious programming sought many of the same benefits from viewing as most television viewers but also used it to support their belief systems and fulfill a need to know themselves better.

Abelman[17] further discovered that disenchantment with commercial television, in conjunction with religiosity, motivated some religious television viewers to seek out purely religious television content. However, George Gerbner and his associates at the University of Pennsylvania discovered that viewers of religious television programming basically had similar viewing tastes as non-viewers of religious programming.[18] One of my colleagues and I found similar results in our study of religious television viewers and talk show viewing. Our research indicated that more than fifty percent of the viewers of one of the most popular religious talk shows in the U.S., *The 700 Club*, were also avid viewers of the Oprah Winfrey Show.[19]

Neal Hamilton and Alan Rubin confirmed the importance of religiosity as an important variable in uses and gratifications research.[20] They discovered that religious conservatives were less likely to watch programming with sexual content but no less likely to watch violent programming content than religious liberals. Unfortunately, there are very few studies that focus on what religious or spiritual uses and gratifications audiences may derive from dramatic television with religious content. Television programs like *Touched by an Angel*, *7th Heaven*, and *Joan of Arcadia*, which regularly incorporated religious or spiritual characters, did very well with religious television viewers and even with some non-religious viewers.

My own research with Dr. Benson Fraser of television viewers in more than 40 nations during the past 25 years shows that people do seek out entertainment media for spiritual uses and edification. A growing number of entertainment media consumers consider themselves to be spiritual but not religious. Thus, entertainment can be a powerful spiritual influence on media consumers, especially when such content features spiritual issues. I will discuss this growing use of entertainment media in more detail in chapter 14.

Media Dependency and Entertainment

Sandra Ball-Rokeach, a media scholar at the University of Southern California, proposed more than thirty-five years ago that that people's degree of dependency on media for information and entertainment determines the extent to which the media will influence them.[21] Her research indicates the social and media environments in which we live determine how important various media become in our lives. For example, a person living in the Los Angeles area will be much more dependent on radio traffic alerts than a person living in Greensboro, North Carolina. The difference between having a successful or unsuccessful day in Los Angles may very well depend on staying abreast of important real time traffic alerts. Media dependency to a great extent determines the impact of mediated messages on a media consumer.

During the past 60 years mass media in the U.S. have increased the public's dependency on entertainment in order to interact in today's American culture. Many of our conversations and social activities center on entertainment. Media dependency is an important research concept that applies to much more than news consumption; it also affects how we form our values.[22] A person devoid of any knowledge of popular television programs, feature films, or well-known celebrities often would be left out of everyday conversations. Many people consume popular media just to keep up with the lives of popular entertainers, so they don't appear ignorant when they interact with friends and colleagues. Consider a typical "water cooler" or "coffee room" conversation in an average office in America, or pre-ZOOM meeting banter. Quite regularly the conversation will relate to some form of entertainment, whether it be about a radio or late-night television talk show, television soap opera, music performance, play, or sports competition.

Powerful Media Effects

Prior to World War II, the dominant thinking among American scholars and media professionals was that the mass media had a powerful and direct influence on audiences. This theoretical perspective was commonly referred to as the hypodermic needle model or magic bullet theory of mass communication.[23] The idea captivated by these phrases is that the mass media has an immediate powerful effect on us, as if injecting a drug into one's bloodstream. This conception of an "all-powerful" media came out of the historical and social milieu of the 1930s and early 1940s, when Hitler, Mussolini, and Hirohito manipulated the mass media to promote fascism and the American and British film industries countered with their own propaganda films to support the war effort for the Allied Powers.

However, during and shortly after World War II, American social scientists discovered that the mass media usually did not have a direct and powerful effect on mass audiences. Elihu Katz and Paul Lazarsfeld found that the mass media were most influential in the lives of opinion leaders, and then opinion leaders would in turn influence individuals and groups of people. In 1946, they published their "two-step flow" model of mass media effects.[24] Subsequent research has shown that mass media effects often follow a multistage process in which there are many intervening variables.[25] Thus, the answer to the question, "Is mass media all powerful?" is "It depends." In some situations media do have a direct and powerful influence on audience members, but such influence is usually the exception rather than the rule.[26] However, when entertainment and education are strategically combined to achieve predetermined outcomes, the result is often a powerful one.

Consider two stories of the powerful life-changing effects of two entertainment drama series, one on radio and one on television. The first story comes from Lutsaan, a small village in the Uttar Pradesh State of India. Like most villages in this Hindu region of the country, the dowry system has been a regular part of Hindi culture. If you had a daughter in Lutsaan, you were expected to give money and gifts to the family of the young man who wished to marry your daughter. Thus, having many daughters could be a financially draining social disposition. The government of India has attempted to curb this practice because the dowry system can be abusive and demeaning to women. However, mere educational programs are not going to change such an entrenched social practice.

The government decided to use an entertainment-education approach to the problem of dowry. I will discuss this approach in more detail later, but essentially, the entertainment-education approach involves intentionally seeking to reinforce or change attitudes, values, beliefs or social practices by integrating educational content into entertainment productions. In order to change beliefs about women and how girls are valued and treated, funding agencies partnered with the government of India to create *Tinka Tinka Sukh (Happiness Lies in Small Things)*, a radio soap opera broadcast in Hindi. Tinka Tinka Sukh, which applied Albert Bandura's social cognitive theory, was broadcast twice a week in 1996 and 1997, gained a loyal following among millions of Hindi-speaking families in India. Not only did millions of people carefully listen to each episode of the drama, but they listened in groups and discussed the content of the program after each episode. These listening groups had a profound influence on the people of Lutsaan.[27] After centuries of collecting dowry, the men in the village decided collectively to discontinue the dowry system after recognizing its destructive influences through Tinka Tinka Sukh.[28]

I will discuss this amazing social transformation, documented by one of my good friends and noted international media scholars, Dr. Arvind Singhal, in chapter six. The point here is that in a few months, the influence of one radio soap opera over-powered hundreds of years of social practice. If the way girls and women are treated can be improved through one soap opera, could we not create dramatic serials to improve education, increase literacy, promote good health, and solve all kinds of other social problems?

That is the very question that Miguel Sabido had after watching the influence of *Simplemente Maria* (Simple Mary), a 1969 Peruvian *telenovela* (television soap opera). Sabido, a talented creative writer, producer, and media scholar in Mexico, observed that viewers of this soap opera strongly identified with Maria, the main character of the series. The series follows the migration of Maria as a teenager from a poor peasant village in the Andes mountains to the capital city of Lima, where she gets a job as a maid for a wealthy family. Through great hardships Maria overcomes abuse and ignorance as an uneducated single mother to become a successful clothing designer. During its broadcast from 1969-1971, *Simplemente Maria* averaged an amazing audience ratings of 85 percent, including some episodes during which almost every television set was tuned into the program.[29] Many versions of *Simplemente Maria* were created and broadcast throughout Latin America. I will discuss this *telenovela* and Miguel Sabido's work a bit more in chapter 6.

These are just two examples among hundreds that show how an entertainment series can produce very powerful social changes. Even a single episode of an entertainment program can create change, and such changes can occur even when the producers were not intending to influence behavior. For example, in an episode of the 1980s U.S. television series *Happy Days*, one of the star characters of the program, Fonzie, decided to get a library card. During the next few days following the broadcast, libraries throughout the U.S. experienced a noticeable spike in applications from school children and young teenagers for library cards.[30] I will come back to this phenomenon later when I discuss the process of identification. Suffice to say that a single television episode had a very positive educational influence on thousands of people, increasing the use of libraries.

These unintended consequences of entertainment can be positive or negative. Depending how you feel about private gun ownership, the 1980s television series *Miami Vice* had a good or bad influence on gun purchases. The popular crime-drama series produced by NBC illustrates that even seemingly insignificant events in entertainment programs may lead to sizable unintended behavioral effects on television viewers. U.S. gun-shop owners noticed a remarkable effect on the gun-buying behaviors of *Miami Vice* viewers during the 1980s. Shortly after detective Sonny Crockett began sporting a shark-gray Australian-made 5.56-mm. Steyr AUG, a semiautomatic assault rifle, on episodes of *Miami Vice*, gun shops across the U.S. were flooded with customer calls asking how they could buy one.[31] Although *Miami Vice*'s producers never claimed they were trying to promote gun ownership, NBC was likely surprised to learn the degree to which *Miami Vice* promoted gun sales and had become the fashion leader in personal protection weaponry in the U.S.

Sometimes the popularity of a single entertainment program can even overcome cultural barriers to produce social change. This occurred with India's first long-running television soap opera, *Hum Log* (We People). *Hum Log* was broadcast in 1984 and 1985 as an entertainment-education program intended to raise the status of women in India. The program also had many other prosocial themes. In one episode of *Hum Log*, a police officer loses his eye in an accident and a family arranges for the donation of an eye from a departed loved one. Organ donation in the Hindi culture is strongly discouraged, yet, as a result of this episode, a young man who was the president of a youth club in Chandigarh began an eye donation campaign to sign up eye donors. The goal of the club's campaign was to sign up 5000 people in one month. At the time the club's president wrote a letter to Doordarshan, India's national television network that was broadcasting *Hum Log*, the Chandigarh Youth Club had already signed up 982 donors.[32] This was one example of many powerful effects in India that we documented through our research of Hum Log.[33]

These stories all illustrate that under certain circumstances the mass media can have a very powerful and direct influence on individuals. Whether it be rejecting a long-held cultural practice like dowry, obtaining library cards, role modeling courage, or donating organs, entertainment media can be a powerful force of social influence that creates prosocial change. Although many scholars and media critics are quick to point out the antisocial effects of entertainment media, and there are many, we cannot underestimate its equivalent power for social good. In the next chapter we will consider the kingpins of the entertainment industry, the entertainers themselves, and how they are the primary brokers of social influence.

Questions for Discussion

1. What entertainment television or radio program has influenced you the most during the past 12 months and why?
2. What type of media are you most dependent on and why?
3. Is there a television program that had a profound influence on your life like *Simplemente Maria* had on viewers in Peru and *Hum Log* had on viewers in India? If yes, please explain.
4. What entertainment television series being broadcast now is the most influential and how do you think viewers of this program are being influenced?

Chapter 3
Entertainers as Post-Modern Moral Teachers

On January 16, 2004, I marveled while watching the news coverage of Michael Jackson's arraignment in court to face charges of sexual assault. A Los Angeles news station took footage of Jackson's motorcade driving down the freeway, reminiscent of the scenes of O. J. Simpson's Ford Bronco being chased by police and broadcast on television news stations prior to his arrest for murder, a drama watched by an estimated 95 million people.[1] I knew Jackson was popular with his fans, but still did not expect such a carnival atmosphere and the blind devotion displayed outside the courtroom. As one typical fan said in an interview, "I don't know what he did, that's his business. I'm just here to support him."[2] Devotion to Michael Jackson by his fans appeared to outweigh the seriousness of the charges of sexual abuse brought against him.

The influence of entertainers today is vastly greater than the influence of entertainers fifty years ago. There are several reasons for this. First, the mass media have expanded internationally at a rapid rate. In China and India alone, there are now more television viewers than the entire population of Western Europe, the United States, and Canada combined. The world's film industries have distributed films, videos, and DVDs to almost every corner of the globe. Music cultural products also are globally distributed, as evidenced by the international popularity of hip-hop music, styles, and artifacts. The fame of world class athletes has penetrated cultural boundaries. Anyone who has followed professional basketball for the past few decades knows Michael Jordan and Lebron James, whether in China, Saudi Arabia, Mozambique, Argentina, Sweden or Sri Lanka. Anyone who likes golf today knows Tiger Woods. If you have been a soccer fan for a long time, you probably know Diego Maradona and David Beckham; and if you're a cyclist, you know about Lance Armstrong and his troubles with the use of performance enhancing drugs. Major sports events are now televised in hundreds of countries. In addition, sports celebrities are contracted by corporate firms to advertise commercial products through radio, television, and print publications. On a trip to Ukraine in 1998, I saw more swooshes, the Nike symbol, than pictures of the hammer and sickle. Advertising reaches virtually every nation on earth, and often features national and international celebrities.

A second reason why entertainers have more influence today than at any time in history is because of the tremendous growth of entertainment media. Regardless of where one lives, wherever media and the arts flourish there is abundant entertainment. The most popular genres of media content are entertainment oriented. Radio serial dramas are more popular than news programs. Latin American *telenovelas* (television novels akin to American soap operas) command more attention than health education programs. Hollywood feature films are seen by many more people than documentary films. People everywhere like to be entertained and seem to consume as much entertainment as they can afford. There simply are more entertainment products on the market this year than there were last; and next year there will probably be even more. With new means of electronic storage, digital cell phone technology, and the Internet companies, our ability to access and consume entertainment is greater than at any other point in history.

In 1985, the late Neil Postman of New York University published *Amusing Ourselves to Death*, a thought-provoking book describing how our consumption of entertainment could eventually kill us intellectually, creatively, and even physically.[3] What Postman discussed more nearly three decades ago is even more relevant today. We devote a substantial amount of time each day to consuming entertainment, which accounts for a large portion of our expenses. Some people now spend more money on entertainment on certain days then they do on food. It's not difficult to do in light of the endless entertainment choices available to us. When we consider the amount of time each week we spend listening to or watching entertainers, it is easy to understand why they are so influential. Entertainers today have more access to more people than at any other time in human history.

The proliferation of media worldwide and rapid growth of entertainment produces a third factor that expands the influences of entertainers: knowledge. We now know more about the lives of entertainers than we probably ever wanted to know. The whole industry of the paparazzi, celebrity news writers, and publications devoted to describing the lives of entertainers, has grown dramatically. In an interview with Michael Jackson, broadcast by VH1 on January 16, 2004, he bemoaned the fact that he cannot go anywhere in public without being mobbed by people. Jackson said he would love to just go to a grocery store himself and buy some food, but even that simple task would create a commotion. Jackson noted that the threat of crowds forces celebrities to "be weird" in that they cannot do the normal activities that other people do.

Elvis Presley had to go to see movies between late night and early morning to avoid being mobbed. He would rent a movie theater for the evening just to maintain his privacy. When he wanted to buy a car, he would arrange for a private night visit to a dealership, surprising one woman on her birthday who happened to be there with a gift of a new car.[4] Thus he developed a schedule of sleeping during the daylight hours and living his life during the nighttime hours, a lifestyle that eventually contributed to his ill health and dependency on prescription drugs. Many celebrities today would say Elvis had it easy. If Elvis lived today, the media scrutiny would be far worse.

As noted earlier, Michael Jackson was just as exasperated by the intense media coverage as was Elvis. If you read the biographical material published shortly after his death in 2009, you will see he often complained that he could not have any resemblance of a normal lifestyle because of his fame.[5] Even walking down the street to the post office or to the bank would create a major event. This kind of scrutiny and lack of normalcy no doubt contributed to some of the bizarre behavior of both Presley and Jackson.

Everything we want to know and don't want to know about the lives of celebrities is disseminated throughout the world every day. One cannot buy groceries without being exposed at the checkout counter to a plethora of news magazines featuring the latest gossip about celebrities on the covers and in the headlines. If you walk into a Barnes & Noble bookstore in the U.S., you will be exposed to displays featuring books about celebrities. If you watch television or listen to the radio, you will no doubt be exposed to many advertisements in which celebrities attempt to sell you products. Wherever you turn, entertainers are there to greet you and tell you what type of soap to shower with in the morning, which deodorant to use, which car to drive, which long distance service to use, where to eat, which car to drive, who to vote for, and what to watch on television when you get home from work. Entertainers are not only those who amuse us, they are our friends, counselors, heroes and role models. They wield a surprising amount of influence in our lives, most of which we do not recognize.

One of the most important roles entertainers have in today's society is the role of a moral teacher. This thought may frighten many parents, but children learn much of their moral behavior from the lives of entertainers they follow. Entertainers are not moral teachers because they are trying to be, but rather, they are moral teachers because those who like them and follow them role model their attitudes, beliefs and behavior. Many entertainers don't want to be role models for moral behavior.[6,7] They don't want to be responsible for those who may copy them, but that is not their choice.[8] The practice of young people receiving their moral cues from celebrities is painfully obvious every day.

The replacement of parents, teachers, and spiritual leaders as sources of moral learning by celebrities is a critically important social change that should not be overlooked. In 2005, Fox News broadcast a story of the growing trend of Hollywood celebrities having children together before they are married.[9] CNN News ran a similar story. The news commentators cited a number of couples such as Tom Cruise and Katie Holmes, who highly publicized having a child before they planned to get married as if this was the normal order of events. The concern raised by Fox and CNN was that these celebrity couples who planned to get married one day, had reversed the normal order of events: romance, marriage, and children, by making marriage an unnecessary component of creating a family, but more of an afterthought. The moral norm set by celebrities in American society clearly expects that people should have sexual relationships and even children before considering marriage. We have only begun to wrestle with the implications of looking to celebrities as the vanguards of our social norms.

Several political, social and cultural changes in western nations like the U.S. have facilitated the power of celebrities to set the moral agenda of our societies. Modernism gave privilege to authority figures in our lives. One of the commonly accepted reasons why people believe what they do is because that's what they were taught in school, or at home, or from community and national leaders. Modernism created a social structure in which the experts and people with official positions of power were given the most amount of credibility.

Post-modern culture does not privilege authority figures, but rather, creates a social system in which authority figures are mistrusted. Consider the low level of credibility of spiritual leaders in the U.S. today. Despite the rise of religious faith and spirituality as important areas of interest in public opinion polls, the overall credibility of spiritual leaders has decreased dramatically. Normative family structure in American culture has radically changed with the sharp increase of divorce in the last half of the twentieth century. When traditional authority structures break down, people look to other sources to help them decide what to believe regarding moral right and wrong. Today, a large percentage of children do not live with both of their biological parents. Because so many parents have struggled to keep their marital and parental commitments, millions of children are reluctant to trust parental guidance and grow into adults who distrust government officials and other forms of authority.

The move away from traditional role models and authority figures has created a leadership vacuum. One group of people who are filling this vacuum, although many have not welcomed this role, are entertainers, including professional athletes. Entertainment professionals are people we often admire and sometimes desire to be like. In the closing decades of the 20th century, actors, musicians, singers, athletes and others in the entertainment business were presented to the public as role models to follow.

This doesn't mean that authority figures have no influence in post-modern culture. Parents, educators, spiritual leaders, business executives and government officials still wield an important amount of social influence. However, the access of millions of people to the lives of others is facilitated through mass media. Therefore, those who receive the most amount of media attention like entertainers have the greatest potential to influence large numbers of people.

We may not like it, but in today's society, the moral lives of entertainment professionals exert tremendous influence on the moral decisions of those who follow their lives. This influence does not need to be negative, however. There are many entertainers who use their social influence to help people promote moral and ethical behavior and to address critical social issues. One of the first mediated celebrities to use celebrity appeal as a positive form of social capital on a grand scale was Kate Smith during World War II. Let me briefly share her story.

Kate Smith and War Bonds

At the outbreak of the United States' involvement in World War II, the U.S. Treasury did not have sufficient funds to finance the war. It became clear to the U.S. Government that the war effort would be impossible to sustain without public support. In response, government-secured savings bonds were issued and eight war bond drives were carried out from 1941 through 1946.

On May 1, 1941, President Franklin D. Roosevelt purchased the first Series E U.S. Savings Bond and the last proceeds from the Victory Bond campaign were deposited to the Treasury on January 3, 1946. The War Finance Committees that oversaw the loan drives sold an astounding $185.7 billion of securities to more than 85 million Americans, a mass mediated sales feat that has never been matched by any other country.[10]

Advertisements for war bonds were created and endorsed by government agencies and by private companies and organizations. Companies contributed advertising space or time and also produced their own advertisements as well as ads for the government. Initially, war bond ads were predominantly found in newspapers and on the radio, two of the primary means by which the public followed the war. By appealing to nationalism through Madison Avenue advertising techniques, war bond ads stirred the conscience of Americans by invoking both their financial and moral involvement in the war.[11]

One of the brilliant advertising strategies implemented in the war bond drives involved Kate Smith, a nationally known singer and stage performer. Smith hosted her own daytime radio program, *The Kate Smith Hour*, which offered her home-spun wisdom and down-home philosophy on women's affairs and current events. On November 11 of 1938, during her radio program, Smith became a powerful symbol of patriotism when she sang "God Bless America," an Irving Berlin song originally written for Berlin's 1918 musical *Yip, Yip, Yaphank*. The song quickly supplanted "The Star-Spangled Banner" as the nation's most popular patriotic song and was formally advocated, unsuccessfully, to become America's new national anthem. It is still popular, as those of us who watched the World Series of 2012 heard it sung during the 7th inning stretch at Candlestick Park in San Francisco. Recognizing the significance of the song, Smith relinquished her right to exclusively perform "God Bless America" and waived all royalties from performances of the song, donating them to the Boy and Girl Scouts of America. She became a perfect choice for selling war bonds.

The overwhelming success of Smith's successful advocacy is unprecedented. No single entertainer has ever come close to her accomplishment in the war bonds campaigns during World War II. Smith sold $107 million worth of war bonds in one 18-hour marathon fund drive on the CBS radio network. In total, her radio broadcasts sold more than $600 million of war bonds.[12] Smith's moral appeals to help those in need and stop evil demonstrated the potential of mass media to communicate powerful motivating influences.

One of the great social scientists of the twentieth century, Robert Merton, analyzed Smith's radio programs and the types of appeals she made. Merton discovered that in contrast to previous war bond campaigns that emphasized investment and future security, Smith challenged listeners to sacrifice and to not let others out-give them, creating competition among various cities.[13] Merton illustrated these themes by publishing the following statements made by Miss Smith during her 18-hour record breaking fund-raising radio broadcast:

"Could you say to Mrs. Viola Buckley ... Mrs. Viola Buckley, whose son Donald was killed in action ... that you are doing everything you can to shorten the war ... that you are backing up her son to the limit of your abilities?"[14]

"We can do it together...We can put this greatest of war bond drives across."[15]

"I was a little disappointed to discover that the good old town of New York was behind Los Angeles ... now we're going to hold the switchboard open to give New Yorkers a chance to catch up to and surpass Los Angeles. Are you with me?"[16]

Kate Smith was born in Greenville, Virginia, on May 1, 1907 as Kathryn Elizabeth Smith. A naturally gifted singer and dancer from a young age, Smith began performing in church socials at age 5 and for World War I troops at age 8 where she grew up in Washington, D.C. Her father, William Smith, unsuccessfully made her take up nursing at George Washington University Hospital. After a few months she quit the program and took a singing job at Keith's Theater, performing in a show which eventually led her to Atlantic City and to Broadway.

By 1926 Smith had signed a contract with a New York City show producer. After successful performances in musical comedies in New York, including *Honeymoon Lane*, *Hit the Deck*, and *Flying High*, Columbia Records vice-president Ted Collin offered her a career in music recording. Smith accepted the offer, and Collins became her career manager and long-time business partner, a 34-year partnership. Smith's career skyrocketed. She broke the record for longevity at the legendary Palace Theatre and recorded more songs than any other performer – nearly 3000 in total, introducing one-third of them for the first time, including 600 hits.[17] Among Smith's biggest hits are "River, Stay 'Way From My Door" (1931), "The Woodpecker Song" (1940), "The White Cliffs of Dover" (1941), "I Don't Want to Walk Without You" (1942), "There Goes That Song Again" (1944), "Seems Like Old Times" (1946), "Now Is the Hour" (1947) and "How Great Thou Art (1965).[18]

Smith launched her own radio program in 1938 and made more than 15,000 radio broadcasts, becoming one of the most recognized voices in the United States during World War II and becoming one of the most popular women in America. When introducing the accomplished singer to King George VI of England, President Roosevelt said: "This is Kate Smith. Miss Smith is America."[19]

Smith's television career was launched in 1950 with a NBC weekday afternoon variety show, *The Kate Smith Show* (1950-1954), followed by a NBC weekly prime-time show on Wednesday nights called The Kate Smith Evening Hour. Smith co-wrote the theme song for her program, "When the Moon Comes over the Mountain," with Harry Woods. Her last television series, *The Kate Smith Show*, was broadcast by CBS in 1960. In addition to her own television programs, Smith made many guest appearances on popular TV shows, including The Ed Sullivan Show, The Tennessee Ernie Ford Show, The Jack Paar Show, ABC Hollywood Palace, The Dean Martin Show, The Smothers Brothers Comedy Hour, The Andy Williams Show, The Tony Orlando and Dawn Show, and The Donny & Marie Show.[20]

By appealing to human values popular among Americans such as sacrifice, teamwork, and competition, Smith was able to motivate an amazing amount of support for the war effort. The effectiveness of celebrity endorsement for a prosocial cause was an important lesson not lost on future campaign professionals.

During the last decade of her career, Smith gave dozens of live concerts in the U.S. and had extended engagements at the largest nightclub in Reno, Nevada, giving two shows each day in 1972 and 1973. Smith ended her career as a professional entertainer in 1976, when she served as Grand Marshall of the Tournament of Roses Parade. President Ronald Reagan awarded Smith the Medal of Freedom in 1982. During the nation's bicentennial celebration in July of 1976, Smith gave her last public performance of the Irving Berlin anthem that cemented her place as a patriotic iconic figure of American culture, God Bless America. She died in Raleigh, North Carolina on June 17, 1986, at the age of 79, several years after becoming a Roman Catholic, and is buried in Saint Agnes Cemetery in Lake Placid, Essex County, New York.

Kate Smith demonstrated the powerful moral force that one popular entertainer can have on millions of people. In the 21st century, there is even greater potential for entertainers to be looked upon for moral leadership. The moral confusion of post-modern society, which grates against the notion of clear moral right and wrong, has created a hunger for moral leadership which has failed within so many social institutions.[21] This fluid socio-cultural milieu, which some social scientists see as a moral vacuum, has created new opportunities for entertainers and celebrities to exert social influence. In the next chapter we will examine the role modeling process and consider examples of entertainers and celebrities who have helped to shape the behavior of millions of people throughout the world.

Discussion Questions

1. Have you ever donated money to support a cause advocated by the appeal of a professional entertainer? If yes, please explain.
2. What entertainer has raised a lot of money for a social cause?
3. What moral lesson have you learned through an entertainer?

Chapter 4
Following Celebrities as Heroes & Role Models

One of the important consequences of mass communication is the increased opportunity mass audiences have to develop relationships with mythic characters, those Mary Kittelson describes as people who "express our deepest goals and values," giving credence to our everyday lives through the power of imagination.[1] Today, popular entertainers become mythic characters through their celebrity status. In the past, mythic characters were based on heroic people, but now they are derived primarily from celebrities. Daniel Boorstin[2] and Joseph Campbell[3] make important distinctions between heroes and celebrities. In Campbell's work, he states that heroes act to redeem society, whereas celebrities live only for themselves.[4] The Greek word for hero denotes one who seeks to protect and to serve, thus connecting the role of a hero with the willingness to sacrifice oneself to benefit others.[5]

In contrast to a hero, a celebrity is simply known for being known and may or may not serve others sacrificially. Boorstin,[6] Campbell,[7] Gamson,[8] Lippmann[9] and others note that a celebrity is not required to have any moral virtue. People who become celebrities today do not do so because of their moral character, but because of their mediated personality and widespread public recognition. Boorstin explains the differences as follows:

> "The hero was distinguished by his achievement, the celebrity by his image or trademark. The hero created himself; the celebrity is created by the media. The hero was a big man, the celebrity a big name."[10]

Whereas heroes are known for great acts of courage or outstanding accomplishments requiring skill and fortitude, celebrities are known for their popularity. Boorstin goes on to explain that heroes by their nature do not seek to draw attention to themselves; their acts speak for them. In contrast, a celebrity is created by media attention and must constantly maintain a certain image that is difficult to sustain in real life. Heroes are provided status through interpersonal relationships, but celebrities are given status by the amount of media coverage they attract. Celebrity status is marked by instability and ambiguity,[11] and some suggest celebrity status is not supported by institutional power,[12] although there are exceptions. The celebrity's status is dependent on public attention, while the hero's is not.[13]

Before the electronic media age, people closely identified with heroes and regarded them as those who should be followed, role modeled, and emulated. Gamson argues that rapid growth of the cinema-television industry in the U.S. spawned America's celebrity culture during the early twentieth century.[14] In a similar vein, Boorstin argues that the growth of popular media has led to a social transition from heroes to celebrities.[15] Famous athletes, musical entertainers, film and television stars, and even controversial and despised political figures have gained an international fan base through the ubiquitous reach of radio, television, print media, and the Internet. Just search the term "international fan base" in Google and you will see how many celebrities, sports teams, music groups, etc. are followed throughout the world.

Creating and maintaining celebrity images has become a major industry in the U.S. and other developed nations, increasing the number of entertainment reporters, publicists, and image consultants.[16] This expansion began during the 1920s and 1930s, when the demand for information about the personal lives of film stars increased rapidly,[17] launching fame as a widely distributed product manufactured by media professionals. Lippmann regarded this new industry as "an engine of publicity such as the world has never known before."[18]

Although the archetype of the hero, or as Campbell discussed, the many different types of heroes, are still prevalent in popular media, the media stars who play the roles of heroes and heroines have to a great extent overpowered the mythic characters they perform. Before his death in 1987, Campbell sadly acknowledged that we seem to worship celebrities, not heroes; observing that young people seek to be known, to have "name and fame," without any concept of having to give oneself for others.[19]

Despite the distinctions between heroes and celebrities, people develop psychological bonds with both groups and seek to emulate their lives. The positioning of celebrities as amoral has negative social implications, however, because moral character is central to the identity of traditional heroes. A celebrity does not need to sacrifice himself or herself to maintain fame. Old heroic figures such as religious, political, and military leaders have been replaced by entertainers.[20] In an 1898 survey of 1440 pre-teens and teenagers ages 12-14, no one listed an entertainer as a person they have heard or read about that they would most like to resemble.[21] By 1948, a similar poll indicated 37 percent of pre-teens and teens wanted to be like an athlete or other type of professional entertainer. In 1986, a similar survey found that 90 percent of the top ten people teenagers wanted to be like were entertainers.[22]

Although celebrities become role models for people to follow, their relation to reality and morality is ambiguous. This moral ambiguity creates what Stuart Ewen refers to as "images without bottoms," leaving the public to project onto the celebrity an interpersonal reality and a moral code, which they then proceed to emulate.[23] When celebrities violate moral norms, the public is thrust into a psychological dilemma in which it is natural to "reject" or "diminish" any moral failure that may have occurred. This diminishment of moral failure explains why it is difficult to convict very popular celebrities of heinous crimes, as demonstrated by those who could not see O.J. Simpson as a murderer[24] or Michael Jackson as a child molester. When celebrities are convicted of crimes, their convictions tend to be for reduced charges and their punishment tends to be less than that given to non-celebrities who commit the same crimes.

"Celebrity" and "success" have become virtually synonymous in media saturated countries like the United States.[25] The probability of an entertainer becoming well known far exceeds that of traditional heroes. Consider original Navy SEAL member Rudy Boesch, who experienced the surprising transition from hero to celebrity during a welcoming home celebration in his hometown of Virginia Beach, Virginia. Boesch tried out for a new television show, CBS's *Survivor*, in 2000. For those of you have not seen the program, *Survivor* is a reality show – in fact, one of the early reality programs before they became standard television fare – in which a group of people are placed in an extreme outdoor living environment and have to survive with very little material support, drawing on their outdoor skills, physical strength and endurance, and ability to build alliances with other competitors. Each week of the program one or more contestants are voted off the program by other contestants. The first season of *Survivor* took place on Borneo, a rugged tropical island north of the Java Sea.

As the first season of *Survivor* progressed, the 76-year-old Rudy Boesch established his image as a cranky non-nonsense pragmatic and likeable contestant. He became very popular with the television audience and came very close to winning the competition. He was one of the last contestants to be voted off the program and was probably more popular than the actual winner of the program, Richard Hatch. Boesch was invited back for a special all-star *Survivor* season in 2003.

Before Boesch became a television star, he had already established his reputation in the Navy with whom those he served. He was a Navy Seal for more than 30 years, becoming one of the most distinguished officers of the original SEAL (Sea-Air-Land) Team TWO. He completed dozens of missions in Vietnam, earning a Bronze Star for his valor. Boesch was a hero long before his participation in the television program *Survivor*. Yet, after Boesch became a television celebrity, the headlines of his hometown newspaper, The Virginian-Pilot, announced Rudy's return to his home after appearing on the final program with the headline "Hometown fans get a chance to honor their hero."[26] A large celebration was prepared for Rudy with extensive media coverage to commemorate his making the final group of four *Survivor* contestants, and the Mayor of Virginia Beach proclaimed a "Rudy Boesch Day. " Reacting to all the attention given to Rudy, one local resident wrote:

> "People seem to think that participating on the show somehow qualifies Rudy as a hero. Rudy Boesch is a true American hero, but not for participating on "*Survivor*." He is a hero for his devoted service to his country and ensuring our survival as a free country. I wonder if Rudy or any of his fellow Navy SEALs made the front page of the newspaper after returning from a mission?"[27]

This resident made an important point. Rudy Boesch has been one of the best role models in one of the most respected elite fighting forces in the U.S., yet he did not receive public recognition until he starred in a television game show. After thousands of people came to greet Rudy with signs such as "Rudy for President" and "Rudy, You Rock," Rudy exclaimed, "Now I know how Elvis felt."

Public perceptions of Rudy Boesch illustrate how both heroes and celebrities function as role models. I define role models as people whose values, beliefs, and behavior are likely to be adopted by others within their sphere of influence. U.S. Navy SEALs viewed Rudy as a role model based on his patriotism and courage; while television audiences viewed Rudy as a role model based on his caustic personality and fame as a game show contestant of the popular television program *Survivor*. In the following section I will discuss some of the important characteristics of the role modeling process.

Modeling Behavior

The process of adopting behavior by modeling others has been extensively researched by Albert Bandura and his students and colleagues at Stanford University.[28] Bandura's social learning theory "emphasizes the prominent roles played by vicarious, symbolic, and self-regulatory processes" that occur in socially mediated experiences.[29] Bandura's theory, more recently referred to as social cognitive theory, has been applied to the study of the most powerful source of these mediated experiences – television. Television provides daily public access to thousands of film and television stars, athletes, and other celebrities.

Choosing celebrities for our role models rather than traditional heroes has important consequences. Celebrities with both good and bad character qualities and behavioral attributes now have enormous social influence. Although there are many celebrities who role model prosocial values and behavior, there are others whose destructive behaviors are adopted by their fans. Even notorious characters can be admired and emulated, as demonstrated by the Columbine High School massacre by two students who idolized Adolf Hitler and rock star Marilyn Manson; or the murder of 6-year-old Tiffany Eunick in Florida by a 168 pound 12-year-old boy who told the jury he was imitating WWF wrestlers he had seen on television.[30]

The recognition that athletes can be positive or negative role models has created great concern among parents, whose children imitate the behavior of athletes they see on television. This has particularly become a problem with young television viewers of WWF wrestling and World Extreme Cagefighting (WEC), some who have seriously injured themselves acting out the violent interactions they have observed on television.[31] As children continue to look toward athletes as their role models for their own behavior, professional sports is placing more recognition that private lives of athletes are just as important forms of social influence as are their professional lives as athletes.[32]

Looking for Heroes among Celebrities

Everyone has a need for heroes. We learn how to act and interact by observing what other people do. There is an innate desire for people to look up to someone who can lead. The rise of the celebrity as society's new leaders has tremendous moral implications. The replacement of parents, teachers and spiritual leaders by actors, athletes and other entertainers indicates a great power shift in today's society. Entertainers now set the example of what kinds of behavior is considered to be appropriate or desirable. Entertainers who practice prosocial behaviors are likely to have a positive influence on society; but those whose behavior is immoral, unethical, or less than desirable, are more likely to have negative influences on others. This double-edged sword is vividly illustrated in the lives of many popular Americans.

The Elvis Phenomenon

Consider the amazing influence of American icon Elvis Presley. Elvis is easily one of the most popular and notable figures of our time, and his impact on the American cultural landscape has been substantive and widespread. Decades after his death, more than 700,000 people each year visit his former home (Graceland) in Memphis, Tennessee.[33] Among private residences, only the White House attracts more visitors each year. Elvis movies, music, books, and other memorabilia continue to sell in the United States and around the world. Newspapers, magazines, television news, and Elvis clubs keep his image perpetually before the American public. In 2007, Elvis' estate earned $52 million, more than any other deceased person.[34]

Elvis fan clubs also have emerged around the world to keep his memory alive. Both in the United States and in other countries, men and women dress up like Elvis and impersonate him in order to entertain audiences at parties, nightclubs and concerts. Based on the various elements associated with those who imitate celebrities, I define impersonation as emulating the appearance and communication behavior of another individual in order to inform, persuade or entertain an audience.

The number of Elvis Presley impersonators worldwide has not been documented, but they have been found in many different nations. One company, B. & K. Enterprises (B-K-Enterprises.com) has sold more than 5,500 Elvis jumpsuits, the average jumpsuit costing $2,800.[35] Visoot Tungarat of Thailand, has impersonated Elvis for more than 42 years in Thailand, Europe, and the United States.[36] He is just one among many international Elvis impersonators. Based on my international observations of Elvis impersonators with my colleague, Dr. Ben Fraser, we concur with other scholars who estimate that there are more than 50,000 Elvis impersonators worldwide. No matter where you live, you can probably find an Elvis impersonator not that far away. These impersonators have become a means by which the persona and values of Elvis are communicated to the larger public. Though Elvis is dead, he continues to entertain and influence a large number of people.

Dr. Benson Fraser and I carried out a five-year study of Elvis Presley impersonators who gathered each summer in Virginia Beach, Virginia, to participate in the Elvis Presley Festival. Through in-depth interviews of Elvis impersonators and fans and our own observations, we have gained insight into the process by which ordinary people role model celebrities. Elvis has been very popular in Virginia both before and after his death. There are more than 20 Elvis fan clubs in Virginia and many fans in the southeast region of the state where Elvis performed. There are also several well-known local Elvis Presley impersonators in the region, and the City of Virginia Beach sponsored an annual Elvis Presley festival during the past six years, bringing internationally known impersonators to the area each summer.

In 2002, we published the results of our study based on interviews with 35 Elvis Presley fans, over half who also are active Elvis impersonators.[37] At least eight of the impersonators have national recognition. The people interviewed were carefully selected in order to include as wide and as diverse a group of fans and impersonators as possible. We over-sampled people from the southeastern United States because we sought to interview what we considered to be a representative group of people we encountered at the Elvis festivals and concerts in Virginia. This purposive sample included: a diverse ethnic representation (including Latin and African American Elvis impersonators), a mixture of different age groups (fans and impersonators from four years old to those in their sixties), and those from a variety of social backgrounds. For example, among those interviewed for this study were: (1) Joan Minnery, the leader of the female impersonation group, "The Graceliners", (2) Brett Fikentsher, a child impersonator of Elvis, (3) Dennis Wise, a professional Elvis impersonator who has been impersonating Elvis for over 20 years, (4) Clarence Giddens, an African American Elvis impersonator, and (5) Robert Lopez, who performs as "El Vez", the Latino Elvis. No group or type of fan was intentionally excluded from the sample.

While the findings of our study were based on the total sample of people interviewed, we drew heavily on certain pertinent or representative interviews from both prominent Elvis impersonators and local performers. We also met with several of the local impersonators in their homes or places of employment. Apart from the festivals, we attended several Elvis performances in Virginia Beach and the surrounding area so that we could get a better understanding of the local Elvis culture. Finally, we visited a shop in Williamsburg, Virginia, that specializes in Elvis Presley memorabilia, and interviewed the owner and a close associate, both experts on Elvis culture. Audio recordings of these interviews were made and several performances of impersonators were videotaped. A number of still photographs were taken for further verification and examination and some of them published. The interviews were transcribed for analysis and provide the basis of my analysis and discussion here.

Identifying with Elvis

Our first research objective explored how Elvis Presley fans identified with him. We also examined what role the mass media played in creating identification with Elvis. Among the 35 respondents in our study, only two had personally met Elvis Presley, and only a few had seen him perform in person. Thus, the images that participants developed of Elvis were predominantly constructed through the mass media. Study participants were repeatedly exposed to Elvis' music and persona through records, tapes, compact discs, radio, television, movies, usually over long periods of time. Dennis Wise articulates what we found to be a common theme among Elvis fans and impersonators when reflecting on his own experience:

> "I have been listening to Elvis every day of my life since I was five years old… We had an old General Electric stereo that had eight or ten records … We would pile them on and go to sleep with Elvis on my mind day and night."[38]

Several other impersonators made similar comments about their involvement with Elvis through various mediated experiences. For example, Clarence Giddons, a popular African American Elvis impersonator, listened to Elvis on the radio, recalling:

> "We didn't have a television set ... I was the only one in my family that liked Elvis. Everybody else was into James Brown, so I kind of had to listen to Elvis by myself."[39]

Another Elvis impersonator, Sterling Riggs, recalled that his mother listened to Elvis music all the time so he grew up listening to Elvis. He reminisced:

> "She had the Elvis 8-track tapes, and I remember that we had a car, and every time we got in that car and went anywhere, I had to put that Elvis 8-track in and listen to it all the time."[40]

Judy Cunida, a long time Elvis fan, remembers immersing herself in Elvis-related media when she was sick with rheumatic fever at age 12 and home from school for six months, stating:

> "Elvis Presley was my salvation during that time. My mom used to buy magazines and records for me, and I spent hours putting photographs in scrapbooks and things like that, listening to the music. I mostly collected books, magazines, the records, photographs, things like that...And those are the things that mean a lot to me, at least $100,000 probably [in value]."[41]

It is interesting to note how many Elvis fans and impersonators were first attracted to him in their youth. As noted earlier, Dennis Wise began listening to Elvis at the age of five; Clarence Giddons and Sterling Riggs both grew up listening to Elvis; Judy Cunida was making scrapbooks of Elvis from popular magazines at age twelve.

One interviewee, Brett Fikentsher, chronicled the process he experienced as a child as he identified with Elvis as a celebrity figure. Brett attended his first Elvis festival in Virginia Beach at age four. He was introduced to Elvis in a very unusual way. As with many four-year-olds, Brett's hero was Superman. Every Sunday he and his mother, Laura, watched *The Adventures of Lois and Clark*, the television series about Superman. One of the characters in the series, Perry White, the newspaper editor, is an Elvis fan. The series often included references to Elvis in the scripts. One day, while watching the program, Brett asked his mother, who was not an Elvis fan, who Elvis was. Although she had not listened to Elvis for years, Laura of course knew who he was and she even had one of his old cassette tapes lying around. When she played the tape for Brett he began dancing around and asked Laura if she would take him to see Elvis. His mother explained that Elvis was dead but that they could rent one of his movies. It wasn't long before Brett was imitating Elvis for the neighborhood children. Superman had been replaced by Elvis.

After Brett performed at the 1995 Elvis Festival in Virginia Beach, both he and his mother decided to forego a trip to Disneyland and visit Graceland instead. At this point, Laura was still not an Elvis fan. The pilgrimage to Graceland changed that. "We learned a lot about [Elvis'] life," Laura says, "and just the multitude of awards that he had won. Not just because of his songs, but because of the person he was..., I found myself in tears every morning at his grave site."[42] Graceland was a turning point for both mother and son. It was a learning experience and helped develop a richer appreciation for Elvis. Besides being there at Elvis' house and at his grave, Laura and Brett were constantly hearing his music in the Memphis stores and in the motel where they stayed. One of the TV channels at the motel played Elvis films 24 hours a day. No place, however, made more of an impression than the meditation garden at Graceland. Laura explained:

> There's something about that meditation garden, and I've tried to figure out what it is, but there is a spiritual presence there of some sort. I've been to Kennedy's' grave and a lot of other peoples' [graves] that I have probably had more admiration for at the time than Elvis, but there's something about—maybe it's the psychic power that people have?[43]

The process by which Brett came to identify with Elvis was sequential, involving several steps. Without a father at home, Brett desired a father figure or role model to help him make sense of his world. His initial fascination with Elvis led the consumption of media products that formed his image of Elvis, eventually leading him to impersonate Elvis and to visit Graceland. With the guidance of his mother, Brett selectively adopted into his personal life attributes and values that he associated with Elvis.

Another impersonator who saw Elvis as a father figure is Dennis Wise. The story of his "relationship" with Elvis began much like Brett's experience, but Wise brings additional aspects of identification into focus not experienced by Brett, who is still a child. Dennis is a 41-year-old Elvis impersonator from Joplin, Missouri.

He has been an Elvis impersonator since March of 1978, when a promoter that his brother knew asked him if he would consider professionally impersonating Elvis. Up until that time he had never sung professionally. Dennis, who has listened to Elvis' music every day since he was five years old, has collected everything he could find about Elvis, including records, audio and video tapes, books, papers, magazines, pictures, posters, and anything with Elvis' picture on it. He has been dressing and acting like Elvis since high school. After impersonating Elvis professionally for some time, Dennis mentioned to his promoter that he had thought of having plastic surgery on his face so he could look more like Elvis. His promoter immediately set up a consultation for the operation. Dennis thought about it deeply. He really wanted to look like Elvis, but he had his doubts about the surgery. Dennis recalled thinking through the decision to go through with the surgery:

> [I thought], "Do I really love this man enough to do that for him?" And you know that's all I thought about. My Dad was a truck driver, y'know, uh, I never saw him. So, Elvis eventually became a father figure to me. So, I did it. And it was phenomenal! I got more press that year than anybody in the country except John Travolta.[44]

Dennis was willing to go through a serious operation in order to more closely identify with Elvis, as revealed in the question he asked himself, "Do I love this man enough to do that for him?" It seems Dennis wants us to believe that he had the operation "for Elvis" and not for himself. He described the operation as an act of love for a surrogate father figure. One wonders about his full array of motives, however, when in the next sentence he elaborates on how much attention he received that year from the facial surgery. Impersonating Elvis reaps other benefits for Dennis, including the fame he receives from his performances. He explained, "when those people are butting, screaming and hollering, that's probably the best reward that money can't buy."[45] For Dennis, Elvis impersonation provides "the greatest experiences a man could have here. You can portray the greatest entertainer in the world and uh, get a little feeling of what it's like to be that man on a very small scale."[46]

Clearly, there are many reasons why a person chooses to identify with a celebrity. This is evident from examining Robert Lopez's identification with Elvis. Robert, who was born in San Diego, identifies with Elvis in quite a different way than Dennis Wise. He performs under the name "El Vez," and has been performing the "El Vez" show for almost ten years. The show has developed and progressed over the years into a Las Vegas/ Mexico review, incorporating Latin sounds and giving Hispanic interpretations to many of Elvis' songs. Robert's colorful show includes a live band, two back-up singers ("The Elvettes"), several costume changes, and social commentary. Interestingly, for a performer of Latino music, Lopez credits punk rock with giving him the idea for the "El Vez" show. When Robert was an adolescent, he performed in a punk-rock band, which he says taught him to take a "do-it-yourself," "anything-goes" approach to performance.

> "I took that do-it-yourself idea and applied it to the Elvis life-style," Robert says. "It's the whole idea [that] you, too, can be King.... I took the punk-rock attitude and applied it to Elvis."[47]

Robert, who had listened to Elvis as a small boy but also liked many other performers and types of music, explained why he identified with Elvis:

> To me, Elvis has always been there, and so I cannot think of a time that he wasn't part of my life. When I was a little boy, my uncles had continental slacks and little pompadours, and so they looked like Elvis, too. And for me [I thought], "Well, Elvis must be Latino, too. He looks just like my uncles. So, to me the idea of Elvis being Latino was always [there].[48]

The idea of becoming an Elvis impersonator came to Robert when he was an art gallery curator and the gallery presented an Elvis Presley theme show. They had paintings, furniture, clothes, a whole multi-media event, and for the opening ceremonies, they hired an Elvis impersonator. "His name was Cashis Elvis," Robert remembers, "and he did it and I go, 'That looks kind've fun. I could do that. I could be "El Vez" the Mexican Elvis.'"[49] So, at the suggestion of some "hard core" Elvis fans, Robert decided to go to Memphis and do a tribute to Elvis as "El Vez." He only intended to do it once, but the act was so well received that Robert decided to launch a career of impersonating Elvis. He has toured both the United States and Europe and has released five CDs.

"El Vez" does more than incorporate different musical styles and Latino dress into his Elvis act. A host of cultural and personal values are embedded in his interpretation of Elvis, as he describes below:

> What I'm doing with El Vez is changing [Elvis' music] for a Latino lifestyle and giving it the Mexican perspective and tellin' the history of my people through the music of Elvis. Elvis is something that's all-American, you know, it's an American idea: an American Dream of a poor-man with nothing coming to be the richest. But I'm showing [in performance] that the dream can be held by a Latino and an immigrant Black, a white [man], a yellow man. The American Dream is for everybody and that's the idea.[50]

Here is a clear illustration of someone taking on the image of a celebrity and merging it with one's own cultural and personal characteristics. Elvis was liked and admired, but in this case, used selectively and purposefully to promote Robert's cultural and social views. Robert was not just interested in "keeping the memory [of Elvis] alive," but he consciously constructed an image to represent a Latin Elvis. In this way Robert was both an impersonator and a translator, both an Elvis fan and an advocate of Latino culture. Robert's identification with Elvis was a means to an end and not and end in itself. For Robert and other impersonators and fans, Elvis is the focal point for constructing a mediated image that is grounded in an historical figure yet is recreated by their own cultural and personal experiences and beliefs.

Another Elvis impersonator who identified with Elvis across cultural boundaries was Clarence Giddens, an African American Elvis impersonator. He identified with Elvis' liberated expression of male sexuality, which he observed was repulsed by many Whites. He describes what he referred to as the "Black sound" of Elvis:

> "Elvis sounds so much like Black, I mean singing those songs and when they told him he couldn't do that, he said, 'I'm gonna do it.' That's why today I pay a big tribute to this guy... I always considered myself the soul side of Elvis Presley. Everybody has a little bit of Elvis in them."[51]

Identification with Elvis also crosses the gender boundary. Women identify with Elvis as a romantic partner. Most women we interviewed have an image of Elvis as a gentleman; few acknowledged him as a womanizer. Carol Miller provides a common perception that we heard repeated by many women. She described Elvis as follows:

> "He was just every teenage girl's dream; and we just fell in love with him. ... When I first got married, my ex-husband was very jealous of Elvis. I said, "That man [Elvis] could put his shoes under my bed anytime. From that day till the day we were

> divorced, I never saw Elvis, I never saw Elvis movies, I never listened to Elvis music. He broke every record I had. I mean, he was insanely jealous of Elvis... he took it for real."[52]

Elvis fan Ronde Fritz explained that Elvis appeared on the scene when she was a young teenager. She both observed and personally experienced how Elvis spurred the sexual awakening of her generation. She explains, "Elvis knew, just seemed to instinctively know, what fed a woman's emotions. The girls were suddenly very, very aware of feelings and emotions that at my 13-year-old age were brand new; they were a brand-new set of emotions."[53]

Many Elvis fans and impersonators identified with Elvis as a lover of music. El John, also an Elvis impersonator, relayed his intense love for Elvis' music, stating, "First of all I love music, I love his music. I love the king of rock n' roll. It will always be alive in my heart. It's just something that pleases me. I hear his music and my problems go away. Everybody has something – I have Elvis." Sean Brickle, the head of a public relations agency, reported becoming an Elvis fan the first time he heard him, recalling, "When *Heartbreak Hotel* came on the radio ...it turned me on to radio and music."[54] Thus Elvis fans and impersonators identified with Elvis in very personal and intimate ways as a father, a relative or culturally similar brother, a lover, and as a lover of music. Elvis was a multicultural symbol of an intimate other with whom fans and impersonators could identify.

Adopting Elvis' Values and Behavior

The second research objective of our five-year study investigated how fans who strongly identified with Elvis Presley seek to role model his perceived values and behavior. Our respondents provided numerous examples of how they had adopted Elvis' perceived values and behaviors as their own. Joan Minnery, a thirty-year-old single mother and the leader of a country and western line-dance team of nine female Elvis impersonators called "The Graceliners," believes that Elvis represents the values of a simpler life when gender roles were more pronounced. She explains:

> "I think that Elvis was the icon of that time. He will always be the king of rock and roll and that's what people want. They want to go back to that time when men could go on stage and wow the ladies and people could just be themselves... He was a gentleman and these are the values that to me, that he carried and the love for his mother and the respect for his father. ...If I could have my son treat me the way Elvis treated his mother, I'd be a happy mom. That's a role model that I want my son to look up to. Elvis is the person I want him to emulate."[55]

Laura Tom believes her and her son Brett have learned generosity and respect from Elvis. She shared sentiments that many other fans expressed when asked how Elvis had influenced her:

> "Yes, he was very generous. He ... never lost respect for his mother. He was always a fair man...I know Elvis himself was a very religious man, but now it [Graceland] has become like Mecca, for people who loved Elvis."[56]

Both Brett and Laura feel that there are some characteristics about Elvis that are not attractive, but they tend to focus on the good attributes in Elvis. Laura encourages Brett to emulate Elvis' out-going character and his charisma. She also points out to Brett that Elvis seemed to really care about people and that he was generous person who was willing to share. Although Laura encourages her son to take on some of Elvis's prosocial behaviors, they also discuss some of the problems Elvis had. Brett is not the only young Elvis impersonator.

Robert Lopez, a.k.a. El Vez, discussed earlier, believes Elvis personified not just the American dream but a global dream of spreading universal values such as good will, helping your fellow man, economic freedom and hope for the poor. In addition to these values, El Vez brings everything from sex education to political commentary into his Elvis shows, explaining:

> "Elvis said, 'Baby let's play house'... But I...say, 'Baby let's play safe.' Ya'know the song "Suspicious Minds" is now about immigration rights, "Immigration Time," for me. "In the Ghetto" is "In El Barrio," so I tell about, you know, problems in East L.A., problems with immigration rights. "Bosinova Baby" turns into "Sez-Cha-vez" [Caesar Chavez]."[57]

In the song "In El Barrier," Elvez sings, "It is now or never, please no more gangs; people are dying, don't you understand? Manana, will be too late. It's now or never, let's stop the hate."[58] This song exemplifies how El Vez reinterprets to address the problem of gang violence and promote the value of non-violence among young Latinos.

Consistently, Elvis impersonators and fans stated they had tried to adopt the positive attributes of Elvis, his love and respect for his parents, his politeness, his generosity, his spirituality, and his multiculturalism, and apply them to their own lives. The negative attributes of Elvis were rarely mentioned by the study participants. When stories of Elvis' drug abuse, eating disorders, or womanizing were mentioned, they were often minimized or thought to be exaggerations or fabrications propagated by media for revenue.

For example, when Joan Minnery was asked about the moral problems Elvis struggled with, she dismissed the notion as arising from rumor or gossip, stating:

> "People can say all sorts of things about him, but he's dead and he's gone. The same thing with Jesus Christ. They say lots of things about him. The man's dead. How can he defend himself? ... I can feel him in my heart. I can see him in my dreams, I can see him on my wall in my posters, that's the stuff that's the real Elvis. The other stuff is a bunch of crap...if he did do that stuff then he should have gotten the help that he deserved. That to me doesn't mean one iota...I am still going to love him."[59]

Joan does what we observed in many other fans and impersonators. She selectively identified with Elvis' prosocial values and downplayed Elvis' antisocial characteristics and behaviors. Thus, Joan has had no difficulty in encouraging her son to be like Elvis, extending the identification process to the next generation.

Results of our study indicate that people selectively integrate the perceived values and behaviors they see in celebrities they admire and adopt them into their own lives. Fans develop self-defining relationships with celebrities and seek to adopt their perceived attributes, resulting in powerful forms of personal and social transformation.

The social and personal lives of those we interviewed have changed substantially. The fans and impersonators we interviewed have a new network of friends with whom they associate and communicate more comfortably. Joan Minnery, for example, indicated that she is more articulate both in the workplace and in her private life as a result of her decision to impersonate Elvis. Several impersonators have even changed their appearance, not only on-stage but also on off-stage, as dramatically exemplified by Dennis Wise's plastic surgery. Most study participants discussed specific values associated with Elvis that they had sought to emulate, including generosity, respecting authority, loyalty, having good manners, being a gentleman, caring for others, patriotism, racial equality, and being a spiritual person. Spigel suggested that, "the Elvis impersonator presents audiences with opportunities to imagine themselves as part of a personal and collective history in which Elvis represents a set of shared beliefs and pleasures."[60] Thus fans and impersonators are able to reinvent their personal history and to involve themselves in a community of shared values.

I note three important findings of our study as they relate to our understanding of social influence through role modeling of popular entertainers. First, we found that many ordinary people develop extraordinary psychological relationships with celebrities, whether living or dead. Second, we found that media consumers regard celebrities as role models. Third, we found that fans tend to adopt a celebrity's perceived attributes, including his or her values and behavior.

There are several implications of our research of Elvis impersonators and fans. The results are consistent with previous studies indicating that following the lives of celebrities can produce profound psychological and behavioral consequences. As noted earlier, media scholars have already observed the effects of celebrities on the adoption of clothing styles, product purchases and health behaviors.[61] Our findings extend beyond the effects found in previous studies that indicate children seek to imitate film stars who play the roles of heroes and heroines;[62] or that adults buy products based on their perceived images of celebrity endorsers; or that people of all ages emulate the appearance and behaviors of media personae they admire.

The Elvis fans and impersonators interviewed in our study have integrated their internal values and beliefs with those derived from a mediated image of Elvis Presley, such that the fabric of their self-identity is intricately interwoven with their image of Elvis, not only as an entertainer, but also as a friend, lover, husband, father, patriot, and citizen. Our results suggest that the image of a celebrity can be more tightly held and more powerful than the real person upon which it is based. This is similar to Baudrillard's concept of simulacra, a copy without an original, except that the copy is a mediated image that is based on an original yet is very different from the original. There seems to be great flexibility in the way that people fill in the details of "the images without bottoms" with whom they relate.

For example, consider the millions of Muslims throughout the world who still regard the late Osama bin Laden as a modern hero of Islam. Bin Laden t-shirts were selling in Islamic countries (I saw them for sale in Thailand) like Michael Jordan t-shirts were selling in western countries during the early 1990s. In spite of the videotape evidence released by Al Qaeda depicting bin Laden's involvement in the September 11, 2001 terrorist attack on the U.S., people still refuse to believe the mediated image of bin Laden as a terrorist because it is inconsistent with their image of him as a hero. Similar to Plato's allegory of the cave, the shadowy figure of bin Laden and his mystique may be more real to his followers than he is in person. Likewise, people we interviewed refused to belief Elvis was a womanizer. Identification with Elvis, Osama bin Laden, or any other celebrity is a process of selective perception, since it is based on a perceived image and mediated reality.

Princess Diana's International Fame

Perhaps no other celebrity's death in the past 25 years since the passing of Elvis Presley has had as much social influence as the tragic death of Diana, Princess of Wales. One could hardly find a news magazine without Princess Diana on the cover in the weeks following her death in August of 1997. Elton John's memorable performance of "Candle in the Wind" at Diana's funeral, a song originally written to memorialize Marilyn Monroe, quickly became the biggest and fastest best-selling single of all time in both the U.S. and Great Britain, selling nearly 3.5 million copies in its first week of release.[63] Just 37 days after its release the Guinness Book of Records declared "Candle in the Wind 97" to be the biggest selling single recording in history.[64]

Princess Diana embodied the archetype of the princess myth. She was a relatively unknown beautiful young woman, discovered by the ruling prince, who became the peoples' princess. Despite her personal moral failures, psychological struggles, and clashes with the house of Windsor, Diana was seen as one who reached out to help those less fortunate. These actions made her a heroine to many admirers who sought to protect her reputation.

More than one million mourners lined the three-mile funeral route in London to pay their respects to Diana. People who had never met the former Princess and who had no personal contact with her traveled to England from around the world to place flowers along the funeral route. Two thousand celebrities attended Diana's memorial service, including fashion designers, film and television stars, political leaders, musicians, and writers. Donatella and Santo Versace, Hillary Clinton, Luciano Pavarotti, Tom Cruise and Nicole Kidman, Steven Spielberg, Henry Kissinger, Tom Hanks, and hundreds of members of royal families from around the world came to pay their respects.[65]

An estimated 2.5 billion people watched the worldwide satellite transmission of the funeral to 200 countries in 44 languages, from small villages in Iceland to giant screens in Hong Kong, making it the most watched event in history.[66] "If the whole world was watching," reported Tom Shales of the Washington Post, "then the whole world was probably weeping, too." In homes, coffee shops, bars, hospitals, restaurants, offices, and wherever television reached them, people mourned the loss of an international celebrity like they mourned the loss of a family member or friend.[67] Books about Diana immediately became best sellers as people consumed media to learn more about her life. Princess Diana is one of the few women in the 20th century whose popularity penetrated every continent in the expanded global marketplace of international fame, making her a great source of social influence. Like Elvis, Diana became one of the few people in history recognized internationally by her first name.

Princess Diana's international fame enabled her to use media to do some extraordinary works, which I will discuss later. The widespread social influence of celebrities like Diana is important given the large numbers of people who follow their lives through the mass media and who look to them as people to emulate. Very few people attracted more media attention than did Diana, who as a result, became one of the most influential role models for millions of people in history, both during her life and at the time of her death.[68]

Agenda Setting Influence of Celebrities

One of the ways in which celebrities gain an extensive social influence is by drawing the news media's attention and hence public attention to the values and behaviors they promote. This would not be possible without the news media's cooperation and the public's infatuation with the lives of celebrities. Journalists seek out celebrities to satisfy the demand for captivating news stories. The need for human interest stories pressures journalists, according to Boorstin, to fabricate or embellish reality, leading to the media's production of "pseudo-events" and to the rise of the celebrity, the "human pseudo-event."[69]

Planned news coverage of a specific event involving one or more celebrities were first referred to by Jun and Dayan as a "media event."[70] The extensive media coverage of the funeral of President John F. Kennedy, the peace trip to Israel by Egyptian President Anwar Sadat, or the wedding of Britain's Prince Charles and Lady Diana, are but a few examples of media events. I extended the concept of media events by noting unplanned media coverage of relatively spontaneous events, such as the Challenger disaster, the bombing of Baghdad during the Persian Gulf War, and the police chase of O.J. Simpson in June of 1995, can have the same influential characteristics as planned media events.[71]

Any event of public interest involving a celebrity has the potential to become a media event, even when the celebrity has no control over the event. For example, the media coverage of Bruno Hauptmann kidnapping and murder trial became a media event because Charles Lindbergh's son was the murder victim. The trial became one of the greatest media events in history because Lindbergh was one of the most popular celebrities in American history. The police chase of O.J. Simpson became the media event of 1994 and his murder trial the media event of 1995, only because of Simpson's great celebrity status. The Jon Benet Ramsey murder case gained national and international attention because Jon Benet was herself a young upcoming celebrity and her parents were wealthy. Even regional and national celebrity status can attract widespread attention and extensive media coverage.

An important consequence of media attention created by celebrities is their influence on the public agenda. The study of agenda-setting was birthed more than four decades ago by two scholars who theorized that media coverage of specific issues could predict public opinion during a presidential election.[72] More recent agenda-setting research indicates that the media not only influence "what we think about" but can also frame issues and influence "how we think" about specific issues.[73] In the past two decades, several studies demonstrate how celebrities can influence the media agenda and public agenda. For example, the analysis of the diffusion of AIDS news stories indicated such news greatly increased when a celebrity, Rock Hudson, died of AIDS.[74] My own research with my colleague Michael Basil indicated that the diffusion of the story of Earvin "Magic" Johnson's HIV infection promoted an increase in concern about HIV among the heterosexual community.[75] Concern about spouse abuse and the U.S. legal system increased during the extensive media coverage of the O.J. Simpson criminal trial.[76] These examples demonstrate how celebrities can have an agenda-setting effect by virtue of their popularity. We refer to the influence of celebrities on the public more generally as "the celebrity effect."

Since the images or personas of celebrities are created, marketed, and sold, the demand for celebrity journalists and celebrity photographers, commonly known as paparazzi, has increased during the past decade. Newspapers, magazines, and news entertainment television programs have created what Shenk calls the "celebro-journalist," a person who reports celebrity news.[77] The roots of celebrity journalism can be traced to the work of Walter Winchel, the father of the gossip column. Boorstin traces the first "interview" of a celebrity to Horace Greeley's question and answer session with Brigham Young in August of 1959, published verbatim in the New York Tribune.[78] Shenk contends that the growth of magazines featuring celebrities such as Andy Warhol's Interview, precursor to *People Magazine*, Jann Wenner's *Rolling Stone*, and Tina Brown's *Vanity Fair*, expanded rapidly during the 1960s and has continued to grow during the past two decades.[79] Many of the most popular magazines and news programs in the U.S. focus on celebrities. The focus on personality rather than substance is affecting many areas of journalism, including coverage of business, politics, and culture. Neimark claims our celebrity culture provides the public with "more and more information about people who are less and less real."[80] Detailed information about the superficial characteristics of famous people "strips them of the sacred and heroic," claims Neimark, creating an illusory world where fact and fiction about people are nearly inseparable.[81]

From Illusion to Sales

The 'larger than life' nature of celebrities creates an illusionary media environment in which they can persuade people to spend money. As former tennis great Andre Agassi said in his advertisements for Canon, "Image is Everything." Advertisers seek to affect consumers' self-images through the brand images they create with celebrity promotions and other marketing schemes.[82] Advertising research indicates celebrities can effectively promote sales and social causes by creating more consumer awareness and favorable attitudes of the products and causes they endorse.[83] Marketing studies have documented the persuasive influences of celebrities such as actor Al Pacino,[84] singer and songwriter Johnny Cash,[85] and actress Mary Tyler Moore[86] for a variety of products. By seeking to match endorsers' public exposure, attributes and lifestyle with the type of product or service being promoted, celebrities have been shown to be effective influencers of purchasing behavior.[87]

Corporations that employ celebrities as spokespersons also tend to increase their profits.[88] Celebrity endorsements have become a ubiquitous feature of marketing. By 1997, the use of celebrities in advertisements reached 25 percent in the U.S.[89] and 70 percent in Japan.[90] This may be because celebrity endorsers are perceived as more trustworthy and competent as compared to non-celebrities, enhancing product image and increasing product use.[91] During the 1990s, advertisers turned to dead celebrities to promote product sales.[92] Albert Einstein, W.C. Fields, Marilyn Monroe, James Dean, Steve McQueen, John Wayne, Humphrey Bogart, Louis Armstrong, Groucho Marx, James Cagney, Greta Garbo, and Babe Ruth have all sold products after their deaths; and, unlike living celebrities, they do not get themselves into trouble, a major concern of companies who hire celebrities to endorse their products.

The income-generating power of celebrities can extend long after their deaths. The top-earning dead celebrities from October 2005 to October 2006 were musician Kurt Cobain, whose beneficiaries received $50 million; Elvis Presley, whose estate earned $42 million; cartoonist Charles Schultz, who earned $35 million; singer-songwriter John Lennon, who earned $24 million, and Albert Einstein, who earned $20 million.[93]

Revenues generated by American-born celebrities are not restricted to the U.S. Leonardo DiCaprio, for example, celebrity king of *Titanic* fame (which grossed nearly $5 billion in total sales worldwide), appeared in a series of television advertisements in Japan in the late 1990s to increase the sales of Orico credit cards and Suzuki wagons.[94] *Titanic*'s big splash in

Japan made DiCaprio a wealth generator for Japanese companies. Other celebrity's marketability extends to places they have never visited. The largest Elvis Presley fan club exists in London, where all kinds of Elvis memorabilia are sold, yet Elvis never visited London.

Celebrities are particularly effective sales promoters when their attributes "match" the attributes of the product they are advertising. For example, Andre Agassi is better at selling tennis rackets than selling cars. Dale Earnhardt Jr. may be very good at selling motor oil but not as good at selling jeans. The reason so many companies use celebrities to sell products is because many people will buy a product advertised by a celebrity they like, even if they are not enthusiastic about the product. Thus, celebrities regularly influence how we spend money.

There are many other things more important than our buying behavior that celebrities can influence. They can influence how we think about ourselves and others and how we act toward one another. They can also influence how we dress, what we eat, how much we exercise, whether or not we use tobacco, alcohol, or illegal drugs, and our sexual behavior. These aspects of our lives can become life and death issues. It is this process of celebrity influence that I will explore further as we consider exactly how this influence works. In order to increase our understanding of celebrity influence, in the next chapter I will discuss how people become psychologically and emotionally involved with celebrities.

Discussion Questions

1. Who is one of your favorite celebrities and do you try to follow his or her life?
2. What celebrity has influenced your life the most and why?
3. What celebrities are being modeled the most by teenagers today and why?
4. How would you get young people to think about the celebrity influence in their lives?

Chapter 5
Involvement with Mediated Personalities

Several years ago, I was explaining to my barber while she was cutting my hair how people become emotionally and psychologically involved with entertainers. I explained to her that when television viewers see the same people on television day after day or week after week, they began to feel like they personally know the people they watch. I then gave several examples of actors and actresses who are approached by strangers who begin to interact with them as if they were good friends. The woman cutting my hair perked up and enthusiastically replied, "I know exactly what you mean. A good friend of mine who looks like a popular soap opera star was approached by a stranger while walking down the street. The stranger stopped her and said, "How dare you treat Erika that way," and went on to scold her for mistreating a character named Erika in a popular soap opera series." My barber's friend was pleased to be mistaken for an attractive professional actress but flabbergasted by the outburst of anger from a complete stranger.

Many other people have similar stories. Once when my wife and I were visiting Scotland, a country music fan was sure that my wife was a famous recording artist and asked for her autograph in a grocery store. My wife, who has been mistaken before for a famous actor, had a difficult time convincing this stranger that she was not a famous singer. What surprised my wife was the perceived familiarity by which she was approached. In addition to much anecdotal evidence about how the public become profoundly fascinated with famous people, there is substantial scientific evidence that demonstrates entertainment media generate intense audience involvement, which can have subsequent effects on the behaviors of audience members.[1] The concept of involvement is a broad one that describes how audience members relate to individuals depicted in and through the mass media.[xi] Alan Rubin[2] describes involvement as a motivated state of anticipated engagement with media messages in which audience members psychologically process media content.

One assumption fundamental to the concept of involvement is that media consumers are active media users rather than passive receivers of information. Two types of involvement are identified by media scholars Alan Rubin and Elizabeth Perse: (1) a motivational state that reflects the attitudes that people bring with them to the communication situation, and

---

[xi] Brown, W. J. (2015). Examining four processes of audience involvement with media personae: Transportation, parasocial interaction, identification and worship. *Communication Theory, 25*(3), 259-283.

(2) the cognitive, affective, and behavioral participation induced by the media during media exposure (i.e. becoming emotionally and intellectually involved with a television character while watching a program).[3]

Research on television effects indicates that television viewers become involved with both television characters and television stars through repeated media exposure.[4] Entertainment television programs have been effective in generating a high degree of audience involvement, particularly when popular media personalities are created. The high involvement of audiences with popular soap opera characters provides substantial evidence of the efficacy of using dramatic serials to induce attitudinal and behavioral changes.[5] Two of the most common forms of audience involvement with mediated personalities are called parasocial interaction and identification. Although closely related, these two types of audience involvement differ substantially.

Building on the work of Alan Rubin, my understanding of involvement is more broadly conceptualized beyond television or any other particular form of media. I define the involvement of an individual with a mediated personality, or persona, whether a real person or a fictional character, as a type of emotional and psychological attachment that occurs through prolonged media or event exposure. For example, a person who attends all the professional football games of Peyton Manning, and who watches all his news conferences and television commercials, and who reads every news story he or she can find about Manning, and who searchers the Internet to visit websites that provide information about Manning and opportunities to discuss him with others, will develop a strong degree of involvement with Manning.

Suppose a music fan becomes deeply involved with Bono and the band U2. That involvement could be cultivated by listening to U2 music, attending U2 concerts, reading articles about U2 in magazines and newspapers, exploring U2's website, keeping a blog on U2 and responding to the posts of those who read the blog, using social networking sites such as Instagram, Facebook, and Twitter to share and exchange U2 pictures, stories, experiences, contacts and ideas. Involvement is not merely an individual psychological state but can include an entire web of relationships, both genuine and imagined.

Several important theories and related studies suggest that people who become involved with celebrities are more likely to be influenced by the celebrity's values, beliefs and practices. Several theories of involvement that are particularly useful in the study of celebrities are basking in reflected glory, parasocial interaction, transportation, identification, and worship. I will now discuss these five processes of involvement that are all powerful forms of social influence and will provide examples from studies that have explored these various processes.

Basking in Reflected Glory

The first type of involvement that is an important form of social influence is called basking in reflected glory, abbreviated BIRG. Social scientists have observed that sports fans of specific sports teams and athletes commonly see "their" team as an extension of themselves.[6] This phenomenon can be as simple as wearing a Boston Red Sox or New York Yankees baseball cap, having a Dallas Cowboys or Los Angeles Lakers sticker on your car, or wearing the team jersey of your favorite soccer star. BIRG takes place all the time between sports fans and their favorite teams and athletes but is especially strong when teams win and athletes are successful. This is because people tend to see themselves more closely associated with teams that win.

As evidence for this, Robert Cialdini and his colleagues discovered that fans use terms such as "we won" to refer to the team's performance on a previous day and are more likely to wear the team's apparel following a win.[7] Conversely, in a corollary concept called "Cutting off Reflected Failure" (CORF), Snyder, Lassegard, & Ford[8] discovered that fans distance themselves from losing teams. Growing up in Boston, I can completely relate to both BIRG and CORF. For many years Bostonians were strongly tied to the Boston Celtics. While I was growing up in the Boston area, the Celtics won an amazing 11 NBA championships over a 13-year period, a feat that has never been reproduced by any professional sports team. My friends and I played many hours of basketball each week and went to many Celtics games – we felt a part of the team. When the Celtics won, we won, and when they lost, we lost. During those same years, the Boston Bruins had some great players and won the Stanley Cup in the 1969-1970 and 1971-1972 hockey seasons.

In contrast, the Boston Patriots, who later became the New England Patriots, and the Boston Red Sox, had a history of heart-breaking and embarrassing losses. The Patriots finally reached their first Superbowl in the 1985-1986 football season, but lost badly to the

The Boston Red Sox, although a team with a great winning history, suffered some of the most excruciating and well-known defeats in sports history during the 1970s, 1980s and 1990s, creating all kinds of jokes about Red Sox fans. In the 1919-1920 off-season, the Red Sox owners made one of the stupidest decisions in sports history – trading one of the greatest baseball players of all time, Babe Ruth, to their hated rivals, the New York Yankees. The resulting "curse of the Bambino," referencing Babe Ruth's nickname, became part of baseball lore and was often used to explain the many inauspicious failures of the Red Sox to win another World Series.

In 1967 the Red Sox had a miraculous season, winning the American League Pennant, but lost the World Series to the St. Louis Cardinals, 4 games to 3, losing 3 times to the magnificent Cardinal pitcher, Bob Gibson. Again, in 1975, the Red Sox made it to the World Series, losing in 7 games to the Cincinnati Reds. The final game 7 was tied 3-3 into the ninth, when Cincinnati scored one run to win the game, 4 to 3. It was another heart-breaking loss for Red Sox fans.

Chicago Bears, 52-10, in Superbowl XX. During the many years of Patriot losses, I heard my high school classmates often say, "I can't believe those guys lost again" or "they were embarrassing" or "they suck."

The most famous and gut-wrenching Red Sox loss occurred in another World Series game, this one, game 6 of the World Series with the New York Mets in 1986. The Boston Red Sox were determined to shake the "curse of the Bambino" once and for all. Boston led the Mets 3 games to 2 and took 5-3 lead over the Mets in the top half of the tenth inning. At the bottom of the tenth, they were one out away from winning their first World Series since 1918 when all hell broke loose. Through bad relief pitching and the most famous error in baseball history, the Mets scored 3 runs in the bottom of the 10th and won the game, 6 to 5. The Mets escaped with a little help, many said, from "The Babe," and went on to win game 7.

I was one of the Bostonians who was a Red Sox fan who had experienced these painful losses in 1967, 1975 and 1986, and I'm sure I said, "I can't believe they lost again!" It probably never occurred to me to admit that "we lost," not "them," but such is the nature of CORF. Only the truest sports fans stick closely to their teams when they lose. I think my Uncle Joe was one of those true fans. He was always hopeful and stayed an avid Red Sox fan season after season of terrible losses. After a while, Bostonians became so used to heartbreakers that they did begin to identify with the Red Sox, even in their losses. Of course, our pain ended during the amazing 2004 baseball season when the Red Sox grew from a Boston franchise team into Red Sox Nation, gaining fans throughout the U.S. (see the feature film *Fever Pitch* (2005) to get a feel for being a Red Sox fan). In one of the most miraculous and improbable come-backs in sports history, the Red Sox beat the New York Yankees, their hated rivals and the richest team in baseball with a plethora of best stars, after being down 3 games to none in the American League play-offs. When the Red Sox finally won the World Series that year, its first in 86 years, Bostonians could be heard shouting in the streets of Boston, "We did it!" "We finally did it!" Such is the nature of basking in reflected glory; it is no longer "they did it" but "we did it!"

The tendency to BIRG or CORF may help to explain an additional mechanism through which people may come to develop an imagined association with a successful team or athlete. The BIRG phenomenon may shape associated affective responses such as the heightened joy and emotional exhilaration that fans may experience from a dramatic win.[9] Even with losing teams, fans may develop a strong attachment that motivates fans to remain loyal even to mediocre teams, such as what occurred between my Uncle Joe and the Boston Red Sox. Only God knows how much money he lost on them during those mediocre years, but my uncle was as faithful a fan as you would ever find. This kind of psychological and emotional attachment creates a long-term involvement that can occur with individual athletes as well as teams.[10]

Processes of Involvement

In my 2015 article in *Communication Theory* cited earlier, I explain four distinct but closely related processes of audience involvement with real people and fictional characters we are exposed to in the media, also called media personae. These four types of involvement are transportation, parasocial interaction, identification and worship.

Transportation

A first important process of involvement with media personas is when audience members transport themselves through their imagination into the perceived world of a media persona. This process involves being emotionally and psychologically transported into another person's world, imagining what it would be like to be another person. The world may be fictional, as it would be in a soap opera, or real, as it would be at a rock concert. For example, I could transport myself through my imagination into the world of my favorite athlete, or film star, or writer. Suppose I was mesmerized by the great composer Amadeus Mozart. I could read every book written about him, immerse myself in his music, go to Mozart concerts, and watch the 1984 film about his life, Amadeus, over and over again. Through this immersion in various media, I could construct in my imagination what it would be like to be in the world in which Mozart lived.

In this process of transportation, audience members can develop such a strong emotional and psychological connection with the persona that they imagine themselves in the presence of the persona. I could even imagine myself listening to Mozart play the piano in his home. The idea that people can actually transport themselves into imaginary worlds is explained by transportation theory, which utilizes a travel metaphor of moving from one place to another. Transportation theorists have viewed this process within the framework of media enjoyment.[21] Some communication scholars discuss the process of transportation under the more general theory of social presence.[22] Social presence occurs when audience members experience a sense of being with a media persona. Although transportation theory and the theory of social presence have been primarily applied to the study of communication processes in virtual environments, they have an important application to the study of involvement with media personas in any mediated environment.

Green and Brock describe transportation into a narrative world as a "distinct mental process" that involves an "integrative melding of attention, imagery and feelings."[23] These psychological processes of transportation can occur just as easily with real people as with fictional characters. Millions of golf enthusiasts, for example, may be so deeply involved with Tiger Woods that they can enter his world of golf through their imagination. Elvis Presley impersonators would "feel like Elvis" as soon as they adorned themselves with an Elvis suite as a part of their impersonation performances.[24] Athletes who perform amazing athletic feats often report that they "visualized themselves" performing the feat, sometimes with the aid of seeing themselves as the star athlete they were seeking to emulate. Thus, transportation into the world of another person can occur with both fictional characters and real people.

It is clear that entering the imaginary world of a media persona is a form of involvement that takes place when people intensively immerse themselves in narrative worlds. Transportation can be understood as "a form of experiential responses to narratives."[25] Exactly where the process of transportation fits with respect to other forms of involvement is not obvious. I place it as an initial involvement process, although it could be experienced concurrently with one or more other involvement processes. For example, an audience member must learn about a media persona and develop an initial relationship with him or her in order to think and feel what it is like to be in the same place as that person.

Although focused on written narratives such as novels, the process of entering the world of another person, whether that world be the fictional of a character of the actual world of a celebrity, transportation can take place through immersion in any type of media.

Green, Brock and Kaufman suggest that with fictional media personae, transportation may be a prerequisite to developing parasocial relationships with personae and identifying with them.[26] Drawing on Jonathan Cohen's[27] conception of identification, they propose that an audience member must achieve an altered state of awareness by being transported into the world of a fictional character in order to identify with that character. Suppose we take a popular fictional character like Jack Bauer, the special agent and star of the television series *24*. We first would get to know Jack Bauer by watching the television program, *24*, and by perhaps reading more information about the character on websites, in news magazines, and on entertainment news programs. Through repeated immersion into Jack Bauer's world, one can begin to feel the conflicting emotions regarding the ethical and moral choices he must make as an agent assigned to stop terrorist attacks through all available legal means at his disposal. I have talked to others immersed in this series about these ethical and moral conflicts exposed by the writers of *24*.

When we think about identifying with Jack Bauer, it is clear that without immersing ourselves in his narrative world, identification would be difficult. How could we consider adopting Bauer's philosophy of interrogating terrorists without understanding his world? This is why it makes sense that the process of transportation precedes the process of identification. If identification with a media persona involves seeing the persona's perspective as one's own, then transporting oneself into the world of the persona is necessary before the process of identification takes place.

In summary, transportation can be viewed as a process that precedes or develops concurrently with the development of a parasocial relationship with a persona, whether with a real person like a celebrity or with a fictional person like a television character, and precedes identification with that persona. Melanie Green and her colleagues also note that the process of transportation can have either a positive or negative valence.[28] They theorize that one can just as easily enter the world of Osama bin Laden or Charles Manson as one could enter the worlds of likeable personas. Thus, negatively-valenced parasocial interaction may follow or develop concurrently with negatively-valenced transportation. Attention will now be turned to the process of identification.

The ability to explore the narrative world of a fictional character or celebrity depends on a number of factors. One factor should be obvious – the development of parasocial relationships in the fictional world. Transportation will feed parasocial relationship development with personae which also will support more transportation.

A second factor influencing transportation is the vividness of a narrative world. The more vivid a narrative world is portrayed, whether through words, sound, or pictures, the more easily a media consumer can immerse himself for herself into that world. Obviously, the type of medium being employed to create another narrative world can affect vividness. The use of HD television and other digital media technologies is increasing the ability for creative artists to create vivid narrative worlds.

A third factor is the amount of energy it takes to immerse oneself into another's narrative world. Entering the fictional world of a Sherlock Holmes novel will require a different amount of energy than entering the fictional world of Dr. Robert Langdon in the film, *The DaVinci Code*. First, since *The DaVinci Code* takes place now, in the 21st century, it is much easier to imagine being a Harvard University Professor who is an expert in symbology. In addition to the great acting ability of Tom Hanks, who plays Dr. Langdon in the film, we do not have to draw on our imagination to conceptualize the world in late 19th century and early 20th century England (1875-1907), as we do with a Sherlock Holmes' novel or film. In addition to imagining various time periods in history, reading a novel requires more imagination and visualization that watching a film. The great media theoretician Marshall McLuhan discussed these distinctions when he talked about "hot" and "cold" media, explaining that hot media are low in participation because the media consumer is provided with more information, but that cold media requires more participation from the audience to complete and process the communication.

Parasocial Interaction

During the past six decades, many dozens of communication scholars have studied a phenomenon called parasocial interaction, a process first conceptualized in 1956 by Donald Horton and Richard Wohl, two psychologists, as a type of involvement of television viewers with television personalities. More specifically, they defined parasocial relationships as the imaginary relationship between a television viewer and a television personality or "persona."[11] Parasocial interaction includes both the affective and cognitive forms of involvement of audience members with mediated personalities. Over decades of research, parasocial relationships have been observed between television viewers and newscasters,[12] talk show hosts,[13] soap opera stars,[14] and situation comedy characters.[15]

The concept of parasocial interaction has been extended during the past couple of decades. My own research demonstrates that individuals establish parasocial relationships with media personas such as celebrities through a variety of mediated contexts.[16] For example, audiences develop parasocial relationships with sports celebrities through their attendance of sports events, by watching televised sports, movies, and commercials featuring sports celebrities, and by collecting sports memorabilia.[17] They also develop strong parasocial relationships with beloved public figures.

> Many people remember exactly where they were or what they were doing when they first heard about the death of a famous person with whom they had a strong parasocial relationship. I remember a friend of mine telling me how he had learned about the tragic car accident that killed Princess Diana. He was having breakfast in the city of Norfolk the morning of August 31st when he noticed the waitress serving his table was crying. My friend asked her what was wrong, and she shared that she had just heard earlier that morning that Princess Diana had died. Although she had never met the Princess, this waitress had developed a strong parasocial relationship with Diana and was visibly distraught over her death. To the waitress, it was as if a close family member had died. If she had lived in the United Kingdom, she no doubt would have placed flowers and wept at one of the many Princess Diana public memorials that were spontaneously created by those who loved her and felt they knew her as a friend.

Long-term media and event exposure can create strong bonds between sports celebrities and their fans. After Dale Earnhardt died in a tragic crash into the wall at the Daytona Motor Speedway, two of my doctoral students joined me in studying how NASCAR fans responded to his death. We were amazed by the strong emotional connections to Earnhardt. People who had never met Earnhardt were seen weeping at memorial services organized by thousands of fans at racetracks throughout the United States.

Participants interviewed in these memorial services said they felt like they had "lost a brother" or "lost a close friend."[18] H.A. (Humpy) Wheeler, president of Lowe's Motor Speedway near Charlotte, North Carolina, described Earnhardt's death as "a terrible, terrible loss," stating "for me, it ranks right up there with the death of JFK."[19] Public responses to Earnhardt's death indicate that many racing fans had strong parasocial relationships with him. Concern for driving safety and discussion of harnesses for drivers became a nationally debated topic after the death of Earnhardt, which may have been prevented if he had greater protection.

We will return to a discussion of Earnhardt later when we consider the effects of parasocial relationships, but suffice to say that, like Elvis Presley, Princess Diana, and most recently,

Michael Jackson, deaths of famous people whose careers we follow and admire can be as emotionally impacting as the death of a member of our own family.

In addition to immediate reactions and short-term effects, the emotional and psychological dimensions of parasocial interaction also can be very powerful and enduring. One of my colleagues and friends with whom I have conducted research, Dr. Arvind Singhal, travelled to Peru a number of years ago to interview television viewers about Peru's powerful soap opera, *Simpelemente Maria* (*Simple Mary*). This soap opera, more accurately called a telenovela (television novel), was a phenomenal program that will be discussed in more detail later. One of the amazing effects of *Simplemente Maria* was the enduring parasocial relationships that television viewers formed with Maria, the star of the program. Almost two decades after its broadcast, Dr. Singhal found that viewers retained vivid memories of Maria and recalled many stories of how Maria had influenced their lives.[20]

Because of the nature of parasocial relationships, this form of involvement and social influence is considered to be a more powerful form of involvement than basking in reflected glory. Involvement with sports teams, athletes, game show contestants, war victors, or other personas through BIRG is usually less predictive of social influence than strong parasocial relationships.

Identification

The third process that explains how individuals become involved with mediated personalities, which for short I have referred to as "personae," is called identification. The process of identification is easy to understand but because the term "identification" is used to describe so many different ideas, I need to explain how social scientists define and understand this process. Identification can best be understood of a process of social influence in which one person adopts the attitudes, values, beliefs or behavior of another person in order to maintain a desired relationship. Although the concept of identification dates back to the work of psychologist Sigmund Freud[29] and political scientist Harold D. Lasswell,[30] it has recently gained renewed interest by communication scholars, particularly those who have been studying people's use of entertainment media and participation in entertainment events.

Cohen[31] provides an excellent review of the concept, beginning with the work of Freud and its development in particular by Richard Wollheim.[32] I particularly draw on the work of Herbert Kelman, who developed a theory of identification during the 1950s, explaining identification as a type of social influence. Kelman conceptualized three processes of social influence in which a person adopts the behavior of another individual because of an actual or perceived relationship with that person: compliance, identification, and internalization.[33] Compliance occurs when someone has power over another, such as when a military commander gives an order or a coach calls for a certain play to be run. The social influence occurs through the submission of one's will to an authority. The second form of social influence conceived by Kelman is identification. He proposed that identification occurs when a person likes or wants to be like someone else.[34] Thus, a person might seek to emulate his or her military commander or coach because of admiration for that person The third social influence process Kelman called internalization, which occurs when a person adopts the values and motivations of another as their own. This process can best be seen in successful parenting when teenagers must take greater responsibility for their lives and use wisdom in their transition into adulthood by living out some of the same values as their parents.

Although Kelman presents these processes as distinct, he did not identify the specific conditions under which each process takes place. Also, Kelman did not conceive his theory of social influence within the context of the highly mediated world fostered by the information explosion of the late 20th century. Thinking through his predictions, all three processes can occur without face-to-face interaction. We often submit to the authority of people we have never met. We identify with people we admire whose lives are portrayed by the media. We internalize the values of people we have read about who are no longer living.

Both Bettelheim[35] and Kelman[36] studied the process of identification through studying prisoners' behavior during World War II. They discovered that prisoners coped with their imprisonment and mistreatment by adopting the attitudes, beliefs, and perspectives of their captors. While Bettelheim focused on the role of imagination and surrender of identity in the identification process, Kelman focused on the social influence aspects of identification. Kelman explained this process as follows:

> Identification can be said to occur when an individual adopts behavior derived from another person or group because this behavior is associated with a satisfying self-defining relationship to this person or group. By a self-defining relationship, I mean a role relationship that forms a part of the person's self-image. Accepting influence through identification, then, is a way of establishing or maintaining the desired relationship to the other, and the self-definition that is anchored in this relationship.[37]

Kelman further described two means of identification; the first he called "classical identification," defined as "attempts to be like or actually be the other person."[38] This kind of identification is illustrated by the many thousands of Elvis Presley impersonators who seek to "be like" Elvis. The second form of identification Kelman called "reciprocal role identification," in which "the roles of two parties are defined with reference to one another."[39] This second means of identification is illustrated in the case of a soap opera character and his or her fans, in which both parties understand their respective roles in the relationship, played out in soap opera magazines and on soap opera websites.

Based on these conceptualizations, identification represents a more powerful form of social influence than parasocial interaction and transportation. Parasocial interaction will likely influence a person's television viewing behavior or media consumption habits. People want to see and read about those with whom they have formed parasocial relationships. They arrange their schedules so they can "be with them" through media involvement. They seek out stories about them to stayed informed about the lives of those they like. Once parasocial interaction takes hold, people imagine what it is like to be like the person with whom they relate. They immerse themselves in the world of their favorite media personalities or personas, transporting themselves into the narrative worlds of these personas.

Identification then follows transportation and parasocial interaction, resulting in an even deeper level of involvement. When people engage in identification, they adopt a persona's attitudes, beliefs, and behavior. Although Kelman's theory of identification is conceptually similar to Horton & Wohl's theory of parasocial interaction, there are two distinct differences. First, a parasocial relationship is conceived of as a psychological state of involvement with a media personality through an imagined or perceived friendship. The relationship is an entity in itself and not a facet of persuasive influence. Second, parasocial interaction does not require adopting another person's attitudes, values or behaviors, although this often occurs. Emulating the behaviors observed in close friends is common but is a consequence of a friendship, not a condition of friendship. Kelman sees the role modeling of behavior exhibited by others with whom we relate as central to the process of identification. Therefore, there may be many entertainers with whom experience parasocial relationships that we do not seek to be like; and others, with whom we do want to emulate. When we take on the values, beliefs or behaviors of entertainers, we enter into the process of identification.

Perhaps you are thinking, "No way, just because I like watching Tiger Woods play golf or Mel Gibson act or Britney Spears sing, I don't want to be like them!" That is exactly my point. What makes you think you know what Tiger Woods is like, or Mel Gibson? Have you met them? Have you ever personally interacted with Britney Spears, or whatever entertainer, newscaster, or athlete that you think you know? Except for a few individuals whose professions put them in contact with celebrities or unless you are an avid fan that seeks autographs, you most likely have never personally interacted with the people you follow through media whom you think you know. We rarely actively think about the process of parasocial interaction. You may think you don't have any parasocial relationships, but you probably do, even with people you don't want to emulate.

A number of scholars have concluded that parasocial interaction does not always lead to identification; often it does not.[40] I may love watching Jay Leno or David Letterman, and I may watch their television shows four or five days a week and really feel like I know them, but never move further into the process of identification.

Worshipping Personas

A fourth type of involvement studied by communication scholars, especially with celebrities, is worship. This common word used in religious communication studies and its corresponding characteristics is perhaps the most intense form of involvement with media personas. Focusing on audience involvement with celebrities, a specific group of media personas, Maltby and his colleagues have explored how media consumers tend to idolize celebrity personas, even to the point of what some might consider to be worship.[41] Although the operationalization of celebrity worship overlaps substantially with other forms of persona involvement, the concept is important to communication scholars who study involvement with media personas and should be extended beyond the study of celebrities.

Building upon the observations of Giles[42] and Jindra,[43] celebrity worship is defined as relegating to celebrities the attention and status normally given to God or some other form of deity.[44] Maltby and his colleagues describe the phenomenon of celebrity worship as "an abnormal type of parasocial relationship, driven by absorption and addictive elements and which potentially has significant clinical sequelae."[45] McCutcheon and colleagues define celebrity worship similarly, indicating it is "a form of parasocial interaction in which individuals become obsessed with one or more celebrities, similar to erotomanic type of delusional disorder."[46] As indicated by these definitions, celebrity worship is regarded by these scholars as an extreme and unhealthy type of parasocial interaction.

When thinking about the act of worship, because the concept of worshipping personas, whether celebrities, avatars or fictional characters, is qualitatively different than other forms of involvement, celebrity worship might best be considered as a unique process of involvement that follows transportation, parasocial interaction, and identification. Careful examination of Horton & Wohl's initial description of the perceived relational development of an audience member with a mediated personality reveals nothing close to worship. In fact, much of the research on parasocial interaction indicates it is a common process that most media consumers experience to one degree or another.[47] An audience member who feels like she knows Oprah Winfrey well, who sees her as a friend, and who appreciates her company every day when she watches her talk show, experiences a form of involvement with Oprah that is qualitatively different than an audience member who venerates Oprah as the most important person in her life whom she believes and follows without question.

An analysis of the 22-item celebrity attitude scale (CAS) created by Maltby and colleagues[48] indicates measurement items that span a range of involvement processes, including selective exposure ("I enjoy watching, reading or listening to my favorite celebrity because it means a good time"), parasocial interaction ("I share with my favorite celebrity a special bond that cannot be described in words"), transportation ("When something good happens to my favorite celebrity I feel like it happened to me"), identification ("the successes of my favorite celebrity are my successes also"), and obsession ("If someone gave me several thousand dollars to do with as I please, I would consider spending it on a personal possession (like a napkin or paper plate) once used by my favorite celebrity"). Although none of the 23 items from the CAS appear to be taken directly from published parasocial interaction and identification scales, the conceptual connections to other involvement scales appear to be strong.

Through the use of a statistical procedures, Maltby and his colleagues divide celebrity worship into three dimensions, which they label as the "entertainment-social" component of CAS (low intensity celebrity worship), the "intense-personal" component of CAS (intermediate intensity celebrity worship), and the "borderline pathological" component of CAS (high intensity celebrity worship).[49] The entertainment-social dimension represents how individuals have incorporated their exposure to and relationships with celebrities into their daily lives. This added dimension of audience enjoyment distinguishes the CAS from other involvement scales. Some of the involvement activities measured by the CAS seem to be quite common, while others are borderline pathological dimensions. Maltby et al., in fact, report low correlations among the three dimensions, particularly between the entertainment-social and borderline pathological dimensions, meaning they do not vary in unison with each other.[50]

Despite the conceptual overlap of celebrity worship with multiple forms of involvement and indications from previous studies that the CAS measures different kinds of involvement, Maltby and his colleagues have made a very important contribution to understanding involvement with media personas such as celebrities, athletes, and other professional entertainers and media personalities. Responding to personas as one would respond to a superhuman deity is certainly taking place, as Giles and others have observed. Our study of Elvis Presley impersonators indicated one of the Elvis fans perceived Elvis as a god-like deity.[51] There is an Elvis Presley temple in Bangalore, India, where it is believed Elvis was once a past king.

There is also a Church of Maradona that worships the soccer god Diego Maradona. Maltby and his colleagues no doubt have many interesting stories of extreme cases of celebrity worship. There likely are other cases of extreme persona involvement throughout the world that we have not yet discovered. One example in the United States is that of John Hinkley's psychological involvement with Academy-award winning actress Jodie Foster. Hinkley developed a strong and dangerous psychological involvement with Foster, nourished through repeated viewings of the film Taxi Driver. After writing many letters to Foster to express his love for her, in his mentally ill state he attempted to assassinate President Ronald Reagan to gain her attention and affection. Hinckley explained in one of his letters to Foster that "there is a definite possibility that I will be killed in my attempt to get Reagan."

Hinckley's abnormal attachment to Foster developed into a destructive pathological state, which can become a type of celebrity worship in which you are even willing to give your life to please the object of your worship.

Although Maltby and his colleagues[52] report that "celebrity worship is not an uncommon phenomena" as they measured it, they may have actually found that selective exposure to celebrities, parasocial interaction with them, and transportation into their worlds are not uncommon phenomena, but that identification with them is less common and that actual worship of them (the borderline pathological dimension of the CAS) is rare.

In conclusion, the concept of celebrity worship takes us one step further into understanding the way in which people become involved with personas, particularly if the concept of persona worship was refined to more specifically indicate reverence and unquestionable obedience to a persona, as one would give reverence and unquestionable obedience to either God or a supernatural being. Since common definitions of worship include words such as adoration, veneration, homage, to glorify, and to be considered worthy, the worshipping of personas can best be understood using similar language.

As we conclude this discussion on involvement, you may be thinking: "So what? So, we are involved with mediated personas. What does that matter?" What we are going to see, is that these processes of involvement through transportation, parasocial interaction, identification and worship can lead to individual behavioral changes that result in social change. On a personal level, your involvement with mediated personas can affect your lifestyle, your health, what you eat, who you marry, how your raise your children, what you do for work, and how you think about yourself and others. In the next chapter we will consider how one powerful form of entertainment, dramatic serials or soap operas, can have an important influence on our health beliefs and practices.

Discussion Questions

1. Have you ever basked in the reflected glory of a winning team? Please explain.
2. What story have you been transported into through the process of transportation?
3. What media persona do you have the strongest parasocial relationship with and why?
4. What media persona have you identified with the most and why?

Chapter 6
Soap Operas for Prosocial Change

Prior to the advent of television, popular radio dramas set the stage for the entertainment function of television. Although radio initially was conceived as an important information service to communicate to the public, over the years radio became less about information dissemination and more about entertainment. Television also was envisioned as an important source of news and information, but like radio, its greater entertainment potential was immediately recognized. As governments, media professionals and educators throughout the world deliberated on how to harness the entertainment function of radio and television to encourage prosocial change and development at the end of the Second World War and into the 1950s, two entrepreneurs emerged who each systematically used a popular entertainment genre, the soap opera, to disseminate prosocial messages. These creative media professionals, Elaine Perkins in Jamaica and Miguel Sabido in Mexico, transformed serial dramas from a pure form of entertainment to a powerful means of prosocial change. Prosocial change is defined as socially beneficial transformations in collective attitudes, beliefs, and behaviors that advance the development goals of communities, people groups and nations.

Elaine Perkins' *Radionovelas*

Elaine Perkins began writing radio serial dramas in Jamaica in 1958. A gifted creative artist, storyteller, and scriptwriter, Perkins body of work has given her international acclaim.[1] Perkins, who does not rely on professional actors for her radio soap operas, attributes her success to her ability to relate closely to the audience. The creative talent she employs is familiar with the problems she addresses through her dramas. In an address at John's Hopkins University, Perkins explained that in Jamaica, radio is still an important medium because of its oral culture and its history of communication important values and beliefs through storytelling.[2]

Perkins believed that serial dramas like radio soap operas could expose large numbers of people to important health information. Her work spanned four decades, enabling her to address a number of important health related issues. Some of the subjects her soap operas dealt with were mosquito control, learning how to be self-sufficient, self-determination, sexual responsibility, and family planning. Perkins created interesting characters that common people could relate to and made her stories dramatic and highly entertaining. Although some of the subjects she dealt with were not talked about openly, her dramas broke the "taboo communication" barriers in Jamaica by openly discussing women's health and sexual behavior through her story plots.

Perkins' *radionovelas* (literally radio novels, akin to radio soap operas) provided educational content to address specific development needs of Jamaica. One of her first creative programs was a radionovela called *Raymond, the Spray Man*. At that time Malaria prevention was an important health issue. The soap opera was part of an organized effort to promote the government's mosquito eradication campaign in 1959.

In 1963, Perkins broadcast a radionovela called *Hopeful Village* to promote integrated rural development. The program aired for 13 years. *Stella*, a third radionovela, addressed social issues important to the middle-class in 1967 and 1968. *Stella* was followed by a fourth radio series called *Dulcimina*, a radionovela that addressed problems faced by rural-to-urban migrants caught in the mass urban migrations of the 1960s and 1970s. *Dulcimina* was broadcast from1967 to 1980. In order to help promote tourism in Jamaica, Perkins created *Life at the Mimosa Hotel*, which was broadcast in 1984.

One of Perkins most famous radio soap operas was *Naseberry Street*. Open discussion about sexual practices was not normative in Jamaica at the time when *Naseberry Street* came on the air. The four-year series, broadcast from 1985 to 1989, promoted family planning and encouraged sexual responsibility. Perkins' characters in the series discussed sensitive issues such as the use of contraceptives, the deceptive practices of older men luring young women into illicit sexual relationships, and the trauma of unwanted pregnancy. Such topics were considered "taboo communication" at the time, hidden practices that weren't talked about openly.

The effects of Perkins' radio soap operas were powerful. Research of her programs showed that they were extremely popular and met a wide variety of educational goals.[3] Perkins was instrumental in demonstrating how soap operas could promote development and serve as an important source of health education. Entertainment-education radio programs like Perkins' *radionovelas* seek to promote specific beliefs and practices that are often lacking and encourage social discussion about conflicting values.[4] In this sense radio programs that address controversial or sensitive topics such as sexual responsibility and family planning have a greater potential to promote social change than less salient programs.

Sabido's *Telenovelas*

In chapter two I introduced you to Miguel Sabido, one of the early pioneers of using television to promote health and development. Sabido grew up in a rich intellectual environment. His father was an activist for the rights of indigenous Mexicans, his mother was a teacher and actress, and his network of friends was a group of post-revolutionary Mexican artists and intellectuals. Sabido began writing plays in the 1960s, focusing on Mexican folk stories, and at the same time became interested in the telenovela (literally television novel). Sabido observed that "the telenovela is one of the most amazing phenomena in communication in the history of mankind."[5]

While Sabido was Vice-President of Research for Televisa, Mexico's national television network, he became fascinated with and inspired by *Simplemente Maria (Simply Mary)*. the Peruvian telenovela that I introduced in the second chapter. *Telenovelas* are similar to television soap operas in the U.S. in that the production values and dramatic story plots are similar, yet the characters and story lines are often quite different from their American counterparts. Latin American serial dramas evolved from folletín, print versions of serialized fiction that were exported by France and Britain during the nineteenth century.[6] Newspapers or magazines would print installments of a dramatic story over time. This practice would be similar to publishing a single chapter of a fiction book today on a weekly or monthly basis. In order to read the entire book, you would need to buy each installment as it was published, thus insuring the continued sale of newspapers and magazines. Serial fiction was published by leading metropolitan publications such as the *Illustrated London News* (1842) and *Harper's Weekly* (1857), as well as through syndication in regional weekly papers[7] The United States was also a big importer of feuilleton fiction from France and Britain during the mid-1800s.

Elizabeth Garrels traces the publication of folletín in South America to the 1830s and 1840s, when newspaper serial novels were published in Argentina and Chile.[8] Latin American dramatic serials on radio and television that eventually evolved from the folletín were not primarily stories about the rich and socially elevated, but stories about common people with whom large numbers of common people could identify and understand. These stories are quite different from American soap operas in which the characters have high-paid jobs, live in palatial homes, have an abundance of material possessions and are all physically attractive and fit.

If you have not watched any *telenovelas* produced in the 1970s, it may be difficult to fully grasp how strongly television viewers could relate to the characters in *telenovelas*. Perhaps the easiest way to in explain the power of *telenovelas* and Miguel Sabido's fascination with them is to describe *Simplemente Maria* in more detail. My colleague and friend Arvind Singhal identifies *Simplemente Maria* as the most famous telenovela of all time. A total of 448 one-hour episodes of the program were produced and it received high broadcast ratings in 18 Latin American countries.[9] At its most basic level, *Simplemente Maria* is as a Horatio Alger story in which an uneducated poor teenage girl working as a maid in Lima, Peru, becomes a successful clothing designer. Others may see *Simplemente Maria* as a Cinderella story; but it was regarded by viewers as much more than simply a modern fairy tale.

During the 1960s, there was mass migration in many developing countries like Peru as people moved from rural areas into urban areas to look for work and to improve the quality of their lives. Maria, the central character of *Simplemente Maria*, was a teenage girl caught up in this migration. She left her home in the countryside to find work in the city of Lima. Maria was severely disadvantaged without a completed high school education and was unfamiliar with the harsh realities of life in the city. In the first episode of the series, Maria was taken advantage of and deceived by a wealthy medical student who falsely proclaimed his love for her. She ended up tragically abandoned and pregnant.

Abortion was not an option for Maria as a Catholic, nor was giving in to debilitating despair. Instead, Maria found a steady job as a maid, learned how to read and write, finished her high school education, raised her child as a single parent, and worked her way out of poverty. The effects of *Simplemente Maria* on not only television viewers, but on the whole nation of Peru, were stunning. The program received high audience ratings and became a commercially successful television program. Although the production budget was not high, people enjoyed the program and the storyline attracted a strong following and committed commercial sponsorship. It was not the commercial success of *Simplemente Maria* that was profound, but rather, its social influence.

During the course of the program, as Maria joins a literacy program and completes her high school education, viewers throughout Peru sent letters to the television network broadcasting the series and addressed letters to Maria and to the actress who played her in the series. Audience responses to *Simplemente Maria* as reflected in the viewer letters was remarkable. Peruvians indicated that they had joined literacy programs, completed high school educations, creating sewing businesses, and formed literacy clubs because of the inspiration they received from Maria. The working-class women of Peru strongly identified with Maria, a poor struggling made who eventually became socially and financially successful through her work ethic, values, and determination.

One of the characters in the series, a schoolteacher named Esteban, falls in love with Maria in secret but eventually asks for her hand in marriage, more than once, during the course of the series. Maria declines, partly due to her previous experience with unscrupulous men. The audience loves Esteban because he is a good man and truly loves Maria, and therefore began writing letters to Maria (the character) and to Saby Kamalich (the Peruvian actress who plays Maria), urging Maria to accept Esteban's proposal. She finally says yes, much to the delight of the audience, and the series' producers find a shooting location for the wedding episode.

Somehow the shooting location, which the producers had tried to keep secret, leaks out to the public. On the day that her wedding episode was to be filmed, the church was so mobbed with fans that the camera crew initially could not make their way into the church. An estimated 10,000 people had showed up to the wedding, many dressed in wedding clothes with wedding gifts in hand.[10] The following day a major newspaper in Peru featured a picture and story of the wedding on the front page as the major news story of the day. When the wedding episode was finally broadcast, its television ratings were higher than the final game of the World Cup.[11]

In addition to these powerful overt behavioral effects on Peruvian society, *Simplemente Maria* also had a positive economic influence. The Singer Sewing company purchased advertising time on the program once it realized its potential. In the story line, Maria eventually makes enough extra money through her sewing activities while working primarily as a maid that she is able to buy a Singer sewing machine. Once Singer began advertising their sewing machines on the program, they had the perfect pitch woman, Maria, even though she was a fictional character. The sale of Singer sewing machines in Peru dramatically increased, as well as in other countries where *Simplemente Maria* was broadcast.[12] The Singer Sewing Company was so grateful for the program that they gave the actress who played Maria a gold sewing machine as an appreciation gift.

All these aspects of the program, its popularity and entertainment appeal, its financial success, and its social influence and educational benefits captured Sabido's intrigue. He reasoned that if a telenovela like *Simplemente Maria* could promote literacy, education, and micro-businesses on accident, then *telenovelas* could be designed to promote education, prosocial values and beliefs, and national development, intentionally. In 1974, he was able to convince Emilio Azcárragah, the President of Televisa, Mexico's national television network, that prosocial values and beliefs with educational and development goals could be infused into *telenovelas* without sacrificing audience ratings. Sabido's realization of the potentially powerful influence of televised serial dramas was a critical discovery that led him to develop a series of educational *telenovelas*, or what we now call entertainment-education programs, in Mexico.[13]

Sabido was uniquely positioned to systematically implement the entertainment-education communication in television. As Vice-President of Research for Televisa, he had the resources and knowledge to test the effects of entertainment-education programs. He also was familiar with important theories of communication and social influence that he could build into his programming designs and use to guide character development.[14] In one sense, Sabido had a working laboratory at Televisa to not only try to replicate the positive effects of a program like *Simplemente Maria* but also to test various social influence and communication theories to be able to more effectively predict and control the effects of *telenovelas*.

Sabido's ambitious program at Televisa resulted in the production of a series of *telenovelas* from 1975 to 1986 to address multiple social and development needs, including many health beliefs and behaviors.[15] Five of these television series promoted family planning beliefs and practices. During this time period, the birth rate in Mexico decreased by 34 percent.[16] Sabido's programs also promoted healthy lifestyles devoid of alcohol and drug abuse. His *telenovelas* were systematically "prosocial" in that they all promoted socially beneficial beliefs and practices that were role modeled by the characters in the programs.

Although Televisa successfully used entertainment-education during the 1970s and 1980s through Miguel Sabido's leadership, the research conducted on his *telenovelas* was "in-house." Thus, outside of Mexico, not many people realized the potential of entertainment-education soap operas and those who did, were somewhat skeptical because the research was conducted by Televisa and not by independent researchers that could assure more objectivity.

India's First Television Soap Opera

Fortunately, for the rest of the world, Sabido had a strong advocate in the person of David Poindexter, an influential visionary leader who was working with national leaders to promote health and social welfare through family planning. Poindexter founded a private non-profit organization called Populations Communications International (PCI), which was headquartered near the United Nations center in New York City. Poindexter was highly impressed with the work of Sabido and encouraged him to share what he had learned about entertainment-education *telenovelas* with other nations.[17] Sabido was somewhat reluctant, but through Poindexter's persistence, agreed to help train a creative team from India that Poindexter had arranged to come to Mexico through his relationship with Rajiv Gandhi, then the Prime Minister of India. Gandhi wanted to use Indian television to promote health and development and saw the tremendous benefits of learning from Sabido and his creative team at Televisa.

The result of Sabido's collaboration with Indian writers, producers and social scientists led to the development of India's first long-running television soap opera, *Hum Log (We People)*. *Hum Log* had a phenomenal influence on the nation of India.[18] The story lines of

Hum Log addressed many social issues, particularly for women. The series had tremendous commercial success and promoted women's status and the cast members became very popular in India.

The scriptwriter for *Hum Log*, Manohar Joshi, created characters that represented positive, negative, and transitional role models for women. The series focused on the life of one family with two sons and three daughters.

Hum Log quickly captured the attention of Indian television viewers. The program achieved extremely high audience ratings, ranging from 65 to 90 in North India (predominantly a Hindi-speaking area) and from 20 to 45 in urban areas of South India (predominantly a non-Hindi speaking area).[19]

Through the leadership of Dr. Everett M. Rogers, who at the time was the Walter H. Annenberg Professor of Communication at the University of Southern California, the Rockefeller Foundation sponsored research on the effects of *Hum Log*. A fellow doctoral student that I have noted earlier, Arvind Singhal, and I traveled with Dr. Rogers to India in the summer of 1986 and traversed the country, conducting a national study in collaboration with the University of Delhi, University of Madras, and University of Poona. In addition to collecting survey data, we interviewed those involved with the production of *Hum Log* and conducted quasi-experimental viewing groups.

We heard many amazing stories about the program. One story about an Indian college student returning home from the U.S. to Delhi epitomizes the popularity of *Hum Log*. After being away from home for a considerable amount of time, he happened to walk into his home at an inopportune time – during an episode of *Hum Log*. Before he could say a word and exchange proper greetings with his family, his family members shooed him into the living room with hushed voices, telling him that *Hum Log* was on, and that he should sit down with them and watch the program. Not until it was over was he able to properly greet his family.

Everything stopped when *Hum Log* came on the air. Even retail shops, offices and industrial sites took a break so that workers could follow the series. In addition to being highly entertaining, "*Hum Log*" changed the way women were perceived by its viewers in Indian society.[20] The positive role models in the *Hum Log* family were independent and self-sufficient young women. One of the intended negative role models was Bhagwanti, the mother of the family. She was always taken advantage of by others and served their needs first, even at the expense or her own well-being.

Hum Log addressed a number of social issues in addition to women's status. *Hum Log*'s prosocial messages promoted (1) the importance of building strong committed families and family harmony, (2) fair and equitable treatment of females, (3) the acceptance of cultural diversity and national unity, and (4) the adoption of family planning practices. In addition, the series dealt with other topics like alcohol abuse and dowry. For example, Basar Ram, the father of the family, had a serious problem with alcohol. Nanhe, the eldest son, was irresponsible. Responsibility was a strong value promoted by the story lines in the series. Each episode had a moral or educational lesson that was reinforced by a short epilogue at the end of every program. The epilogues were monologues performed by Ashok Kumar, a well-known and well-liked film star. Kumar would pose the question to the viewing audience, "What can we learn from this episode of *Hum Log*?" He would then explain the moral lesson.

In one *Hum Log* episode, a police inspector loses his eyesight in a bomb explosion while attempting to save a child. At the end of the episode, an epilogue by a famous Indian film star encourages audience members to sign eye donation cards. In the two weeks following the program some 200,000 people signed eye and organ donation cards, including one youth club member, who I mentioned earlier, who personally recruited more than 900 donors.[21]

Our research indicates that *Hum Log* did promote prosocial beliefs, particularly pro-women's beliefs, and was viewed as an important educational source by viewers in India.[22] There was hardly a place we went where people were unaware of the program. We randomly selected and examined 400 viewer letters among the many thousands of letters received by Doordarshan, India's national television network. The network received so many letters that they had no space for them, so they put them in bags on the roof of Doordarshan's headquarters building in Delhi. The letters provided a fascinating look into how audience members were affected by the program. There was no doubt that people were identifying with the characters in the series and learning values and beliefs through the program.

On almost every level, *Hum Log* was considered a success. There was one exception. In the first several weeks of the series, there was a strong family planning message. Our interviews with audience members and program planners indicated the message was too strong or what some people perceived as "preachy." Although India's national government wanted to promote family planning through *Hum Log*, a serious problem developed that made this nearly impossible. The actress playing the female role model for family planning unexpectedly became pregnant. The producers either had to drop the family planning theme or replace the actress and bring in a new character. They decided to drop the family planning messages. Our research substantiated that the program had no effects on family planning beliefs and practices.[23]

Hum Log also had other profound effects on India beyond the social effects of individual viewers. Before *Hum Log* was produced, the Indian television industry, headquartered in Delhi, and the Indian film industry, headquartered in Bombay (now called Mumbai), were virtually independent of one another. *Hum Log* used film actors and media professionals from both industries, paving a way for the two industries to begin collaborating on future media productions.

Hum Log was also a commercial success. One of the sponsors of the program, the Nestle Company, marketed a new product called Magi Two-Minute Noodles. Almost every college student in the U.S. is familiar with this type of product, which was a staple for college students like me living on a meager budget. Just add boiling water and an egg and you have an instant meal. Instant noodles were unknown in India before *Hum Log*. Now, you can purchase them virtually anywhere in the country.

Nestle's success with Magi Two-Minute Noodles demonstrated to other advertisers that television soap operas could successfully market products. This led to the commercialization of the television industry in India, which was incepted as an educational tool and primarily funded by the government. The positive audience responses to *Hum Log* and its commercial success paved the way for other commercial soap operas with educational goals.[24] One such television soap opera that followed *Hum Log* in India was *Hum Raahi (Co-Travelers)*, which promoted the status of women and smaller family-size norms. Today, soap operas are a regular staple in the Indian television diet and many are created to promote or enhance specific educational goals.

India's Entertainment-Education Radio Soap Operas

Although India began its experimentation with entertainment-education soap operas through television, the use of radio dramas for education and development followed the successes of *Hum Log*. Much of India's population still lives in rural areas where radio is more accessible than television. While *Hum Log* tells the story of India's launch into entertainment-education television serials, "*Tinka Tinka Sukh*" *(Happiness Lies in Small Things)* tells the story of India's successful launch of entertainment-education radio soap operas. You may recall I introduced you to this radio program in chapter two when I briefly shared the transformation of the village of Lutsaan.

Many of the issues addressed by "*Hum Log*" related to the status of women have been an ongoing concern in India. Traditional practices such as demanding dowry for women, child marriage, female feticide, and poor treatment and physical abuse of wives, have concerned government leaders that are committed to making India, the world's largest democracy, a fair and just society. The success of "*Hum Log*" convinced government leaders that entertainment-education could address these social issues. Supported with funding from both private agencies and the government, "*Tinka Tinka Sukh*" was broadcast twice a week in Hindi on All India Radio, rapidly gained a loyal following. In all 104 episodes were broadcast in 1996 and 1997 on 27 radio stations that covered seven Indian states in the mostly densely populated Hindi regions of India, with a potential audience of 100 million households (about 600 million people) at that time.[25]

Let me return to the story of the transformation of Lutsaan and provide a more detailed account. The setting for "*Tinka Tinka Sukh*" is the village of Navgaon, or "new village." The main character of the series is village girl named Champa, who despite difficult family circumstances, including a drug-addicted brother, works her way out of poverty to become a successful singer. The program openly showed the evils of dowry and the systematic discrimination against girls, which Champa overcomes.

A few months after my friend and colleague, Arvind Singhal, at that time a professor at Ohio University, began to study the effects of the program, All India Radio received through the mail a poster-size letter from Birendra Singh Khushwaha, a tailor in the small village of Lutsaan in the state of Uttar Pradesh. In his amazing letter testifying of the changes in their village brought about by "*Tinka Tinka Sukh*," Khushwaha stated: "For the past ten years I had lost my way, but '*Tinka Tinka Sukh*' showed me a new path of life. I used to be delinquent, aimless, and a bully. I harassed girls .... After listening to the drama, my life underwent a change .... All my other drawbacks and negative values were transformed.[26] Not only was the letter signed by 183 Lutsaan villagers, but they also added their thumbprints.[27]

In order to validate the change in Lutsaan, which the producers of "*Tinka Tinka Sukh*" surmised was a hoax, the radio network sponsored a research team, led by Dr. Singhal, to visit Lutsaan in 1997 and interview the tailor, Birendra Singh Khushwaha, and other listeners of the program. The research team estimated that among the 1000 homes in Lutsaan, there were 65 radios, 5 television sets, and many radio listening groups. Khushwaha's tailor's shop was close to the intersection of the two main roads that ran through Lutsaan, so many villagers would stop in his shop to listen to the program.[28]

Among the many stories collected by Dr. Singhal and the research team, one story was particularly poignant. The villagers had begun to understand that Lutsaan had similar antisocial characteristics to the fictional village of Navgaon in "*Tinka Tinka Sukh*." When the radio series broadcast the suicide of Poonam, a young bride who was falsely accused of infidelity and beaten by her in-laws because they were not satisfied with her dowry, the villagers if Lutsaan widely discussed the story. In a subsequent episode of the series, the postmaster of Navgaon has a son who gets married. Instead of receiving the traditional dowry given by the family of his daughter-in-law, the postmaster refuses, believing it is not right to receive dowry. After much discussion, the consensus among the villages in Lutsaan was to side with the postmaster and also reject the traditional dowry system.

In one of the subplots of "*Tinka Tinka Sukh*," the daughter of a widow named Lali has to contend for her education and eventually perseveres to the extent of going to college and becoming a doctor. When Dr. Singhal first arrived in Lutsaan, he talked to a seven-year old girl, also named Lali, who had to stay at home and do chores so her brothers could attend school. On Dr. Singhal's next visit he checked up on Lali and to his surprise, found her at school. He found out that the people of Lutsaan had secured a government grant for a child-care center so that girls would not have sacrifice their education in order to take care of their brothers and sisters. Singhal, reflecting on his research that showed the percentage of girls from Lutsaan attending school had quadrupled, from 10 percent to 40 percent, commented: "It was so wonderfully gratifying. It took some period of time, and then the magic began. The conversations led to certain decisions; the decisions led to certain actions. This is what we hope for."[29]

Soap Operas for Health, Education and Development

Once research of the positive effects of entertainment-education soap operas in Jamaica, Mexico and India were disseminated during the 1980s and 1990s, the use of soap operas to promote health, education, and development through both radio and television rapidly diffused internationally.[30] Other countries saw the potential to use soap operas to address important health, education and development issues.

Miguel Sabido continued to share what he had learned with other media professionals, buoyed by strong encouragement from David Poindexter, who had comprehended the great potential of using Sabido's entertainment-education methodology to promote family planning. After Sabido's interaction with the producers of *Hum Log*, Sabido hosted another workshop in Mexico to help others create entertainment-education soap operas. During the workshop, plans were developed to create both a radio soap opera and television soap opera in Kenya. The radio soap opera that resulted, *Ushikwapo Shikamana* (Hold on to He Who Holds on to You), broadcast from 1987 to 1989, reached 7 million people, about 40 percent of the population of Kenya in 1987.[31] By 1989, the series was reaching 60 percent of the population, of which a projected 75 percent reported that they understood the family planning messages.[32] Several other health-related themes were addressed by the serial, including the benefits of smaller family sizes, husband and wife communication and respect, and the disadvantages of polygamy.

Through the efforts of a number of different individuals and groups, including Miguel Sabido, Elaine Perkins, David Poindexter, other NGOs using media for education and development, and a network of academic scholars working at universities and related institutes, entertainment-education soap operas were produced in many different nations. These soap operas include Turkey's *Sparrows Don't Migrate*, watched by 20 million television viewers. A study of its effects indicates 250,000 Turkish women said the program encourage them to adopt modern contraception methods.[33] Other entertainment-education television serials included Mexico's *Polite Society*, which promoted sexual responsibility; Egypt's *And the Nile Flows On* and Ana Zanana (I'm a Nag), which promoted family planning; Brazil's *High Stakes*, which encouraged viewers to overcome drinking problems and to help alcoholics; Pakistan's *Hawwa Ki Beti* (*Daughter of Eve*), which promoted self-reliance, dignity, and adult literacy among the underprivileged in Pakistan and *Aahat* (*Approaching Sound*), which promoted family planning in Pakistan; Kenya's *Tushauriane* (*Let's Discuss*), which promoted responsible sexual behavior; and Japan's *Oshin*, which promoted sacrifice and self-reliance.

Oshindrome

The diffusion of *Oshin* is a particularly fascinating story. The series tells the story of one family's endurance and survival during the hard times the Japanese endured from the Meiji of Japan in the early 1900s through the Second World War. The star of *Oshin* is a female character by the same name, whose life story is told from the time that she was a little girl through her elderly years. Oshin's family had so little food that her pregnant mother felt forced to commit kuchiberashi, an induced abortion by immersing oneself in a cold body of water so the family has one less mouth to feed. This tragedy was compounded when at age seven Oshin had to be sold to a rich timber merchant for a bale or rice. Throughout Oshin's life she faces tremendous hardships, including abuse by the timber merchant from whom she ran away, the young man she loved and wanted to marry falling in love with her best friend, her and her husband losing their successful business to the great Kanto earthquake of 1923, and her oldest son's death and her husband's suicide during the Second World War. Oshin showed great fortitude, resilience, and dignity through each hardship, not succumbing to overwhelming despair but always believing in a brighter future. After the war she is able to slowly build up a fish business establish a highly successful supermarket chain called Tanokura.

Let me briefly share one episode of *Oshin* to provide an understanding of the program's appeal. Everyone in Oshin's family had to work hard in the rice fields and doing other chores just to earn enough food to survive; but often, they were still short. You can imagine the agony of having to collect rice through hard labor for other families that you yourself could not eat. In one episode of the television series, Oshin's grandmother gives up her ration of food, explaining that she is old and useless because she can no longer work, and therefore it is not important if she lives or dies. The family accepts this sacrifice, but not Oshin. She comes to her grandmother in secret with her own food and tells her grandmother that she must eat, that she needs her grandmother and that her life is out great value. The grandmother begins weeping because of Oshin's expression of love and sacrifice, and they share their food together. Thus, Oshin helps preserve the life of her grandmother by sharing her food through the famine period.

It is not difficult to understand why *Oshin* became a television phenomenon, not only in Japan but throughout the world. Following Oshin's remarkable life through age 83, the series diffused to 47 countries by 1996, achieving audience ratings of 65 percent in Japan, 70 percent in Poland, 81 percent in Thailand, and 89 percent in China, Mexico, and Iran.[34] *Oshin* reminded the Japanese people, whose nation had developed into a prosperous and leading economic powerhouse during the 1970s and 1980s, of the great sacrifices made by their parents, grandparents and great grandparents. Rising from the devastation of World War II, Japan's extraordinary economic recovery had captured the world's attention, but so had Oshin, the woman who symbolically represented one of the important reasons for that recovery

The immense popularity of the television series created the "*Oshin* fad" or "Oshindrome" as it became known as during the mid-1980s. In order to understand this phenomenon, it is necessary to first understand the power of archetypes. Noted Swiss psychologist and scholar, Carl Jung (1875-1961), developed a rich understanding of archetypes during his journeys across Europe, Africa, America and India. Jung theorized that everyone is born with a collective unconsciousness, a reservoir of collective human experiences and knowledge that we are not consciously aware of but that influence our experiences, especially emotional ones, leading to "patterns of instinctual behavior."[35] Jung believed that archetypes, organizing principles through which we see the world and through which we understand people and relationships, exist within the collective unconscious.[36] Although our archetypes are formed independently with individual variations, there are also universal "identities of experience" that are shared by peoples throughout the world.[37] Common archetypes featured in melodramatic television series include heroic personas such as the reluctant warrior, the virgin daughter, the sacrificial savior, the evil tyrant, the secret lover, and the unselfish saint.[38]

Oshin tapped into the archetype of a self-sacrificing woman and mother who always puts the interests of her family first, even at her own peril. This archetype had a global appeal across geo-political and socio-demographic boundaries, providing a heroine that people could identify with throughout the world. In order to understand the powerful influence of archetypes in television serials, consider the unexpected popularity of *Oshin* in Iran as a positive role model for women's emancipation.[39] Although the program promoted the values of hard work and self-determination, regarded highly in Iran, the character Oshin conflicted with the role of women in Islamic society.

When *Oshin* was imported into Iran, the government, under the watchful eye of Ayatollah Khomeini, was very selective about the television programs it imported. Very few foreign programs met the approval of the Islamic religious leaders, but *Oshin* provided the positive values of sacrifice, hard work, and endurance, values appreciated by the Islamic revolutionary leaders. As a result, the character Oshin became a positive role model for women in Iran. Although the program values were highly regarded by Iranian television viewers, the self-determination and independence of Oshin conflicted with the subservient role of women promoted by the Islamic Iranian leaders.

Oshin might have survived this conflict had not the Ayatollah heard an Iranian woman on a radio talk show explain that Oshin was a better role model for her daughter than the prophet Mohammed's daughter Fatima. The Ayatollah was incensed, immediately stopped broadcasts of *Oshin*, and punished the Director of Iran's broadcasting agency with 50 lashes for importing the program.[40] At the height of its popularity, *Oshin* had achieved a television audience ratings of 70 percent in Iran.[41] One of the important lessons of Oshindrome is that entertainment programs can have unintended effects, perceived as both positive, as in the case of Iranian women who identified with Oshin; and negative, as in the case of the Iranian religious leaders who were fearful of women's rights and freedoms role modeled by Oshin. The unintentional effects of *Oshin* in Iran, as in other nations where the program was exported, were regarded as positive by most television viewers and national leaders, but also negative by some government officials who objected to *Oshin*'s message about women's status.

Three important lessons emerge from the "Oshindrome" phenomenon. First, research on *Oshin* indicates that entertainment media programs with educational messages can have powerful audience effects, especially in nations such as Iran and China where the mass media is perceived as an important educational and ideological tool. Second, these effects are difficult to predict. *Oshin* was not expected to achieve the high audience ratings of 50 percent in Japan to 70 percent in Poland and Iran.[42] The 16 different countries outside of Japan that have imported *Oshin* demonstrates the program's widespread popularity.[43] The third lesson from "Oshindrome" is that prosocial entertainment programs can have unintended effects perceived as negative by certain audience segments. For example, *Oshin* was not intended to promote women's status in Iran in opposition to Islamic norms, just as the U.S. television program Miami Vice was not intended to promote the sale of semi-automatic weapons. Likewise, the entertainment-education soap opera "*Hum Log*" was not intended to commercialize India's television industry, yet commercial sponsors flocked to sponsor more than 30 soap operas broadcast during the two-year period that followed "*Hum Log*."[44] The challenges of unintended effects as exemplified by "Oshindrome" and similar programs must be considered when weighing the benefits and potential risks of the entertainment-education media strategy.

The international phenomenon of *Simplemente Maria* and *Oshin*, two dramatic television serials with unplanned prosocial effects, coupled with Sabido's successful planned entertainment-education *telenovelas*, inspired a number of other entertainment-education soap operas throughout the world. These programs, many which I have already mentioned, include: China's Ke Wang (Aspirations),[45] India's *Hum Raahi (We Travelers)*,[46] Nigeria's *Cock Crow at Dawn*,[47] Kenya's *Tushauriane*,[48] Turkey's *Sparrows Don't Migrate*,[49] Brazil's *High Stakes* and Pakistan's *Hawwa Ki Beti* (*Daughter of Eve*).

Today, large development agencies such as USAID, UNAIDS, the Ford Foundation, BBC Trust, and the Rockefeller Foundation have funded numerous entertainment-education programs to promote health throughout the world. The Centers for Disease Control in Atlanta also is keenly interested in the use of entertainment to reduce the spread of sexually transmitted diseases The use of soap operas is just one genre of programming that has been used to promote health, education, and development. In the next chapter I will focus particularly on health issues, showing how many different kinds of entertainment genres are now being used to promote health throughout the world.

Discussion Questions

1. What serial drama do you think has had a great influence on the U.S.? Please explain.
2. Can you think of a specific social need that was powerfully addressed by a radio or television drama in the U.S. or overseas that is not discussed in this chapter?
3. Can you think of a powerful fictional role model like Oshin that inspired self-sacrifice? Please explain.

Chapter 7
Promoting Health through Entertainment

Perhaps one of the most successful uses of entertainment for educational purposes and prosocial change is to promote beneficial health beliefs and behavior. Most of us have heard about the detrimental health effects of heavy media consumption of entertainment media, including heart disease and obesity. However, few people have learned about the numerous health benefits brought about through entertainment media and the arts. Communication scholars and other social scientists have documented many of these benefits during the past several decades. In this chapter I will provide examples from around the world that show how entertainment media is being used to address important health issues and promote healthy lifestyles.

Advocating Family Planning

Learning how to plan and prepare for family growth and prevent unplanned pregnancies has been a major health issue in much of the world, particularly in poor nations seeking to curtail uncontrolled population growth. John Cleland and his colleagues, writing for the World Health Organization, report that the promotion of family planning in countries with high birth rates can potentially reduce poverty and hunger and avert 32% of all maternal deaths and nearly 10% of childhood deaths; and in addition, promote women's empowerment, education for young children, and long-term environmental sustainability.[1] During the past five decades family-planning campaigns have played a major role in helping couples to choose the number of children they want to have, when to have children, and how to manage their size of their families. Even a little change in family size can make a big difference in reducing poverty. For example, research of 45 countries estimated that during the 1980s, the number of people living in poverty could have one reduced by one-third if the crude birth rate had decreased by five per 1000 population.[2] In poor countries where populations are doubling every 25-30 years, family planning is of the highest priority to alleviate extreme poverty and suffering and improve family health, education, and economic development.

A number of organizations that focus on family planning education such as Population Communication International actively use and promote the entertainment-education communication strategy.[3] Perhaps the most famous family planning radio drama was *Naseberry Street*, which I introduced in the last chapter as one of the many *radionovelas* written and produced by Elaine Perkins in Jamaica. *Naseberry Street* was a fictitious street in a poor neighborhood of Kingston. One of the main characters of the dramatic series was a health educator and nurse who provided family planning information to people in the community. The program reached an audience of about one million people daily, which at that time was 40 percent of the total population of Jamaica. The program was especially popular with women of lower socio-economic status, those in greatest need of family planning information. A study of the program's effects indicated that listeners were more likely to adopt family planning practices, to be more sexually responsible, and to delay sexual relations until marriage than those who did not follow the program.[4]

Educators in Costa Rica decided to use a radio talk show to promote sexual responsibility and provide family planning information. They created a ten-minute radio program called *Dialogo (Dialogue)* and broadcast it weekdays at 7:00 a.m. on five national and regional stations from 1970 to the mid-1980s. The host of the program was an Episcopalian minister named Padre Carlos. It was quite a change for the public to heart a Christian minister leading open discussions about sex on the radio. The program drew a large audience estimated to be 40 percent of the population, and just as many men regularly listened to the program as women. Although *Dialogo* was only a 10-minute program, the daily reading of letters on the air from audience members who wanted to learn about sex, reproductive health, pregnancy, and having children by Pastor Carlos created a trust between the audience and host. Felipe Risopatron and Peter Spain conducted a study on the program's effects in the 1970s and concluded that the program effectively increased knowledge of and positive attitudes toward family planning among Costa Ricans.[5] Like *Naseberry Street* in Jamaica, *Dialogo* created the space for public dialogue about topics traditional considered taboo.

In 1977, Indonesia, one of the most populated countries in the world, created a radio soap called *Butir Pasir di Laut (Grains of Sand in the Sea)* to promote family planning. A total of 3,500 episodes of the program were aired over a 12-year period, providing useful information about family planning issues.[6] Although we don't know how many couples adopted family planning as a result of the program, it is likely that the longevity of the program had a cumulative effect in encouraging people to seek out family planning information.

In addition to using radio soap operas to promote family planning during the 1970s, some countries began to experiment with incorporating family planning messages into television drama.[7] Through Miguel Sabido's leadership, Mexico was one of the first nations to use entertainment television programs to promote family planning. In August of 1977, Mexico began broadcasting *Accompáñame (Come Along with Me)*, a 30-minute television serial. There was a total of 180 episodes broadcast through late April of the following year. *Accompáñame* attracted a loyal audience, achieving an average audience rating of 29 percent.[8]

The setting of the drama was a lower-class neighborhood in Mexico City where three sisters lived. One sister was intended to be a negative role model who suffers through an unwanted pregnancy and the resulting stress that follows. A second sister plays the positive role model who enjoys a happy marriage and discusses with her husband how to plan their children and use contraception methods to prevent unwanted pregnancies. The happy life and unhappy life of these two sisters are contrasted in the series. The third sister in the series was a transitional role model, one who begins in a state of conflict with her husband because of their growing family but who transitions over time to a happy and peaceful marriage. In one dramatic episode of the series, this transitional character, named Martha, has an emotional breakdown when she fears she is pregnant with their fourth child. Already stressed out with the burden of three young children, Martha moves her bed into the kitchen to prevent her husband from having sex with her. The conflict is resolved when the couple agreed to visit a family planning clinic to receive counseling on what other means they could use in addition to abstinence to have a healthy sexual relationship and yet prevent unwanted pregnancies.

Through these dramatic narratives, *Accompáñame* promoted the value of family harmony and showed that married couples who plan their families are much more likely to achieve harmony in the home. The program also provided valuable information about resources available to couples to help them learn about family planning methods and motivated couples to go to family planning counseling centers and seek out family planning advice.

While a masters' student at Iboamerican University in Mexico, Heidi Nariman conducted research on the effects of *Accompáñame* on a sample of 800 adult viewers. She found that viewers of the program had a higher knowledge of family planning methods than non-viewers and also had more positive attitudes about family planning methods.[9] Mexico's national family planning program also received an average of 500 calls a month during the time period of the broadcasts and gained 2500 volunteers to help promote family planning, both dramatic increases; and more than 562,000 individuals adopted family planning methods provided by government health clinics, a 33 percent increase in one year.[10] These results demonstrated that even a sensitive topic that delved into sexually responsibility issues could be addressed through entertainment television. Televisa's positive experience with Sabido's methodology and production of *Accompáñame* encouraged them to broadcast a second telenovela to promote family planning in 1981 and 1982 called *Por Amor (For Love).*

Nigeria was one of the first countries in Africa to use entertainment television to promote family planning. In collaboration with Johns Hopkins University's Population Communication Services (JHU/PCS), the National Television Authority (NTA) in Nigeria launched a family planning campaign through an existing television variety show in the Enugu region. The program, called *In a Lighter Mood*, integrated family planning content in 39 of its episodes during a four-month period of 1986-1987. Some of the themes dealt with included showing the benefits of adequately spacing the birth of children, discussing various methods of contraception, and promoting the acceptability of smaller family sizes. The program also advertised the family planning clinics in Enugu, Ilorin and Ibadan, where viewers could get family planning information.

In a survey of visitors to the clinics in Enugu and Ibadan, about half them said they had watched episodes of *In a Lighter Mood*; and among those who watched, 79 of the Enugu respondents and 99 percent of the Ibadan respondents recalled the family planning messages in the program.[11] Both clinics experienced dramatic increases in the number of clients.

Inspired by the successful use of entertainment for health education in other countries, and concerned about population growth, the government of Kenya produced its first entertainment-education radio soap opera, *Ushikwapo Shikimana (When Given Advice, Take It)*, in 1987. The dramatic program reached an estimated 7 million people, about 40 percent of the population of Kenya in 1987.[12] By 1989, the series was reaching 60 percent of the population, of which a projected 75 percent reported that they understood the family planning messages.[13]

The setting for the radio series was the home of Mzee Gogo and his four wives, children and grandchildren. Each broadcast reached 40-50 percent of the population of Kenya. A mailed survey study sponsored by the Kaiser Family Foundation found that 84% of the survey respondents had listened to the program and 72% of them felt that the program helped listeners to adopt family planning.[14] The series lasted 219 episodes.

A summative study of *Ushikwapo Shikimana* conducted at the end of the broadcasts indicated that many women said the radio program motivated their husbands to permit them to seek family planning services.[15] An analysis comparing the 1984 and 1989 Kenyan Demographic Health Surveys revealed that the decline in desired family size from 6.3 children to 4.8 children and the 58% increase in contraceptive usage are due in substantial part to mass media family planning messages such as those contained in the television and radio serials.[16]

In another collaborative project with JHU/PCS, Turkish television produced *Sparrows Don't Migrate*, a three-part family planning television serial produced through as a joint effort of the Turkish Family Health and Planning Foundation and Turkish Radio and TV (TRT). Broadcast in 1988, the television series had an estimated 20 million viewers in Turkey and nearly 60 percent of all adult viewers watched the program.[17] Research shows that the viewers liked the TV serial and comprehended the family planning messages correctly.[18]

One of the most interesting experiments with an entertainment-education family planning campaign was Egypt's television mini-series called *Ana Zananna (I'm Persistent)*, also the name of the lead character of the series. If you have ever seen the Taster's Choice commercial mini-series in the U.S., you will have an idea of the nature of the *Ana Zananna* campaign dramas, except that *Ana Zananna* used humor. Egypt produced 14 of the one-minute mini-dramas and broadcast them repeatedly nationwide in 1988 with each episode being broadcast about 100 times.[19] At that time 90 percent of Egyptian households had television sets, so the mini-series reached most of the population.

Egypt has a long history of using television to promote health messages.[20] Memorable television commercials in Egypt with their popular jingles have promoted family planning, oral rehydration solution (ORS), and immunizations. In an effort to make these health commercials more entertaining, the producers increasingly incorporated sophisticated story lines, settings, and characters representing rural peasants, played by popular and well-liked actors.[21]

A study of Egyptian television viewers indicated that nearly all of them had seen the series, 98 percent of them understood the family planning messages, and 74 per cent could recall the specific phrases used the lead role model for family planning, Ana Zananna.[22] The respondents were also able to correctly identify the positive and negative role models in the mini-drama series characters, which they found to be both entertaining and educational.

JHU/PCS, one of the leading agencies in producing entertainment-education programming, was also involved in a number of other family planning projects, collaborating with family planning associations of various African countries to launch several highly effective radio soap operas. These programs include *Fakube Jarra (Wise Man)* in Gambia (1990); *Family Affair* in Ghana (1990-1993); *Ezi-na-Uno (Our Family)* in Nigeria (1988); and *Akarumwa Nechekuchera (You Reap What You Sow)* in Zimbabwe (1989-1992). Audience ratings were high for each of these radio soap operas and listeners of these programs demonstrated sharp increases in knowledge and more favorable attitudes toward family planning and slight to modest increases in adopting family planning methods.[23] For example, a study of *Fakube Jarra* by Tom Valente and his colleagues showed that 35 percent of the programs' listeners adopted family planning methods during the year it was broadcast, a 16 percent increase from the previous year.[24]

During the late 1980s, Kenya followed its foray into entertainment-education radio with its first entertainment-education television series, *Tushauriane (Let's Discuss)*, its first long-running television soap opera. The program promoted family planning and sexual responsibility, achieved high audience ratings, and was frequently discussed by Kenya's print media.[25] Although no evaluation of *Tushauriane's* influence on family planning and sexual responsibility issues was conducted, the program's popularity made it a model for other African entertainment-education television soap operas.

In summary, the family planning soap operas on radio and television around the world achieved both commercial suggest and modest health benefits, depending upon the degree of audience involvement with the characters in the series, as discussed in chapter five, and how effectively family planning was modeled by the characters. More importantly, experiences with entertainment-education during the 1980s inspired new entertainment-education projects in the 1990s that took on a variety of health education needs.

Reducing Sexually Transmitted Diseases

Among the most critical health issues of the 21st century is the need to reduce the spread sexually transmitted diseases, particularly HIV/AIDS, which has become the number one cause of death in many nations. By the beginning of 2009, more than 60 million people have been infected with HIV, more than 25 million people have died of AIDS-related illnesses worldwide, and more than 33 million people are living with HIV.[26] To put this in perspective, ten million more people have died of AIDS than the estimated total number of people who died as a result of World War I. Before this epidemic is over, the total number of people killed by AIDS will likely surpass the estimated 48 million people killed during World War II. Consider the devastation of a single region, sub-Saharan Africa, where there are now more than 14 million children who have been orphaned because of AIDS.[27]

Although efforts to reduce other sexually transmitted diseases besides HIV are important, policy planners and health educators have focused their use of the entertainment-education communication strategy to slow the rate of HIV transmission; and more generally, to promote sexual responsibility, which reduces the transmission of all sexually transmitted diseases.[28]

Tanzania was one of the first countries targeted for an HIV-prevention entertainment-education campaign. With both private and government funding for both research and production, Tanzania launched a five-year radio project in 1993, leading to the broadcast a highly popular radio soap opera, *Twende na Wakati (Let's Go with the Times)*. The series overall promoted sexual responsibility and addressed a number of issues, including family planning and empowerment of women, but developed a very powerful storyline that addressed HIV and AIDS.

The star of *Twende na Wakati* was a truck driver named *Mkwaju* who transported goods up and down the trans-African highway, which runs north to south through the center of Tanzania. The well-travelled truck route is notorious for its brothels at major truck stops and it became one of the primary ways in which HIV was transmitted throughout East Africa.[29] In the soap opera series, Mkwaju is not only a truck driver but also a sexual adventurer who has many sexual encounters with girlfriends along his truck routes. Unbeknownst to his wife, Tunu, Mkwaju wastes his money on alcohol and gifts for his girlfriends. As he drifts away from his wife and children, Mkwaju begins to get sick repeatedly. Although he does not understand what is happening to him, the radio audience eventually discerns that he has all the symptoms of being infected with HIV.

The drama is heightened when the *Twende na Wakati* listeners begin to speculate which girlfriend transmitted HIV to him, and whether or not his wife Tunu would also become sick. Eventually Mkwaju develops AIDS and despite his irresponsibility, his wife cares for him until he dies. But the dramatic story does not end with his death. *Twende na Wakati* continues the HIV/AIDS theme with Mkwaju's son, Kibuyu, who at first seems to be following in the irresponsible lifestyle of his father. However, Kibuyu becomes a transition role model who changes his behavior before he acquires the same disease that killed his father.

The program writers created Kibuyu as an empathetic character so the audience would identify with him. They also developed the character arcs slowly to facilitate high levels of involvement with the characters through parasocial interaction and identification. They then began to deal with the various health issues addressed, especially HIV and AIDS.

One of the advantages the producers of *Twende na Wakati* had is the project sponsors funded formative research. Formative research involves collecting data from targeted audience members through surveys, in-depth interviews, and focus groups to learn their existing levels of knowledge, attitudes, beliefs and behaviors regarding any specific issue or set of issues. Through formative research the creators of *Twende na Wakati* were able to address the specific needs of radio listeners in Tanzania. In addition to the formative research, the effects of *Twende na Wakati* on its audience were evaluated at multiple points in time during the life of the series to ensure that the characters and story lines were effectively promoting the health information and other prosocial messages.

A second important advantage given to the producers of *Twende na Wakati* was being able to set up a randomized controlled study for HIV prevention by blocking the broadcast of the radio series in one city of Tanzania, Dodoma, whose radio listeners became the control group. Thus, direct comparisons could be made of the heath beliefs and practices of those who listened to the radio series and those who did not. Dr. Everett M. Rogers led a team of researchers to Tanzania over a five-year period to create one of the most comprehensive studies ever of an entertainment-education campaign. Rogers and his colleagues found that *Twende na Wakati* had a measurable effect on reducing HIV in Tanzania, including: (1) increase perceptions of personal risk of contracting HIV /AIDS, (2) increasing self-efficacy with respect to preventing HIV and AIDS, (3) increasing interpersonal communication about HIV and AIDS, (4) increasing identification with the role models of the program, (5) decreasing the number of sexual partners by both men and women, and (6) increasing condom use.[30] The series also promoted the adoption of family planning.[31] An amazing 82 percent of the listeners of *Twende na Wakati* adopted at least one method of HIV-prevention and 23 percent adopted one or more family planning methods.[32] During the same time period there was a 153 percent increase in condom distribution in the country.[33]

Across the border, Kenya was inspired by the success of Tanzania's *Twende na Wakati*. Kenya's past experiences with using dramatic serials for health education had also been positive. Thus, in 1998, with the sponsorship of Populations Communications International (PCI), who also helped to fund *Twende na Wakati*, and First Voice International (FVI), Kenya resurrected the radio drama it had first broadcast in the late 1980s. The new radio series, *Ushikwapo Shikamana (If Assisted, Assist Yourself)*, a slightly different name, focused on HIV and AIDS. *Ushikwapo Shikamana* addressed multiple health-related issues in addition to HIV/AIDS, including teen sexuality and gender discrimination. The program featured three typical settings for life in Kenya: an urban centre, a community in the outskirts of a major city, and a poor underdeveloped rural area. Radio was the most effective way to reach Kenyans at that time.

Based on the early success of *Twende na Wakati* in promoting HIV and AIDS prevention practices, Tanzania launched a new radio soap opera called *Mkwaju (Walking Stick)*. Like its predecessor, Mkwaju features the life of a truck driver and his battles with sexual responsibility and HIV. The program has achieved great national popularity and according to one study, has persuaded three-fourths of its regular listeners to change their sexual practices.[36]

Kenya aired four episodes of *Ushikwapo Shikamana* each week over a 26-week period each season during a five-year period, which ended in June 2004. Storylines included the challenges of urban life such as crime, loneliness, promiscuity, and drug trafficking; the hardships of peri-urban life such as poverty, poor housing, and inadequate social services, and the disadvantages of traditional rural life such as narrow thinking, lack of innovation and opposition to change. The ongoing themes of HIV and AIDS transmission, having compassion for people living with AIDS, and caring for children orphaned by AIDS are addressed by the characters in the three settings.

In addition to the radio series, the program sponsors and creative team produced comic strips that were published three times a week in Kenya's leading Kiswahili newspaper, *Taifa Leo*. These weekly comic strips were eventually compiled into one comic book which was printed in December 2001. The comic book was then distributed through a variety of outlets, including bookstores, church groups, and literacy programs.

Initial feedback from listening groups indicates *Ushikwapo Shikamana* increased awareness of the causes of HIV and AIDS and helped girls protect themselves from HIV and sexual abuse.[34] Primary and secondary school children also created soap opera drama clubs based on the series.[35] In April of 2005, Kenya began rebroadcasting *Ushikwapo Shikimana* by satellite.

Children and HIV/AIDS Education In July of 2000, the South African version of the Sesame Street children's television series, *Takalani (Be Happy)*, was launched through a collaboration of the South African Broadcasting Corporation, the Department of Education, and the Sesame Street Workshop. Funding for the series was also provided by USAID and Sanlam. There are more than two million children living with HIV in South Africa, which had an HIV prevalence rate among children age 2-9 of 5.6 percent by 2005.[37] Educators are concerned about the potential discrimination of these children. In order to help children understand other children living with HIV, the producers of *Takalani* created an HIV-positive muppet.

Glynis Clatherty and Ann Kushlicj conducted formative research with young children to help the creative producers understand how children would relate to the HIV/AIDS messages in the program.[38]

Puppets have been used for many hundreds of years to serve as a theatrical form of entertainment during which deep feelings, values, attitudes, and beliefs are communicated to an audience. Ancient cultures used puppets in rituals to create a connectedness within a community and to reinforce cultural norms. Ester Dagan believes puppets have a universal appeal because all people have a need to visualize the overcoming of a crisis through illusion.[39]

Across many different cultures and regions of the world, puppets have been used to serve three main functions: entertainment, education and to provide therapy.[40] Puppets have been used in HIV/AIDS campaigns in many countries, including India, Kenya, Namibia, South Africa, Thailand, Togo, and Zimbabwe. One of the founders of the African Research and Education Puppetry Program (ARREP), Gary Friedman, notes that puppets have an immediate effect on an audience because they provide a visual metaphor that is an international language.[41] Puppets are able to discuss very sensitive issues without offending the audience, and thus can open up a dialogue about HIV/AIDS and other sexually transmitted diseases. Puppet presentations are often a form of interactive community theater. Due to the tremendous versatility of puppets to address sexual responsibility issues, ARREP's first long-term project, Puppets against AIDS, was diffused to several African countries.[42]

Kenya has an organization called the Community Health Awareness Puppeteers (CHAPS). The organization uses puppet performances to raise awareness of sexually transmitted disease. Thailand has a youth organization called Making Dreams for a New Future. The group holds regular puppet shows in schools and community centers to promote sexual responsibility.[43] In Togo, puppets are used in a popular play called, AIDS, If I had only Known![44]

South African health educators also have been reaching out to children with HIV/AIDS prevention messages through the use of comic books. Through the creation of *eKasi*, a comic that tells the serialized story of Thandi, a teenage girl, researchers have been able to study the use of comics for HIV/AIDS prevention. A total of 24 issues of the comic were produced and 180,000 comic books were distributed to school children each month by the Daily Sun, South Africa's largest newspaper.[45] The main character of the comic series, Thandi, encountered numerous sociocultural contexts where she had to deal with HIV/AIDS. During the series, the children established strong identification with Thandi, who eventually reveals that she is HIV positive. Research of the effects of *eKasi* by Kirti Menon through in-depth interviews with children indicate that the comic series increased HIV/AIDS knowledge, dispelled harmful myths about the disease, and reduced the stigma of those infected with HIV. Readers also felt the characters were real and thus learned from them.[46]

HIV/AIDS Prevention Theatre is one of the oldest means of disseminating health information. Since the inception of theatre as an organized form of public entertainment and social commentary writers of plays and short skits have addressed health related issues. Theatre is still one of the most powerful educational mediums, especially in rural communities in developing nations. Today, live drama is being used throughout the world to promote beneficial health beliefs and practices.

In a number of countries, live drama is playing a critical role in the fight against the spread of HIV/AIDS. The subject of HIV/AIDS has been addressed by theatre groups in the U.S. for several decades. Playwright Gillette Elvgren, former head of the MFA program in Theatre at the University of Pittsburgh, wrote an HIV/AIDS prevention play during his tenure as Director of Pittsburgh's Shakespeare's Theatre. Elvgren applied the skills he had developed entertaining audiences with Elizabethan theatre to help audiences grapple with the AIDS epidemic.

Encouraged by positive responses in the U.S., Elvgren incorporated Hindi cultural theater forms and wrote an HIV/AIDS prevention play for Nepal.[47] A drama team has been travelling throughout Nepal and Northern India for more than five years performing his adaptation. Hindi audiences enjoy this production, which elicits much humor, while they are learning about a life and death subject.

In addition to Nepal and northern India, stage dramas dealing with HIV/AIDS have been used effectively in Ethiopia, South Africa, and other parts of India.[48] Mobile teams can reach millions of people through stage dramas, which can be performed in schools, parks, churches, stadiums, public squares, stadiums, market places, and on college and university campuses. They are relatively inexpensive to produce and can be made more culturally relevant than most mass media through the involvement of local performing artists.

In South Africa, a NGO called DramaAidE, a collaborate venture of the University of Zululand and the University of Natal, has used theatre to promote HIV/AIDS prevention and to provide care and support for those infected with HIV.[49] DramaAidE has organized thousands of events featuring theatre with music, dance and poetry in secondary schools in the KwaZulu-Natal Province, one of the hardest hit areas for HIV-infection. The theatre company also conducts theatre workshops that allow participants to engage in the creative process in a non-threatening environment to help them deal with the threat of AIDS by reflecting on their own sexual behavior. The goal of these workshops is to empower teenagers to become sexual responsible and not merely react to the pressures they may feel from others to be sexually active. The workshops not only involve acting and role playing, but also initiate active discussion of the subject matter and ideas they are seeking to communicate.

This form of theatre used by DramAidE, often referred to participatory theatre, is intended to not only influence the direct participants, but also their parents, teachers, community officials, spiritual leaders, and health professionals. DramAidE volunteers also help to organize health clubs in local schools and communities to promote healthy lifestyles. A number of these health clubs have organized fund-raising activities to teach good hygiene, dispose of harmful waste, and disseminate disinfectants and protective gloves.[50]

One of the keys to DramAidE popularity with teenagers is the opportunities for direct involvement that the organizers facilitate. Instead of students having to listen to teachers lecture to them on what they should know, how they should feel, and how they should behave, the educators simply create a means for teenagers to collaborate with each other in communicating through performing arts the thoughts, feelings, and actions they know they need to engage in order to live more healthy lifestyles. Research shows this strategy is very effective. DramAidE interventions have reduced high-risk sexual behaviors and have empowered participants to take control of their own beliefs and practices rather than be led by their circumstances or peer pressure.[51]

In Brazil, theatre also has been successfully used to promote HIV/AIDS prevention. Ranulfo Cardoso, Jr., with financial support from the MacArthur Foundation, created a group called Bricantes Contra a AIDS (Street Artists against AIDS) to train artists to deal with this issue through their writing and performing arts skills. The group initially focused on training artists in the Ceará State. The success of the program eventually spread across the country. Now thousands of Brazilian writers and performing artists are telling powerful stories through participatory theatre, folk media, and radio that promote sexual responsibility and generate understanding and support for those infected with HIV.[52]

In the State of Tamil Nadu in south India, a street theatre group called Nalamdana (Are you well?*)* has educated audiences about a number of health-related subjects, including cancer, maternal and child health, and HIV/AIDS.[53] The group often performs in outdoor community gathering places such as village squares. In addition to performing dramas, Nalamdana performers solicit participation from audience members and conduct follow-up workshops, providing audience members with a way to receive more assistance and support in dealing with the health issue targeted by the presentation. For example, after a two-hour performance dealing with HIV/AIDS, performers provide audience members with telephone numbers and locations where they could make arrangements to be tested for HIV and/or receive counseling.[54] During its first ten years, Nalamdana has performed health education dramas for more than a million people. A study of the effects of Nalamdana dramas indicated they helped to increase accurate knowledge about HIV/AIDS, change misperceptions about the disease, and reduce the stigma associated with those who are infected with HIV.[55]

Increasing Breast Cancer Awareness

One important health issue that has emerged in entertainment storylines is breast cancer. Breast cancer is one of the most critical health issues among women in the U.S. One of the first times that breast cancer was featured in an entertainment program was in an early 1970s episode of *All in the Family*. Edith, Archie Bunker's wife in the series, gets breast cancer and has to have a mastectomy. In a scene between Edith and one of her good friends, she breaks down in tears because of the fear that Archie may not love her in the same way after she has a breast removed. In a dramatic twist, Edith's friend reveals that she had had a mastectomy and that her husband loved her in exactly the same way. Edith tries not to look at her friend's bust several times to see if she can notice one breast is real, but she can't help herself, to the roaring laughter of the live audience.

The magic of Norman Lear's *All in the Family* was its combination of humor, real life, and important issues dramatized that people did not openly discuss. Through the genre of a situation comedy or sitcom, taboo communication was broken about breast cancer as well as many other sensitive subjects. The characters exposed commonly held prejudicial attitudes, beliefs, and stereotypes in a way to create self-reflection among audience members, although the satirical content also reinforced racial stereotypes among some viewers.[56]

A decade after Norman Lear's first experiments with entertainment-education in the U.S., one of the most popular situation comedies in the U.S., *Thirtysomething*, featured a story plot in which one of the main characters gets ovarian cancer. Viewers who followed the cancer storyline were both cognitively and emotionally influenced, creating a greater awareness of the issues surrounding ovarian cancer.[57] The telephone hotline provided to viewers lit up with a dramatic increase of telephone calls, mostly from women requesting more information on cancer.

Popular daytime television soap operas such as *One Life to Live* and *The Young and the Restless* also have dealt with the issue of breast cancer. In 2002, producers of *The Young and the Restless* launched a storyline in which Ashley, one of the program's major characters, is diagnosed with breast cancer. The audience walks through this challenge with Ashley for several weeks as she goes through her treatments to a successful conclusion. During the storyline, accurate information was provided to viewers on breast cancer screening, diagnosis and treatment options. In order to facilitate behavioral responses to the storyline, public service announcements on breast cancer were broadcast by the Cancer Information Service providing a toll-free 800 number for viewers who wanted further information.[58]

Alcohol Abuse Prevention

One important health issue featured in entertainment productions is alcohol abuse. One of the first organized communication campaigns designed to promote responsible drinking and driving through entertainment was created during the 1980s by the Harvard School of Public Health. Stung by the tragic death of a popular faculty member, husband, and father, who was killed by a drunk driver, the Harvard faculty searched for a way to address this growing national tragedy. The faculty of Harvard's School of Public Health realized that the most powerful means of influencing a large group of people was through the entertainment industry. One of the school's leaders visited with Hollywood producers and asked them to make room in their scripts to launch the designated driver concept. The Harvard Alcohol Project Harvard was incepted as a result of this collaboration, and in late1988, the Harvard School of Public Health launched the National Designated Driver Campaign (NDDC), also called the Harvard Alcohol Project, to advance the social norm that drivers should abstain from alcohol and that groups of friends planning to drink should choose a designated driver.[59]

One of the first presentations of the drinking and driving concept was given through a 1989 episode of *My Two Dads*, a popular U.S. television series. In the episode, two dads get drunk and then drive home together in their inebriated condition. Their irresponsible drinking and driving angers their daughter, who tells them they should have decided who would be the "designated driver" before they began drinking. Similar prosocial messages encouraging the designated driver concept were included in 76 other U.S. television programs as part of a two-month campaign between Thanksgiving and New Years (the heavy drinking season in the U.S.) of 1989, causing an increase in viewer awareness of the designated driver concept.[60] Through the partnership of Hollywood leaders, the national campaign, valued at over $100 million dollars in advertising space, placed designated driver messages in more than 160 entertainment programs.[61] Many famous actors and actresses were involved in promoting the no drinking and driving concept. An assessment of the campaign indicated the adoption of the designated driver practice was successfully diffused, especially among males.[62] Now the idea and practice of choosing a designated driver is quite common. Not only has it helped those who don't like to drink alcohol go out with a group and not feel pressured to drink, but it has saved lives by reducing the number of drunk drivers on the road.

Portrayals of alcohol consumption on entertainment television programs in the U.S. are common.[63] Researchers examine how entertainment contributes viewers' perceptions of various social norms such as drinking alcohol. For example, one episode of the program, Party of Five, portrayed a detailed drinking and driving incident in which Bailey, one of the main characters, gets in a drunk driving accident, injuring his girlfriend. The episode made the abstract problem of drinking and driving very real, particularly to college students targeted by the episode.[64]

The popular 1980s U.S. television situation comedy *Growing Pains* included a powerful episode on drunk driving.[65] In the episode, the oldest daughter of the family, Carol Seaver (played by Tracey Gold), had a boyfriend named Sandy who had dropped her off from a date the night before. Due to his over-consumption of alcohol during the evening, he gets in a serious car accident and is hospitalized. When Carol visits Sandy in the hospital during the next day, he is conscious and appears to be on the road to recovery. Carol tells him he narrowly escaped death and now has a second chance on life and makes him promise never to drink and drive again. Later that evening, Carol's brother Mike receives a shocking call from the hospital informing him family that Sandy had died from internal hemorrhaging. When Mike breaks the terrible news, Carol cries out in anguish, asking her family through her tears, "What happened to his second chance?" The episode was so powerful that NBC Nightly News ran a story about it, indicating the producers had intended to send a powerful message about drinking and driving.

Hollywood writer, producer and director Peter Engel not only took on the issues of alcohol and drug abuse, but addressed a host of relevant topics that teenagers struggle with from day to day in his popular series, Engel purposefully sought to blend high quality entertainment for teenagers with stories involving everyday moral issues that teens encountered. By showing the struggles of his characters in making the right moral decisions, the program promoted responsibility among its teenage viewers who followed the lives of the program's characters into adulthood. *Saved by the Bell* and its many spin-offs became some of the most highly rated television programs among teenagers in television history. Engel's creative use of satirical humor demonstrated that popular entertainment and comedy could effectively help teenagers to discuss important moral issues such as drinking and driving.[66]

The designated driver campaign, *Growing Pains* and *Saved by the Bell* are but a few examples among many in which entertainment has been used to reduce the abuse of alcohol. Although not all dramatic stories dealing with alcoholism or drunk driving necessarily communicate abuse prevention messages, those that do can be very effective.

Television programs overseas also have dealt with alcohol abuse. For example, India's first long-running television soap opera, *Hum Log*, discussed earlier, aired several episodes with an alcohol abuse subplot.[67] In the epilogues, film star Askok Kumar warned viewers about the disastrous effects of alcohol abuse. In one of Tanzania's first television soap operas, *Maisha*, alcoholism and drug abuse were prominently featured.[68]

Oral Rehydration Therapy

Dysentery is one of the leading causes of death among young children in the world today. The lack of potable water has contributed to alarming rates of dysentery deaths in much of the underdeveloped world. Diarrhea-related diseases such as cholera, dysentery, typhoid fever, and rotavirus claim the lives of nearly two million children each year and account for a high percentage of infant mortalities worldwide.[69] One simple but effective technique to save a child's life when dysentery strikes is through oral rehyradation therapy (ORT), a sodium and glucose solution developed by medical researchers in Bangladesh and India during the 1970s. By mixing salt, sugar and water, common ingredients in every household, an oral rehydration solution can save a dehydrated child's life.

Egypt, a country with a high infant death rate, successfully implemented a $50 million ORT campaign using entertainment to teach parents how to administer ORT. By using well-known film and television stars to promote ORT, the public service announcement campaign attracted a great deal of attention. Results of the campaign were phenomenal. Awareness of ORT reached 98 percent of the population in five years and usage of ORT reached 82 percent.[70] Infant mortality rates were cut almost in half during the campaign and by 1991, at the end of the campaign, nearly all mothers (more than 99%) knew about ORT and more than 96% used ORT. Infant mortality rates were reduced by 70 percent by the end of the campaign, saving the lives of more than 100,000 children in the first two years of the entertaining public service television ads.[71] Other countries have also made ORT a commonly-know life-saving technique through entertainment-education media.

Environmental Safety

One of the most important health issues of the 21st century concerns environmental safety. The increased toxicity of our environment through the accumulation of waste and toxic compounds has contributed to the increase of cancer and other harmful diseases, costing some developed nations billions of dollars each year in health care costs and the tragic loss of life. Embedding environmental safety messages in popular entertainment has become an increasingly effective means of raising awareness about the environment.

One of the early and most successful experiments in mixing entertainment and environmental education was a television special broadcast in 1977 called *The Great American Values Test*. Created by Milton and Sandra Ball Rokeach, two social scientists and university professors, the program was designed to persuade the viewing audience to self-reflect on the values of equality and a world of beauty and motivated viewers to increase the importance that they placed on those two values. The Rokeaches had conducted numerous studies of how media messages could change people through a process of self-reflection. They theorized that if people realized how important the value of a clean and safe environment was to those around them, and saw that they did not value the environment as highly as others did, that they would be motivated to become more environmentally concerned and active.

In order to test their theory, they decided to simulcast a one-hour television special in the tri-city area of the northern Washington state. This experiment took place in the days before cable television took hold and when ABC, CBS, and NBC dominated television broadcasting. All three major networks broadcast the program so that if you lived in that area and watched television you were likely to see the program, which was hosted by Ed Asner and provided viewers with information about how much people in their area valued the environment. The effectiveness of *The Great American Values Test* was stunning. Those who watched the program not only increased their value of a clean and healthy environment, but also increased their donations to environmental causes after watching the program. The powerful results of this experiment in using popular media to promote environmental safety were published in a book by Rokeaches and their colleague, Joel Grube, in1984.[72]

In the NBC comedy series *My Two Dads*, noted earlier, Joey Harris, one of the main characters in the series, was revealed as a dedicated environmentalist. Joey's environmental activism even landed him in jail on one episode, a storyline promoted by a Hollywood lobby group called The Environmental Media Association. Noting the popular series ability to address social issues such as irresponsible drinking and polluting of the environment, producer David Steven Simon explained, "We can create consciousness and prompt activity."[73]

One important dimension of environmental safety is safe working conditions. Industrial safety is an extremely large industry that seeks to promote safety in the workplace environment. One of the leading producers of these videos in the U.S. is Coastal Video based in Virginia Beach, Virginia. The company markets hundreds of videos throughout the world to teach workers important work policies and procedures such as fire safety, handling hazardous materials, electrical safety. Dr. Timothy Wright, a trained actor, writer, and professor of communication, has produced numerous award-winning entertainment-education videos for Coastal Video during the past 20 years. The videos are extremely popular with workers because instead of the dry educational fare they are accustomed to, Dr. Wright's videos are humorous, thought-provoking, informative, irreverent, and highly entertaining.

Perhaps the most recognizable pro-environmental entertainment production is the Hollywood film, *Erin Brockovich*. Based on a true story about a young woman who dared to take on the corporate powerhouse that controlled the town in which she lived, the film dramatizes the tragic effects of environmental irresponsibility. Played by actress Julia Roberts, who won an academy award nomination for her role, Ms. Brockevich becomes a hero for standing up for the rights of those whose lives have been destroyed by chemical wastes.

These are but a few of the many examples in which popular media has been used to effectively promote pro-environmental attitudes beliefs and behavior. Most of these efforts, for example, the several pro-environmental films produced by Disney, have not been studied. What is clear is that the media and the arts can strongly influence how much we value our environment.

Promoting Care for the Handicapped

The nation of Nepal, the small country to the north of India and a favorite destination for Himalayan mountain climbers, has more than 30 million people. Estimates of the number of Nepalis with disabilities range from 5 to 10 percent of the population, or 1.5-3.0 million people.[74] The average family size in Nepal is 6.6 people; therefore, many Nepali households are directly affected by someone with a disability – either a family member or a close relative. Only 4.9% of Nepal's budget is allocated for health care and virtually none is provided for those with disabilities.[75] Most disabled persons in Nepal have little or no access to rehabilitation.

Many Nepalis still view disability as a form of penance for the sins they committed in previous lives. People with disabilities are often shunned or treated as objects of pity. Most disabled persons have no education as compared to the general population, in which only a small percentage have no education. Although the human rights of disabled people are upheld by the Nepalese Constitution, in practice disabled people remain severely disadvantaged and marginalized in society. The rights of people with disabilities to participate fully in society have not been realized. In terms of health accessibility, education, and employment opportunities, people with disabilities are treated much like the lowest caste citizens of their culture.

One of the powerful means for changing attitudes toward the handicapped in Nepal is through television. Television is an integral piece of household furniture in many Nepali homes. Where electricity is available in the country, among approximately 80% of the population, practically every house has at least one television set. Affluent families usually possess one or more television sets. In many homes, the television stays on from the moment one family member wakes up until the last family member goes to bed. It is the number one and often the only form of entertainment for most families. Nepali children are born into a world in which television has a major presence.

In 2007 Nepal began airing a television program called *Khushi Ko Sansar (Happy World)*. *Khushi Ko Sansar (KKS)* is the Nepali version of the Hindi program, *Khushi Ki Duniya (Happy*

World in Hindi), a thirty-minute weekly children's TV show produced by the Christian Broadcasting Network in India. *Khushi Ki Duniya* has been on air in India since 2005 with great success. In India, 20,000 letters were received from audience members in 2007.[76] The first two month's airing of the TV show also promised to be successful with several hundred letters received from audience members. This TV show is a biblically based character education program presented in an entertainment-education format which has wide appeal to children. Music, song, dance and brightly colored, amusing sets appealing to children are shown throughout the show keeping their attention on the program. It covers such topics as speaking no evil; sowing and reaping; using things properly (not being destructive with other's property, books, household items, tools and school items); choosing good role models; good health; honesty; stealing; friendship; respect for their elders and other subjects relevant to a child's character development.

In addition to the above topics, some shows contain a specific educational element which discusses persons with disabilities. These programs explore the lives of deaf people; blind people; physically and mentally disabled people; accident victims who are now in wheelchairs or use other walking aids; autism and other health concerns. These shows are intended to educate children about disabilities, so they understand the importance of respecting those different than themselves, showing the importance of everyone's right to dignity in life. They emphasize how every person has worth and value and that someone with a disability can live almost as normal a life as can a non-disabled person.

In my 2008 study of the effects of involvement with *Khushi Ko Sansar (Happy World)* with my colleagues, we collected pre-test and post-test survey data from 357 Nepali children from seven communities in the country were analyzed. Results show children role modeled the prosocial beliefs of the program's star character, Kush. As was expected, media exposure increased identification and was effective in changing the thinking and perceptions of children toward people with disabilities, primarily through two means: (1) creating an increased sense of positive beliefs about with people with disabilities, and (2) increasing more positive intended behavior toward those with disabilities.[77] Overall, our findings of the study are encouraging and optimistic with regards to the use of an entertainment-education television program to promote positive thinking and favorable treatment of people with disabilities.

Media Centers, Health Communication and Entertainment-Education

Media centers are creating unique opportunities for universities, higher educational institutions, media organizations, and government agencies to collaborate on health-related entertainment-education projects. For example, media centers throughout the U. K.

bring together artists, fi1m-makers, academics, publishers, and other communication specialists to collaborate on specific media projects, providing unique opportunities for research on the use of entertainment to address important social needs.[78] Joint efforts between communication scholars and creative artists can make important contributions to the development of future entertainment-education projects. Many entertainment-education productions for public health are now either being designed and/or created by media centers, including independent centers and those housed in universities. A number of centers exist within universities or foundations while others are independent. Let me discuss a few pertinent examples of media centers that promote and study entertainment-education as a primary means of health communication.

One of the leading media centers in the world is the Center for Communication Programs (CCP), housed in the Bloomberg School of Public Health at John Hopkins University in Baltimore, Maryland. CCP collaborates with organizations worldwide to design and implement communication programs that promote beneficial health practices by seeking to influence public health policies, community health practices, and individual behavior. CCP, which receives substantial funding from USAID, is the creative force behind dozens of entertainment-education projects throughout the world. Scholars and media practitioners who develop and study entertainment-education have made enormous contributions to entertainment-education theory and research.[79] As noted earlier, CCP also has been instrumental in organizing and supporting the four international conferences on for social change.

Dozens of studies referenced in this chapter were funded and produced through JHUCCP. With projects in 36 countries, a perusal of their website reveals a great breadth of health-related entertainment-education productions that they have created.[80] The Center also provides dozens of publications and research reports written by media scholars who work there and carry out evaluation studies throughout the world. Although JHU/CCP has multiple funding sources, a substantial amount of its budget is provided by the U.S. government. For example, in 2009 USAID awarded JHU/CCP a five-year $100,000,000 grant to implement Malaria prevention programs in 28 countries.[81]

One of the European centers for entertainment-education collaboration is the Center for Media and Health in the Netherlands. The Center is an example of an independent media center that works closely with the Netherlands Entertainment-Education Foundation (NEEF), a non-profit organization that promotes the study and use of entertainment-education, and several Dutch Universities. NEEF brought together more than 100 media professionals and communication scholars from 22 countries when it hosted the Third International Entertainment-Education Conference for Social Change in Arnhem and Amsterdam in 2000.[82] The Center organizers ongoing entertainment-education workshops and soap opera summits, develops and assesses entertainment-education curriculum at Dutch universities, hosts Fulbright scholars who are entertainment-education experts, and collaborates with health communication scholars and media professionals to design, implement and evaluate entertainment-education projects.

The Dutch Entertainment-Education Foundation was established in the late 1990s to create collaboration between media professionals and health educators in Europe, focusing on the Dutch television industry in Hilversum, the Netherlands. Although Hilversum's population hovers around 84,000, it is the center of Dutch radio and television broadcasting as well as a manufacturing center. Pioneered by Dr. Martine Bouman, a communication consultant of Bouman Development and adjunct professor at several Dutch universities, the Dutch Entertainment-Education Foundation and closed linked Center for Media and Health have conducted training seminars and workshops with media and health professionals, initiated a number of entertainment-education projects in the Netherlands, collaborated on entertainment-education projects in Europe and Africa, and has conducted research on the effects of entertainment-education messages. In many aspects European health educators are leading the way in creating educational training and university curriculum to help health and media professionals understand the tremendous potential of popular media to advance health education and benefit society.

Recently, the Center for Media and Health designed, created, produced, and implemented a sound effects campaign to raise awareness of the need to use earplugs to protect against permanent hearing loss brought about by repeated exposure to loud music in bars, clubs and discothèques. The campaign featured a web-based entertainment-education drama mini-series, a media campaign called Go Out and Plug In, and extensive formative and summative research on the campaign effects.[83] The innovative internet-based campaign attracted media attention which prompted a discussion on the floor of the Dutch Parliament about hearing loss in 2009.

Another example of an independent media center that specializes in entertainment-education is Population Media Center (PMC) in the United States. PMC, founded in 1998 and headquartered in Vermont, has produced and implemented entertainment-education projects in the eastern Caribbean, Ethiopia, Jamaica, Mali, Mexico, Niger, Nigeria, Rwanda, Senegal, the U.S., and Vietnam. PMC's focus is on using Miguel Sabido's entertainment-education methodology to promote environmental preservation, family planning, HIV/AIDS prevention, women's empowerment and child protection. PMC collaborates with local producers and writers in the countries where they work to create indigenous serial dramas that are broadcast locally and nationally. The Center has a board of experienced entertainment-education experts from around the world, including David Poindexter, one of the international leaders in diffusing the entertainment-education strategy. Although PMC programs address many different issues, their focus is on population planning, as illustrated by the running total of the world population on the opening page of their website. PMC also provides academic publications, newsletters, training guides, and samples of entertainment-education programs for media professionals and health educators working on entertainment-education projects. Their 2008 Annual Report shows health and education projects in a dozen countries.[84]

Population Services International (PSI), headquartered in Washington, D.C., is another leading center for health campaigns. PSI operates in 67 countries with more than 100 overseas staff and 200 support staff in the U.S., with a budget that exceeded $400 million in 2008.[85] Many of their ongoing projects involve behavior change communications brought about through media campaigns that draw on elements of the entertainment-education communication strategy, although they do not stress the use of entertainment-education. Some of their major donor include USAID, the U.S. Centers for Disease Control and Prevention (CDC), the Canadian International Development Agency (CIDA), the Department for International Development (DFID), the Netherlands Government Ministry of Foreign Affairs, the Federal Republic of Germany through KfW Entwicklungsbank (the German development bank), and the Global Fund To Fight AIDS, Tuberculosis and Malaria.

Among the most successful of media centers for entertainment-education production is the *Soul City* Institute for Health and Development Communication in South Africa.[86] The center was founded in 1992 by Garth Japhet and Shereen Usdin, two medical doctors and health communication specialists, to help meet critical health needs in southern Africa. *Soul City* uses a variety of entertainment-education media, which they refer to as edutainment, to promote health education, including radio, television, film, billboards, and print media. *Soul City* is one of the world's leading health promotion organizations, subscribing to the principles of the World Health Organization's Ottawa Charter, which recognized that public health requires a supportive environment, advocacy for health policies, community action, interpersonal communication skills, and focusing health services on health promotion.[87]

In 1994, *Soul City* began broadcasting its first entertainment-education television series, also called *Soul City*. Within 15 years the organization had produced nine television drama series reaching more than 16 million South Africans.[88] *Soul City* has an impressive network of funding organizations for its programs, including government entities like the European Union, the U.S. State Department's PEPFAR program, the United Kingdom's Department for International Development, the Royal Netherlands Embassy, Development Corporation Ireland, AUSAID, Japan Official Development Assistance, and South Africa's Department of Health; and private organizations and corporate sponsors like De Beers, British Petroleum, MTN Group, Joseph Rowntree Charitable Trust, Kagiso Trust, Cordaid, Save the Children, UNICEF, UNHCR, the Rockefeller Foundation, and the Nelson Mandela Children's Fund.

In addition to creating entertainment-education programs and health campaigns, *Soul City* conducts formative research on the use of entertainment media to promote HIV/AIDS prevention, sexual responsibility, spousal abuse prevention, maternal and child health practices, and substance abuse prevention, and hires independent scholars to conduct summative research of its programs.[89] Research of *Soul City* entertainment-education projects indicates its media programs have led to the adoption of a number of important beneficial health practices.[90]

Soul City Campaigns have produced numerous multimedia campaigns, including ten *Soul City* radio and television series, four *Soul Buddyz* radio and television series, nine African films from nine countries, and print materials and advertising the accompany the media productions.

The first 13 dramatic episodes of *Soul City's* television broadcasts focused on children's health and HIV/AIDS prevention. *Soul City's* second television series, broadcast in 1996, focused on HIV/AIDS, TB, and smoking prevention; followed by a third series in 1997, which also concentrated on HIV/AIDS prevention messages as well as other health-related themes. All three series achieved high audience ratings, became some of the most popular prime-time television programs on South African television, and reached an estimated 20 million people.[91]

In 1999, *Soul City* launched its fourth entertainment-education television series on all nine of the SABC (South African Broadcasting Corporation) regional language radio stations. In addition, *Soul City*'s print material was distributed by 11 partner newspapers, including *The Cape Argus*; *Daily News*; *Echo*; *Ilanga*; *Sowetan*; *Daily Dispatch*; *Diamond Fields Advertiser*; *Evening Post*; and *Pretoria News & The Star*.[92] The series addressed the issues of gender sensitivity and empowering women, community activism, racial discrimination, parenting, violence and substance abuse.

In 2001 and 2003, the fifth and sixth *Soul City* television series were produced and broadcast in South Africa. Like the first four series, the programs consistently achieved high audience ratings and won numerous awards for excellence in television drama. Extensive social scientific research indicates the programs have increased knowledge, discussion and adoption of HIV/AIDS prevention practices.[93] *Soul City* has conducted evaluation studies of each television series to document the influence of the programs on viewers. In addition to promoting sexual responsibility, family planning, HIV/AIDS prevention, drug and alcohol abuse prevention, and other prosocial beliefs and practices in South Africa, *Soul City* media have been used in neighboring Botswana, Lesotho, Namibia, Swaziland, Zambia and Zimbabwe.

The success of *Soul City* inspired the KBC national television network in Kenya to produce the dramatic television series *Heart and Soul*. Sponsored by 24 United Nations agencies, *Heart and Soul* was produced through the creative leadership of Matthew Robinson, a veteran BBC director of television soap operas. The program is intended to reach an estimated 50 million television viewers in 23 English-speaking African nations to address key development issues, including HIV/AIDS prevention.[94]

The Norman Lear Center

Some media centers involved in entertainment-education endeavors serve as resource centers and networking sites for those seeking to collaborate on entertainment-education projects. One such center is the Norman Lear Center at the University of Southern California (USC), home to the Hollywood, Health and Society (HH&S) project, an ongoing service for the American entertainment industry. Results of a 2001 study by Porter Novelli on health styles indicated that more than half of regular prime time and daytime drama viewers recalled learning something about a disease or how to prevent it from a television program.[95] About one-third of regular television viewers said they took some action after hearing about a health issue or disease on a television program. The HH&S project provides a website with updated accurate health information for writers and producers of entertainment content. The Norman Lear Center also provides individual consultations, group briefings, and panel discussions for and with communication scholars and media and health professionals.

HH&S resources include a quarterly newsletter with health updates called Real to Real, an expanding list of tip sheets written specifically for writers and producers that can be accessed through the Center for Disease Controls' website and for the National Cancer Institute's website. Information at these websites cover a broad range of topics, including facts about influenza, toxic mold, smallpox, cancer, autism, motor vehicle crashes, obesity, adolescent health issues, antibiotic resistance, and clinical trials.

Film and television students at USC can access these resources to learn how to address educational issues through their creative productions. More importantly, students can learn theory and research behind the entertainment-education communication strategy in coursework offered by the Annenberg School for Communication. One of the courses, Entertainment-Education & Marketing, is taught by Professor Michael Cody, who has served with his colleagues on the Board of Advisers for the office of Hollywood, Health and Society. He also judges the Sentinel Awards, an annual award given for promoting health in entertainment programs.

CDC in Atlanta The Centers for Disease Control in Atlanta recognizes the power of popular entertainment in shaping the perceptions and practices of its viewers. Television shows, movies, and music not only command the attention of their audiences, but also reinforce existing behavior, demonstrate new behavior, and affect audience emotions. The CDC often partners with Hollywood executives and academic, public health, and advocacy organizations to share information with writers and producers about the nation's pressing health issues. The CDC Entertainment Education Program works in partnership with Hollywood, Health & Society project (HH&S) at the University of Southern California's

Norman Lear Center to provide expert consultation, education and resources for writers and producers who develop scripts with health storylines and information.[96]

The Hollywood, Health & Society project resulted from years of research that shows popular entertainment provides an ideal outlet for sharing health information and affecting behavior. The website for the project states that its goal is to provide information that covers a variety of topics, including violence against women, suicide, lead poisoning, hospital infection, bioterrorism, youth health issues, and HIV/AIDS. Since an estimated 88 percent of people in America learn about health issues from television, HH & S scholars believe that prime time and daytime television programs, movies, talk shows and more, are great outlets for our health messages.

CDC Sentinel for Health Award One of the goals of the HH&S project is to show how television can be a powerful means to reach those at risk for preventable diseases. Spurred on by findings of a 1999 Healthstyles Survey, which indicated that regular viewers of soap operas had more health concerns than individuals who do not watch soap operas, HH&S created the CDC Sentinel for Health Award for Daytime Drama. This award recognizes the exemplary portrayal of health issues in television soap operas. The first award winner, given in 2000, was an episode of ABC's *One Life to Live* titled "Viki's Breast Cancer." In 2001, HH&S partnered with the CDC to recognize "Raul's Diabetes" from CBS's *The Young and the Restless*. The following year, the award went to "Tony's HIV" from CBS's *The Bold and The Beautiful*. The diabetes episode in 2001 generated scores of letters from viewers who said the storyline helped them or a loved one to recognize early signs of the disease and to receive a diagnosis and treatment. The response to the HIV episode in 2002 was even more dramatic. An 800-number public service announcement was aired with Tony, one of the main characters in the series, resulting in the largest spike in callers to the CDC's national AIDS hotline for the entire year. In 2003, the Sentinel for Health Award was awarded to "Neil's Alcoholism" from *The Young and the Restless*. An episode of *Law & Order* on fetal alcohol syndrome won the 2004 prime time drama award.

The following year, the CBS prime time drama *Without a Trace* received first place in the prime-time drama category for "Volcano," a storyline on autism. Also in 2005, the ABC soap opera *All My Children* took first place in daytime drama for a storyline about a teen with autism and the WB drama *7th Heaven* took first place for prime time minor storyline with "Leaps of Faith," a storyline about sickle cell anemia. In 2005 the Sentinel Awards committee created a Spanish language programming award. The first winner was given to *Telemundo's* Anita, no te rajes, for its breast cancer storyline. The seventh Sentinel Awards were given to the CBS soap opera *As the World Turns* for a storyline about breast cancer diagnosis and treatment in a major character, to the NBC drama *ER* took for its primetime minor storyline with "BRCA – Breast Cancer Risks," and to ABC's George Lopez for its primetime comedy storyline about preventing kidney disease. *Telemundo* took home its second Sentinel Award in the Spanish-language telenovela category, for "Don Pedro's Diabetes."

Publicity for the Sentinel Awards encourages television writers and producers to consider integrating important health messages into the television episodes of the programs they are creating. Once they decide to do so, the resources at the Norman Lear Center and at the Centers for Disease Control make it easier for creators of television fiction to find the factual information they need regarding the health issue they are featuring. The Sentinel for Health Award is just one example of how media producers use entertainment to educate people about public health concerns that affect their daily lives. Through the Hollywood, Health & Society program, public health and medical experts offer expert consultation, education and resources for writers and producers who develop scripts with health storylines and information. The HH&S project is creating more than 130 tip sheets on a broad range of topics, including skin cancer, sudden infant death syndrome, smallpox, and antibiotic resistance, with many of these already available online. The HH&S staff also holds meetings with the creators of TV shows and network campaigns, conduct expert briefings for writers, and respond to inquiries for health information. These meetings inform television networks and their creative staff about the services provided through the Norman Lear Center and the CDC. Experts collaborate with writers and producers in person, by telephone or through e-mail correspondence. Program staff also arrange expert briefings for the writing staff of television shows and arrange one-on-one conversations between a producers and health experts and between writers and those directly dealing with specific health issues.

Communication and health scholars at the University of Southern California collaborate on various research projects to assess the effects of entertainment-education television episodes on television audiences. National studies in the U.S. have shown that daytime and prime time television viewers pay attention to the health information they are exposed to, learn from it and act on it. They also share the information they learn from television with others.

These examples of leading media centers from different parts of the world are but a few of the dozens of media centers that are involved in entertainment-education productions. Such centers are important because they provide focal points for ongoing entertainment-education collaboration, training, and research. In our final section we will discuss the future of entertainment-education, international synergies, and consider opportunities for both media academics and media practitioners who desire to become involved in entertainment-education projects.

International Entertainment-Education Synergies and Opportunities

The use of entertainment-education for social change, particularly with the application to promoting beneficial health practices and healthy lifestyles, has become an international industry. There are more entertainment-education collaborative projects today than ever, and the growth of entertainment-education will likely continue as entertainment media continues to become a powerful source of social influence. The international gatherings include a large network of entertainment-education scholars, experts, and practitioners. To date, there have been five international entertainment-education conferences, with the last one being held in New Delhi in 2011 (EE5). The synergies created by these conferences include the development of explanatory entertainment-education theories, more shard principles of successful entertainment-education interventions, more understanding of productive collaboration processes, more shared knowledge of effective entertainment-education strategies, and more interpersonal relationships among entertainment-education scholars and practitioners throughout the world.

Entertainment-education is an international practice bound to expand in the 21st century. Media centers, universities, government health and development agencies, and non-profit organizations are looking for media academics and practitioners who have experience, knowledge, and skill in the design, production and evaluation of entertainment-education media and arts. More entertainment-education experts will be needed in the near future who can provide valuable training programs and skills for producing and researching entertainment-education. The use of entertainment-education as an important health and development communication strategy will continue to increase in the foreseeable future. In the following chapter, I will focus specifically on one piece of the entertainment-education puzzle – how we learn through athletes who become sports celebrities.

Discussion Questions

1. Have you changed a health-related behavior in your own life as a result of watching an entertainment television program?
2. What one fictional character would you say has influence your diet and exercise lifestyle the most?
3. Can you think of a health storyline that motivated a family member or friend to change a health-related behavior? Please explain.
4. If you were given a health-education award to a producer or entertainment programming, who would you award and why?

Chapter 8
Learning through Sports Stars

Participating in sports and following sports teams and individual stars is a worldwide phenomenon that has touched virtually every country on the planet. Sports stars can have a very powerful influence on millions of people. In this chapter I will examine the influence of several prominent athletes and explain the kinds of things we can learn through their lives.

Learning about HIV from "Magic" Johnson

Earvin Johnson Jr. grew up with nine siblings, but he was the one who usually slept with his basketball. He dribbled it both on and off the basketball court, taking it on errands around where he lived. By the time he entered high school, Junior had developed into an excellent player. After watching him work his "magic" on the court as an outstanding high school player, a local sportswriter nicknamed him "Magic," much to the chagrin of his mother. Johnson developed into a complete player, excelling at scoring, rebounding, and giving assists to others. He could see plays as they were unfolding, anticipating the movements of other players on the court. His passing skills were phenomenal, as enjoyable to watch as his own scoring. The basketball statistics term "triple double" (indicating that a player's total points, rebounds, and assists in one game reached double digits) described the common play of Magic Johnson, who personified the term. Johnson played every position on the basketball court.

Johnson led his high school to the state championship and his college, Michigan State University, to the 1978-79 national championship. He then went pro after his sophomore season and helped lead the Los Angeles Lakers to the NBA championship in his rookie season, winning the Most Valuable Player award for the playoffs. During his hall of fame career as an NBA superstar, Johnson led the Lakers five NBA titles.

On Nov. 7, 1991, two months after getting married and still very much at the top of his game, Johnson shocked the world by announcing that he had tested positive for HIV and that he was retiring from basketball. At the time Johnson was one of the most well-known and well-liked athletes in the world. He was one of the first celebrities to make such an announcement and disclosed that he had foolishly engaged in unprotected sex with dozens of women.

After Johnson's stunning announcement, the news spread quickly of his infection. Instantly the world had a well-liked, high-profile celebrity who demonstrated that heterosexuals were at risk for HIV/AIDS. This event appeared to be a potentially critical turning point in people's perception of the disease. The press predicted that Magic would be immensely effective in conveying this risk to the public. They speculated that his charisma would personalize the concern to other heterosexuals who had otherwise rationalized that the AIDS risk was limited to gay men. Magic's immediate interviews with the press, public service announcements, and appointment to the President's AIDS Council reinforced this hope.[1] Johnson also pledged himself to be a spokesperson for HIV/AIDS prevention and established The Magic Johnson Foundation to raise funds for AIDS education.[2]

Before Magic Johnson's stunning announcement, the U. S. government had spent a considerable amount of money promoting HIV/AIDS prevention. However, the government's efforts to curtail the spread of HIV through health campaigns in the middle to late 1980s fell short of what was needed. Televised PSAs and printed materials raised knowledge of AIDS and HIV transmission but did not effectively promote change in high-risk sexual behaviors.[3] These campaigns primarily focused on providing knowledge about the disease and sought to convince people through a cognitive-rational approach to change their high-risk sexual behaviors.

In contrast to the limited effectiveness of informational HIV/AIDS prevention efforts, Magic Johnson had a much more powerful influence. One of the dilemmas for health educators seeking to slow down the diffusion of HIV infection was that the general public viewed AIDS as a homosexual disease during the 1980s. Although many people knew that HIV could be acquired through heterosexual relations, the disease was not perceived as much of a threat to heterosexuals except for drug users. This false perception, that HIV/AIDS was not a threat to non-drug using heterosexuals, was very difficult to overcome. In a few short minutes, Magic Johnson obliterated this false perception. When Magic Johnson became a spokesperson for HIV prevention, giving talks and producing an HIV-prevention video, *Time Out*, with Arsenio Hall, high-risk teenagers and young adults listened to Johnson. Everyone knew Johnson was an athletic, healthy and active heterosexual. There was no evidence that he was a drug user. Heterosexuals, especially men, not only listened to Johnson, but they were more likely to change their high-risk sexual behaviors in response to his appeals to do so.

Several studies have documented Magic Johnson's influence on HIV prevention. The day after Johnson held the news conference indicating he was HIV-positive, the National AIDS hotline logged some 40,000 calls, a 10-fold increase from the average number of daily calls received.[4] I conducted research on the effects of Johnson's announcement with Michael Basil, a colleague of mine at the University of Hawaii. We found that those who had a higher degree of emotional involvement with Johnson demonstrated increases in their personal concern about AIDS, concern about the risk of AIDS to heterosexuals, and intention to reduce high-risk sexual behaviors.[5] Michael Basil replicated our study a year later and again found that those who identified more strongly with Johnson were more likely to exhibit attitudinal and behavior changes in their lives to reduce their risk of HIV-infection.[6]

Working with an additional data set, Mike and I conducted a third study on Magic Johnson's influence on HIV/AIDS prevention. We found that identification with Johnson affected both social and personal concern about AIDS. Public responses indicated the heterosexual population felt "if it could happen to Johnson (a heterosexual becoming HIV-positive), it could happen to me."[7] Magic Johnson clearly had a more powerful influence on motivating heterosexuals to reduce their high-risk sexual behaviors than the multi-million dollar HIV/AIDS prevention campaigns that preceded his announcement.

The influence of Magic Johnson on HIV/AIDS prevention is an excellent example of how a famous athlete can change health behaviors. No one knows how many thousands of lives Johnson might have saved as a result of his courage in the face of public embarrassment and steadfast efforts to fight the spread of AIDS.

Learning through the O.J. Simpson Nightmare

Orenthal James Simpson was born on July 9, 1947, in the city of San Francisco. Named by his aunt Eunice after one of her favorite French actors, Simpson had a difficult childhood, contracting rickets at age two. The sickness left Simpson with legs that were skinny, bow-legged and pigeon-toed. Eunice, a hospital orderly who helped her sister raise Simpson, couldn't afford to give Simpson braces, so she made him wear a pair of shoes connected by an iron bar for a few hours almost every day until age five. He lived with his mother, brother and two sisters in an impoverished section of San Francisco called Potrero Hill.[8]

Simpson was a problem child, joining his first gang at age 13. He said in a 1976 interview for Playboy Magazine that nearly every weekend he would "beat up dudes who deserved it," noting that "If there weren't no fight, it wasn't no weekend." At age 15 he was sent to a Youth Guidance Center for one week for fighting. Fortunately, football provided a positive outlet for his aggression, and he excelled at it while playing at Galileo High School. Although his poor grades dissuaded scholarship offers after high school graduation, Simpson enrolled in the City College of San Francisco where he broke junior-college football records. Then the recruiters came knocking on his door, and Simpson accepted an offer from the University of Southern California (USC), the school he had dreamed about playing for since he began playing football.

At 6-foot-1 and 212 pounds, Simpson was a record-setting back at USC. One of his greatest achievements came while playing against unbeaten UCLA. USC trailed the Bruins when Simpson broke through the line, scampering down the left sideline and then cutting back to the middle of the field before entering the end zone. His 64-yard touchdown run gave USC a 21-20 victory and its berth in the Rose Bowl, where it defeated Indiana.

Simpson won the Heisman trophy in 1968 by one of the largest margins ever in his senior season, in which he set NCAA records for most yards rushing in the regular season (1,709) and most carries (355). Counting the two Rose Bowls, Simpson finished his two-year career with 3,423 yards. In 17 of his 21 games, the two-time All-American ran for more than 100 yards, five times (four as a senior) gaining more than 200. USC coach John Mckay recalled, "Simpson was not only the greatest player I ever had – he was the greatest player anyone ever had."[9]

The Buffalo Bills drafted Simpson as the number one pick in the 1969 National Football League (NFL) draft. In 1972, Simpson led the NFL with 1,251 yards rushing. The following year he passed 1,000 yards midseason. In his next-to-last game of the season he ran for 219 yards, leaving him 197 shy of 2,000. In the last game of the season, Simpson established a new threshold, running in the snow of Shea Stadium for 200 yards, giving him an amazing season total of 2,003 yards in only 14 games. Although there are now 16 games in a season, Simpson's record for the highest number of yards in 14 games still holds. He led the NFL in rushing four times in a five-year span and finished his 11-year career with 11,236 yards.[10]

After retiring from professional football, Simpson turned his attention to acting and broadcasting. He had minor roles in several films, including Cassandra Crossing, The Towering Inferno and his comical scenes in *Naked Gun*. Interestingly, Simpson also acted in The Klansman, a film in which he played a man framed for murder by the police. Simpson also became a television sportscaster, and although he was not articulate on air, his bubbling personality kept him popular with many viewers.

Perhaps Simpson's most successful post-football career was in advertising. He landed a large contract with the Hertz car rental corporation and became their most recognizable spokesman. During and after his professional football career, Simpson made a conscious decision to project a positive image and to distance himself from the teenage O.J. who was a troublemaker and spent time in a correctional center. He had an ability to communicate warmth and charm that elevated his celebrity appeal to such a degree that he became the first African American athlete to market products on a grand scale across cultural groupings.

The Hertz commercials pictured a dapper O.J. Simpson running through airports and hurdling guardrails on his way to catch a rent-a-car, smiling as people cheered him on. He was a Black man interacting easily with people across cultural boundaries. Simpson sidestepped issues of racial inequity, choosing instead to avoid politics and controversy. The business community and the public eagerly accepted him, propelling him to a level of financial success that exceeded that of most other athletes of his time, irrespective of their ethnicity.

While Simpson's professional life was accomplished, his personal life suffered. His first marriage ended in separation and divorce. In 1979, a year after his separation, Simpson's first child drowned in the Rockingham mansion pool. While still married to his first wife, Simpson met seventeen–year-old waitress, Nicole Brown. Simpson married Nicole in 1985. Their first child was born 7 months later.

In the same year of his marriage to Nicole, Simpson was inducted into the Pro Football Hall of Fame. He credited his mother Eunice with his success. His mother responded by saying: "I didn't really think he'd turn out the way he did, but he always said you'd read about him in the papers someday and my oldest daughter would always say, 'In the police report.'"[11] Simpson's outstanding achievements seemed to have completely erased the difficulties of his troubled youth.

In 1989, Simpson's image as a friendly successful sports icon began to crumble. O.J. and his wife Nicole began to have serious relational problems, and Simpson was formally charged with beating Nicole. According to police, he hit and kicked Nicole as he yelled, "I'll kill you."[12] Simpson was placed on probation for two years and ordered to undergo psychiatric counseling and perform community service after pleading no contest. During the next several years Simpson's spousal abuse infractions became well known to the Los Angeles Police Department, but not to the general public. Nicole Brown Simpson often complained to friends and family of beatings by Simpson, who did not approve of her apparent flirtatious association with other men. After what was described as a "rocky marriage," Nicole filed for divorce in 1992.

For those of you who may not be familiar with the case, let me briefly review the stunning events that made O. J. Simpson the lead news story for many days. On June 12, 1994, shortly after the murder of Nicole Brown Simpson and Ronald Goldman, Simpson flew to Chicago for a promotional engagement just before midnight. The next day, just past noon, the bodies of Nicole and Ron were found outside Nicole's Brentwood condominium. Four hours later, Simpson checked into a hotel near Chicago's airport. He checked out after being contacted by the Los Angeles Police Department and flew back to Los Angeles. Thirty minutes after arriving at his home, two miles from the crime scene, Simpson was taken away by the police for three hours of questioning. News reports indicate blood stains found in O.J. Simpson's vehicle and in his driveway matched the types discovered at the crime scene. On June 15, police sources confirmed a match of the blood stains found at the crime scene and at Simpson's home.

On Friday, June 17, Simpson was charged with two counts of murder with special circumstances but did not surrender as was planned by his lawyer, causing the police to declare him a fugitive. At approximately 6:45 p.m., the police spotted a white Ford Bronco belonging to Simpson's friend Al Cowlings on an expressway. Simpson was a passenger and was reported to have a gun. They took the police on a 60-mile low speed pursuit through southern Los Angeles, which was referenced earlier in this book. At 8:00 p.m., the vehicle arrived at Simpson's Brentwood mansion and the negotiations with the police began. At 8:51 p.m., Simpson surrendered, clutching a family photo. He was arrested and jailed without bail.

The influence of O. J. Simpson's life on millions of Americans was substantive. Sportscaster Bob Costas, who worked with Simpson as an NFL commentator for NBC, astutely remarked, "You'll never be able to hear O.J. Simpson's name or even watch the great vintage footage of O.J. Simpson as one of the very greatest players who ever lived without thinking of this tragedy."[13] Simpson quickly became the central player, the celebrity, at the center of one of the greatest news stories of the 1990s.

The Influence of Media Events

Details of the drama that unfolded on the day of O. J. Simpson's arrest show how the media gravitated to the police chase and arrest. At 1:50 pm on Friday, June 17, a spokesperson for the LAPD held a news conference to inform the news media that Simpson was fleeing his arrest after he had agreed to turn himself in to the police by noon. Simpson left an apparent suicide letter which was read to the public during a news conference held by his attorney, Robert Shapiro, at 5:00 pm. This immediately set off a frenzied search for Simpson. About an hour later, the police pinpointed Simpson's location with Cowling in a car by tracing cellular-phone calls and a citizen's tip. Soon the police were pursuing them on a Los Angeles freeway with more than a dozen police and news helicopters.

All regular programming on ABC, CBS, NBC, and CNN was interrupted by live television coverage of the LAPD following Cowlings and Simpson. News reporters stated that Simpson held a gun to his head. NBC's broadcast of a championship series NBA playoff game between the New York Knicks and Houston Rockets began shortly before the television news helicopters picked up Simpson. The game was interrupted and boxed off to one corner of the television screen for viewers while the main picture was provided by a camera crew covering the chase scene from a helicopter. An estimated 95 million television viewers watched the live coverage of the dramatic chase which ended at Simpson's home in the Brentwood area of Los Angeles.[14]

During the next two weeks the news media were saturated with stories about O.J. Simpson and his arrest for two counts of first-degree murder. Virtually every major print news publication, every radio talk show, and most of the television talk shows discussed multiple aspects of the O.J. Simpson case in depth. The overwhelming shock of Simpson's arrest for two brutal murders generated so much media attention that there is little doubt the O.J. Simpson story was first on the media agenda and dramatically affected what people talked about and thought about throughout the country.

Immediately after Simpson's arrest, I devised a study with two colleagues to determine how people were being affected by Simpson's arrest. Our interest was primarily focused on how the public concerns and communication behavior was influenced by the media coverage of Simpson. Specifically, we examined the types of issues constructed by the public in response to news coverage of the O.J. Simpson case. Regardless of Simpson's degree of guilt or innocence regarding the tragic death of his former wife Nicole Brown and Ron Goldman, Simpson was an influential celebrity admired by the public and emulated by those who perceived him as a positive role model.

Athletes and the Public Agenda

One of the ways in which communication scholars assess the influence of famous athletes is by studying how athletes draw attention to certain issues through the media coverage of their lives. What the public thinks about, is concerned about, and talks with one another about is commonly referred to as the "public agenda." Our public conversations in the office at work, with our friends, and at home often reflect the news stories we read about in the paper or on a news website, see on television, or hear discussed on the radio. Commonly known as "agenda-setting research," studies reveal that the mass media influence what we talk about and how we think about certain issues.[15] Research also indicates that the public agenda, commonly conceptualized as the issues that the public thinks about, have a measurable influence on public opinion.[16] Although the seminal agenda-setting study conducted by Max McCombs and Donald Shaw[17] in Chapel Hill, North Carolina, focused on the news media's ability to determine the importance of an issue in the mind of the public, decades of agenda-setting research indicates the news media also influence the public's attitudes and perceptions about issues and events portrayed by news media.[18]

The public agenda is generally comprised of multiple issues of concern. However, the more dominant a specific issue becomes, the more likely other concerns will be of less importance to the public.[19] For example, during the air attacks on Iraq by U.S. forces during the Gulf War in 1991, news coverage was completely dominated by the Gulf War story.[20]

Celebrities who become the center of a media event or who are involved in major news stories can have a powerful influence on public attitudes, beliefs, and behaviors. For example, the importance of the issue of HIV infection and AIDS in the public agenda has been affected by celebrities in the news. Everett M. Rogers and his colleagues documented the increase in media coverage of the AIDS issue through Rock Hudson's death and the behavioral impact this coverage had on the homosexual community.[21] Arthur Ashe's battle with AIDS raised the importance of the AIDS issue among those who have received blood transfusions and brought attention to the safety of the nation's blood supply. Magic Johnson's HIV infection focused attention on the risky sexual practices of heterosexuals.[22]

In each of these examples, a media celebrity who became infected with HIV/AIDS became the focus of media attention, influencing public attitudes toward HIV/AIDS, beliefs about how the disease is contracted, and behaviors that reduce the risk of infection. Although thousands of people had contracted HIV during the 1980s and 1990s, it was the deaths of celebrities like Rock Hudson and Arthur Ashe, and the premature retirement of Magic Johnson, that attracted the immense media coverage and focused public concern on HIV prevention.[23]

Tracking OJ's Influence

In the case of O.J. Simpson, rather than focusing on the traditional research question regarding the public agenda (i.e., What is the most important issue that people are thinking and talking about?), a colleague and I assessed public responses to the media coverage of the O.J. Simpson case. Our interest was not whether the media set the public agenda, but rather how the public agenda was influenced by the media coverage. Specifically, we examined the types of issues constructed by the public in response to news coverage of the O.J. Simpson case.

As was discussed earlier, parasocial interaction with athletes can create a strong influence on the public's perceptions of them. Parasocial interaction with O.J. Simpson provided an important variable we used to predict the impact of his arrest on the public agenda. We hypothesized that those who were more psychologically involved with Simpson would be more sympathetic toward him, more desirous that he be found innocent, and more personally concerned about two of the public agenda issues raised by the Simpson case: domestic violence and spouse abuse.

In order to test our predictions, we surveyed by telephone 574 residents from five distinct geographical regions of the country: Southern California, Denver, Atlanta, Buffalo, and Hampton Roads, Virginia.[24] Of the total sample, 64 percent were women and the average age was 39 years old. The ethnicity of the sample was very diverse: 55 percent Caucasian, 34 percent African American, four percent Hispanic American, three percent Asian American, and the rest Pacific Islanders and other cultural minorities. Nearly two-thirds of the respondents had some college education or a college degree.

Our survey had 48 questions, both open-ended and closed. We asked people about their perceptions of O.J. Simpson, how much they liked or admired him, how much they felt they knew him, and how much they thought about the issue of spouse abuse. We also recorded the demographic information of all those surveyed. The telephone interviews began on June 21, four days after Simpson was arrested. The interviews were conducted each day until July 1, two weeks from the arrest date.

Results showed that the news about Simpson's arrest diffused rapidly to the public. Nearly 85 percent of the respondents learned of Simpson's arrest the same day he was arrested on June 17th. Contrary to the pattern of other major news events, most respondents learned about Simpson's arrest from a media source rather than through an interpersonal conversation. In addition, results showed that once they learned about his arrest, 55 percent of the respondents sought additional information from a media source. Approximately 99 percent of the respondents knew that Simpson was arrested for murder.

We also wanted to know how people responded to the issues of spouse abuse and public role models in the aftermath of the Simpson case. Our study indicated that respondents talked to an average of one person every two days about the issue of celebrity role models and talked to an average of four people over the 11-day interview period.[25] Clearly media coverage of the Simpson case, especially reactions to the announcement of the final verdict in the criminal trial, caused the public to think about and talk about whether or not athletes should be role models.

A final research concern was to assess how media coverage of Simpson's arrest affected the public's concern about spouse abuse. We found that our respondents talked to an average of 3-4 people about spouse abuse during the 11-day interview period. In addition, 46 percent of the respondents who were married or who had a romantic partner discussed the issue of spouse abuse with their partner in response to the Simpson case. When respondents were asked who they discussed the issue of spouse abuse with besides their spouses or romantic partners, the most common group was family members, followed by same sex friends and opposite sex friends. Overall, the 574 people we interviewed talked to an average of 13-14 people about issues related to the Simpson news story.[26] This represents a very powerful agenda-setting effect. People throughout the U.S. were thinking about and openly discussing a serious issue in our country, spouse abuse, as a direct result of O.J. Simpson's arrest.

Perceptions of Innocence

One of the intriguing questions we pursued in our study was whether or not those who exhibited strong parasocial relationships with O.J. Simpson would be more sympathetic to him and more likely to believe in his innocence. Our study again demonstrated the powerful influence of parasocial interaction. Those who had the strongest parasocial relationship with Simpson were more likely to believe in his innocence and did express more sympathy for him.

Concern about Domestic Violence

We also discovered that strong parasocial interaction with Simpson predicted more concern about domestic violence. However, consistent with the sentiments expressed by many women who have been abused by their husbands or boyfriends, our findings do not seem to support the likelihood that long-term behavioral changes took place as a result of the Simpson case. Respondents seemed to disassociate the trouble between O.J. and Nicole from their own personal relationships.

Perhaps the negative social desirability of acknowledging a high risk of being involved in an abuse situation biased the responses of the respondents. Or perhaps almost all of the respondents were happily married or had peaceful romantic relationships. Whatever the case, we simply did not find a relationship between personal concern about spouse abuse and involvement with Simpson.

Learning about the U.S. Justice System

The extensive media coverage of Simpson's criminal trial focused an enormous amount of attention on the justice system of the U.S. One of our research questions examined how much people learned about the U.S. justice system while following the trial. Our results showed that people did learn about the U.S. legal system, and the more they learned the more they talked to others about the U.S. legal system.[27] Lance Ito, the judge in Simpson's criminal trial, became a celebrity as a result of his extensive time on television. The second trial of Simpson in which he was held responsible for the deaths of Nicole and Ronald Goldman and ordered to pay $33.5 million in compensatory and punitive damages to their families, also informed the public about the differences between criminal and non-criminal trials.

In summary, the tragic story of O.J. Simpson influenced public knowledge, attitudes and beliefs about a host of issues, including spouse abuse, the fairness of the U.S. legal system, the influence of famous athletes, and the effects of media coverage of celebrity athletes.[28]

Following Mark McGwire's Quest

The year of 1998 will be remembered as one of the greatest baseball seasons and one of the worst political seasons in American history. The baseball training season began in the late winter at about the same time that the public became aware of President Clinton's sexual infidelity with White House intern Monica Lewinsky. Both culminated in October with very different types of public responses. The President struck out in trying to appease public disgruntlement, while Mark McGwire and Sammy Sosa crushed home run after home run, both breaking Roger Maris's 37-year home run record and making them American heroes. The massive public outpouring of attention directed toward McGwire and Sosa brought welcomed relief from the heat of a presidential impeachment inquiry. In these years before the intensified controversy of performance enhancing drugs in American baseball, both McGwire and Sosa were highly esteemed and held up as public role models, representing not only the best of baseball but the best of American culture and society.

To the non-baseball fan, the mass hysteria about McGwire and Sosa's feats may be difficult to understand. Sportswriter Tom Verducci explains the cultural significance of home runs that led to the extensive media attention given to McGwire and Sosa:

> "The single season home run record is the most revered mark in sports. It's engraved on Maris's tombstone, just 61 in '61. The home run is America – appealing to Americans' roots of rugged individualism and their fascination with the grand scale."[29] (p. 30).

Very few people thought Babe Ruth's record of 60 home runs in a single season would ever be broken in this century. Ruth, renowned as one of the greatest players ever to play the game of baseball, also played in a shorter season than today. When Roger Maris eclipsed Ruth in 1961 with 61 home runs, the baseball commissioner put an asterisk by Maris' name (which was later removed) in the record book since he had more games to hit in than did Ruth. McGwire tied Maris' record of 61 home runs and then surpassed the record in less games than it took Ruth to hit 60. In his last 40 games, McGwire hit 23 home runs, blasting five home runs in his last 19 at-bats on his way to a phenomenal total of 70 for the season.

The media attention given to McGwire was not just due to the record he chased, but also due to the way in which he pulverized the record with public grace and humility. McGwire demonstrated patience with the media and fans, acknowledged the efforts of his teammates, and showed genuine friendship and good sportsmanship toward his competitor in the home run race, Sammy Sosa. His words and actions displayed his respect for the man whose record he broke and for the entire Maris family, and demonstrated his love for his parents, his family, and his son, who also served as a bat-boy for McGwire's team, the St. Louis Cardinals. Media attention to these positive character qualities of McGwire helped catapult him to a celebrity's status, and to some, made him a hero.[30]

Yet the news media also made known to the public two interesting facts, one positive and one negative, about McGwire. First, McGwire has been a strong advocate and supporter of child abuse prevention programs. Child abuse is a national concern in the U.S., costing the nation some $94 billion per year.[31] Sexual assault has been one of the most rapidly growing crimes in the U.S., affecting more than one million children in 1999.[32] To combat child abuse, McGwire launched the Mark McGwire Foundation for Children in 1998 and donated over a million dollars per year of his salary and his book proceeds to the foundation while playing baseball.[33] He has also recorded several child abuse prevention PSAs[34] and assisted Starbucks Coffee Co. in raising funds for children's literacy.[35]

A second aspect of McGwire's life that came into public scrutiny was his use of a muscle-building dietary supplement, androstenedione, an androgenic steroid hormone. Although the supplement at that time was legally sold in health food stores and Major League Baseball allowed players to use androstenedione, it was banned by the NCAA, the NFL, and many international sports federations. In 1998, the International Olympic Committee became alarmed by McGwire's public admission that he used androstenedione, fearing many young athletes would role model McGwire's example.[36] The long-term effects of androstenedione are not well understood, but short-term effects can be detrimental.[37] Thus McGwire's use of androstenedione was expected to be viewed negatively by segments of the public and yet role modeled by others.

McGwire's Social Influence

During McGwire's record-breaking year, Mike Basil and I, along with the help of one of my doctoral students, Mihai Bocarnea, conducted a study of McGwire's influence on the public.[38] The purpose of our study was to assess the degree to which involvement with McGwire might have affected two public health issues: child abuse prevention and steroid use. We also wanted to explore how two types of audience involvement with sports celebrities, parasocial interaction and identification, influenced health-related awareness, beliefs, concerns and intended behavior.

At the end of the1998 baseball season, we administered a national survey that consisted of 55 questions, both closed questions and open-ended ones. A total sample of 356 people provided completed questionnaires for our study from several different geographical locations in the U.S The data were collected in September and early October of 1998 within a three-week period after McGwire hit his 62nd home run, breaking Maris' record.

Our study participants represented a diverse group of people throughout the United States. Nearly 56 percent of the sample was in the 18 to 40-year old age group, with another 18 percent in the 41 to 60-year old age group. About 55 percent were men and 38 percent were married. The educational backgrounds and ethnicity of the sample was diverse, with 87 percent Caucasian, eight percent African American, and about two and a half percent

Hispanic American and the same percentage of Asian Americans. Most respondents had some college courses or a college.

Child Abuse Prevention

Our first research goal explored the extent to which segments of the American public increased their concern about child abuse and its prevention through learning about Mark McGwire's work with abused children. Results indicated that 8.4 percent of the respondents reported that they are now more concerned about child abuse prevention after learning about this problem through Mark McGwire.[39]

A related research goal was to examine the extent to which segments of the American public believed that Mark McGwire helped them to realize the importance of speaking out against child abuse. Our results showed that 13.3 percent of the respondents reported that McGwire helped them to recognize that speaking out against child abuse was important.[40]

Our study shows that the extensive media coverage that McGwire attracted positively affected the issue of child abuse by raising public awareness of the problem and by getting people to openly discuss the problem. This would not have occurred if McGwire had not been in the race to break Maris' home run record.

Steroid Use

Our analysis of McGwire's unintentional negative influence also yielded interesting results. We investigated the degree to which segments of the American public became aware that McGwire used a muscle-enhancing dietary supplement. Results indicated that 65.1 percent of the respondents became aware that McGwire used androstenedione, an anabolic steroid that enhances muscle development. Even more revealing was our finding that 24 percent of the respondents in our study were interested in learning more about androstenedione.[41] Unknowingly, McGwire created a great interest, especially among young athletes, in anabolic steroids.

Reasons for McGwire's Influence

Like Magic Johnson and O.J. Simpson, we reasoned that media exposure to Mark McGwire would lead to the development of a parasocial relationship with him, which we found to be true. We also predicted the degree of parasocial relationship with Mark McGwire would be positively associated with identification with him. Our study showed that both men and women who had a greater degree of parasocial relationship with McGwire more strongly identified with him.

We also predicted that the degree of identification with McGwire would be positively associated with concern for child abuse prevention and belief in the importance of speaking out against child abuse. Again, results supported our prediction for both men and women.

Our last set of predictions sought to explain McGwire's public influence regarding the use of steroids. We thought that respondents' identification with McGwire would be positively associated with their awareness of the benefits and risks of androstenedione, which we found to be true. We also expected that respondents who more strongly identified with McGwire would more likely be (a) more aware of androstenedione, (b) more aware of McGwire's use of the drug, (c) more interested in learning more about the drug, and (d) more interested in taking dietary supplements to enhance athletic performance. All four of these predictions were supported by our results.

Learning from McGwire

Our study of Mark McGwire builds on the findings of previous research that indicates famous athletes can have an important influence on the health-related knowledge, attitudes, and behavioral intentions of media consumers. The extensive news coverage of McGwire' home run record exposed millions of people to aspects of his life that probably would never be known by a large percentage of the American public. There were likely many contributing factors to the public's exposure to McGwire. It is important to note here that about 60 percent of the respondents in this study did not consider themselves to be big baseball fans.

The use of the dietary supplement androstenedione was discussed in the media's coverage of McGwire. Almost two-thirds of the respondents were aware of McGwire's use of this supplement, 24 percent wanted to learn more about it, and 22 percent were interested in taking it. The fact that 11 percent of the respondents agreed or strongly agreed that as a result of following McGwire in the news they had learned about androstenedione is an important finding. If this percentage is multiplied by the millions of people who followed the McGwire story, it becomes clear that McGwire did promote awareness of androstenedione, desire to learn more about it, and desire to try it.

U.S. News & World Report's story on McGwire's use of the muscle-enhancer raised public awareness of the benefits and detriments of this anabolic steroid.[42] Parents were concerned that McGwire's use of a steroid may promote the use of such substances among their children. One parent responded:

> "I was heartbroken to have been 'left out' of the national celebration of Mark McGwire's extraordinary achievement. I have an 11-year old son, and he is aware of both the magnitude of the achievement and of McGwire's use of steroids. That awareness placed me in the painful position of either celebrating the historical milestone, and subliminally endorsing my son's future use of performance-enhancing or life-threatening drugs, or rejecting the achievement outright and sending a clear

> message to my son that substance abuse was both unacceptable and dangerous. For a father, that's no choice."[43] (Turner, September 28, 1998, p. 5).

Turner's letter published *in U.S. World & News Report* succinctly articulates the belief that a sports celebrity is a public role model and that his or her behavior will likely be emulated by others, particularly young people.

Our results also provide further evidence that the public does establish parasocial relationships with sports celebrities, and parasocial relationships lead to identification, a predictor of cognitive, affective and behavioral adaptation. As expected, the results support the notion that audience involvement with sports celebrities can promote the health-related knowledge, awareness, concern, and intended practices endorsed and modeled by these athletes.

There are other convincing data that links McGwire with fostering changes in public sentiments toward these two health issues, particularly with regards to taking androstenedione. Concern for child abuse has grown in the U.S. during the past several years, sparking an organized coalition of national organizations fighting child abuse.[44] Our data show McGwire clearly played an important role in raising public concerns and motivating people to become involved in child abuse prevention programs. Other data suggest McGwire had a powerful influence on promoting androstenedione use. Barry McCaffrey, Director of the Office of National Drug Control Policy in 1999, reported that androstenedione use by youngsters increased 5-fold after McGwire's publicized admission of his use of the supplement,[45] and the sale of androstenedione substantially increased.[46]

We continued to be amazed by the potential influence of a single athlete, for good and for bad. If only a few children are spared an abusive situation through the efforts of athletes like McGwire, that few is still extremely important and worth the effort. Popular athletes who use muscle-building dietary supplements should consider their influence on those who may role model their steroid use. Unfortunately, many young people who regarded McGwire as a role model may not have understood the risks of steroids. It is a credit to McGwire that after learning about his influence on young peoples' experimentation with muscle-enhancing steroids, he immediately discontinued his use of androstenedione. Despite McGwire's efforts, he paid a heavy toll in his public image after refusing to answer certain questions before Congress about his own steroid use, implying that he used other performance drugs in addition to androstenedione.

Barry Bonds and Steroid Use

Our research sheds some light on the intense interest in steroid use by a great athlete like Barry Bonds, who went on the break Mark McGwire's single season home run record by hitting 73 home runs in 2001. As Bonds surpassed Babe Ruth's career home run total of 714, thousands of news stories, published articles, and radio and television talk shows discussed the issue of his reported steroid use. Some people may wonder, why all the hoopla about Barry Bonds? The answer is clear. Millions of young people are watching him closely and see the tremendous results of his "reported" steroid use. Regardless of whether Bonds took steroids, and if so, how much and what kinds of steroids he might have used, millions of impressionable teenagers and young adults believe he took steroids and believe it enhanced his career. Bonds eventually became the greatest home run hitter in the history of baseball with his 756th home run, breaking Hank Aaron's record. Like Mark McGwire, young people will try it to "be like Barry."

NASCAR Driver Dale Earnhardt

NASCAR, the National Association for Stock Car Auto Racing, is now the most attended sport in the United States and one of the most watched professional sports in the world. According to Nielsen Media Research, NASCAR events are the second highest rated regular season televised sports in the U.S. The NASCAR NEXTEL Cup Series events attract more fans the Superbowl, World Series, and NBA Finals combined. An estimated 75 million adults in the U.S., about one third of its adult population, are NASCAR fans, 40 percent of whom are female.

Earlier in chapter 5, I discussed some impacts of the death of NASCAR driver Dale Earnhardt. Perhaps no other NASCAR driver captured the personality of the sport as did this former racing star. Earnhardt's tragic death on February 18, 2001, shook the nation and moved thousands of fans to organize memorial services at racetracks throughout the United States, as I noted earlier. At age 49, he had won 76 races, including the prestigious Winston Cup seven times. He was a man who was loved, but also hated. "Earnhardt's aggressive driving style, which often entailed perilously threading his famous black No. 3 Goodwrench Chevrolet Monte Carlo between cars, angered many of his fellow drivers, who believed that he was crossing the line of recklessness... Earnhardt once said by way of response to his critics. 'It's not a sport for the faint of heart.' It was a style that fed his mystique as perhaps the most gifted driver ever to strap himself into a stock car."[47] "He had massive, irresistible appeal. He brought fans into the sport who wouldn't know NASCAR from NASA. He was the rebel soul of a sport that had gone corporate"[48]

J. Saward summed up Earnhardt's enormous influence as follows:

> Dale Earnhardt was a modern American folk hero. He was the most popular driver in the biggest motor-racing series in the United States, the NASCAR Winston Cup, and he made his name playing the bad guy. His car was black, his racing suit was black and tens of thousands of fans loved to hate him. His nicknames included "The Intimidator" and "Ironhead" ... Earnhardt's popularity was based on his toughness.[49]

After Earnhardt's death fans flocked to NASCAR memorabilia stores to buy hats, shirts, jackets, stickers and model cars. One owner commented: "I have never seen anything like this. It was wild in here when Davey Allison and Alan Kulwicki died in '93, but Earnhardt was God." A couple who had bought a baby size t-shirt with Earnhardt's #3 on explained that they were expecting a baby and that they were going to name him Dale.[50] A family in the St. Louis suburb of Fenton, MO, confided: "We have life-size stand-ups of Dale and Dale Junior in our living room. We have curio cases full of cars, we have tires from their cars we've bought. You would think our house is a shrine to NASCAR."[51] Another fan in Palm Beach Gardens, FL, exclaimed: "I've been married 43 years… Besides my husband, Dale Earnhardt is the only man I've ever loved."[52]

These expressions of friendship and affection for Earnhardt indicate strong parasocial relationships. Most of these fans had never met Earnhardt personally, but had developed a sense of connection to him through exposure to him in the media. As was the case with Magic Johnson, O.J. Simpson, and Mark McGwire, fans who become psychologically involved with celebrity athletes can adopt their attitudes and values. They can also be deeply moved by their deaths.

Dale Earnhardt and Racecar Safety

As discussed earlier, an important consequence of the media attention given to famous athletes is their influence on the public agenda, i.e. what issues are considered important and how these issues are framed in the media. In the aftermath of Earnhardt's death, NASCAR safety features soon became a hot topic. There was much debate over whether Earnhardt might have survived had he been using a state-of-the-art piece of head and neck safety equipment, which restrains the head in relation to the torso during a crash. He had died instantly from a basal skull fracture from a head-on collision into a concrete wall.

Ed Miller of The Virginian Pilot wrote:

> "The fact that his death extends a string of recent racing tragedies is reason enough for drivers and the corporate interests that rule NASCAR to take a sober look at what their sport has become… Earnhardt shunned basic safety innovations as unsuitable for a tough guy who had bounced back from more than his share of scrapes and brushes and crashes. He refused to wear a head-and- neck safety brace that some other drivers are starting to wear."[53]

His seat belt had apparently broken during the crash, possibly contributing to his death. In addition, the open-face helmet he wore did not protect him from hitting his face in the steering wheel, which may have been another factor in his death. The results of two different reports published a few months after the accident were inconclusive and partially contradictory. NASCAR's own report stated that there was no guarantee Earnhardt would have survived if he had been wearing the head-and-neck restraint feature.

Immediately after Earnhardt's crash, I initiated a study with one of my doctoral students, Dr. Gina Barker, to assess racing fans' degree of parasocial interaction and identification with Earnhardt and to explore how the extensive media coverage of Earnhardt's death may have affected the issue of racecar safety. We administered a survey questionnaire to a sample of 159 internet users from throughout the U.S. In addition, another one of my doctoral students, Dr. Kara Presnell, followed our study with a qualitative analysis of Earnhardt fans. We combined the results of our two studies to provide an in-depth analysis of the influence that Earnhardt had on NASCAR fans.[54]

All respondents in our survey research identified Earnhardt's profession correctly and knew of his accident. More than three-fourths of the respondents in our survey found out about Earnhardt's death it by 9 p.m. Sunday night on the day of the crash. Interestingly, we found that women reported a higher level of psychological involvement with Earnhardt than did men.

As we predicted, we found that those who were more psychologically involved with Earnhardt were more concerned about driving safety. We also found out that 50% of the respondents reported that they owned NASCAR memorabilia and were big NASCAR fans and 56% reported that they were planning on watching the memorial services.[55] More revealing was the close personal connection that our study participants felt they had with Earnhardt. Many of these fans considered him to be like a family member, resulting in a sense of deep loss.

Results of our research show how sports fans can intensify involvement with athletes through memorabilia such as autographs, pictures, t-shirts, etc. It also shows how a celebrity's life and death can focus a tremendous amount of attention on a specific issue, in this case seat belt safety. As a result of Earnhardt's death and the public debates about NASCAR safety that followed, changes were made to increase the safety of NASCAR drivers.[56]

Soccer Legend Diego Maradona

The rise of Diego Maradona from the slums of Buenos Aires to the pinnacle of the World Cup soccer championship is the story of a beloved mythic hero both in his native country and throughout the soccer sports world. "Diego Armando Maradona" was born on October 30th, 1960 in Lanús, Buenos Aires, Argentina's capital city. He was the fifth of eight children of a factory worker and, as legend has it, he was given his first football as an infant and slept with it under his arm.

Growing up in one of the poorest slums in Buenos Aires, Villa Fiorito, Diego had to overcome many obstacles throughout his childhood. "If I were asked to sum up Fiorito in one word," he once said, "it would be struggle. If there was food you ate it and, if there wasn't, then you went hungry."[57] Maradona was a gifted soccer player from an early age. In

December 1970, when he was only 9 years old, he began playing with the Los Cebollitas (The Little Onions), an amateur junior league team belonging to an organization that also handled another team called Argentinos Juniors in the professional category. Los Cebollitas became legendary and remained unbeaten for 136 matches, largely due to Maradona's performance. His prowess was so outstanding that he was invited as a guest onto the most-watched television show of the 1960s, Sabados Circulares (Circled Saturday) hosted by Pipo Mancera. Sabados Circulares introduced Maradona to what would later become his constant companion - media coverage. In 1971, at age 10, his surname (albeit misspelled) appeared for first time in a sports report in a national newspaper.

By 1976, at age 16, he was Argentina's youngest-ever international soccer player. A few years later he captained the Youth Championship of the World Cup. Later, in 1978, Argentina's National Soccer team coach excluded him from the list of the 22 players who would represent the nation in the World Cup on the grounds that the 18-year-old Diego was too young to handle the pressure.

Despite not making the national team, Maradona was soon transferred to Boca Juniors, one of the best soccer teams in Argentina, and assisted them in winning the Argentinean Professional Championship of the year. Maradona's nicknames included "El Pibe de Oro" (The Boy of Gold or The Kid of Gold), "The God of Soccer ", "The 10" (meaning the top), "King" and "God."

Maradona's Career Blossoms

Internationally, Maradona´s career in professional soccer began in 1979 with the national youth team that exposed him for first time to the world. Later in 1982, he joined the Barcelona soccer team in Spain, where he suffered the worst injury of his career, breaking his left ankle and a tearing its ligaments. Two years later, in 1984, he joined the Naples soccer team in southern Italy where he continued to excel as an athlete and gain international recognition. In 1986, the World Soccer Cup was held in Mexico and Maradona played as a member of the Argentinean National Team (for playing in the World Cup, national teams can call out their players when the players are playing overseas).

In the quarterfinal, Maradona scored his most famous and controversial goal with his hand. Despite doubt and protest from the British, the referee considered the goal to be valid, not seeing Maradona's hand, following his colleague's assurance that the hand did not touch the ball. Maradona later admitted in an interview that what became known as the 'hand of God' was actually his hand. Soon after this controversial score, Maradona followed it up with a magnificent second goal in a 2-1 victory over England. Argentina's triumph over England was very significant and memorable because the country had just lost the now infamous four-year Malvinas Islands (or Falkland Islands) war against England over their possession. This point will be further discussed later on. In the finals, Maradona led Argentina to victory over West Germany, 3-2, winning the 1986 World Cup.

In Buenos Aires, people danced and car horns hooted, street posters declared Maradona Presidente! and Monsignor Jorge Caseretto of the diocese of San Isidro declared that "he had already arranged a victory with God.[58] When the national team arrived in Argentina it was received by the President at the Presidential Palace as a crowd gathered outside to celebrate the champions.

After the 1986 World Cup Maradona returned to Italy, where he led Naples' soccer team to the first of two national championships in that club's history. He helped them also earn their first victory in an international competition. In 1990, the World Cup was played in Italy. Though he played professionally for an Italian team, Maradona guided Argentina's National Team to the finals. They lost 1-0 to West Germany. Afterwards, he returned to Naples for a third season.

Maradona's Tragic Downfall

It was while playing for Naples in 1991 that Diego Maradona faced his first 15-month ban after a positive drug test. About a month later, Maradona was detained in Argentina for cocaine consumption. One year later, still banned from playing, Maradona was transferred to Sevilla, a Spaniard soccer team. He would last in Sevilla less than a year. By September 1993, Maradona moved back to Argentina. There he joined Newells' Old Boys, a respectable soccer club, though not one of the greatest. In 1994, the World Cup was played in the United States and Maradona, at age 34, once again joined the Argentinean National Team and played in two matches. Sadly, he was ejected from the tournament after testing positive for Ephedrine, a substance disallowed by FIFA, the organization governing the World Cup. The symbolic consequences of Maradona's turbulent life are discussed extensively in Marcela de Matviuk's doctoral dissertation on fans' involvement with Maradona.[59]

Back in Argentina, Diego Maradona began a career as a soccer coach, but he resigned from two separate clubs after only a few months. In 1995, Maradona returned to play for the Boca Juniors team and his fans eagerly prepared a massive party with fireworks to celebrate his return. He played with them for two years, and in 1997 started the new season with Boca in great shape and at peak performance levels. However, at the beginning of the season he tested positive in a drug screening test for the third time. Then Maradona booked into a Swiss drug rehabilitation clinic. During 1996, Maradona had made promises to change his lifestyle and even declared on TV that he had defeated his bad habits. Threats to his health were serious.[60]

In October of 1997, on his 37th birthday, Maradona officially retired from playing. However, his fame did not diminish. In a poll conducted by FIFA three years later, Maradona tied with Pele as the greatest soccer player ever. After Maradona retired from professional soccer, he became more involved with a risky lifestyle of heavy alcohol and drug use. While vacationing that same year, an overweight and out of shape Maradona suffered a severe cardiovascular crisis due to a cocaine overdose and was required to begin a lengthy rehabilitation process. In 2000, Maradona voluntarily went to Cuba to seek treatment for cocaine addiction because, as he was reported to have said, "the dignity of its people" and his confidence in its medical services. Cuba's president, Fidel Castro, was reportedly pleased that Maradona chose his country, and the visit is seen as a propaganda coup for the President.

During the next few years Maradona gave little impression of making any real progress in permanently overcoming his addiction. However, far from vanishing, his appeal as a living myth increased even more. Today, even after his pre-mature death in 2020 due to poor health, Diego Maradona is still a legend and hero to millions of people.[61]

Maradona's Influence on Drug Use

Dr. de Matviuk's study of Maradona in Argentina is revealing. She administered a survey questionnaire to 359 Argentineans, 168 (55.6%) males and 191 (63.4%) females. Most of the participants in her study were high school and college students in the 18-25-year-old age group. Results of her study indicated that men with less education showed the strongest parasocial relationship and identification with Maradona. Matviuk found through a series of statistical analyses that parasocial interaction with Maradona predicted personal concern about drug abuse, awareness of drug abuse, support of drug abuse prevention programs, abstinence from drug use, and involvement in soccer. In addition, she found that identification with Maradona predicted support for his social causes, awareness of drug abuse, and support of drug abuse prevention programs. Surprisingly, women were more receptive to awareness of drug abuse, support of drug abuse prevention programs, and abstinence from drug use than men.

Selective Media Exposure and Parasocial Interaction

Dr. Matviuk allowed me to conduct more in-depth statistical tests with her data to further explore the relationships among selective media exposure to Maradona, parasocial interaction and identification with him.[62] We determined that there were likely many contributing factors to the public's exposure to Maradona. In fact, one would think that exposure to Maradona may be linked to an affinity matter such as being a soccer fan, or the issue of interest such as concern about the pervasiveness of drugs in sports.

However, more than half of the respondents in her study did not consider themselves to be soccer fans. Nonetheless, parasocial interaction still occurred. One explanation for this is because of the agenda-setting effect of the media which I discussed earlier. Studies on agenda-setting have shown that the number of times a story is repeated in the news will affect peoples' perception of the story's importance, regardless of what is said about the topic. The regular presence of Diego Maradona in the news media and, in consequence, in the interest of people, confirms these findings.

In the study we measured selective media exposure by asking respondents to respond to two statements using a 1-5 agree-disagree scale: "I have been seeking out information in the media to learn more about Diego Maradona," and "I go to the Internet to obtain more information about Diego Maradona." In this case, selective media exposure described how media consumers were motivated to seek out information about Maradona. Exposure to media messages in general (TV, radio, and newspapers and other sources) did not have association with parasocial interaction with Maradona. Many respondents were young people and did not have a chance to see Maradona play professionally and did not have a generational connection with him. Thus, Maradona's appeal to younger generations may be found in his condition as a living myth more than active celebrity.

In fact, at the time when the data were gathered, Argentina's best players in less popular sports such as tennis and basketball were flourishing. For example, the finals of the French Open in 2004 was disputed by two Argentineans, while six Argentinean male tennis players ranked in the world's top 50. Also, during the 2004 Olympics, Argentina conquered the gold medal in basketball, a widely played sport but not as popular as soccer.

In light of the fact that these other sports figures were gaining international prominence, why did this younger generation of Argentineans still establish parasocial relationships with Maradona? Explanations for this phenomenon point — in addition to the agenda-setting effect of the media — to the active nature of media consumers. Audiences are not passive absorbers of media messages but selective processors of arts and media. As active media consumers, they construct their own individual meanings from media messages.

Some Argentineans believe that the rhetoric of Argentina as a nation relies on a historical series of world sports heroes: national representatives who are supported by the community and the media.[63] Diego Maradona is the quintessential sports hero in which debate about Maradona's role in society "is also a debate about Argentina's soul, according to Daniel Grech."[64] He explains that in a country whose past was filled with promises and whose present is marked by despair, two perspectives, one nostalgic and the other pessimistic, compete to define Diego Maradona's legacy. The media is an ideal tool to set these two perspectives on stage as the epic narrative of the sports hero. Maradona embodies the hopes of a social sector for which sports (especially soccer) became a possible road to economic success and fame and the re-assertion of the belief in equality. He appeals to audiences not only with his status of celebrity, but also with his vulnerable condition as a flawed human being with struggles that are common to millions of people. This helps to explain why people who have not seen Maradona play still experience parasocial interaction with him.

Our extensive statistical tests comparing different forms of involvement with Maradona affirm that parasocial interaction with a popular athlete is often positively associated with identification with that person. Studies on social influence of athletes have found that the two types of audience involvement with athletes, parasocial interaction and identification, are often difficult to separate. As noted earlier, scholars have argued that when studying sports stars whose overall image is good, identification with their attitudes and behaviors flows almost naturally from parasocial interaction and makes it difficult to separate parasocial interaction and identification.[65] It has also been suggested that comparing widely admired athletes who are rejected as role models, because of moral failures, might make these two types of involvement more easily distinguishable.

Maradona is a case in point. Many people who feel they know him do not identify with him. The separation between parasocial interaction and identification very likely resulted from many converging factors. One of them is the moral character of Maradona. Months before the data for this study were gathered, Maradona was severely sick and hospitalized because of his drug addiction. Maradona did not present an admirable persona to emulate as a role model. Identification with Maradona meant having a personal desire or fantasy to be like him or recognized as someone who is "one with him" or similar to him.

The result is that media consumers can feel they know somebody famous, as Maradona, but it does not mean that they want to be like that person. Wanting to be like a celebrity is much deeper than simply knowing, imitating or emulating a celebrity. Identification involves adherence to specific values and beliefs taken from the object of the identification. Because values and beliefs emanate from moral constructs, identification with celebrities has to compete with other sources of moral standards.

Previously I explained the influence of sports celebrities through a phenomenon called "basking in reflected glory" (BIRG). Theorists have proposed that fans see "their" team as an extension of themselves.[66] In his study of this phenomenon, Cialdini and his colleagues found that fans use terms such as "we won" to refer to the team's performance on a previous day and are more likely to wear the team's apparel following a win.[67]

The tendency to BIRG may help to explain an additional mechanism through which people may come to develop an imagined association with a successful team. As implied earlier, the literature indicates that the BIRG phenomenon has many qualities that may shape associated affective responses. For example, Wann and Branscombe observed the BIRG phenomenon determines a fan's sense of enjoyment derived from following a winning team.[68] Some research suggests that the BIRG phenomenon is not entirely determined by winning and losing, indicating that a fan's identification with a team is not necessarily related to that team's professional record.[69] This research helps explain the behavior of fans who continue to remain loyal to mediocre teams.

To the extent that an attitude toward a team is established, this attitude may be seen to apply to phenomena such as "affect transfer" and "balance." Thus, a positive attitude toward a sports team is likely to transfer to a particular sports celebrity. This "affect transfer" may also occur with products or issues endorsed by the sports celebrity.[70]

Because of the importance of sports figures as sources of identification, the world of sports is an especially likely area to investigate the process of identification.[71] Zillmann and Paulus believe that the defining characteristic of fans is the formation of imaginary alliances where fans perceive themselves to be members of an existing group.[72] This approach, then, supports the importance of identification with the group of athletes that makes up a sports team. It is quite reasonable that strong identification with even one member of a sports team may be the key to developing a commitment to an entire team. This explains the strong fan reaction to superstars who leave their teams to accept more lucrative contracts on other teams. Fans often feel betrayed when this occurs, as when NBA star Lebron James left the Cleveland Cavaliers to play for the Miami Heat.[73]

Influence of Maradona's Mediated Life

Clearly Argentineans basked in the reflected glory of Argentina's World Cup win over England, led by Maradona's extraordinary play. The extensive news coverage of Maradona's career, his long-term struggle with drug abuse, and the life-threatening crisis he faced in March of 2004 exposed millions of Argentineans to aspects of his life that probably would never have been known by a large percentage of the public. As a living icon, Maradona offered to television audiences an exciting narrative that provoked excitement and captured the public's attention as they followed the saga of a fallen hero. In this process, Maradona became the embodiment of the struggle and consequences of drug abuse. As the people followed updates on Maradona's health condition, he put a face and a name to the dangers of drug abuse and made the public aware of drug abuse as a critical health issue.

Argentina has the highest rates of illegal drug use and addiction among South American countries. More than one million Argentineans have consumed marijuana at least once in their lifetime, while four thousand have tried cocaine.[74] To compound this problem, Argentina also has the third highest HIV/AIDS rates in Latin America, after Brazil and Mexico, and more than 39% of these cases were due to drug use with contaminated needles.[75] Within this social and public health context, Maradona's struggles contributes to raising awareness of an acute social need. As was discussed earlier, parasocial interaction with Maradona accounted for a high degree of awareness of drug abuse and promoted support of drug abuse prevention programs, while identification promoted support for Maradona's social causes as well as support of drug abuse prevention programs.

Through his professional career, Maradona called attention to a number of social problems that received extensive media coverage. Among these social problems, Maradona openly –

but not systematically– talked about drugs in sports and the pressures of the sports business on the players to perform. However, his prevention message was mixed because he never seemed to repent of his own drug use. Maradona suffered a truncated career as the world's best soccer player and even now risks a premature death due to his long-term drug abuse.

The media's role in retelling the saga of Maradona's story as a fallen sports' hero illuminated the dark side of the man who was once known as the "Kid of Gold." Consequently, Maradona not only remained in the public eye as a polemical national icon but transcended to the status of a myth. For many, Maradona's addiction took away his condition of god yet he remained an icon. For others, his mistakes and self-afflicted wounds did not diminish the collective imagination of Maradona as a hero.

Seeing Maradona as a myth does allows him to transcend the laws that apply to simple human beings. He is "beyond good and evil," as one of his fans said.[76] However, Maradona the person is caught in the deceptive web of drug addiction. It is this flaw in the mythical character that brings Maradona down to the realm of mere mortals in the minds of millions of his admirers. But even as a mortal being at the edge of life and death, Maradona managed to reinforce his mythical status by cheating death twice during his two serious bouts of illness.

Maradona's Influence on Drug Abuse Prevention

When a celebrity becomes aligned with a health issue, then the media attention given to that celebrity draws public involvement into his or her health issue. In the case of Maradona, however, there are three elements that mitigate against Maradona's potential influence over drug abuse prevention. First, Maradona has not actively pursued opportunities to communicate a drug abuse prevention message. Second, media messages about Maradona are mostly oriented to reinforce and recreate his image as national hero rather than to deal with his struggles with drug addiction. Finally, Maradona has not yet won the battle with drug abuse and may not be perceived by the public as one who has made a committed effort to do so. Thus, he has not been sending a strong message to his fans and to the general public about the dangers of drug abuse, even though he is fortunate to be alive.

Nevertheless, our study shows that Maradona's celebrity status gives him the ability to influence millions of people regarding several health-related issues. Moral character is required in order for a celebrity to provoke change in beliefs and behaviors in a prosocial manner. There is always the potential to influence the public negatively. If Maradona continues to fail to overcome his addiction, he will establish a negative precedent about recovery from drug addiction, and in turn, this will worsen the situation of those who establish parasocial relationships and identification with him. For example, in the month after Hollywood star Marilyn Monroe killed herself, the national suicide rate went up by 12 percent. Other studies have shown that suicides go up by about 2.5 percent following mass coverage of a suicide story.[77]

When celebrities lose their moral standing, it is difficult to rehabilitate their status. Communication scholar William Benoit, a professor at the University of Missouri, who has done quite a bit of study on image restoration, shows that it is possible to rehabilitate one's public image with a carefully constructed media campaign.[78] The fallen celebrity must be re-framed or repackaged with the help of promoters and publicists. Rehabilitation in the public sphere is contingent, however, upon the celebrity's admission of guilt. For example, Pete Rose will never be admitted to Major League Baseball's Hall of Fame without saying he is sorry for gambling on baseball. Likewise, Maradona needed first to make significant progress in his drug recovery and take responsibility for his condition, something he had struggled with for much of his life. Unfortunately, Maradona was never able to completely overcome his addictions and become that international spokesperson for drug abuse prevention that he wanted to be.

Opportunity for Advocacy on a Global Scale

As celebrities increase their involvement as social activists to promote social causes of which they are passionate, they have the opportunity to use their celebrity capital for social change. The efforts of actor George Clooney to move political leaders and the United Nations to increase their efforts to stop the genocide taking place in southern Sudan is a good example of how important celebrity influence can be. Clooney, who personally talked to Sudanese victims of the violence perpetrated by the Sudanese government, spoke a powerful message of social responsibility to the United Nations in September of 2006, urging them to end the mass murders. The association between celebrities and critical social issues has expanded over the past couple of decades as evidenced by publicized celebrity causes.[79] The strategic use of celebrity influence to bring about social change shows no signs of abating as new forms of communication technology further extend celebrity influence.[80]

Discussion Questions

1. What famous athlete has influenced you the most and why?
2. What famous athletic event did you follow closely that had a strong effect on you or on someone close to you?
3. Do you think athletes should be role models in our society? Why or why not?
4. How can we make athletes more aware and more responsible for their public behavior that is being watched by millions of young people seeking to emulate them?

Chapter 9
Moving Millions through Popular Music

My friend came to me,
With sadness in his eyes,
He told me that he wanted help,
Before his country died,
Although I couldn't feel the pain,
I knew I'd have to try,
Now I'm asking all of you,
To help us save some lives.

-George Harrison

The worldwide popularity of music makes it a potentially potent form of social influence. Music, like other forms of entertainment, is pervasive and carries messages to every corner of the globe. A single song can move millions of people to adhere to a certain political belief, experiment with a certain drug, march in the streets to change a government policy, or give food to the hungry. Music and lyrics are much more than a popular form of entertainment; they are powerful sources of learning and social change. Major issues addressed through music include the growing disillusionment of government ideology, advances in civil rights, increased influence of the women's movement, and a heightened concern for the environment.

There are intrinsic attributes of popular music that accentuate its teaching capabilities. The human brain has a tremendous capacity to store and recall musical notes, melodies, tempo, and rhythm. Advertisers have known for decades that music enhances memory. Marketers constantly search for "jingles," short musical signposts that people will easily remember and associate with specific products. If you are a baby boomer, for example, you will find it difficult to forget such phrases as "Things go better than Coca Cola, things go better with Coke," "Winston tastes good like a [pause pause] cigarette should," or "You'll wonder where the yellow went when you brush your teeth with Pepsident." Many people in media-developed environments have more jingles in their heads than many I-pods have in their music memories.

Beyond radio, television and film advertisements is the world of television programs and popular films. Ask a baby boomer to hum the theme song to the television program, Gilligan's Island, and he or she will likely sing the song for you with many of the correct lyrics, even after many years of having not seen the program (if you forgot and want to recall the song, just google it to refresh your memory). Consider the Broadway play and film *West Side Story*. How many adults would one need to ask before finding one who could sing the first lines of Maria or I want to Live in America? Are there any baby boomers in the U.S. who would not know be able to finish the phrase, "Somewhere, over the rainbow, …." Songs that combine melodic music with poetic lyrics are easy to remember after multiple exposures. Each time a person recalls a song or repeats the words, he or she is once again exposed to its message.

Educators have found that music is a great tool to enhance learning.[1] The popular learning program *Hooked on Phonics* demonstrates the positive roll music can play in learning how to read. Part of the big success of children's television programs like *Sesame Street* and *Electric Company* is the music used to enhance memory and learning. These programs and others like them have diffused all over the world, teaching millions of children how to read and write. *Sesame Street* has been seen by children in more than 120 countries.[2]

Many of the ideas of the 1960′s, considered radical at that time, won wider acceptance in the hearts and minds of the American public during the 1970′s through popular music. Some of these "radical" ideas, styles, and practices are now a part of mainstream American life and culture. Protest movements of the 1960's and 1970's, especially the Civil Rights movement and the Vietnam War, were fueled by music groups, musicians, and songwriters. Among some of the most popular protest songs are *If I had a Hammer* (1962) by Peter, Paul and Mary, *Where have all the Flowers Gone* (1962) by The Kingston Trio, *Blowin in the Wind* (1963) and The *Times they are a-Changin* (1964) by Bob Dylan, *Eve of Destruction* (1965) by Barry McGuire, *Universal Soldier* (1967) by Donovan, *Fortunate Son* (1969) by Creedence Clearwater Revival, *Give Peace a Chance* (1969) by John Lennon, and *War* (1970) by Mr. Edwin Starr/Agent Double-O Soul. These songs focused the attention of millions of people on military conflicts around the globe. Individual songs have a way to break through the clutter of chaotic events and focus attention on symbolic events. Few people who lived through those turbulent times, for example, will ever forget the four students killed in a Vietnam War protest at Kent State University on May 4, 1970, thanks to Crosby, Stills, Nash and Young's song, *Ohio*(1970). Even more than the tragic deaths alone, it was songs like Ohio that galvanized public opinion against U.S. military involvement in southeast Asia.

In late May of 1969, John Lennon and Yoko Ono held a week-long protest-in bed against violence at the Queen Elizabeth Hotel in Montreal. The former Beatle and his wife recorded their song, *Give Peace a Chance*, declaring to millions of television viewers, "We're here as a protest against violence. If we say peace often enough, if I, John Lennon, say peace, it's going to make all those people who love me say peace. Now think about it. At least, they're going to think about it which is the most anybody can count on."[3]

The Emergence of Rock Benefit Concerts

The year following John Lennon and Yoko Ono's media event in Canada, with the encouragement of Ravi Shankar, George Harrison organized the "Concert for Bangladesh" in the U.S. to raise funds for UNICEF's relief efforts in Bangladesh.[4] War, famine and a devastating cyclone that killed 300,000 people had left Bangladesh in ruins and on the brink of mass starvation. Harrison cut a new song titled *Bangladesh* and performed it in New York City to bring attention to the crisis and began to organize his friends to raise funds for the relief efforts.

On August 1, 1971, 40,000 people attended Harrison's two benefit concerts in Madison Square Garden to help raise funds for famine relief. A host of rock stars joined in the effort, including Bob Dylan, Eric Clapton, Ravi Shankar, Leon Russell, Billy Preston, and fellow Beatle Ringo Starr. By organizing this first "rock-for-benefit" concert, Harrison inspired many other rock stars to use their celebrity influence to meet other important social needs.[5] Shankar marveled, "Within hours of the show, Bangladesh was known all over the world."[6] Ticket proceeds for the Concert for Bangladesh raised $243,418 for UNICEF, but the continuing donations in the form of artist royalties, a movie, and a music album of the concert has exceeded $15 million.[7] A documentary film of the event, directed by Saul Swimmer, was released in 1972.

The 35th anniversary of the concert was celebrated in August of 2006, when Jay Marciano, president of MSG Entertainment, installed a plaque on the MSG Walk of Fame. Marciano, publicizing the event, declared "George Harrison's wife, Olivia Harrison, will help us remember how music can help create change."[8] The plaque was the first of its kind given to an event rather than a person or group. In 1973, George and Olivia Harrison founded the Material World Charitable Foundation to continue giving to the poor. According to Olivia, her husband quietly donated the proceeds from three concerts on his 1974 U.S. tour to the Foundation.[9] In reflecting on the significance of the event, Rolling Stone reported that the Concert for Bangladesh was "brilliantly put together," demonstrating that an enjoyable rock show could be "a vehicle for aiding starving refugees" without any incongruity, because the musicians and audiences conducted themselves with self-respect.[10] Clearly Harrison had found the right mix of entertainment and education to create a powerful and beneficial social influence.

Harrison's pioneer work in formulating a successful entertainment-education music event was replicated by many entertainers in the following decade.[11] In December of 1984, Harry Belafonte saw a news report on the devastating African famine, that like Harrison a decade before, moved him to action. Belafonte contacted Ken Kragen, who managed entertainment superstars, who immediately agreed to help create a relief effort. On December 20th Belafonte and Kragen decided to record a song to raise funds to alleviate the devastating effects of the famine. By January 10, 1985, Belafonte and Kragen had founded United Support of Artists for Africa (USA for Africa). Kragen solicited the help of Lionel Richie, who in turn contacted Michael Jackson and Stevie Wonder. Jackson and Richie collaborated to write the song, *We are the World*, and Jackson asked Quincy Jones to produce it. The song was recorded on January 28th in A & M Studios in Hollywood, only a few weeks after Belafonte and Kragen had conceptualized their idea to once again use music to motivate a massive disaster relief appeal. A total of 45 musical superstars were involved in the recording, including Bob Dylan, six of the Jacksons, including Michael, Bob Geldof, Waylon Jennings, Billy Joel, Cyndi Lauper, Kenny Logins, Bette Midler, Lionel Richie, Kenny Rogers, Diana Ross, Paul Simon, Bruce Springsteen, Tina Turner, and Stevie Wonder. Three weeks after the single was released on March 8, 1985, it hit number one on the Billboard Hot 100, and went on to become the bestselling record in music industry history. *We are the World* won Grammys for Song of the Year and Record of the Year in 1985 (inthe80s.com). The song has generated more than $62 million, 90 percent that has been distributed to Africa for famine relief.[12]

A few months after *We are the World* was released, Bob Geldof staged another Africa relief concert, Live Aid, in London. The concert was described as "the Woodstock of the 80s," drawing 72,000 people into London's Wembley Stadium. Geldof was moved by BBC news reports and Michael Buerk's BBC documentary of the African famine. Geldof, lead singer of the Boomtown Rats, teamed with Midge Ure from Ultravox to write the song, *Do They Know it's Christmas?* to help raise funds. The song was recorded by Band Aid, a group of 37 songwriters, singers and musicians from the U.K.[13] The song raised many millions of pounds and became the biggest-selling single in UK chart history. (It has since been passed by Elton John's tribute to Diana, Princess of Wales).

During the London Live Aid concert, a second Live Aid concert was held simultaneously in Philadelphia's John F. Kennedy Stadium. Within five minutes of the Beach Boys taking the stage in Philadelphia, 22,000 pledges were received. The event drew participation from dozens of celebrities, including Prince Charles and Lady Diana, David Bowie, Bono, Wham, Dire Straits and Mick Jagger in London, and Bob Dylan, Lionel Richie, Tina Turner, Pail Simon and the Beach Boys in the U.S. The 16-hour marathon event, which was satellite broadcast to 1.5 billion people in 160 countries, raised $100 million in pledges for African famine relief from donors in 30 countries.[14] For his efforts, Bob Geldof was given an honorary knighthood in 1986.

The year after *We are the World* was released, Kragen organized *Hands Across America*, a benefit event staged to raise additional funds for famine relief and for homelessness in America. The planned even was announced on January 26th during the Super-bowl half-time shows. On Sunday afternoon of Sunday, May 25, 1986, an estimated seven million people joined hands for 15 minutes to form a line that stretched from New York City's Battery Park to a pier in Long Beach, California, 4,152 miles in total. President Reagan, his family, the White House staff and their families joined the line. At 3:00 pm EST on the same day, the song *Hands Across America* was played on hundreds of radio stations across the U.S. Corporate support for the event totaled $30 million and individual participants donated another $20 million, which was distributed to 1651 organizations by May of 1987.[15]

Inspired by the success of USA for Africa's *We are the World*, and Band Aid's *Do They Know it's Christmas*, Jimmy Bain, Vivian Campbell, and Ronnie James Dio organized Hear 'N Aid, another famine relief effort for Africa. All three artists had taken part in a 48-hour charity radiothon for KLOS, an FM radio station in Los Angeles. Bain and Campbell had noticed that the representation of heavy metal stars was scarce during the event and decided to team with Dio to create a focused fund-raising effort with heavy metal artists. The result was the song *Stars*, which was recorded on May 20-21 at A & M Records Studio in Hollywood with 40 artists. The project included members of many popular heavy metal bands, including Dio, Quiet Riot, Iron Maiden, Mötley Crüe, Twisted Sister, Queensrÿche, Blue Öyster Cult, Dokken, Night Ranger, Judas Priest, W.A.S.P., Journey, Y&T, Vanilla Fudge, and Spinal Tap.

Farm Aid in the U.S.

Farm Aid was initiated when Bob Dylan said on stage, "Wouldn't it be great if we did something for our own farmers here in America."[16] Partnering with Willie Nelson, Neil Young and John Mellencamp, Dylan organized the first Farm Aid concert on September 22, 1985, in Champaign, Illinois, home of the University of Illinois. The concert drew 80,000 participants, and Dylan, Nelson, Mellencamp, Billy Joel, BB King, Loretta Lynn, Johnny Cash, John Denver, Glen Campbell, the Beach Boys, Alabama and others raised more than $7 million for farmers.

Since that first concert, there has been at least one Farm Aid concert in the U.S. every year. Farm Aid II was held on Independence Day in 1986 in Austin, Texas, and broadcast live on VH-1. Austin also was home to another large agricultural university, the University of Texas. Farm Aid III was held in Lincoln, Nebraska on September 19, 1987, home of the University of Nebraska. It also was broadcast live via satellite. In 1989, Farm Aid President Willie Nelson took Farm Aid on the road to 16 cities, holding press conferences at each site.

In many ways Nelson was a good choice to head up Farm Aid. The controversial yet popular Texan has created more than 200 albums and has won six Grammys. He also was given a President's Merit Award, a Grammy Legend Award, and a Lifetime Achievement Award. Nelson is both knowledgeable and passionate about helping farmers and has a tremendous amount of creative energy. In addition to his long-time work with Farm Aid, Nelson and his wife Annie became partners with Bob and Kelly King in 2004 and built two Pacific Biodiesel Plants, one in Salem, Oregon, and the other at Carl's Corner, Texas. The following year Nelson and several other business partners formed Willie Nelson Biodiesel (also known as BioWillie), a company that is marketing Biodiesel biofuel to truck stops. The fuel is made from vegetable oils, mainly soybeans, and can be burned without modification in diesel engines.

Nelson and Mellencamp have brought family farmers before Congress to testify about the state of family farming in America. Congress subsequently passed the Agricultural Credit Act of 1987 to help save family farms from foreclosure. Farm Aid has continued to influence public policy through its concerts, relief efforts, and media coverage. The 1990 Farm Aid concert, which sold out in 90 minutes, was broadcast live on the Nashville Network and re-broadcast to ten million viewers on CBS. The 1992 Farm Aid concert brought Dallas Cowboys owner Jerry Jones. Farm Aid brought to the attention of America and the Clinton Administration to devastating rate of farm closures – some 500 per week.

In September of 2000 Farm Aid brought together Crosby, Stills, Nash and Young, with a host of other entertainers, to interact with political candidates and to educate the public about synthetic Growth Bovine Hormone. Five years later the 20th Farm Aid concert was held in Tinley Park, Illinois. At the press event Farm Aid recounted 20 years of solid work and announced the release of Farm Aid: A Song for America. The book chronicles 20 years of the Farm Aid music that galvanized the grassroots movement for family farms and good food. Farmers and advocates also tallied Farm Aid's accomplishments, from direct aid to farmers in trouble, to fighting factory farms to building up the good food movement. Concert attenders brought donations of food for Katrina victims. The concert concluded a full week of activities from Champaign to Chicago, with farm visits, music and chefs at Chicago's farmers markets, films at the Cultural Center, a tractor parade leading to the County Fair at the Garfield Conservatory, and over 20 restaurants offering their guests a "family farm" menu item.

Farm Aid has now raised tens of millions of dollars to help American farmers.[17] The organization, founded in 1985 by Mellencamp, Nelson and Neil Young, has provided an enormous amount of public education about protecting the people and land resources that feed the United States and peoples in many other nations. The emphasis of the 2006 Farm Aid concert in Camden, NJ, which featured rock pioneer Jerry Lee Lewis, was to educate the public on the food production and eating healthy food. From its inception, Farm Aid has focused educational mission advanced through its annual concerts. Farm Aid 2012 was staged from the popular Hershey Park in Pennsylvania.

Social Justice and Hip-Hop Music

Songs about social justice issues date back to the beginning musical performance. Perhaps the best known international creative artist whose social justice songs touched the world was Bob Marley. When Marley was inducted into the Rock and Roll Hall of Fame, Robert Palmer wrote in a tribute, "No one in rock and roll has left a musical legacy that matters more or one that matters in such fundamental ways. He was particularly moved throughout his career by the gulf between haves and have-nots, a culture of oppression that was particularly glaring in his poverty- and crime-ridden Jamaican homeland."[18]

In a 1976 interview with Timothy White, Marley explained his passion with these words: "We should all come together and creative music and love, but [there] is too much poverty. The most intelligent people [are] the poorest people...[but] people don't get no time to feel and spend [their] intelligence...The intelligent and innocent are poor, are crumbled and get brutalized daily."[19]

Marley's influence contributed to the development of a new genre of music, hip-hop, that emerged in the streets of New York in the late 1960's and early 1970's. Hip-hop is a broad term that covers several kinds of youth cultural expressions, including rap music, break dancing, graffiti, fashion, video, crime and commerce.[20] Fernando traces the origins of hip-hop music "back to the concrete jungles of the Bronx in the late '60s and early '70s, an era now fondly remembered as the old school."[21] Although hip-hop is a term commonly associated with the generation of Black Youth who grew up during that era, hip-hop culture has grown to encompass youth from multiple cultural backgrounds.

African Americans, Caribbean and Latino Americans have been prominent in the development of hip-hop culture, which is now part of mainstream American culture. The artist Flash explained one of the reasons for hip-hop's popularity, stating "Hip hop is the only genre of music that allows us to talk about almost anything. Musically, it allows us to sample and play and create poetry to the beat of the music."[22]

Hip-hop music emerged from the confluence of several social, political and artistic conditions. Tricia Rose contends that the "de-industrialization" of New York, accelerated by the growth of powerful information service corporations and media industries and the decline of manufacturing factories and related infrastructure, exacerbated the decline of blue-collar jobs.[23] In the South Bronx, populations of economically depressed ethnic minorities poured in from other areas of New York City. The Cross-Bronx Expressway cut through heavily populated working-class ethnic residential communities in the borough, further depressing real estate value and creating slums. Along with the razing of old blue-collar homes, "subsequent 'White flight,' devastated kin networks and neighborhood services," vast social and economic inequalities were created.[24]

David Toop notes that it was in this social, musical and cultural context of the 1970's that South Bronx youth found themselves that led to the development of their own alternative to the increased gang warfare that had arisen from poverty.[25] Outdoor parties in public parks were common in the Bronx during the late 60s and early 70s.[26] DJs would connect their sound system into a streetlight's power box and play 7-inch or 12-inch vinyl records as youth danced, rhymed or wrote graffiti. It was an inexpensive alternative to community centers and an escape from the obvious poverty that surrounded them. It also was a source of alternative local identity and community.

Three individuals are consistently recognized as the founding fathers of rap: Clive Campbell (a.k.a Kool Herc), Afrika Bambaataa, and Joseph Saddler – all with Jamaican roots.[27] This "old school" era of hip-hop, as it is called, started in 1974 at these street parties or "hip-hop jams."[28]

Grand Master Flash, who loved tinkering with electronics, developed an inexpensive cue monitor that allowed him greater precision and speed in spinning the break beats. Along with his showmanship, he also had an exceptional hand-eye coordination that enabled him to mix records (thus the moniker "Flash"). Flash and his crew are credited with several innovations. For example, they developed the art of "scratching" or using the noise of a turntable needle working back and forth to create its own rhythm for entertainment. Additionally, according to Nelson George, "'Punch phrasing' – playing a quick burst from a record on the turntable while it continues on the other- and "break spinning" -alternately spinning both records backwards to repeat the same phrase over and over- are credited to Flash."[29] As with Herc, the use of MCs for toasting and developing catch phrases was also a norm. Rapping came after graffiti and breakdancing but it is the enduring and the most central element of hip-hop.

Afro-Diaspora Cultural Concerns

Recognition of the Afro-Diaspora elements and how it interacted with hip-hop cultural development is an important consideration. Two areas to note are the concerns within the community for authenticity and the search for Black priorities and the creation of new identities. One of my doctoral students, Dr. Raymond Anderson, mapped identification with hip-hop culture in his dissertation work, drawing on Kembrew McLeod's examination of the hip -hop music community's claims of authenticity that are rooted in cultural concerns."[30] Both Anderson and McLeod discuss the range of discursive meanings associated with this concern, recognizing it as socially–agreed upon construct. I will draw extensively on Anderson's analysis here. Utilizing Sietel's conceptual apparatus of semantic dimensions, Anderson approached authenticity through six semantic dimensions: social psychology, racial identification, the political-economic aspects of the music industry, gender and sexual roles, social location and cultural concerns.[31]

"Keepin' it real" is a versatile signifier that means different things based on the context in which it is used. The social- psychological dimension of "keepin' it real" is when one stays true to themselves instead of following mass trends, valorizing individualism over conformity. The racial dimension of the phrase considers "the real" as tied to Black cultural expression. Underground movements, which are important incubators for social change, are also considered real in a political –economic dimension, whereas artists who position themselves with commercial interests of the dominant multinational corporations are considered to have sold out. Independent distribution is more real than MTV and radio and popular award shows. From a gender-sexual dimension, assimilation occurs when an artist is being soft, representing female attributes, with an emphasis on love songs as against harder homophobic songs. Social location involves the street versus the suburbs with the ongoing need to associate with the African American dominated inner cities.

Finally, there is the cultural dimension of old school as consideration of authenticity, with "discourse that addresses hip-hop's status as a culture that has deep and resonating traditions, rather than as a commodity."[32] Old schoolers are a close-knit community of break dancers, DJs, MCs and graffiti artists who helped nurture the movement and who understand it as "cultural tradition rather than treat [hip-hop] as merely a product."[33]

Chuck D., The Public Enemy spokesman, grew up listening to protest music, and later used it as inspiration for his own work. "*Fight the Power* by the Isley Brothers was the song that inspired me to write *Fight the Power* by Public Enemy," he says. "But, being a child of the Sixties, there's so many great protest songs. *People Get Ready* and a lot of Curtis Mayfield's songs touched my soul. James Brown had a protest song against drugs with *King Heroin*, and Peter, Paul and Mary struck me as a kindergartener. How could those songs not mean so much?"[34]

Yo MTV Raps ran from August 1988 to August 1995 on MTV. It was hosted by Fab 5 Freddy on the weekend show, and Ed Lover and Doctor Dre on the weekday show. The program featured interviews with rap stars, Friday live studio performances, and comedy. Before this show MTV rarely had any videos or performances from hip hop or rap artists. Run-DMC hosted the pilot episode. Hip Hop and Rap became widely popular with this exposure. With his first solo album, 1992's The Chronic, Dr. Dre established himself as the premier hip-hop producer of the mid-'90s it also introduced the word to the talents of Snoop Dogg.

In 1992, Ice-T released a song *Cop Killer* that was a commentary on police violence and brutality. The lyrics were directed at "bad cops" whom by their actions were themselves criminals. Before performing this song live in concert Ice-T always made it clear that there were also "good cops" and that he was not advocating violence against anyone. This song caused an international controversy and was eventually dropped from his 'Body Count' album.[35] Police picketed and protested Time Warner, Ice-T's then record label. Even then President Bush angrily lambasted it.

Ice-T now later went on to play a police officer on Law & Order Special Victims Unit on NBC. In September of 1996, West rapper Tupac Amaru Shakur was shot to death in a drive by shooting in Las Vegas. Then in March of 1997 East rapper Christopher Wallace, aka Notorious B.I.G., was shot to death. They both were killed in a feud between East Coast and West Coast rappers. That was a wakeup call to many other rappers that music should be a positive force for people.

Rose argues for an appreciation of Black cultural priorities, especially in the use of sound organization.[36] Use of sampled sounds and "the prolific use of collage, inter-textuality, boasting, toasting, and signifying in rap's lyrical style" are informed by Black traditions.[37] Anderson describes in his dissertation how the rhythmic and percussive density and organizational nature of the music differs from harmonic Western classical music. Rose discusses the short and repetitious nature of African melodic phrases noted by others, characterizing them as not simply stylistic effects, but as "aural manifestations of philosophical approaches to social environments."[38] She regards repetition as an important aspect to cultural groups, providing a sense of security or coverage against assimilation or loss of identity. In Western classical music, rhythm is used as an aid in developing a sense of progression to a harmonic cadence and resolution with repetition being suppressed; whereas in Black cultures, foreground repetition is perceived as circulation [that provides] equilibrium.[39] (p. 69). The ritual, dance or beat is there to be picked up when you return for it, so it continually "cuts" or breaks, in a seemingly accidental fashion, back to the start. Snead observed that "Black culture, in the 'cut,' 'builds' accidents into its coverage, almost as if to control their unpredictability."[40] Rap music uses repetition and rupture in "new and complex ways ... with break beat deconstruction and reconstruction ... [makes] repetition more accessible."[41] This is achieved with reliance on looping (continuously repeating the sampled sound) on the circularity of rhythm and the break beat. It is used in ways that affirm Black cultural priorities.

Although hip-hop music became more accepted in the entertainment industry, the attributes of its resistance and critique of the dominant culture continued to draw negative public responses, especially the antipolice raps of KRS-One (*Who Protects Us from You*, 1989), LL Kool J.(*Illegal Search*, 1990) and NWA ("—The Police", 1988). These songs provided social commentary and challenges to perceived institutional control. Rose claims that discussions of rap and rap-related violence in the popular media are linked to spatial control of Blacks out of a belief that Black people are a threat to social order.[42] Black urban teenagers are the most volatile symbolic referent for internal threats to social order. The lyrics of NWA's — *The Police* received negative responses from the authorities. Public debate of rap and hip-hop and their mediated projections of violence, materialism and sex has taken place within the broader context of an American cultural environment that promotes gratuitous expressions of sex and violence through popular music, prime time television, and youth marketed films.[43]

Rising out of this cultural tension in the 1990s, a new urban Black entrepreneurial persona emerged. Hip-hop label chiefs or "Big Willies" as they were called, were "often as famous as their signings."[44] These artists include Bad Boy Entertainment's Sean "Puffy" Combs, No Limit's Master P, Russel Simmons at Def Jam and Priority Record's Bryan Turner. They have become celebrities with social influence through their music and fashion, eventually penetrating sports apparel. Successful and longstanding Big Willies like Simmons and Puffy also provided role models of the possibilities within hip-hop for commercial success. Simmons initiated a Hip-hop Summit to focus on the political aspects of hip-hop along with a coalition of hip-hop artists, civil leaders (including the Congressional Black Caucus and NACCP), scholars and music industry representatives.[45]

Hip-hop's continued growth in mainstream American culture and cultures of other nations gives it a tremendous potential for initiating social change. It will also continue to represent celebration and controversy, but also incorporate entertainment-education elements. Rap, which lies at the center of the culture, has evolved into several sub-genres over the past several decades. Although the history of hip-hop culture has strong African American roots and evolved from urban environments, Caucasian artists and audiences have openly embraced the culture and its music. Hip-hop is no longer a sub-culture but is now part of the fabric of American culture and of international culture.

Music for Political Involvement

During the last thirty years of the 20th century, voter turnout in American presidential elections steadily decreased. From an overall participation rate of 69.3% of eligible voters in 1964 to 55% in 1992, Americans become steadily less active in voting in elections.[46] Although this decline involves Americans from all racial, social, and demographic groups, research indicated that young voters aged 18-24 was the group for whom the decline has been greatest.[47]

However, in the 1992 presidential election, the decline not only stopped, but dramatically reversed. For the first time in two decades, voter turnout among young people actually increased from 36.2 percent in 1988 to 42.8 percent.[48] Although we could consider many possible reasons why this decline was reversed, we do not that two years preceding the election, one of the most watched cable networks among youth, MTV, became engaged in a massive voter education and promotion campaign called Rock the Vote.

The Rock the Vote campaign targeted young voters and aired solely on MTV. Unlike any preceding voter enhancement campaign, Rock the Vote featured a host of celebrities who were employed to solicit the political involvement of young people. The campaign also featured some of the most popular bands at that time who donated their time to reinforce the importance of voting. Each Rock the Vote public service announcement (PSA) reflected the style and culture of MTV music videos, their featured artists, and the MTV viewing audience as a whole.

Rock the Vote was officially founded in 1990 by members of the recording industry in response to a wave of attacks on freedom of speech and artistic expression. Rock the Vote expanded its focus to the political empowerment of young Americans. Eight years later, Rock the Vote expanded its focus and organization and rewrote its mission statement, dedicating itself to protecting freedom of expression and helping young people realize and utilize their power to affect change in the civic and political affairs of their communities.

Rock the Vote supported the National Voter Registration Reform Act (NVRA) in 1991, also known as the Motor Voter Bill. The PSA (public service announcement) campaign distributed "Dear Senator" postcards on the now-defunct CD longboxes, urging members of Congress to pass the Motor Voter Bill. The bill was ultimately vetoed by President Bush but later signed by President Clinton in 1993.

In 1992, the Rock the Vote campaign produced PSAs with artists including R.E.M., En Vogue, Aerosmith, Queen Latifah Eddie Vedder and others. The PSAs aired on networks such as MTV, VH-1, BET and Fox. The campaign also partnered with the National Association of Secretaries of State to produce additional PSAs for local television broadcast. In addition to the public service announcements, Fox Television broadcast a one-hour, Peabody Award-winning Rock the Vote television special hosted by Queen Latifah and featuring celebrities Michael Douglas, Madonna, Robin Williams, Tom Cruise, Whoopi Goldberg, Chris Rock and others.

Rock the Vote PSAs began airing on MTV at most commercial breaks about six months preceding the 1992 presidential election. The variety of Rock the Vote PSAs produced allowed the campaign organizers to show the commercials repeatedly. Although such repetition might annoy most television viewers, the re-airing of popular videos several times a day made the MTV audience accustomed to repeat programming. Also, Rock the Vote was able to develop many different PSAs because of the variety and depth of music personalities, actors, music bands, and production companies that donated their time to the campaign. The more than 75 commercials produced by the campaign enjoyed extensive amount of airtime at peak programming hours.

Young people responded to the Rock the Vote message, which employed a specific rhetorical strategy to create an effective appeal.[49] Following the 1992 presidential election, Rock the Vote touted its success with full-page advertisements in the Washington Post, New York Times, and Los Angeles Times, claiming that 17 million young adults had voted. Rock the Vote and its partner organizations registered 350,000 young people and helped motivate more than two million new young voters to the polls in the November 2002 election. On Election Day, these young people reversed a 20-year cycle of declining participation. A Bureau of the Census report confirmed MTV's claim, reporting that turnout among voters in the 18-24-year-old age group had increased by more than 6.5 percentage points over 1988, the largest percentage increase of any demographic group surveyed.[50]

Emboldened by President Clinton's signature of the Motor Voter Bill into law on May 20, 1993, the Rock the Vote campaign joined activist groups to lobby for the National and Community Service Trust Act. The bill, designed to encourage volunteerism, was signed into law by President Clinton on September 21, 1993.

The next year the campaign created and distributed some one million free copies of "Rock the System: A Guide to Health Care for Young Americans," a pamphlet on health issues affecting young people. That same year, the First Annual Rock the Vote Patrick Lippert Awards was held in memory of Rock the Vote's founding Executive Director, Patrick Lippert, who died of AIDS-related pneumonia in 1993. R.E.M. accepted the inaugural award, honoring those making a significant contribution to empowering young people.

The campaign continued its health education efforts in 1995, producing the Peabody Award-winning "Out of Order: Rock the Vote Targets Health," a series of short dramatic films focusing on health care issues and featuring up-and-coming stars Giovanni Ribisi, Cuba Gooding Jr., Joey Lauren Adams and Amy Smart. The Second Annual Rock the Vote Patrick Lippert Award was given to Pearl Jam and Queen Latifah.

In 1996, Rock the Vote debuted the first program to register voters by phone, 1-800-REGISTER. Closer to the election, the campaign converted the number into 1-800-ROCK VOTE to give callers the number of their local elections office to request absentee ballots or locate their polling place. Working with MCI, the campaign also developed the first website to offer on-line voter registration, dubbed NetVote '96. Rock the Vote PSA's in 1996 featured celebrity entertainers Drew Barrymore, Seal, LL Cool J, Chuck D, Joan Osbourne, Coolio and Hootie & The Blowfish, airing on MTV, VH1, ABC, CBS, USA Networks and DIRECTV. The multi-media campaign, which included both radio and television, registered some 500,000 new voters. Rock the Vote and MTV published 200,000 copies of a free non-partisan voter guide, educating young people about the issues and candidates in the 1996 election. Chuck D of Public Enemy and Hootie & The Blowfish were honored at Rock the Vote's Third Annual Patrick Lippert Awards.

By the late 1990s, the Rock the Vote campaign had tremendous momentum. The campaign continued to mobilize the participation of young people in the political process. They included sports celebrities in their efforts, honoring Steve Young and the NFL Quarterback Club in 1997. The campaign also expanded their use of the Internet, winning Computerworld's Smithsonian Award for Innovation in Technology, and began reaching out to older people through partnerships with MCI and AARP.

The campaign also developed a new political activism guide, titled "Use Your Power to Rock the Vote Every Day," and distributed it through record stores, community organizations and schools. They also organized artists such as The Murmurs, the cast of the "The West Wing," Rah Digga, Outkast, Hootie & The Blowfish joined the campaigns' 25-city, four-month bus tour to educate and register new young voters. Through a new series of PSAs, its concert tours, bus tour, radio partners, website, and volunteers, Rock the Vote registered more than half a million new voters in 2000 and called nearly 200,000 young people in the days before the election.

The following year, the campaign launched 15 Community Street Teams across the country to mobilize and increase youth political participation. The 120 team members conducted peer-to-peer organizing activities through organizing tactics and guerilla street marketing. The team collected 31,565 hate crime petition signatures and distributed 79,000 "Fight for Your Rights: Take a Stand Against Discrimination" guides. The campaign also partnered with the Los Angeles County Commission for Human Relations to combat discrimination and intolerance and build an infrastructure for youth to develop interpersonal skills, cultural sensitivity, peace building and peacekeeping skills.

The hip-hop music community again joined their efforts with the Rock the Vote campaign in 2002. The NAACP's Russell Simmons and Def Jam Records re-launched the Rap the Vote campaign. As part of the re-launch, The Beatnuts and Non-Phixion partnered with Rock the Vote campaign for a nationwide Rap the Vote Tour in the fall. The conducted hundreds of community festivals, concerts and parades in 35 cities. The next years the campaign created a partnership with Ben & Jerry's ice cream franchise to register new voters.

Rock the Vote launched the 2004 campaign by partnering with CNN to produce a Democratic presidential candidates forum at Faneuil Hall in Boston in November of 2003. The debate was considered by many to be the liveliest and most informative of the entire race. That year there were more than 1.2 million on-line voter registrations. At the campaign's peak in late September of 2004, nearly 40,000 people came to Rock the Vote's website in one day to fill out voter registration forms. Partnerships with more than 1000 web partners coupled with innovative media campaigns. The campaign also instituted a Voter Call system through which volunteers made Election Day reminder calls to our Online Voter Registration list in Ohio, Pennsylvania, Wisconsin and Oregon. In October of 2004, the Rock the Vote website had 27.4 million hits from people registering to vote, learning about the issues, and finding ways to get involved. According to an online Polimetrix survey with 20,000 participants, more than 45% of 18- to 24-year-olds surveyed had visited the campaign website in the months leading up to the election.

In 2004, there also was unprecedented celebrity involvement in the Rock the Vote campaign. Celebrity participants included Kate Bosworth, Eva Mendes, Maroon 5, Q-Tip, Paul Van Dyk, Ben Jelen, Jada Pinkett Smith, Joss Stone, Josh Hartnett, Jill Scott, Snoop Dogg, Eliza Dushku, Christina Applegate, Tamyra Gray, Alyssa Milano, LL Cool J, Vanessa Carlton,

Black Eyed Peas, Amber Tamblyn, Leonardo DiCaprio, Ben Affleck, Justin Timberlake, Benicio del Toro, Samuel L. Jackson, Ricky Martin, Lil' Kim, Paris Hilton, Angie Harmon & Jason Sehorn, Rosario Dawson, Jake Gyllenhaal, Maggie Gyllenhaal and stars from all The WB shows.

The tremendous success of Rock the Vote inspired other entertainers to become politically active. For example, Sean "P. Diddy" Combs founded Citizen Change, a national, non-partisan and non-profit organization created to educate, motivate, and empower the more than 42 million Americans aged 18 to 30 that are eligible to vote. The mission of Citizen Change, which has promoted its message through t-shirts, is to make voting relevant to a generation that hasn't reached full participation in the political process. The influence of the music industry on political involvement during the past 25 years is nearly impossible to scientifically measure but obviously is substantial.

Social Causes of the 21st Century

During the 1980's and 1990's, a number of professional artists became involved in various social causes. These include Willie Nelson for Farm AID, Bono for Third World Relief, hunger and HIV/AIDS, The Dave Mathews Band for global warming, Sheryl Crow for landmine removal, Moby for environmental protection, Elton John for HIV/AIDS, Sting for protection of the Rainforest, and Don Henley for the Waldon Woods Project.

These efforts have continued into the 2lst century. In April of 2002, the Dave Matthews Band, SaveOurEnvironment.org and Ben & Jerry's launched One Sweet Whirled.org — one sweet ice cream and one sweet campaign to fight global warming. This unique campaign is a product and the product is a campaign.

Bono, leader of the Rock group U2, has been active in many social issues, including reducing the debt of third world nations. In his commencement address to Harvard University in 2001, Bono, dressed in olive-green clothes, a camouflage hat and his trademark shades, told the graduates that "we've got to follow through on our ideals or we betray something at the heart of who we are," noting that "the culture of idealism is under siege."[51] Bono continues to use his popularity as a Rock Star not only to rally assistance for the poor in Africa, but also to change public policy. Bono's well publicized trip to Africa in 2002 with US Treasury Secretary Paul O'Neill, his ongoing friendship with former Senator Jesse Helms of North Carolina, and his frequent contact with government officials, demonstrates that he is constantly turning his celebrity capital into political influence to persuade policy makers to point more resources towards the needs in Africa. During Bono's keynote address at the National Prayer Breakfast in Washington on February 2, 2006, attended by President Bush and other influential US government officials, he laid a biblical foundation for releasing poor African countries from their debts to western nations, saying "this is not about charity, it is about justice and equality."[52]

Actor Chris Tucker also accompanied Bono and Treasury Secretary Paul O'Neill on their ten-day trip to Ghana, South Africa, Uganda and Ethiopia. When Tucker received his 2002 MTV movie award, he dedicated it to the mothers and children he had met on this trip. He also urged everyone to call their elected officials to urge them to support aid to Africa.

Bono gave the speech to the closing ceremony of the African Development Bank Meetings in Ethiopia, stating:

> "This is where it all started for me. Seventeen years ago, I came to Ethiopia on a wave of tears and compassion, flowing from the rich countries to the poor from soccer stadiums taken over by musicians to refugee camps taken over by the starving war weary people of Ethiopia. The brilliant Bob Geldof taught me then the importance of being focused, angry, persistent. We raised 200 million dollars, and we thought we'd cracked it. It was a great moment; it was a great feeling. Then I discovered that Africa pays 200 million dollars every five days repaying old debts. Can I repeat that, 200 million dollars every five days? Tears were obviously not enough" (Solcomhouse, 2006).

Live 8 for Poverty Alleviation

LIVE 8 was a world-wide event designed to draw attention to the poor around the world. The event sought to galvanize the fight against global poverty, promoting the goal to "make poverty history." The event began with The Long Walk to Justice and a call to leaders of the world's richest countries to help the poor when they met in Gleneagles on 6th-9th July. On July 2, 2005 in London, Edinburgh, Philadelphia, Berlin, Paris and Rome, millions of people came together to call for Third World debt cancellation and increased financial aid and trade incentives for the world's poorest people. LIVE 8 called for people across the world to unite in one call – it is your voice we are after, not your money.

Bono, one of the organizers of the event, described its significance:

> "Live 8 was and remains a brilliant moment but what is more important is the brilliant movement of which it was a part. This gives the poorest of the poor real political muscle for the first time. It is this movement of church people and trade unionists, soccer moms and student activists, that will carry the spirit of Live 8 on. It is this movement, not rock stars, that will make it untenable in the future to break promises to the most vulnerable people on this planet. That was always why we put on the concerts."[53]

An estimated three billion people watched LIVE 8, which featured 10 venues, 150 bands and 1250 musicians who played across the globe to ask people not for their money but for their names. More than 30 million people from all around the world provided their names for the live 8 list which was presented to Tony Blair, the chair of the G8, by representatives of LIVE 8.[54] Blair was also presented with a document, entitled, The Global Call to Action against Poverty.

The Live 8 concert was produced by a number of individuals internationally, including Richard Curtis, Sir Bob Geldorf, Harvey Goldsmith, John Kennedy and Kevin Wall with Ken Ehrlich, Larry Magid, Tim Sexton, Greg Sills and Russell Simmons. The beneficiary of excess revenue after the costs of the concerts is the Band Aid Charitable Trust.

Organizers said that in addition to the three billion people who watched on TV and an estimated 1.5 million attended the concerts in person. Barbara Stocking, Director of Oxfam GB, felt that "Live 8 made people realize that they could do something about poverty. I think that was the difference," she says. "I don't pretend that everybody's remembered that, but I think there was a change in attitude."[55]

Celebrities, Youth and Human Rights

In November of 2004, 19 year-old creative artist Taron Lexton released a five-minute film/music video called *United*, which he directed as an entertainment education projected targeted toward youth. The video, which fuses together hip-hop music and a powerful human rights message, tells a moving tale of children fighting for their rights around the world. The video features cameo appearances from a host of celebrities, including soul legend Isaac Hayes, movie actress Erika Christensen (*Traffic*), and television actresses Catherine Bell (*JAG*), Jenna Elfman (*Dharma and Greg*), and Lynsey Bartilson (*Grounded for Life*).

Taron Lexton traveled across 14 countries on four continents to obtain the footage he needed. Everyone involved in the project donated their time and talents, including the entire multi-ethnic cast and crew and more than 2,000 volunteers.[56] Lexton was overwhelmed with the positive response, realizing that his passion to raise concern about human rights was shared by many professional artists and millions of their fans. The song featured in Lexton's video, also called United, was written by up-and-coming artists Charles Gee and Chris Thomas. Additional lyrics were contributed by 14-year-old female rapper Lai Lai. The video was produced by Hiroko Hayata and award-winning musician Geoff Levin.

Mr. Craig Mokhiber, Deputy Director of the Office of the High Commissioner for Human Rights at the United Nations in New York, described the work as "brilliant" and as "an important contribution to human rights education"[57] Some civil rights leaders believe the video has the potential to dramatically curb youth violence. In California alone, the Department of Justice estimates there are 300,000 gang members.[58] Six thousand young people in the state are hospitalized each year for some form of violent injury.

Lexton used his production company, TXL Films, to create the music video as a project for Youth for Human Rights International (YHRI), an organization that teaches kids human rights and encourages youth-to-youth mentorship. At the United Premier event in New York City, Lexton earned the prestigious "Outstanding Youth Humanitarian Award" award from YHRI. Mary Shuttleworth, founder of YHRI, is making the work available to schools, youth organizations, and others concerned to advance human rights for youth. International distribution is now underway. With tens of thousands of copies in circulation in 15 languages, UNITED is already generating an international grass roots movement for human rights.

Popular Music and Health Campaigns

The strategic use of music for social change has been implemented in a number of entertainment-education health campaigns throughout the world. One of the first strategic campaigns took place in Mexico during the late 1980s. Mexican communication and health professionals, familiar with the success of entertainment-education *telenovelas*, began to experiment with the music video as a genre for promoting health education. In 1986, Mexico launched a unique campaign utilizing rock music. The campaign featured two rock music videos, *Cuando Estemos Juntos* ("When We Are Together") and *Detente* (*Wait*), which promoted sexual abstinence and contraception. The first song was number one on the pop music charts within six weeks of its release in Mexico and became a top-rated song in 11 other Latin American countries.[59]

Johns Hopkins University's Population Communication Services (JHU/PCS) provided the impetus for launching *Cuando Estemos Juntos*. First, researchers conducted formative evaluation research in Latin America to determine the best way to reach young people with a message about sexual behavior. Their research revealed that the common denominator for young people throughout Latin America was rock music. The lyrics of the songs and the two singers were carefully selected. The two teenage singers, Tatiana, a 16-year old female singer from Mexico, and Johnny, a 17-year old male Puerto Rican singer, urged their teenage audience not to have sex but to wait until they are older. Radio and television stations could play the song without paying a broadcast fee if they accompanied the music with an announcement of the address and telephone number of a local family planning counseling center that offered services to teenagers. This strategy helped channel the teenage audiences' knowledge and attitudes into action.

A typical Mexican radio station played the song about 14 times per day for about four months, providing massive audience exposure to the sexual responsibility messages.[60] An evaluation of the song's effects in Mexico indicated that it encouraged teenagers to talk more freely about teenage sex, reinforced teenagers who already had decided to use restraint, sensitized younger viewers to the importance of the topic, and disseminated information about contraception.[61]

Building on the prior experience of Tatiana and Johnny in Latin America, JHU/PCS launched a popular music campaign in 1988 in the Philippines to promote sexual responsibility among Filipino teenagers. Two songs, *That Situation* and "I Still Believe," were sung by a 16-year old female Filipino artist named Lea Salonga and members of the Puerto Rico-based rock group Menudo, which also featured a young artist by the name of Ricky Martin. Both songs became number one on the popular music charts in the Philippines.

JHU/PCS's entertainment-education efforts in the Philippines had two components: commercial and institutional. The commercial component established each song as a commercial hit with a social message. The institutional component linked the songs and their messages to a telephone hotline where young adults received information, counseling, and referrals about their problems. In addition, television spots (centered on sequences of *That Situation* and *I Still Believe*) showed teenage crisis situations associated with premarital sex and unwanted pregnancy, encouraging the teenagers to "Dial-a-Friend" for counseling. Trained professional counselors manned four telephone hotlines that averaged more than 1,000 telephone calls a week from teenagers wanting to discuss sexual responsibility. A study of the campaign indicated that the songs positively influenced knowledge, attitudes, and behaviors related to sexual responsibility among Filipino teenagers.[62]

Following the success of their efforts in the Philippines, JHU/PCS launched two popular music videos in Nigeria in1989, titled *Choices* and *Wait for Me*. Both songs promoted family planning. Sung by King Sunny Ade, a famous singer of West African music, and Onyeka Onwenu, these two songs were part of an integrated communication campaign. Research of the effects of these songs indicated they were highly popular both in urban and rural areas, encouraged couples to talk more freely about sex and family planning, and persuaded couples to adopt contraceptives.[63] The success of these early music video projects in Mexico, the Philippines and Nigeria led to dozens of similar projects throughout the world. Following are several examples from different regions of the world that demonstrate the power of music to address critical health needs.

UNAIDS and Janoon

On July 1, 2005, the lead singer of one of south Asia's biggest rock bands, the Pakistani group Junoon, agreed to assist UNAIDS in its efforts to reverse the spread of HIV by raising awareness about HIV and AIDS through their music and celebrity status. UNAIDS Pakistan commemorated World AIDS Day that year with the launch of a new music video on AIDS by Salman Ahmed, renowned Pakistani rock star who was recently appointed UNAIDS Global Goodwill Ambassador.

Ahmed, the founder of Junoon, decided to use a music video format to increase HIV/AIDS awareness. The result was a music video entitled Al Vida, which depicts the struggle of a woman living with HIV, emotionally battling against stigma and discrimination as she seeks to access anti-retroviral treatment.[64] The music video, released in Karachi in December of 2005, was made possible through the financial assistance from the Swiss Agency for

Development and Cooperation and with the collaboration of Family Health International. Federal and provincial government officials, diplomats, and representatives from the media, NGOs and young people, attended a launch ceremony at the Marriot Hotel in Karachi. The director of the music video, Ms. Ruhi Hamid, is a renowned director in the field of social and human rights issues. Her work includes documentaries on people living with HIV and AIDS (Living Positively), life after the tsunami (At the Epicenter), Muslims in America post 9/11 (This is my country too) and the softer and moderate image of Islam (The Rock Star & the Mullahs).

Bollywood Music Video for Women at Risk

In India, government campaigns for HIV/AIDS prevention still commonly target "high-risk" populations, such as commercial sex workers, men who have sex with men (MSM), and intravenous drug users, but married women among the general population also are greatly at risk. In 2012, India was home to the second-largest AIDS epidemic in the world (after Africa), with more than 2.4 million people living with the disease and the number of HIV-infected women rising fast.[65] While the prevailing notion is that the majority of HIV-positive women are commercial sex workers, statistics show that they comprise only around one per cent of the total of those who are HIV-positive. The prevailing gender norms in Indian society put many married women at risk for HIV. The majority of women infected are married women whose husbands or primary sexual partners are engaging in high-risk sexual behavior outside marriage and are, in effect, "bringing home" the virus.

The Economist magazine predicts that women will soon be a majority of those infected by HIV/AIDS the world over, with male chauvinism largely to blame. Smita Jain reported that women are more vulnerable epidemiologically, biologically and socially to contracting HIV/AIDS; and that young women are nearly 2.5 times more likely to contract HIV than their male counterparts.[66]

In a society where discussion of sex is largely taboo, women have only limited access to reliable information about HIV/AIDS. "Far too many women do not know how AIDS is spread," notes Irfan Khan of the Naz Foundation. "There need to be more spaces where women and girls can access information about HIV/AIDS, and also engage in open discussions on sexual health and sexuality."[67] Government campaigns still mainly target traditionally stigmatized "high-risk" populations: sex workers, men who have sex with men (MSM), intravenous drug users and migrant populations. Yet the reality is that the new face of AIDS is that of a young, married woman, who may live in a home near you.

In order to address this issue, the Bollywood community produced *Maati*, a beautifully crafted music video that describes the love story of a happily married couple, enacted by celebrities Mandira Bedi and Samir Soni. The award-winning lyricist Prasoon Joshi wrote the theme song of the video and Arjun Bali of Red Ice Films directed the work. The video also features the dramatic voice of Shubha Mudgal. A first impression of the music video causes most audiences to categorize it as an engaging Bollywood Indi-pop single, but the video's powerful message makes it quite different than the common music video fare. Married men are challenged with the following question: Are you the kind of man who wouldn't use a condom for the safety of your wife, putting her at risk for HIV/AIDS?

Maati is actually part of a broader multi-media campaign sponsored by human rights group Breakthrough in response to the growing risk faced by young and married women. The overall campaign, entitled "What Kind of Man Are You?" sought to promote dialogue and equality within marriage and encourage condom use among married men. "The purpose of the campaign is not to place the blame on men," explained assistant director Alika Khosla, "but simply to sensitize them about the issues that women face and ask them to sit up and think about the needs of a woman."[68]

While men usually contract the disease by engaging in high-risk sexual behavior, Indian women, who rarely are sexually active before marriage, often encounter their biggest risk of contracting HIV after they are married, with nearly four-fifths of new infections being amongst married women. Indian women who do become HIV-positive, often face violence, stigma and abandonment by their families and societies. Jain interviewed two such women, Meena and Usha, whose stories she found to be all too common. Meena's husband threw her out of the house after she shared her HIV status, which she had discovered during a pregnancy-related checkup. Rather than getting tested himself to see his own status, her husband placed the entire blame of the infection on Meena and abandoned her along with their three children. He filed for a divorce from her on the grounds that she was HIV-positive and married another woman. Usha, a 26-year-old married woman, found out her HIV positive status two years ago, as her husband lay dying of tuberculosis. "We sought treatment for months and months and couldn't understand why he wasn't getting better. At a bigger hospital, they confirmed his HIV- positive condition. Immediately after, they tested me."[69]

Usha had only had sexual relations with her husband and was completely unaware of his other sexual partners. Out of fear of possible rejection and blame, she has not told her family members about her condition. Usha explained to Jain:

> "I don't want to burden people with my pains. Due to God's grace, I have not yet had a reason to think about my condition. I work hard every day, with the knowledge that my daughter may study and have a better life. I want to show people that even we can lead happy, positive lives. Women need to know more about AIDS, and myths need to be dispelled. I know that I will never marry again as I do not want to afflict anyone else with the disease. Men need to begin to think the same way."[70]

More music videos like *Maati* will help to stem the growing threat of HIV/AIDS to married women in India and prevent an epidemic of African proportions.

Music Contest in Uganda

The nation of Uganda has also been promoting HIV/AIDS education through popular music for a number of years. In late May of 1995, six young amateur performers leapt onto a high-tech mobile stage in Kampala, Uganda and performed the song, *Ray of Hope*, before 10,000 young Ugandans. The performers were some of the finalists among 237 contestants who entered a contest to find the best campaign song for an AIDS prevention campaign. In June the group, House Lane B, was declared the winner of the first Hits for Hope music contest organized by the Delivery of Improved Services for Health (DISH) project. Their song, *Ray of Hope*, became the theme song for the Safer Sex or AIDS Campaign that was launched that year.[71]

Six months later, *Ray of Hope* became the informal theme song for the IXth International Conference on AIDS and STDs in Africa. A music video was produced and distributed to televisions stations throughout Uganda and East Africa and to video halls in targeted districts of Uganda. Audio cassettes of the most popular songs from the contest also were distributed to radio stations throughout the country. One of their songs, *Through a Child's Eyes*, shares the spiritual struggle and hope of children battling the terrible consequences of AIDS.

Uganda is one of the world's success stories for limiting the spread of HIV/AIDS in Africa. Uganda's policies are credited with helping to reduce the adult HIV-prevalence (the proportion of adults living with HIV) from around 15% in the early 1990s to around 5% in 2001.[72] At the end of 2005, UNAIDS estimates that 6.7% of adults were living with the virus.[73] The Hits for Hope contest was an important part of the highly visible and successful HIV/AIDS prevention campaign for young men and women in Uganda that began in May 1995.

In addition to the music contest, campaign planners produced posters, Straight Talk newsletters in English and three local languages, radio spots, and a weekly radio program for youth, also in English and local languages. Each newsletter addressed youth and sexual responsibility issues in an innovative, exciting, frank and informative manner. The project distributed 247,500 copies of the first issue with strong support from youth, parents, teachers and government representatives.[74]

In April of 1996, the project began broadcasting an entertaining weekly radio program in English, *Luganda and Runyankole*. The program incorporated an ongoing serial drama called *Kafunda Stage*, popular music, and answers to listeners' letters by Dear Auntie (for girls) and Dear Big Brother (for boys). The radio programs and posters were integrated with the music contests, drama contests and tours, video shows, and bicycle rallies. Safer sex bicycle rallies were particularly popular, drawing contestants from "boda bodas," the many young men who use their bicycles as two-wheeled taxis.[75] More than 15,000 people attended the local bicycle rally in Mbarara, which was co-sponsored by Coca-Cola. In

Masaka district, a school drama entitled *The Lifesaver* was performed for more than 4,000 secondary school students and drew such high praise from district officials that the script was translated into Luganda and distributed to primary schools as well.[76]

The campaign message and media strategy, developed as a collaborative effort of District Health Educators, representatives from the Health Education Division of the Ministry of Health, various non-governmental organizations, The Johns Hopkins University Center for Communication Programs directed the effort with financial support from the United States Agency for International Development.

In an August 1995 survey of 1,723 youth in seven targeted districts of Uganda, 40% of in-school youth and 31% of out-of-school youth had heard about the first Hits for Hope concerts and, of those, 54% had attended. Males were somewhat more likely than females to attend the concerts (38% vs. 33%), an important fact since the intended audience was primarily young men.[77] The Delivery of Improved Services for Health (DISH) HIV/AIDS prevention campaign has drawn wide acclaim, becoming a model for other nations.

In summary, music is one of the most powerful forms of persuasive influence known to man. Music has played an integral role in promoting social values, beliefs and practices and has been used for many centuries to promote social change. More recently, music has been combined with visual images to address many critical health issues throughout the world and rally people to fight poverty, hunger, ethnic strife, violence, and the spread of HIV/AIDS. In the next chapter we will explore the world of film as another powerful source of learning and social change.

Discussion Questions

1. Which performing artist has influence you the most and why? Please explain.
2. Name a 21st century recording artist that you believe has had one of the greatest positive influences on young teenagers and explain the influence.
3. Since the outbreak of COVID-19, what have performing artists been doing to make up for the lost face-to-face interaction with their fans through their live performances?
4. Do you think most performing artists are aware of the great amount of influence they have on the values, beliefs and behaviors of their fans? Please explain.

Chapter 10
Teaching through Film and Video

Despite the rapid global expansion of television, personal computers and the Internet, feature films and videos remain some of the most popular modes of entertainment in both developed and underdeveloped countries. Driven by a focus on profits, commercial feature films rarely promote educational- development themes in a conscious manner. Educational messages are usually a by-product of a film's entertainment appeal. Some notable examples include *Cry Freedom* about Apartheid in South Africa, *Gorillas in the Mist* about preserving the environment, *Mississippi Burning* about the civil rights movement in the South, *Children of a Lesser God* about physically disabled people, *Schindler's List* about the Holocaust, *Philadelphia* about AIDS in the workplace, *Hotel Rwanda* about genocide in Rwanda, *Blood Diamond*, about child soldiers and the exploitative diamond trade in West Africa, and *Amazing Grace* about the abolition of the slave trade in the British empire.

Long before the blockbuster Hollywood films of the late 20th century, entertainment films were recognized as important sources of learning. The strategic use of entertainment films to promote moral education or raise social consciousness has an extensive history. Even in the silent film era film was a mass influence tool to raise consciousness of social issues. Consider the 41-minute 35 mm film, *The Invaders* (1912), restored by the Library of Congress. The film chronicles one of the many broken treaties between Native American tribes and the U.S. government, focusing on railroad men as they encroached on Native American land. The filmmakers present a surprisingly more accurate portrayal of the way the "white man" handled the follow through of treaties with the Indians, a portrayal the U.S. government would like to be swept under a rug and forgotten.

Other great historical film epics have embedded important social messages, including: Carl Dreyer's Joan of Arc, which sculpted a spiritual message while addressing the struggle between the individual and the government; D. W. Griffith's *Intolerance*, which addressed the evil of the idea of cultural superiority; Thomas Ince's *Civilization*, a powerful anti-war film; Frank Capra's *It's a Wonderful Life*, which makes a strong statement against suicide; Edward Dmytryk's *Crossfire*, which exposed anti-Semitism and bigotry; and John Grierson's socially conscious documentaries.

Interest in how films affect mass audiences grew during the 1930s and 1940s. Between 1929-1932, the Payne Fund studies were organized by the Motion Picture Research Council, which was working on the development of a national policy for motion pictures, especially concerning children. A series of 13 studies was conducted to explore film content, audience characteristics, and the influence of film on children.[1] Results of these studies showed that films could effectively create emotional responses, foster learning, change attitudes, and influence the behavior of children. At the time of the research, information sources were limited, and the movies were still a novelty. The experience of sitting in the movie theater activated multiple senses unlike radio or print publications, the common media at that time. In the period between the first and second would wars, there also was a fear of the power of mass media to manipulate people. The public was highly aware of the potential of media for propaganda and also was concerned about the media's ability to erode moral standards. Children, who often attended movies without the supervision of parents or other adults, were seen at risk from the influences of this powerful medium. The general public was still relatively unfamiliar with film technology and its potential effects.

The methodology for each of the Payne Fund studies varied based on the specific research question being addressed. Qualitative analysis of the movies was used to determine the categories of movie content. Census and survey data were used to analyze audiences attending these movies. Effects were measured using experimental design, questionnaires, case studies and personal interviews. Emotional stimulation was measured using laboratory techniques.

Based on audience research in more than fifty Ohio communities, researchers found that children attended the movies more frequently than adults, and from 1929-1930, children went to the movies on average of once a week. The film research also indicated that children acquired and retained a lot of information while they were being entertained. In addition to learning, children's attitudes concerning ethnic, racial and social issues were changed by watching films. Emotions also were stimulated, especially those related to fear and tension. Health effects were measured by examining the sleep patterns of children after watching movies, and certain movies disturbed healthy sleep. Children who attended movies regularly were found to behave poorly in school compared to those who attended less frequently. Children imitated favorable behavior they saw in movies, but movies also appeared to play a direct role in delinquent careers. Overall, researchers found that movies influenced both children's attitudes and behaviors and are moderated by the social background and personality of movie viewers.[2] These effects were cumulative and persistent over time.

During this same time period national governments became very interested in the potential influence of popular films. Lenin was among the first political leaders to declare film and mass media as important instruments for social policy and education in the years following the 1917 Russian Revolution. In 1927 the BBC was created by Royal charter in the United Kingdom to "educate and enlighten" the public. The 1934 Communications Act of the United States mandated that radio (and eventually television) broadcasters should provide programs "in the public interest."[3] The Canadian Broadcasting Corporation was founded in November of 1936 to both entertainment and diffuse valuable information to its rural communities spread across great distances, particularly to its farmers. Three years later John Grierson founded the National Film Board of Canada to produce dramas and comedies for prosocial purposes.[4]

Hitler and his propaganda machine made extensive use of film to promote his fascist ideology.[5] Under Hitler's leadership, he appointed Dr. Joseph Goebbels to be Germany's Minister of Propaganda and National Enlightenment. Goebbels controlled film production in Germany during this time and used film to promote pro-Nazi messages. Films released to the public concentrated on certain issues such as the Jews, the greatness of Hitler, and the way of life for a true Nazi, especially children. As World War II approached, the Nazi propaganda machine also portrayed the ill-treatment of Germans who lived in Eastern Europe. Hitler could not have used film as a powerful medium for reaching millions of people without the talents of exceptional filmmakers. Perhaps none were more talented in Germany at that time than Leni Riefenstahl, a famous dancer, actor and up-and-coming film producer and director.[6] Riefenstahl had been in the entertainment business for many years as a multi-talented creative artist whose career blossomed during the 1930s, but she was uninvolved in national politics.

Leni Riefenstahl was one of the most gifted creative artists that Germany has ever produced. She was truly a Renaissance woman, excelling in everything she put her had to do. She was born Helene Amalia Bertha Riefenstahl on August 22, 1902, in Wedding, a sooty workers' district on the industrial edges of Berlin. The population of the city was then two million going on four, with growth so rapid that street maps were obsolete before printers could produce them. A gifted athlete from a young age, there has hardly a sport that Riefenstahl did not passionately master once she embraced it. At the age of five, she learned to swim and became a member of the swimmers' club "Nixe," where she won numerous swimming competitions. She later joined the gymnastics club and became the best among her peers on all apparatus. Her athletic prowess spanned the sports of tennis, roller skating, ice-skating, climbing, skiing, horseback riding, and scuba diving.

Riefenstahl began her artistic career as a dancer and painter. She became so famous after her first dance hat Max Reinhardt engaged her for the Deutsches Theater. Her father, in the plumbing business, opposed her goal to train as a dancer, but she pursued this education anyway at Berlin's Kunstakademie where she studied Russian ballet and, under Mary Wigman, modern dance. Riefenstahl appeared on stage in many European cities as a dancer in the years 1923 through 1926. A knee injury ended her sensational dancing career. Riefenstahl was impressed with the work of film-maker Arnold Fanck, whose "mountain" films presented a mythical struggle between humans and nature. She talked Fanck into giving her a role in one of his films, playing the part of a dancer. Then she went on to star in five more of Fanck's films and became a well-known actress. After staring in *Der heilige Berg* (1926), *Der große Sprung* (1927), *Die weiße Hölle vom Piz Palü* (1929), *Stürme über dem Mont Blanc* (1930), *Der weiße Rausch* (1931), *Das Blaue Licht* (1932) and *SOS Eisberg* (1933), Riefenstahl became well-known.

In 1931, Riefenstahl formed her own production company, Leni Riefenstahl-Produktion. A year later she produced, directed and starred in *Das blaue Licht* (*The Blue Light*). This film was her attempt to work within the "mountain" film genre, but with a woman as the central character and a more romantic presentation. *Das blaue Licht* showcased Riefenstahl's skill in editing and in the technical experimentation that became a hallmark of her work. Hitler corralled Riefenstahl's skill to produce a number of documentary propaganda films for Nazi Germany, including *Sieg des Glaubens* (*Victory of the Faith*) in 1933, *Triumph des Willens* (*Triumph of the Will*) in 1934, *Tag der Freiheit: Unsere Wehrmach* (*Day of Freedom: Our Armed Forces*) in 1935, and *Olympische Spiele* (*Olympia*) in 1936. Riefenstahl started a number of film projects during World War II but none of them were completed and she received no more government assignments for documentaries. In 1944, Leni Riesenstahl married Major Peter Jakob, a dashing Wehrmacht ski instructor and her sole comfort during the end of World War II. Before her marriage, Riesenstahl was believed to have slept with innumerable young men but had avoided falling in love, having been jilted by her ace cameraman, Heinz Schneeberger. Tragically, her husband Jacob proved to be unfaithful and broke her heart. They were divorced in 1946.

Although Riefenstahl was briefly imprinted immediately after the war because of her pro-Nazi contributions, a German court found that she had not been actively a Nazi and cleared her of Nazi involvement in 1948. Four years later, another German court officially cleared her of any collaboration that could be considered war crimes.

Later in life Riefenstahl turned her focus to photography, eventually achieving a world renown status as a photographer. In the Nuba people of southern Sudan, Riefenstahl found opportunities to explore visually the beauty of the human body. Photos taken during her stay with the Nuba were published in major print news magazines such as Stern, *The Sunday Times Magazine*, *Paris Match*, *L'Europeo*, *Newsweek* and *The Sun*. Her two illustrated books, The Nuba and The Nuba of Kau, earned her further honors and awards. In 1972, the London Times had Riefenstahl photograph the Munich Olympics. But it was in her work in Africa that she achieved new fame.

At the age of 71, Riefenstahl fulfilled a life-long dream and learned scuba diving so could both enjoy the sport and pursue underwater photography. She soon became an outstanding diver and underwater photographer, completing more than 2,000 dives. Diving became her favorite sport which she practiced into her 90s, and her underwater photography resulted in two award-winning illustrated books, *The Coral Gardens* and *The Wonders Underwater*. At the age of 94, Riefenstahl dived off the coast of Cocos Island in Costa Rica and took pictures of sharks.

In 1987, Leni Riefenstahl published Memoirs, her life story; followed by a documentary of her life five years later entitled, *Die Macht der Bilder*, in which she expressed her opinions about her life and her artistic work. This film too received several international awards, including an Emmy Award in the USA and a special film award given by film critics in Japan. Leni Riefenstahl continued to insist, to her last interview, that art and politics are separate and that what she did was in the world of art. She died on Monday 8, September 2003, in her home in Poecking, Germany, just a few weeks after her 101st birthday.

A couple years after Riefenstahl became an independent film producer, she heard a young leader of the Nazi Party, Adolf Hitler, give an electrifying speech at a Nazi party. Mesmerized by Hitler's dynamic speaking style, Riefenstahl contacted Hitler and asked him if she could make a film of a major Nazi rally. Hitler obliged, resulting in the 1933 documentary film, *Sieg des Glaubens* (*Victory of the Faith*). The film was later destroyed and in her later years Riefenstahl described the film as having little artistic value. Leni Riefenstahl's next film, *Triumph des Willens* (*Triumph of the Will*), gave her an international reputation as a filmmaker. This documentary of the 1934 Nazi Party convention in

Nuremburg (Nürnberg) is regarded as the best propaganda film ever made. Riefenstahl disliked the term propaganda and referred to this work a documentary film.

Despite her denials that *Triumph des Willens* was anything but a work of art, Riefenstahl later admitted in a book she collaborated on with a ghostwriter about the making of the film, *Hinter den Kulissen des Reichsparteitag*, that she helped to plan the Nuremberg rally as a staged event that could be properly filmed.[7] Film critics such as Richard Meran Barsam and others described *Triumph des Willens* as cinematically dazzling but ideologically vicious, portraying Hitler almost divinely as a larger-than-life figure glorified by the German people.[8] Other critics less judgmental of Riefenstahl such as David B. Hinton noted that Riefenstahl's skillful use of the telephoto lens captured genuine emotions through the facial expressions of those attending the rally, enabling her to record the fanaticism already present in the hearts of people.[9] The film is technically brilliant, especially in the editing, and the result is a documentary more aesthetic than literal. The film glorifies the German people, especially those who look Aryan, and invigorates patriotic and nationalistic emotions in its images, music, and structure.

Triumph des Willens showed very little of the German armed forces; but Riefenstahl's next work a year later, *Tag der Freiheit: Unsere Wehrmach* (*Day of Freedom: Our Armed Forces*), featured the German army.

In 1936, Germany hosted the World Olympics, and Hitler once again called on Riefenstahl to film the event. Giving her much latitude to try special techniques — including digging pits next to the pole-vaulting event, for instance, to get a better camera angle — they expected a film that would once again show the glory of Germany. However, Riefenstahl insisted on and received an agreement to give her much freedom in making the film. This enabled her to resist Goebbel's advice to diminish the emphasis on the African American athlete, Jesse Owens. Riefenstahl managed to give Owens a considerable amount of screen time though his strong presence worked against the prejudicial pro-Aryan Nazi position. The resulting two-part film, *Olympische Spiele* (*Olympia*), won acclaim for its technical accomplishments and artistic merit and criticism for its "Nazi aesthetic."[10] The film received the highest film awards: a gold medal in Paris in 1937, recognition in Venice a year later as the world's best film, the Olympic Award (a gold medal and diploma) by the International Olympic Committee in 1939, and in 1956 its recognition as one of the world's best ten films.[11]

Throughout her amazing career, Riefenstahl always maintained that she was a creative artist and a documentary filmmaker during the Hitler years, not a tool of political propaganda. Nevertheless, Riefenstahl's documentaries certainly promulgated a German nationalism that Hitler was able to manipulate to propel Germany to its own destruction and to orchestrate the murder of millions of innocent civilians throughout Europe. The German film industry clearly demonstrated the tremendous power of employing the entertainment-education concept in film to create social change, in this case, to promote antisocial values and beliefs.

The Films of Frank Capra

While Riefenstahl captured the German imagination, on the other side of the Atlantic, Frank Capra was working his own magic among film audiences in the United States. More than any other filmmaker, Capra motivated Americans to strongly oppose the fascist dictatorships of Hilter, Mussolini, and Hirohito. During the 1930s Capra established himself as one of the most proficient and influential filmmakers in the United States.[12] When the U.S. entered World War II, Capra was pulled into the war effort to produce documentary propaganda films for the American public. Capra's creative work achieved stunning success.

Frank Capra was one of the most influential film directors of the 20th century. He was born Francesco Rosario Capra in May of 1897 in the town of Bisacquino in Palermo Provincia, Sicily, Italy. In 1903, he moved to the United States with his father Salvatore, his mother Rosaria Nicolosi, and his siblings Giuseppa, Giuseppe, and Antonia. His oldest brother, Benedetto, had already immigrated to California. The Capra family settled in Los Angeles, where Frank attended school and sold newspapers to support his education. After graduating from Manual Arts High School, Capra worked his way through college, attending the Throop Institute (later renamed the California Institute of Technology). He graduated in 1918 with a B.S. degree in chemical engineering. In October of that same year, he joined the U.S. Army, teaching math to artillery officers. While at the Presidio, he contracted Spanish influenza and was discharged on two weeks before Christmas. In 1920, he became a naturalized American citizen.

After working at various jobs after World War I, Frank began making short films in San Francisco in 1922. He also became an editor and gag writer for Bob Eddy. Capra's first film, *Fultah Fisher's Boarding House*, was a 12-minute black and white silent film comedy that he directed in 1922. Capra maintains that this short feature was his first exposure to film, a job he bluffed his way into out of poverty-stricken desperation. Four years later Capra directed another silent film comedy, *The Strong Man*, a 75-minute silent feature film about a shy young Belgian soldier during World War I who searches for the American girl who wrote him a love letter during the war. Harry Langdon starred in the film, whose success brought Capra his first notoriety as a filmmaker.

He signed a contract with the small "Poverty Row" studio Columbia Pictures led by Harry Cohn and Sam Briskin, and made *That Certain Thing* and Columbia's first sound picture, *The*

Submarine, in 1928. Capra's background in physics made him comfortable with sound when it came as an innovation to motion pictures. Capra`s films in the 1930`s enjoyed great success at the Academy Awards. *It Happened One Night* (1934) was the first film to win all five top Oscars, Best Picture, Best Director, Best Actor, Best Actress and Best Screenplay. Two years later Capra won his second Best Director Oscar for *Mr. Deeds Goes to Town* (1936), and in 1938, he won his third Best Director Oscar in just five years for *You Can't Take It with You* (1938), which also won Best Picture. Capra was a major creative force behind other highly popular films, including the classics *It's a Wonderful Life* and *Mr. Smith Goes to Washington*.

Between 1942 and 1945, Capra directed or co-directed eleven war documentaries including *Prelude to War* (1942), *The Nazis Strike* (1942), *The Battle of Britain* (1943), Divide and Conquer (1943), *Know Your Enemy Japan* (1945), *Tunisian Victory* (1945) and *Two Down and One to Go* (1945). His Academy Award-winning documentary series, *Why We Fight*, which includes seven of these films, is widely considered a masterpiece of propaganda. Capra was faced with the task of convincing an isolationist nation to enter the war, desegregate the troops, and ally with the Russians, among other things. In 1982 he was awarded the American Film Institute's Life Achievement Award. Lucille died in 1984 and Frank Capra suffered a stroke in 1985 and remained in poor health until he died of a heart attack in his sleep on September 3, 1991 at La Quinta, California.

How Frank Capra Educated Film Audiences

In Capra's first war propaganda film, *Prelude to War* (1942), he sought to convince American troops of the necessity of combating the Axis Powers during World War II. Putting aside the arguments as to why the U.S. should or should not be involved in the war, the film depicted World War II in black and white terms, as summarized by Henry Wallace: "This is a fight between a free world and a slave world" pictorialized with the "free world" of the Allies as a white planet and the "slave world" of the Axis Powers as a black planet.[13]

Capra examined the differences between democratic and fascist states, using footage from Axis propaganda films including *Triumph of the Will*, but with different narration designed to support the Allied cause. The film shows how the Nazis smashed opposing political parties and labor unions and how they persecuted Christians, depicting Hitler as an antichrist figure who sought worship from German schoolchildren and who sought total world conquest.

In Capra's second propaganda film, *The Nazis Strike* (1942), he introduced Germany as a nation whose aggressive ambitions began in 1863 with Otto von Bismarck. He then showed the German political strategy of "softening-up" Western democracies through fascist organizations such as the Belgian Rexists, the Sudeten German National Socialist Party of Konrad Henlein, the British Union of Fascists and the German-American Bund. Parallel with these political efforts, Capra showed how the Nazis implemented a deceptive plan of enormous rearmament, culminating with the Blitzkrieg invasion of Poland, who were helpless against the Nazi war machine and who suffered widespread Nazi atrocities following their defeat.

Divide and Conquer (1943) was the third film of Capra's *Why We Fight* propaganda film series. The film shows the Nazi conquest of Western Europe in 1940, highlighting Hitler's treachery towards the small neutral countries of Europe by using Hitler's own words – to Denmark: "We have concluded a non-aggression pact with Denmark" – to Norway: "Germany never had any quarrel with the Northern States and has none today" – to the Netherlands: "The new Reich has always endeavored to maintain the traditional friendship with Holland" – and to Belgium: "The Reich has put forth no claim which may in any way be regarded as a threat to Belgium". These quotes are repeated after the conquest of each of these countries.

The film then moves on to the conquest of France. In order to avoid depicting France in a negative light to American audiences, the film begins in 1914 at the Battle of the Marne, showing French heroism, then goes on to describe the defensive orientation of 1930s France, exemplified by the Maginot Line. Capra paid special attention to Nazi atrocities such as the bombing of Rotterdam and Nazi attacks on villages and small towns and even a Belgian school, designed to choke roads with refugees and thus impede the Allied troop movements.

The Battle of Britain (1943), the fourth film in the *Why we Fight* series, begins after Hitler's conquest of Western Europe. Capra shows the Nazis massive air assault on the British Isles and the heroic deeds of the Royal Air Force (RAF), outnumbered six to one by the German Luftwaffe. Capra embellishes the deeds of the RAF during the four-month battle, claiming that they fought 200 dogfights in the first thirty minutes of the battle alone and that by the end of the first month they had destroyed 900 German planes.[14] Nevertheless, the success of the British defenses forced the Germans to change strategies, switching to more frightening night raids that terrorized London. Despite the onslaught, Capra shows how the courageous resolve of the British people won the day, defeating a superior German force and forcing Hitler to cancel Operation Sealion, his plan to invade Britain.

The Battle of Russia (1943) was Capra's fifth film in the series and the longest among the seven films. Hitler's attempt to conquer Russia is presented in a way to give a positive impression of the Soviet Union to the American audience. The film highlight's Russia's ethnic diversity and reminds Americans of popular elements of Russian culture such as the musical compositions of Tchaikovsky and Leo Tolstoy's classic, War and Peace. Communism is never mentioned at any point in the film.

The Battle of China (1944), the sixth film of the series, shows the four-step plan for the Japanese conquest of China. The film shows the occupation of Manchuria for raw materials, the absorption of China for manpower, a triumphant sweep to the south to seize the riches of the Indies, and the eastward move to crush the United States. Capra pays special attention to Japanese atrocities such as the bombing of Shanghai and the Nanking Massacre. Although the Chinese communists are never explicitly mentioned, they are implicitly acknowledged with a discussion of Chinese guerrilla warfare behind the Japanese lines.

The final film of Capra's *Why we Fight* series was *War Comes to America* (1945). The film begins by celebrating the American values of liberty and freedom that are threatened by the aggressive forces of Germany and Japan. The film examines how American public opinion gradually changed from one of isolationism to one of support for the Allied cause, and demonstrated by changes in a series of Gallup polls.[15] Capra also exposed Hitler's policy of softening up future targets with political sympathizers, showing one surreal Nazi rally at Madison Square Garden, where paintings of George Washington hung alongside the swastika. Capra shows how an Axis victory in Europe and Asia would leave the Unites States alone and virtually surrounded by enemies ten times stronger than America. The film ends with the Japanese attack on Pearl Harbor, showing the duplicity of Japanese diplomats negotiating in Washington, DC, while the surprise attack was taking place in Hawaii.

Yale University social scientists Carl Hovland, Irving Janis, Harold Kelley, and others developed a substantial body of theoretical work through their study of the effects of Capra's *Why We Fight* series.[16] What the filmmakers in both Germany and the U.S. and the social scientists at Yale concluded was that movies could be a powerful form of entertainment-education. Although the documentary film genre does not have the entertainment value as dramatic film fiction, mass audiences of World War II films still learned and were persuaded as they were being entertained.

Feature Films and Videos for Social Change

Although almost every communication scholar and film professional in the 20th century recognized that films combine elements of entertainment with educational messages, the purposeful use of fictional film narratives to disseminate educational messages did not develop until the decades after World War II. One of the first filmmakers to experiment with the entertainment-education communication strategy was John Riber, an American born in India to missionary parents. Riber acquired his film education in the United States in 1977 but returned to Asia shortly thereafter to make films that would help alleviate some of the suffering he witnessed that he knew was preventable if people understood what to do and what not to do.

Riber's launch into entertainment-education feature films began with *Sonamoni*, a popular film shown in movie theaters throughout Bangladesh in the 1980s and seen by an estimated 20 million people.[17] In *Sonamoni*, Riber told the story of a man named Gafur and his wife Rohima, who were persecuted by a village ruffian and cut off from safe drinking water. Forced to use polluted river water for their family, their baby soon gets dysentery and dehydration threatens the child's life. Fortunately, Gafur learns about oral rehydration therapy (ORT) and saves his child. He then exposes to the community that the villain's cattle had been contaminating their village's drinking water.[18] The film increased knowledge of safe drinking water and dramatically increased the practice of ORT throughout Bangladesh.

Not long after Riber's success in helping parents to save thousands of children in Bangladesh, the AIDS epidemic emerged in the U.S. The son of a well-known entertainer and President of the U.S., Ronald Reagan, Jr., was a professional entertainer at that time and decided to produce a short film that would be both entertaining and educational, disseminating important facts about HIV and AIDS. Reagan produced *AIDS: Changing the Rules*, and distributed it in a video format through video stores and schools, specifically targeting teenagers and young adults. The film utilized humor and short dramatic narratives to captivate audiences, effectively increasing knowledge and concern of HIV/AIDS.[19]

These two examples of the purposeful use of film to fuse entertainment and education has diffused to filmmakers all over the world. In the United States, a few filmmakers sought to systematically utilize the entertainment-education strategy in film during the 1980s.[20] Randall Frederick, a Los Angeles-based producer, produced several entertaining films on the topics of alcoholism, drug dependency, and substance abuse. His films sought to promote awareness and solutions to these critical societal needs.

Another American film producer, Sarah Pillsbury, advocates that Hollywood producers acknowledge the moral messages of their productions.[21] Pillsbury's first short dramatic film, which addressed the plight of those with Downs Syndrome, won an Oscar. One of Pillsbury's controversial films, *River's Edge* (1986), a story with a strong moral message for teenagers despite its R-rated content, was based on the true story of the tragic murder of a teenage girl. Pillsbury's *Eight Men Out* (1988) addressed greed, fame, and peer pressure through its depiction of the Chicago "Black Sox" scandal; and in *Immediate Family* (1989), she addressed the complex issue of adoption.[22]

In *The Tic Code* (1999), Pillsbury told the story of a 10-year-old gifted boy, Miles Caraday, who wanted to be a jazz pianist much to the chagrin of his more classical oriented piano instructor. Miles solicits his mother's help so he can play jazz piano as a regular at a local nightspot, though he is underage to perform where alcohol is served. While there, he teams up with Tyron, a sax superstar. Both come to learn that each suffers from Tourette's Syndrome (thus the film title). The older man has developed mannerisms to cover up his own fallibilities and resents the boy and his mother's acceptance of the disease. Miles and his mother learn the reason for his defensiveness, discovering that Tryron's father has not really accepted his son's odd behavior. Pillsbury hoped to help film audiences to see the beneficial and detrimental responses to debilitating diseases.

During the 1990s, film critics such as Michael Medved, author of *Hollywood versus America* and co-host of PBS's *Sneak Previews*, and Ted Baehr, publisher of a family-oriented film and video review called *MovieGuide*, encouraged Hollywood producers to increase their production of films that promoted moral messages.[23] Recognizing the public demand for more prosocial entertainment, political leaders called for similar actions during the 1990s, including President Bill Clinton and former Senate leader and presidential candidate Bob Dole.

Entertainment-Education Films in Africa

Media have been widely used as a development tool in Africa. In documenting the history of the British and Rhodesian film units following World War II, Kedmon Hungwe explained how development communication was carried out through films in Eastern and Southern Africa.[24] For example, the British established the Central African Film Unit (CAFU) to make films primarily for rural audiences to promote agricultural methods and beneficial health practices. A limited number of their films targeted urban audiences and concerns like road safety. One of the scriptwriters, Denys Brown, thought Africans had a "thirst for knowledge and 'a special ability' to learn and remember visually presented information" and a "highly developed tendency for emulation," making film an ideal medium for Africans.[25]

After creating a number of influential and award-winning entertainment-education films in Asia as discussed earlier, filmmaker John Riber moved to Africa in the late 1980s. During the past 30 years Riber has developed into one of the most accomplished creators of commercially successful entertainment-education films is the world. Riber, who now lives in Tanzania, previously lived and worked as a filmmaker in India and in Zimbabwe, has focused his creative work on developing convincing characters who role model prosocial beliefs and behavior. Encouraged by his initial success in Bangladesh as noted earlier, Riber has produced numerous award-winning dramatic films to address a number of critical social and health-related issues. In addition to promoting oral rehydration therapy, Riber's African films have advocated family planning (*Consequences*, 1988), AIDS prevention (*It's Not Easy*, 1990; and *More Time*, 1994), increased status and rights for women (Neria, 1993), the rejection of western materialism (*Everyone's Child*, 1996), and sexual responsibility (*Yellow Card*, 2000). Each one of these commercially successful films promoted specific educational goals, drew large audiences, and increased the adoption of prosocial health beliefs and behavior.[26]

From 1979-1981, Riber produced five documentary films in India. He then moved to Dhaka, Bangladesh, to direct a media center called the World International Foundation. In Bangladesh, Riber produced several 16mm educational films and videos. He then moved back to Madras, India, where he produced more entertainment education films to promote health and environmental education and behavior change from 1984-1987. During the eight-year period that Riber lived in India, he made films with specific educational goals and objectives. His international recognition followed the success of *Sonamoni* in

Bangladesh. Riber has developed a successful career at producing and directing entertainment-education films in Asia and Africa.

John Riber is perhaps the most experienced creative artist in the world at using the medium of film to produce social change and promote beneficial health practices. Riber was born in south India to missionary parents in 1955. Fascinated with the rich visual imagery of the Indian continent, from a young age he wanted to be a filmmaker. He graduated from Kodaikanal High School in Tamildadu, India, in 1973, and later that year returned to the United States to pursue cinema studies at the University of Iowa. Riber completed his B.A. degree as a film and broadcasting major in 1977 and continued working another two years at the University of Iowa as a lab technician. He also produced several independent films during that time. He then returned to India to make films that would help to alleviate the social and health problems he observed growing up that were due to a lack of knowledge and education.

Many of these films are available through Media for Development International (see www.mfdi.com), a non-profit organization he and his wife Louise developed with his close friends Steve and Sally Smith. MFDI established offices now in Dar es Salaam, Tanzania, where the Ribers lived and in Glenwood Springs, Colorado, where the Smiths lived.

MFDI now stocks about 1,000 VHS videos, over a dozen 16mm films, and a small number of 35mm prints. The videos are available to purchase and the 16mm films can be borrowed for educational purposes. All titles are available in English and many titles are available in several other languages. Most of the titles are available in the VHS PAL and NTSC formats. The SECAM format also is available with special order for some French titles. Prices are set low to cover the reproduction and distribute costs rather than to make profit. MFDI's goal is to distribute its films and videos to the maximum number of people. MFDI is always looking for new titles and adds up to a dozen a year. Proceeds of MFDI films and videos also support the growth of the African cinema industry and generate royalty checks for African filmmakers. Riber and his African filmmaking colleagues also actively work with government agencies and development foundations seeking to improve the quality of life of peoples in developing nations.

Consequences in Zimbabwe

The feature film *Consequences*, a 54-minute fiction drama directed and produced by John Riber, was intended to encourage African adolescents to take precaution to avoid unwanted pregnancies by demonstrating the consequences of such a pregnancy.

Consequences tells the story of Rita, a 16-year old who lives in a high-density urban area in Africa. She is bright, talented, has a steady boyfriend and will soon graduate from secondary school. Rita has plans to go to a university and is very happy about her life until she discovers that she is pregnant. Through Rita's story, *Consequences* offers adolescents insights into the reality of teen pregnancy and urges them to consider either postponing sex or taking precautions to avoid getting pregnant.

More than 3,300 copies of *Consequences* have been distributed since 1988 through a variety of means, including distribution through nongovernmental organizations, television and film distribution companies, mobile van systems, home video sales/rental firms, and official cinema halls. The film is available in English, French, Setswana, Swahili, Shona and Ndebele. *Consequences* has won seven international film awards and continues to be popular with audiences throughout southern Africa. The production budget for the film was $350,000 and it was shot on 16 mm film.

Three major studies were conducted to assess the effects of *Consequences* on audiences.[27] First, telephone surveys and fax letters were used from 1989 through 1992 to measure exposure to the film. Results indicated that 25,000 people in South Africans had seen the film, 39,000 Ethiopians had watched it, and nearly 50,000 people in Burkina Faso had seen the film.

In 1991, interviews, surveys and participant observation of film viewings were conducted in Kenya to evaluate the impact of *Consequences* in educational settings. The Kenyans responded very favorably to the film, finding it to be both highly entertaining and educational. Participants in the study said they understood the message of the film and linked the positive role models in the film with sexual responsibility. Identification with the positive role models in the film was associated with responsible attitudes and intended behavior related to sexuality. The film was believed to have increased the number of people going to family planning clinics and decreased rates of pregnancy in schools.

In 1993, a sample of 34 schools out of 75 who had received a copy of *Consequences* in Zimbabwe agreed to take part in a survey to assess students' responses to the film. Results of these studies indicate that all the schools surveyed had used the film and 85% of these schools had organized discussion groups to openly talk about the sexual responsibility themes in the film. More than 19,000 students had seen the film through the project.

The Yellow Card Campaign

Perhaps more than any other film he has produced, Riber's film *Yellow Card* demonstrates the powerful difference that cultural context can have on the overall influence of an entertainment-education film. One of my doctoral students, Dr. Deborah Buenting, focused her dissertation work on the effects of *Yellow Card* in Nigeria. The film has won numerous awards and has played in theaters in Kenya, Tanzania, Uganda, Zambia and Zimbabwe. The motivation for producing *Yellow Card* actually began after observing the effects of an earlier film. Years before producing *Yellow Card*, Development Through Self Reliance (DSR, the predecessor of Media for Development International), a non-profit media and development organization, produced and distributed a film called *It's Not Easy*. The film told the story of a young African business executive whose life changes when his son is born with the deadly AIDS virus. Just before DSR was about to begin filming *It's Not Easy*, they experienced the wrath of a Zimbabwean government official who attempted to stop their effort to publicly address AIDS as an important health issue. The official denied there were any AIDS cases in his country, and in a Voice of America interview, he called DSR liars for claiming that AIDS was a legitimate concern in Zimbabwe. The official also petitioned the World Health Organization (WHO) to lower its AIDS figures for Zimbabwe. Thousands of dollars were lost and the film was put on hold until it could be shot a few years later in another African country.

Slowly the climate began to change in Africa and many information and education campaigns were launched to fight the spread of HIV/AIDS. In the late 1990s, Pathfinder International, a non-profit organization that works to make family planning and reproductive health information and services available in Africa and other regions, approached Media for Development International (MDFI) about making a feature entertainment-education film for a younger audience. Thus, began the pre-production phase of *Yellow Card*, a film that was specifically targeted at young men to dramatize both the potential reproductive and disease consequences of promiscuity. Additional funding for the film came from the United Kingdom's Department for International Development (DFID), the United States' Agency for International Development (USAID), and the Ford Foundation. British Petroleum, Western Union, United Parcel Service and Air Zimbabwe added additional support.

Pathfinder and MFDI had previously collaborated on *Consequences*, a 54-minute film on teenage pregnancy and responsibility produced in1987. The purpose of both films was to challenge young Africans to adopt responsible attitudes and behavior towards sex. Associate producer Steve Smith explained their collaborative strategy:

> We're just filmmakers, and do what we think will entertain audiences first, and secondly to deliver social messages. Well [sic] both entertainment and education are pretty equal, but we always stress the entertainment side to counterbalance our funders who stress the message side. Pathfinder… understood what works well, and didn't get in our way, trying to get us to deliver a message a minute.[28]

MFDI has a long track record of producing EE films and distributing socially conscious films throughout Africa, with its 2000 annual report citing sales of more than eighty titles. Maintaining a mailing list of some 2,000 names, MFDI was well situated to distribute the film to social development agencies and broadcasting entities.[29] In researching the script for *Yellow Card*, twenty-six discussion groups and one-on-one interviews were conducted with young people throughout Zimbabwe. Young people were queried about their views on sex, morality, school, pregnancy, ambition, relationships, HIV and other moral and social issues. From these taped interviews, producer/director John Riber worked with Andrew Whaley, a Zimbabwean playwright and director whose previous work had centered on social and political struggles.

MFDI hired Hollywood Director of Photography Sandi Sissel, whose credits include *Mr. & Mrs. Smith*, *Master and Commander*, *The Far Side of the World*, and *Salaam Bombay*, a film shot in India that won several awards, including the Golden Camera Award at the Cannes Film Festival in 1988 and a nomination for the Academy Award Best Foreign Language Film in 1989. Shot on 35mm film, *Yellow Card* was MDFI's most ambitious and expensive project to date.

Feature-length *Yellow Card* was very similar to melodrama in that it is centered on relationships, romance and life struggles. It was intentionally emotionally charged so it would be easily understood by the average African youth. It was strategically aimed at young men, stressing their responsibilities in reproductive health burdens that are traditionally carried by women in African culture.

Yellow Card is about a high school soccer star named Tiyane who, despite his low-income beginnings, dreams of one day "making it big" and playing for the famous Manchester United Football Club in Britain. The title of the film was strategically chosen to provide a metaphor for a risky sexual life. A yellow card is cautionary soccer foul used to warn players to stop inappropriate behavior. A player who receives two yellow cards is shown a red card and ejected from the game.

Tiyane, the lead make role in the film and central character, is a good student with a bright future. But his big dreams are cut short when he is forced to deal with the unwanted pregnancy of a one-night stand with his classmate Linda, even after he has become romantically involved with Juliet, a mixed-race girl from an upper-class family. After a failed abortion, Linda abandons the baby on Tiyane's doorstep and leaves town with another man. Tiyane is forced to raise the child despite his dreams of fame and fortune. Writer Whaley explained the story as follows:

> The whole point of this story is that Tiyane ducks and dives away from responsibility. Morally, I guess he's blameworthy. But he's human. And a lot of young people are like that – scared to face the truth. The whole film works its way to that overwhelming moment when he realizes his is isolated by his own lies. He can't go on. He knows he has been wrong, but he must put everything right, however painful it is for him.[30]

A secondary storyline surrounds Tiyane's promiscuous friend Skido, the jokester of the film who is always making people laugh, but who is also promiscuous with young women. Skido falls ill and becomes hospitalized. During an emotional visit, Tiyane learns that his friend has tested positive for HIV and will probably never recover. When Juliet comes to visit Tiyane at his parents' house, she learns of the child and rushes off in anger. The film ends with Tiyane engaged in a soccer match while his friends Skido, Linda and Juliet all listen on radio to his scoring victory. The film ends in a freeze frame of Tiyane playing football and the audience is left to speculate on what eventually happened to Tiyane and the other characters. The ambiguous ending was a strategic decision on the part of the filmmakers. The ambiguous ending was designed to encourage viewers to actively think about and discuss possible implications of the characters' choices and relate them to their own lives.

The *Yellow Card* campaign comprised of several components including the film, support materials a soundtrack CD, a theme song music video, promotional materials, including posters, flyers, and postcards, and a website with background information, photos, bios, e-cards, competitions and a chat room. The website was not a planned part of the *Yellow Card* strategy, but rather a last minute experiment proposed by associate producer Steve Smith as a forum for making promotional information to distributors and film festivals, and for gathering viewer feedback, however limited that might be. MFD had never hosted a website with any of its campaigns before and had not seen the web integrated into any EE project at all, let alone in Africa. No one knew if viewers would log on to the site, participate in chats or send emails to the three major characters, Tiyane, Linda and Juliette. (It was 2000, the same year *Big Brother* in the U.S. and U.K, and *Attachments* in the U.K. began experimenting with the web.) Viewers were invited to log onto the sites to read articles, look at photos and web cams and send emails, in what parasocial researchers would call a deliberate attempt to "create an illusion of interaction."[31]

The film was distributed commercially to cinemas and was broadcast on television. It also was distributed on a grassroots level to development agencies, schools and community groups with an accompanying support video and booklet which were designed to help trained facilitators lead discussion about issues raised in the film such as youth identity, sexuality, teen pregnancy, male responsibility, AIDS, and communication with friends and family. A spokesman for the United Kingdom Department for International Development (DFID) said the innovative training package increased the power of the campaign.

Originally produced in English, the film was translated into French, Portuguese, Swahili, Ndebele, Shona and Pidgin English for wider distribution within Zimbabwe, where it was shot, and other African countries. The budget for promotion and distribution was about equal to the cost of production (about US $900,000), with funds designated for advertising and support materials.

The film premiered in Harare, Zimbabwe in April 2000. It played on all six screens of a six-plex and ran for a record-breaking fourteen weeks. During its first television broadcast in Zimbabwe during Easter weekend in 2001, the audience was estimated at five million. It played in theaters in Zimbabwe, Kenya, Uganda, Zambia and South Africa, as well as Senegal and other French-speaking countries. *Yellow Card* was shown in 750 neighborhood cantinas in Mozambique, where it was also distributed informally on video. It was screened by traveling mobile cinemas in hard-to-reach rural areas and townships in Zimbabwe, Kenya and Nigeria. It aired on national television in Nigeria with the support of UNICEF to an estimated 25 million viewers. Producers planned for 50 million Africans to see the film during the first two years of its release. However, associate producer Steve Smith thought *Yellow Card* was seen by at least 50 million viewers in West Africa alone.[32] These are known distribution facts. However, because of widespread piracy and little to no broadcast and sales data gathering in Africa, the true number of viewers will never be known.

Effects of *Yellow Card*

Yellow Card was nothing less than a cultural phenomenon throughout much of sub-Saharan Africa, having been seen in movie theatres and video cantinas, on television and on videocassette and VCD (video-CD) in many nations since its release in 2000. According to associate producer Steve Smith, it is likely one of the most watched African films of all time.[33] *Yellow Card* also garnered the support of NGOs, local governments, and schools, making it the centerpiece of the most popular African entertainment-education campaigns ever. According to viewer feedback, many teenagers appear to have watched the film multiple times. Despite limited access to computers and the Internet, hundreds of viewers logged onto a forum on the *Yellow Card* website, where they were able to write emails to the characters and express their thoughts about the film. Many *Yellow Card* viewers expressed a strong desire for a sequel film.[34]

One of the NGO's that used *Yellow Card* was Filmaid, an international nonprofit organization which screens films as a strategy to entertain, educate and empower audiences. Filmaid showed *Yellow Card* to an estimated 14,000 residents of refugee camps (filmaid.org). In 2004, Media for Development International founders and *Yellow Card* associate producers Steve and Sally Smith visited the Kakuma refugee camp in northern Kenya. Most of the camps residents, estimated at 80,000, were what is commonly called today the "lost boys of the Sudan." Residents of the camp were able to talk about the main character of *Yellow Card*, Tiyane. The Smith's gave the refugees a new copy of the film because the copy they had was worn out, having been played over and over again. The refugees pleaded with the Smiths to send Tiyane to visit them.

Yellow Card's influence in Mozambique was studied by Ngenge using focus groups.[35] Participants between the ages of ten and twenty-four were picked randomly for selection in the focus groups. *Yellow Card* was being show with many other films in cantinas, including three other prosocial films. Ngenge found the normal fare of these cantinas consisted of Asian Kung Fu movies, American action films, music videos, and some pornography. The cantinas screened the Portuguese-language version of *Yellow Card* (*Cartao Amarelo*) through the efforts of FilmAfrik, a film distributor working to gather and show locally relevant media content throughout Mozambique. Population Services International (PSI), a Washington-based non-profit organization addressing health problems among low-income populations in some seventy countries, help to sponsor *Yellow Card*'s distribution along with other HIV/AIDS prevention films, including *Night Stop, Dancing on the Edge*, and *A Miner's Tale*.

The participants expressed a strong liking for *Yellow Card*, recognizing both its high entertainment appeal and its educational messages. Of the four films Ngenge studied, *Yellow Card* was by far the most popular, with audiences liking the humor and general entertainment value, learning about relationships and "seeing people like themselves." The close identification between audience members and the film that Ngenge found was especially significant since *Yellow Card* was the only film not produced in Mozambique. The researchers were not surprised when one cantina owner said the cultural understanding of *Yellow Card* was much greater than with Asian and white characters portrayed in films he regularly screened at his cantina.

Ngenge noticed that whenever he showed the films in a certain location, many audience members would return to see the film again and again, often in the same day. When power outages made showing *Yellow Card* impossible, he relied on the memories of those who had previously seen the films to advance the focus group discussions. In one discussion group, a nine-year-old boy who had seen *Yellow Card* several months earlier said he could "retell the story as if he was reading the script!"[36] Many other young people also knew the story well and could recount not only the plot but also the educational messages of the film. Focus group participants made comments such as, "It shows the situation of everyone" and "It teaches us about our daily lives, when to play and when to be serious."[37] Even the teenage boys responded positively to *Yellow Card* and the other entertainment-education films.

One important observation made by Ngenge was how freely his focus group participants engaged in discussing "epidimia silenciosa," the silent HIV/AIDS epidemic. When asked how Tiyane and Linda could have avoided the pregnancy, the children and teenagers in the focus groups would mention "Using Jeito," Mozambique's national condom brand. They seemed to feel more comfortable discussing sex and related subjects with their peers after viewing the film. Ngenge concluded that *Yellow Card* was effective in reaching the target audience of adolescent males in Mozambique.

As cited earlier, Debra Buenting conducted an extensive study of the effects of *Yellow Card* in Nigeria for her doctoral dissertation in 2006. First, she conducted a content analysis of approximately 1800 viewer emails that had been sent by *Yellow Card* viewers to the three main characters of the film. Buenting discovered that the *Yellow Card* website had received 1,377,384 hits in the first year of the film's released, between May 2002 and April 2003. Most emails were received from Nigerians following the 2002 broadcast of the film in Nigeria by Africa Independent Television.[38]

Several themes emerged in Buenting's analysis of the emails. Audiences not only loved the film, but also made strong emotional connections with its characters, addressing most of their emails to the characters in the film and not to the names of the actors who played those roles. It was evident to Buenting that film viewers had developed parasocial relationships with the characters of *Yellow Card* by watching it multiple times. Second, Buenting noticed that perceived similarity seemed to enhance the parasocial relationships with the film's characters. The more audience members saw the *Yellow Card* characters as being similar to themselves, the stronger parasocial relationships developed.

Buenting pursued further study of these two processes, parasocial interaction and perceived similarity, in Nigeria, where most of the viewer letter had come from. In 2006, she set up focus groups in Nigeria to watch the film and then discuss it afterwards. Her qualitative study involved 56 Nigerian film viewers between the ages of 16 and 25. In addition to conducting eight one-hour focus groups, Buenting conducted one-on-one in-depth interviews with eight of the focus group participants.

Results of her Nigerian study confirmed her earlier findings. The Nigerian participants were strongly attracted to the *Yellow Card* characters because they perceived them to be similar to themselves. In addition, both attraction and perceived similarity facilitated intense parasocial involvement with the *Yellow Card* characters, leading to a desire to continue the perceived relationships; and more importantly, producing a strong motivation to practice responsible sex, the central educational message of the film.

Buenting's Nigerian study demonstrates that exposure to a film with a clear social responsibility message can be very effective in promoting health behavior change when the film's stars are attractive and perceived to be similar to the audience. Both attraction and perceived similarity facilitate parasocial interaction and eventually identification with the characters of a film, leading to the acceptance of the film's educational message and role modeling of the film's characters.

As a result of the tremendous positive influence that *Yellow Card* has had on audiences throughout Africa, the story line of *Yellow Card* is being developed into a television series to further promote sexual responsibility and reduce the spread of HIV/AIDS. Producers of this new series are also focusing on creating realistic characters with whom audiences can realize perceived similarity, parasocial interaction, and identification.

HIV/AIDS Prevention Films in East Africa

One of the organizations that funds entertainment-education projects is the Henry J. Kaiser Family Foundation. In collaboration with John Riber, the foundation sponsored the production of an HIV/AIDS prevention film called It's not Easy. This is the same film mentioned earlier that the government of Zimbabwe resisted because they did not want to publicly address the problem of AIDS. The objective of the film project was to show HIV-positive people as everyday working people just like everyone else. The film was also designed to clarify the basic facts about HIV/AIDS and to encourage attitudinal changes towards people who are HIV positive. The film encouraged the adoption of safer sexual practices.

It's not Easy was shot on 16 mm film and was 48 minutes in length. It is available in English, French, Luganda, Swahili and siSwati. The film has won seven international awards and nearly 2000 copies of the film have been distributed in a video format. In 1991, AIDSCOM conducted a study of It's not Easy on an American audience to test if a film targeted for audiences of a developing country could be equally effective in the United States.[39] The study showed that the film was effective in providing correct HIV/AIDS knowledge and also increased viewers' intention to change their sexual practices. Although originally intended for a Black African audience, the film was shown to effectively communicate to people from various cultural backgrounds.

The effects of the film were also studied in the nations of Malawi and Zimbabwe. At the time of the study, approximately 20,500 people in Malawi had seen the film and 44 percent of those interviewed in Zimbabwe had seen it on television. Results of the study show that nearly 90 percent of the viewers of It's not Easy could recall the main message of the film and 77 percent of the viewers indicated that they had changed their behavior in some way in response to the message. The study further revealed that 26 percent of the viewers discussed the film with a friend and 23 percent discussed the film with a sexual partner. Receptivity to the lower-risk sexual practices promoted by the film was favorable, with 33 percent of the viewers reporting that they were going to practice monogamy and 15 percent indicating that they would use condoms now as a result of watching the film.[40]

Kenya and Tanzania

Based on the positive experiences in Tanzania and Kenya with the use of radio soap operas to address sexual responsibility issues, the U.S. Department of Defense, through the work of the Naval Health Research Center in San Diego, sponsored the production and dissemination of two HIV/AIDS prevention films for the Tanzanian and Kenyan militaries. The development model for these projects involved seven phases of research and production. In the first phase of the project, a baseline study of attitudes, beliefs, HIV/AIDS prevention knowledge, and sexual practices was conducted to assess the risk level among military personnel. In phase 2, members of the creative team such as the scriptwriter and producer conducted formative research in each country, conducting in-depth interviews among members of the target audience. In phase 3, the film script was written in collaboration with military health officials. Then began the production phase, during which the film was shot and edited and a rough cut was made for focus group testing. In phase 5, the rough cuts of each film were tested in focus groups in each country to solicit feedback to the films before the final edits were made. These focus groups enabled the produces to make modification to the films in phase 6, before they were reproduced and disseminated. In the last phase of the project, pre-test and post-test studies were conducted in each country among military personnel where the films were shown. This last research phase is also referred to as a summative evaluation of the films' effects in each country. The integration of extensive research with production of entertainment-education media is a technique that has been perfected over the years by Soul City in South Africa.

The Tanzanian research and film production project resulted in a 50-minute film titled *AIDS: The Hidden Enemy*. The formative research commenced in the fall of 2001, the film was completed in the fall of 2002, and the summative research was conducted at the end of 2002. The film was a dramatic story about two close friends in the Tanzania military and the committed and casual sexual partners in their lives. One of the men becomes HIV positive and develops AIDS. Not only must he overcome his tragic health prospects, but he also must deal with the intense shame he feels when he has to tell his wife and his parents of his sickness. Embedded in the film is a traditional Maasai story of an ogre, a creature who symbolizes AIDS in the film. The film also concludes with a dramatic epilog by military officers who have lost comrades and loved ones to AIDS and interviews with HIV-positive soldiers. The film was distributed to 300 military bases in Tanzania and implemented into the military's health education programs.

The Kenyan research and film production project were commenced early in 2003 in Kenya and completed by the end of the year, resulting in a 67-minute dramatic film titled, *Red Card: Sammy's Final Match*. This story centers on the life of a star soccer player, Sammy Masumbuko, who plays in the military soccer league in Kenya. Sammy becomes HIV-positive through his promiscuous lifestyle and eventually dies of AIDS during the film. This film also provides an epilog. At the end of the film, the star goalie for Kenya's National soccer team, Francis Onyiso, goes to a VCT center where he is tested on camera for HIV infection, and found to be HIV negative. The film has been seen by 100,000 military personnel in Kenya and is part of the military's comprehensive HIV/AIDS prevention program.

The Tanzanian film, *AIDS: The Hidden Enemy*, increased accurate knowledge of HIV/AIDS, increased awareness of the HIV/AIDS threat, increase discussion of HIV/AIDS prevention with sexual partners, increased condom use and future intention to use condoms, and prompted audiences to seek out more HIV/AIDS-related information through mass media. The strongest effects of the film were in raising awareness and concern of HIV/AIDS and the weakest effects were in changing sexual practices. Had the film viewers been able to watch the film two or three times, they might have been able to identify more strongly with the characters and increase their role-modeling of the risk prevention practices that were advocated. Subsequent focus-group studies, which generated a tremendous amount of discussion, indicated many of the military respondents wanted to watch the film again.

In the Kenyan film, *Red Card: Sammy's Final Match*, viewers belief that they could adopt risk prevention practices such as abstinence, monogamy, and condom use, substantially increased. The researchers concluded that this was a result of focusing on these prevention behaviors during the scriptwriting phase of the project. The researchers were encouraged that their conscious efforts to implement certain theoretical frameworks for entertainment-education proved to be effective in the field.

Both films effectively increased knowledge of HIV/AIDS and concern about the spread of HIV-infection.[41] This finding is consistent with previous studies that show EE health interventions are quite effective in increasing knowledge and raising health concerns. Our results also indicated that knowledge was associated with increasing self-efficacy.

As anticipated, self-efficacy, the belief that one can make a change in his or her own life, was an important variable in these studies. Results show that those with a stronger sense of their ability to protect themselves against HIV/AIDS were more likely to get a blood test and encourage others to get a blood test. In addition, the more film viewers believed they were able to adopt HIV/AIDS prevention behaviors the fewer sexual partners they planned to have in the future.

The advocacy of monogamous relationships among the married and abstinence among the non-married in both films was well received by members of the Tanzanian and Kenyan defense forces. Both governments are cautious about sponsoring "condoms only" messages because they are concerned about the risks associated with this strategy. Many soldiers are still reluctant to use condoms; thus, inconsistency of condom use is still a major problem. In addition, learning how to use condoms properly is a second challenge to overcome. Study respondents did not indicate that they had any difficulty processing the multiple HIV/AIDS prevention messages of the films, which was first, stay monogamous if you are married and practice abstinence if you are not; and second, use condoms as a last means of protection if you decide to engage in high-risk sexual activities.

Results of these two projects demonstrate that a single film intervention can effectively promote HIV/AIDS prevention. Consistent with past studies, dramatic stories communicated through popular media can be an effective means of promoting health education and of motivating people to adopt beneficial health behaviors. However, the moderate attitude and behavior changes documented also demonstrate that a single film intervention is likely to be less influential than a long-running radio or television serial, unless the film is seen over and over again. These studies suggest that entertainment-education health messages are most effective when audience members have time to develop relationships with the characters who role model the positive health-related beliefs and practices.

Overall, these two projects add to the growing body of literature indicating entertainment films can be an effective means of teaching people about HIV/AIDS, raising concern about HIV/AIDS, encouraging more open discussion about HIV/AIDS, and persuading people to stay monogamous, practice abstinence, and use condoms properly and consistently as a means of protection.

Steps for the Future in Southern Africa

Steps for the Future *is among the largest film projects ever to be undertaken in Africa. The goal of the project is to reach people in Southern Africa and around the world with films that challenge people's perceptions about HIV/AIDS, and the stigmatization and denial that accompany the epidemic. By 2006, there were thirty-six films in the series, ranging in length from five to seventy-five minutes and provided in several languages spoken in Southern Africa.*[42] *The series resulted from the collaboration among Southern Africa and international filmmakers, broadcasters, AIDS organizations and people living with HIV/AIDS. The styles and stories of the films are diverse; however, each film features a strong personal narrative that makes the HIV/AIDS issue highly emotional and personal. As a whole, the films depart from the didactic informational approaches of many HIV/AIDS prevention campaigns common in the 1990s. The* Steps for the Future *organization intend for these films "to open up spaces for critical conversations" about HIV/AIDS and to win awards.*[43]

In many countries these films reinforce other HIV/AIDS prevention messages disseminated over other media such as soap operas, animated comics, and plays. In Lesotho, for example, a team of facilitators, most of whom are characters in a *Steps* film and HIV-positive themselves, have been traveling around the country with a mobile cinema unit to show the film and interact with audience members. In Mozambique, trained *Steps* facilitators are receiving support from NGOs to take these films into both urban and rural communities. Facilitators who are either film subjects or trained HIV/AIDS educators have organized screenings and are training community groups in South Africa to set up further sessions using the series. The outreach program has been extended to several other countries in the region, including Malawi, Zimbabwe, Zambia and Namibia.

One of the goals of the *Steps* initiative was to change the image of people who are HIV-positive. Most of the characters in these films are not portrayed as "a marginalized group" but as people who are not defined by their HIV-positive status. Because these film narratives were developed in collaboration with the targeted audiences, these films have an authenticity that elude many other health education productions. Some scholars see the *Steps* initiative as case-study media activism, although real activism does not necessarily take place in the production process but in the screening rooms and discussions that take place after the films are shown. After each film, one of the film subjects comes before the group of viewers in person and shares some of their personal story. Their physical presence before audience members creates a unique dynamic for discussion that provides another dimension of social influence.

One of the keys to the success of the *Steps* initiative is diversity. First, the *Steps* films encompass multiple genres, including documentaries, music videos, and short fictional works. The screening locations for *Steps* films also are diverse, including church halls, clinics, universities, disabled learner's centers, private homes, police stations and hostels. Third, the relationships between film audiences and the subjects of these films who speak with them also are diverse. Sometimes audience members know each other intimately and sometimes they are complete strangers.

Lucinda Englehart, who teaches Visual Anthropology in the Department of Social Anthropology at the University of Cape Town, has studied the *Steps* initiative extensively.[44] Her research shows that the *Steps* film series helps to close the gap of HIV/AIDS as a distant problem by fitting it into the everyday landscape of peoples' lives, dispelling notions that it is something extraordinary or taboo. The open discussion sessions after the film showings allows audience members to learn more about how people actually contracted HIV and how its transmission can be further prevented. Meeting the actual subjects of these films also creates a compassion among audience members that doesn't victimize for those who are infected.

Bollywood Films for HIV/AIDS Prevention in India

One of the many NGOs involved in the fight against HIV/AIDS is Population Services International (PSI). PSI utilizes the entertainment-education approach in its many communication campaigns.[45] Since 1991, PSI has been working in the red-light area of Mumbai (formerly called the city of Bombay) to reduce the spread of HIV/AIDS. PSI has a drop-in center in the area and supports social workers for outreach efforts to address the area's population.

In the late 1990s, PSI decided to use popular Bollywood celebrities to promote HIV/AIDS awareness and prevention. Cinema halls in the area were booked for popular Hindi films to be shown for free. Entertaining skits on HIV/AIDS were performed during the interval between films, and popular film stars addressed the audiences with sexual responsibility messages. The objectives of the communication campaign were to increase awareness and knowledge about HIV/AIDS, and secondly, to increase motivation for condom use. The campaign was targeted to commercial sex workers (CSWs), madams, pimps and customers of CSWs.

In addition to the outreach in film theaters, a photographic mobile exhibition was created and displayed in red light areas, railway stations, factories, low cost housing societies and crowded markets and streets. Also, a "record dance" event on multiple stages was put at crossroads in the red-light area and professional dancers performed popular dance sequences from films to audiences exceeding 1,000. Between sequences the master of ceremonies would give HIV/AIDS prevention messages and distribute information booklets.

Simultaneously, an AIDS film titled *Bodyguard* made in the popular Hindi film format was played in neighborhood bars that the men frequented before going to the brothels. The film spoke of the importance of condom use and demonstrated the correct way to use a condom. *Bodyguard* won the Best Abby for best public service film 1997 at the Bombay Ad

Club awards. The film also was designated as one of the best five films in India during a two-year period by the Standing Committee on Advertising. Other awareness raising activities included street fairs with games and contests with HIV/AIDS prevention messages and audiotapes that were played by the street side cigarette shops.

Other media and arts used in the campaign included street plays and tamashas ("commotions" in Hindi), posters, fliers, free samples, leaflets on AIDS, taxi stickers, flip charts and puppet and mimicry shows.

A pre-campaign knowledge, attitudes, beliefs and practices (KABP) study indicated that awareness of HIV/AIDS was extremely low, and that reaching clients was critical. Also, because the population in this area was mostly illiterate, with little or no access to the media other than, occasionally, cinema, conventional media were not generally suitable. Results show the campaign was effective in reaching its intended audience.[46]

Senorita Extraviada, Missing Young Women

The 74-minute Mexican human rights film, *Senorita Extraviada, Missing Young Women*, tells the haunting story of the more than 350 kidnapped, raped and murdered young women of Juárez, Mexico. The film is visually poetic and yet unflinching in its gaze of this critical social issue. The film's director, Lordes Portillo, provides a compelling investigation of the layers of complicity that have allowed for the brutal murders of women living along the Mexico-U.S. border. The film exposes the hidden story of the grossly underreported human rights abuses and violence against women in the midst of Juárez's international mystique and high-profile job market. Based on the testimonies of the families of these murdered women, the film shows that if the climate of violence and impunity continues to grow, no women in the region will be safe until justice is served.

Senorita Extraviada, Missing Young Woman has won numerous awards, including a Special Jury Prize at the Sundance Film Festival, an Ariel award from the Academy of Cinematographic Arts and Sciences in Mexico for Best Mexican Documentary, the Nestor Almendros Prize from the Human Rights Watch International Film Festival, a Grand Prize Best Documentary award from the Malaga Film Festival, an Audience Award for Best Documentary from Cinequest and from the Festival International de Films De Femmes in Creteil, and a Gold Gandhi Award from the Barcelona Human Rights Film Festival.[47] The film has certainly raised consciousness of the terrible cost in lives of innocent people when authorities do little to stop a known wave of crime.

University Sponsored Entertainment-Education Films & Educational Programs

In the late 1980s, Dan Georgakas, then the editor of Cineaste, predicted that the first film school that would produce entertainment-oriented films with pro-family messages would come from a group of faculty and graduate students at Regent University (formerly CBN University).Since its founding in 1978, Regent University has experimented with the entertainment-education strategy to promote prosocial messages grounded in the Judeo-Christian worldview. For example, Chris Auer, a Regent University alumnus, applied his knowledge of the entertainment-education concept as a writer to create pro-family themes for the *Cosby Show* and as executive producer of *Big Brother Jake*, staring Jake Steinfeld.

Since the late 1980s, Regent University students have produced several films and videos with prosocial educational messages which have won both regional and national awards.[48] Many universities produce prosocial films and videos. The film programs of Stanford and Temple universities have a tradition of producing socially conscious films. Eighty or so universities have been recipients of the Dore Schary competition, an award that recognizes social issue productions. However, the cinema-television-theatre program at Regent University specifically teaches students to experiment with the entertainment-education communication strategy. Everett Rogers, one of the foremost authorities on entertainment-education before his passing in 2003, noted that very few universities specifically teach students the theoretical basis of entertainment-education. There are many examples of Regent University films and videos that exemplify the use of entertainment to address critical social issues and promote specific prosocial values and practices. I will discuss several of these productions.

Forgiving an Alcohol Parent One difficult social problem that entertainment-education can address effectively is the long-term effects of abusive relationships, particularly those inflicted upon children. *Lighthouse* (1988), directed by Rick Settoon, tackles this problem by relating the story of a grown man's efforts to come to terms with a childhood of physical abuse by his alcoholic father. This film began Regent University's experimentation with prosocial filmmaking.

The backstory to *Lighthouse* concerns the childhood of Alan Kemp, Jr., who at an early age ran away from home, ending all contact with his family. While outwardly pursuing a successful career as a lawyer, inwardly he struggled with self-acceptance and inner peace. His inability to forgive his father, who worked as a lightman at a coastal lighthouse, threatened the quality and longevity of all his interpersonal relationships. For example, Kemp could not fully give himself emotionally to his fiancé. His active and continuing hatred of his father denied him of any genuine contentment.

Early in the film, after learning of his father's death, Kemp travels to his boyhood home to attend his father's funeral and settle his estate. Upon arriving, he discovers that his father, of Caucasian ethnicity, had at a late age experienced a religious conversion and had joined a predominantly African American Pentecostal church. Even more shocking to Kemp, his father had quit abusing alcohol and had legally adopted an African American teenage orphan named Lewis. Initially, Kemp could not believe his father had mended his ways nor could he tolerate accepting an adopted brother. In one scene Kemp explodes in anger at a friend of his father's, shouting, "No! He couldn't behave that way with me. He got some outsider to be decent to. Not his own family. Not us!"

The dramatic resolution of *Lighthouse* comes when Kemp heroically rescues his stepbrother, Lewis, from a capsized boat during a storm at sea. The emotional distance between them is broken and in accepting Lewis as his brother, Kemp accepts the transformation and legacy of his father. Kemp comes to realize that individual moral change is possible and that hate is self-destructive. The primary prosocial message of *Lighthouse* is that hatred of others is ultimately self-defeating; it hurts the one doing the hating more than the object of hatred. Even when the hate is caused by a legitimate grievance for a grave wrong done, the film attempts to show how hatred erodes the moral ground from under the victim.

Accepting Special Needs Children Turtle Races (1990), directed by Jim Lincoln, was Regent University's next major entertainment-education film. It tells the story of Scott Delancy, a former athlete and trainer of physically and mentally handicapped children for the Special Olympics. Andy (short for Andrea) and her boyfriend Tray are self-absorbed track stars at a local university. Tray in particular shows contempt for the children with whom he is forced to share the track. One day Andy severely hurts a leg when Cary, one of the Special Olympics children, runs onto the track in front of her, causing her to fall. Her resulting injury prohibits her participation in qualifying races for a state track tournament. Andy's coach informs her she might be able to convince the officials to let her qualify later. However, there is a catch. In order for Andy to get her coach to talk to the tournament officials, she must help Scott Delancy train the handicapped children for the Special Olympics.

Andy only helps reluctantly, clearly showing her resentment of being forced into this situation. As time passes, she mellows and begins to enjoy working with the kids. She also begins to feel some romantic attraction for Delancy and becomes progressively disillusioned with her arrogant boyfriend, Tray. However, when her qualifying heat is inadvertently scheduled at the same time as the Special Olympics, she chooses to miss the latter event, even though this greatly disappoints the children who had counted on her presence for emotional support. Andy ultimately discovers that getting what she thought she wanted (winning) did not bring her satisfaction or contentment. The film closes with Andy making amends with Delancy and returning to the children whose company had become a gift of joy, helping her to realize what is most important in life.

There are several important prosocial messages conveyed by *Turtle Races*. First, the film conveys the value of each person, regardless of their physical or mental limitations, and that all people ought to be treated with respect and dignity. The film consciously draws viewers into a greater and more compassionate understanding of the world of special needs children. A second recurring theme highlights the choice between selfish ambition and unselfish commitment to others in need.

Families Coping with Cancer Coping with the ravages of cancer is a struggle that millions of Americans face each year. It is particularly devastating when children are afflicted with this horrible disease. The stress and pressure can be enormous, shattering some families, yet ironically strengthening others. Student filmmaker Vickie Bronaugh, now a Hollywood producer, decided to tell a story about a family that, rather than being destroyed by such a misfortune, pulled together to fight the disease and strengthen their family and personal relationships.

Partially based on a true story, the film *Crowning Glory* (1992) portrays the struggles and friendship of two teenage sisters when one is abruptly stricken with cancer. The story opens toward the end of summer holidays. Millie, the sister who has been living with cancer for a while now, must face a new round of chemotherapy. As if the pain of the disease weren't enough, she must also face the cogent fear of losing the acceptance of her peers due to her hair loss. The family experiments with hats and wigs as Millie dreads returning to school with massive amounts of her hair falling out daily leaving unsightly bald patches. Finally, one night, unable to bear her mangy appearance any longer, she asks her father to shave her remaining hair. The father reluctantly complies and breaks down in tears when he sees what has become of his "baby girl."

How does *Crowning Glory* promote prosocial values? Millie's adopted Asian sister, Tyne, is overcome with profound feelings of guilt, feeling that as the adopted family member she should have the cancer, not Millie. She also struggles with compassion and empathy for the pain, humiliation and social isolation that Millie feels. In the final scene of the film, Tyne astonishes the entire family when she comes down the stairs on the morning of the first day of school with a shaved head. Realizing that her love for her sister is more important than popularity, being chic or being "cool," she decided to share Millie's social ostracism and participate in some of her suffering. The film ends with the two bald sisters walking toward the school bus hand in hand.

In describing one of the prosocial themes in *Crowning Glory*, Bronaugh referred to the biblical principle of "bearing one another's burdens." She explained that the film is fundamentally about compassion and thinking beyond one's own needs, even if it means sharing the suffering of others. "Let's face it," said Bronaugh, "when we are up against difficult circumstances, two people can face the challenge better than one person alone."

Compassion for People with AIDS One important prosocial value is having compassion for those in need who suffer from disease and mistreatment. This is embodied in the biblical concept of "loving your neighbor as yourself" and not passing moral judgment on how the need arose. Much of society has been ambivalent about helping people with AIDS, partly because moral behavior is often a factor in contracting the disease. The Regent University film *As I Perish* (1993), shot on video, addresses this very destructive attitude by demonstrating that moral behavior compels us to show compassion toward those infected with HIV and to provide help to those in need, regardless of the circumstances that created the need. At the time this film was made, there was still a great reluctance among religious groups in the U.S. to extend compassion toward people with AIDS because of opposition to homosexuality and pre-marital sexual relationships. This cultural context gave the film a more powerful edge, partly because it was made by students from a Christ-centered film school.

As I Perish is the story of a young woman named Brenda, who after contracting AIDS from her live-in boyfriend, was abandoned by him. Brenda's parents morally disapproved of her living out of wedlock with her "good-for-nothing" boyfriend and her father forbid her to "set foot" in their home again. Although the video was completed in 1992, it was initially conceived and written in 1988 when paranoia about the possible spread of the AIDS virus through casual contact was still widespread. Thus, as the video's back story is revealed, we learn that because of the prejudice and ignorance of others, Brenda has lost her job and her apartment.

The story begins when Brenda, afraid to return home to her parents, finds herself living in the streets. Two sisters who own a business near where Brenda was sleeping, Janice and Sheila, notice her shivering in the rain and in obvious distress. The sisters take her in, offer her a meal and eventually offer her a place to stay. Brenda graciously receives the first responses of compassion and friendship since she had contracted HIV. Janice and Sheila provide her shelter and friendship because of their strong religious convictions of helping those in distress. Janice explained to a friend, "although we don't know Brenda, we know her need."

After Brenda's HIV infection becomes known, Janice and Sheila are shocked when their friends refuse to support their decision to shelter an HIV/AIDS victim. One friend is outraged that he ate at their table with Brenda and was not told she was HIV-infected. Likewise, the members of Janice and Sheila's church show paranoia due to their inaccurate belief about the casual spread of the virus. Their pastor, rather than ministering to Brenda and providing moral leadership, asks Janice not to bring her to the church anymore. The sisters are outraged and disheartened and Sheila even begins to think of herself, wanting the problem with Brenda just to go away, so that their lives can return to normal.

Ultimately, through Janice's moral leadership and her refusal to abandon Brenda, even to the point of selling off her assets to pay Brenda's mounting medical bills, the sisters' friends become ashamed of their behavior. The pastor of Janice and Sheila's church resumes his proper role and ministers to Brenda. Even Brenda's parents are reconciled with her when her father asks her forgiveness for how he had treated her. Compassion for Brenda increases as the disease enters its final stages. She dies in a hospital with her friends and pastor beside her. In the final scene the audience is reminded of the words of her doctor:

"No one deserves to enter into eternity alone." The overriding message of *As I Perish* is that the worth of each person calls for others to give compassion and help, regardless of the mistakes another person may have made and regardless of whether one supports the moral decisions another person has made.

Stopping Sexual Abuse Perhaps no other social issue in the United States in the early 21st century is as sinister as the epidemic of sexual abuse. Every year thousands of children are abused within their own homes, while hundreds more are abducted, sold into sexual slavery, and abused. Dozens of these children are murdered by sexual predators. Within the last two decades several major trials concerning abuse at day care facilities and churches have gained nationwide attention. Regent University student Lisa Bernhard, now Lisa DuBois, decided to produce an educational video to help fight the epidemic of child abuse. Bernhard produced and directed *Simon Says, "Go Ahead and Tell"* for the Children's Performance Workshop, a nonprofit organization founded by Regina Marscheider that creates puppet shows to educate children and address important social issues. Bernhard's video not only provides startling facts chronicled by educators, medical doctors, law enforcement and child abuse experts, but it also tells the stories of survivors of sexual abuse and presents an intervention program to stop abuse.

One of the most serious problems is that children do not understand when they have been victimized. Abused children often think they are bad and caused the abuse situation. Thus, usually a great deal of time passes before sexually abused children are able to come forward and report the crime. The psychological stress children experience inhibits them from seeking help. Bernhard's video teaches children that it is all right to "go ahead and tell" someone about the abuse they are experiencing.

Marscheider uses puppets to provide that education. Through the non-threatening use of marionettes, children who might have been abused are encouraged to recognize that they are victims and come forward to get help. The presentations are performed in schools in the presence of a social worker and police officer, who are there to ensure that there is adequate follow-up and investigation.

Bernhard's video carefully trains teachers to help abused children come forward in a nonjudgmental way so that their sense of shame is not heightened. Careful procedures are illustrated to help teachers recognize indicative behavior of abused children and instructs them about how to properly obtain help for the children. The video has been used by educators and law enforcement personnel in the Virginia cities of Norfolk, Virginia Beach, and Chesapeake.

By combining storytelling, interviews, dramatization, and puppetry, *Simon Says, "Go Ahead and Tell"* provides a powerful tool that teaches adults how to use entertainment-education to stop the sexual abuse of children. As Bernhard explains, "the video has been greatly successful in helping to expose and stop the horrible crimes of child abuse."[49]

Johns Hopkins University's School of Public Health

The John Hopkins Bloomberg School of Public Health, as explained earlier, receives millions of dollars of funding annually from USAID to support its Center for Communication Programs (JHU/CCP), which creates and evaluates entertainment-education films and videos around the world. Through the CORE Initiative of USAID, a federal program designed to enhance the response of community and faith-based leaders and institutions to the causes and consequences of the HIV/AIDS epidemic, JHU/CCP partners with local churches and non-profit ministries to use visual media to promote HIV prevention. In 2008, JHU/CCP had field offices in 25 countries of Africa, Asia, Latin America, Eurasia, and the Middle East.[50]

The website for the Center for Communication Programs listed more than 100 awards and citations for their entertainment-education productions from 1984 through 2008, including awards for many short films and videos. These productions are available for use through the M/MC Health Communication Materials Network (HCMN), an international network of professionals specializing in the development and use of health communication materials – pamphlets, posters, video, radio, novelty items, flipcharts, cue cards, training materials, electronic media, etc. HCMN's website, which is linked to CCP's website, also provides a forum for health communication specialists to share ideas, information, and samples of health communication materials with their colleagues. By the end of 2008, more than 100 short entertainment-education films and videos that address a variety of health needs were listed on HCMN's website.

Several media projects at JHU/CCP demonstrate the expertise they have developed in using films and videos to promote healthy beliefs and lifestyles. In September of 2005, *Kaisay Kahoon* (*How Shall I Say It?*), an entertainment-education television drama series supported by the David and Lucille Packard Foundation, began broadcasting in Pakistan. The romantic comedy series dealt with the lives of two siblings, Zain and Natasha, who must negotiate the pressures of adolescence in a modern world amidst the traditional values of their parents and grandparents. The producers of the series collaborated with the Newlywed Counseling Services at Greenstar clinics in Pakistan to help young married people communicate more effectively and make wise choices as they plan their families. In 2007, *Kaisay Kahoon* won a national film award at the New York Film & Video Festival.

Another JHU/CCP sponsored television series is *Tsha Tsha*, an ongoing television drama in South Africa which began broadcasting in 2006, targeted young people to promote HIV/AIDS prevention. Research shows the series increased abstinence and increased faithfulness to a partner.[51] The series was nominated for 16 awards by the South African Broadcasting Corporation.

During the past several years JHU/CCP has continued to produce entertainment-education films and videos throughout the world, despite more restrictive funding from USAID. In

2012 they reported projects in 38 countries dealing with many different health needs, including sexual responsibility, HIV and AIDS prevention, malaria prevention, water safety, influenza protection, and family planning.[52]

The rapid diffusion of communication technology and the Internet will continue to expand the international influence of film and video productions. In the next chapter I will consider the convergence of news, entertainment and politics and how entertainment media are changing the way we learn about the events occurring in our world and how we should govern.

Discussion Questions

1. What feature film has most powerfully influenced your own life and why?
2. In the 21st century, what film do you think has had the greatest effect on promoting better health and fitness?
3. What filmmaker alive today has had the greatest prosocial influence on American society?
4. What social issue or societal need should filmmakers today seek to address through their filmmaking?

Chapter 11
Entertainment, News & Politics

The intersection of entertainment, news and the political process is one of the most important sociopolitical changes that has taken place in democratized nations during the past fifty years. No longer can a political candidate win an elected office without considering the mediated appeal of his or her persona. Two global trends have precipitated the change in how we choose our leaders. First, is the merger of news with entertainment. Second, is the merger of politics with entertainment. Results of these two mergers have important implications on how we learn about the events that are taking place in our communities, nation, and the world; and also influence the electoral process. The confluence of news, politics and entertainment also dictates the kind of leaders who have risen to lead democratic societies. I will discuss each of these trends.

News and Entertainment Culture

Earlier in this book I examined the research that shows how many societies in developed nations have developed into entertainment cultures. I cannot find any one scholar who was the first to coin the term "entertainment culture," but the concept is growing in popularity as entertainment drives the U.S. economy.[1] I define an entertainment culture as one in which the majority of people who live in the culture either produce, distribute or consume entertainment on a daily basis. My definition is based on previous definitions of an information society, defined by Everett Rogers as one in which at least fifty percent of the population is engaged in producing or distributing information.[2] In the last half of the 20th century, many social scientists divided the world into three basic societal structures: (1) agricultural societies, in which at least half the members are involved in the production or distribution of agricultural products; (2) industrial societies, in which at least half the members are involved in the creation and production of manufactured products (manmade rather than grown and cultivated); and (3) information societies, as noted earlier. The U.S. is probably the first nation that transitioned into an information society, which occurred in around the middle of the 20th century. European nations, Japan, Taiwan and other developed nations soon followed. Today there are dozens of nations that are primarily involved in the information production business, which includes all forms of media and communication networks.

The concept of an entertainment culture subsumes the idea of an information society. Although entertainment does provide information, it is much more than information. Entertainment culture is more descriptive of a way of life rather than simply a means to create and exchange information. In his book, *Only Entertainment*, Richard Dryer states that "any entertainment carries assumptions about and attitudes toward the world."[3] An entertainment culture is one in which the driving force of everyday life is entertainment.

Entertainment becomes as much a part of a person's daily existence as food and water. Many scholars like media and entertainment consultant Michael J. Wolf explain how the mega-deals of global entertainment companies have created integrated entertainment industries that reach people with daily messages through multiple media platforms. It is not difficult to see that what we used to view as "information industries" are now really "entertainment industries." Just look at the programming of radio stations, television networks and cable channels – it's predominantly entertainment-oriented programming, sometimes with an educational mix as is common in talk shows. The film industry and the Internet both thrive on the consumption of entertainment. Music, theater and the performing arts are all forms of entertainment. Even print media heavily relies on entertainment to pay for its production expenses and distribution.

The competitive nature of entertainment gives consumers an increasing number of choices for media consumption. Current trends in the entertainment industry lead scholars to predict the entertainment culture that permeates our American society will continue to grow and transform other societies. For good or for bad, our preoccupation with the creation and consumption of entertainment is not going away soon. Elana Shefrin shows how the culture of media entertainment "is being infused with new modes of authorship, production, marketing, and consumption that are characterized by Internet fan clubs, online producer-consumer affiliations, and real-world legal controversies over the proprietary ownership of digital bits of information."[4] Thus our models of cultural production must change to encompass the increasing reality that more and more people are producing entertainment through the creation of their own websites, their online blogs, and their own music, film and video productions. Access to computer-mediated communication has expanded the dissemination of entertainment across all sociocultural and geopolitical boundaries.

News and Entertainment Merger

If entertainment dominates our cultural landscape, then where does the news fit in? It fits in best when it is entertaining. In the United States as well as in many other democratic nations, news and entertainment have been merging for decades. Consider how news is produced. News programs must compete with other programs to gain the viewership of an audience, which means they must have a strong appeal. News programs that fail to gain an adequate audience will not receive enough advertising support to stay on the air or in print. In commercially dominated media industries like the U.S., news programs, newspapers and news magazines must build a stable number of consumers to maintain commercial viability. News anchors who achieve high ratings stay on the air, while those who don't are let go. News itself is produced, packaged and marketed to captivate an audience. News coverage of major events is advertised and packaged like other entertainment programs, with news anchors becoming celebrated personalities during the events.

Although news consumers do expect to be captivated by the news, they also expect to be informed. Achieving the right mix of news and entertainment is difficult. Consider, for example, the hiring of Katie Couric for *CBS News* for $15 million.[5] Couric's hiring was intended to increase the entertainment appeal of the *Evening News*, but six months after her hiring, the ratings had fallen as compared to her predecessor, Bob Schieffer. Couric, not known for her news reporting skills, had a difficult time reaching older viewers. Nonetheless, ABC hired her away to host a syndicated talk show in June of 2011 for $40 million.[6]

News anchors like Couric are expected to develop a following, just like *American Idol* host Ryan Seacrest is expected to keep his fans for the popular FOX television series, despite the frequent rotation of celebrity judges. Seacrest's popular appeal was well-recognized by rival network NBC, who hired him to help host the 2012 summer Olympics in London. CBS continues to try to rebuild its *Evening News* program, anchored by Scott Pelley in 2012, but sustained audience growth is dependent on finding a trusted news anchor with the right entertainment and information appeal.

The blurring boundaries between news and entertainment has produced some movement toward sensationalism in broadcast journalism.[7] News stories that titillate have a higher entertainment value than those that do not. Thus, the personal lives of news subjects often receive expanded attention when the entertainment potential is high. News directors rarely lose their jobs because of too much entertainment content as compared too little entertainment content that results in poor ratings.

The primacy of ratings and readership drives the news business because it is first of all a commercial enterprise. The increasing conglomeration of the media industry works to reinforce the pressure for commercial success.[8] When I published the first edition of this book, I provided examples of these early mergers between news networks and entertainment companies, *ABC World News*, hosted by Charles Gipson from 2006-2009, was the highest rated evening news program in 2007 with 8.1 million viewers and had nearly seven million evening viewers with anchor Diane Sawyer. Who owns the ABC network that produces and broadcasts *ABC World News*? The Disney Company, at the time of this writing, owns ABC. Disney also owns many other television stations that reach a large percentage of US households. Disney owns many popular news and entertainment programs, including *Prime Time Live*, *Nightline*, *20/20*, and *Good Morning America*; it owns ESPN and half of Lifetime Television; it has minority holdings in A&E, the History Channel and E! Then there are its holdings in the Disney Channel, Disney Television, Touchtone Television, Miramax, Touchtone Pictures, all Disney theme parks, Walt Disney Cruise Lines, and many dozens of newspapers, magazines, music labels, book publishers, and a large stake in one of the major search engines on the Internet. The Disney Company is obviously in the entertainment business. Although Disney's corporate leaders will tell you that they never will interfere with the news, they cannot prevent the corporate entertainment culture from influencing the news.

In 2008, *NBC Nightly News* with Brian Williams took over the number one spot for network news broadcasts and averaged between 7.5 million viewers per broadcast in 2013. NBC Universal purchased a majority of shares of Comcast, an entertainment conglomerate, whose holdings at that time included 24 television stations, several television networks, several cable networks, theme parks, film studios and a host of other domestic and foreign media companies as shown in their annual report.[9]

To avoid the appearance of picking on the three major broadcast networks, consider the number one cable news outlet, *Fox News*. Have you ever seen an unattractive news anchor on *Fox News*? Notice how many FOX news on-air anchors look like the models and celebrities who appear on the covers of *GQ* and *Vogue* magazines. FOX news programs seek to entertain with exceptionally attractive people as well as inform with highly educated and intelligent anchors.

News Corp owns *Fox News* and despite its company name, News Corp is not primarily a news company but an entertainment company. News Corp, headed by Rupert Murdoch and his family, is one of the three largest media conglomerates in the world. They own too many entertainment companies to list here and have a large presence on the Internet through its company, Fox Interactive, which included MySpace, RottenTomatoes.com, AmericanIdol.com and FoxSports.com.

Might I add a third distinctive to *Fox News*' moniker – "fair, balanced, and entertaining"? I doubt that it is a coincidence that Greta van Susteren, after leaving her job at *CNN News*, joined the *Fox News* team after plastic surgery and literally provided a "new face" for her new show with Fox, *On the Record*. Greta had been very happy with her decision (both the move to Fox and with her surgery) and her show did well during the years she was at Fox. She certainly increased her "entertainment appeal" with television viewers, resulting in good ratings that have pleased the executives at Fox. Greta was followed by a host of other talented women that anchored very successful Fox news and commentary programs. This is one more example among many of how news and entertainment come together when news programs are owned by entertainment companies.

In December of 2013, I was invited to give some lectures at Ludwig Maximilian University in Munich, Germany, by Dr. Thomas Hanitzsch, Chair of the Department of Communication Studies and Media Research. During my visit, I gave a 90-minute guest lecture to Dr. Thomas Hanitzsch's journalism research class on assessing the role of celebrities in news creation and consumption.

During my presentation, I put up PowerPoint slides of many of the leading news anchors at Fox News. They were large photographs of seven women. I told the students these women were celebrities in the U.S. and I asked the students what they did for a living. Many of the students guessed that these women were models and/or winners of beauty pageants like *Miss America* or *Miss USA*. I then told them they were all leading news anchors of FOX News. The students were taken aback, as they were so impressed by the attractiveness of these women that they did not consider the possibility of theme being news anchors. They then understood the point I was making – news and entertainment had merged in the U.S.

Print news, including newspapers and news magazines, are also owned by entertainment companies. However, even with the influx of entertainment into print news stories, less people are getting their news through print sources, especially young people. In a 2004 study of 100,000 American high school students sponsored by the John S. and James L. Knight Foundation, 57 percent reported using at least one news source daily and 76 percent reported checking into multiple news sources each week.[10] Television and the Internet were the most important news sources for young people, but these findings don't tell the whole story.

Not only have most young people decreased their print news consumption in the 2lst century, but they are also increasingly getting their news from entertainment television programs such as *The Daily Show* with Jon Stewart, found on *Comedy Central*, and the late-night talk shows hosted by Jay Leno and David Letterman.[11] These talk show hosts make it their primary objective to entertain their viewers by using the news for comedy. Today, late night comedy hosts Stephen Colbert, Jimmy Fallon, Jimmy Kimmel, and others are openly political and left of center ideologically, regularly delighting in bashing whatever conservative leaders happen to be in their gaze and often restraining themselves from skewering political liberals who provide just as much fodder for good satire.

The Internet sites that young people frequent often mix news and entertainment, and some of the news is grossly superficial, often inaccurate and commonly politically biased.[12] Thus news consumption among young people today is vastly different than news consumption among young people 25 years ago. Today's news, created within a dominant entertainment culture, is much more of an "entertainment-information" mix; it entertains us as well as informs us.

One result of the growing celebrity culture is the loss of news reporters to celebrity journalism. Famous entertainers are created, marketed, and sold, therefore, the demand for celebrity journalists has increased during the past couple of decades. Newspapers, magazines, and news entertainment television programs have created what Shenk calls the "celebro-journalist," a person who reports celebrity news.[13] The roots of celebrity journalism can be traced to the work of Walter Winchel, the father of the gossip column. The first "interview" of a celebrity is traced by Daniel Boorstin to Horace Greeley's question and answer session with Brigham Young in August of 1959, published verbatim in the *New York Tribune*.[14] Shenk contends that the growth of magazines featuring celebrities such as Andy Warhol's Interview, precursor to *People Magazine*, Jann Wenner's *Rolling Stone*, and Tina Brown's *Vanity Fair*, expanded rapidly during the 1960s and has continued to grow during the past several decades.[15] Many of the most popular magazines and news programs in the U.S. focus on celebrities. The focus on personality rather than substance is affecting many areas of journalism, including coverage of business, politics, and culture. Neimark claims our celebrity culture provides the public with "more and more information about people who are less and less real."[16]

Detailed information about the superficial characteristics of famous people "strips them of the sacred and heroic," claims Neimark, creating an illusory world where fact and fiction about people are nearly inseparable.[17] The cultural backdrop of the post-modern philosophy emanating from many academics and the educated elite reinforces the culture of the celebrity.

Politics and Entertainment

When I used to listen carefully to the news given by Jon Stewart, Bill Maher and David Letterman, it was not difficult to discern a political slant in the news content. It is beyond debate that many of these television hosts dislike, and in some cases, openly despise Republican leaders such as former President George Bush and his administration, except for the fact that the Bush administration provided them with a continual supply of comic material. Of course, today, President Bush has been replaced by President Trump as the target of derision.

Johnny Carson, who hosted *The Tonight Show* with NBC for nearly 30 years and became one of the longest-running television hosts in history, said that he attempted to equally parody Republican and Democrat presidents and stay above taking political sides. Jay Leno stated that he tried to follow that tradition by being politically neutral, but he entertained within a cultural milieu that leans hard to the left ideologically. Few of today's television talk show hosts have such self-control. News, political views and entertainment are all mixed, as on the ABC news entertainment program *The View*, produced by ABC News correspondent Barbara Walters. There is no pretext of any type of politically balanced discussion of the news on *The View*.[18]

Bill Clinton was one of the first political candidates savvy enough to recognize the importance of the role of entertainment media in political campaigns. His frequent appearances on television talk shows, playing his saxophone on *MTV*, and granting many interviews with entertainment news magazines were not simply manifestations of his love for the entertainment world, but revealed his intuitive sense that entertainment media was critical to creating a desirable public persona.

Senator Bob Dole, who ran an ineffective political campaign for the presidency, delighted audiences with his warmth and humor while appearing on the *Late-Night Show* with David Letterman. Viewers wondered what might have become of Dole's campaign if he had done a lot more talk shows and a lot less campaign speeches. Dole simply did not have the entertainment venues to show his good-natured self-deprecating humor, which attracted people to him. Bill Clinton, who did not hold the reputation among news reporters as someone who was fun to travel with, nevertheless knew how to communicate charm through the mass media and took advantage of entertainment venues.

Even before Bill Clinton, the merging of entertainment and politics was very much a part of the U.S. presidency during the Kennedy administration. John F. Kennedy regularly interacted with Hollywood celebrities, sometimes very closely as his friendship with Marilyn Monroe later revealed. Growing up in the Camelot presidency of his father, it should have been no surprise when John F. Kennedy, Jr. launched the political news magazine *George*, which perfectly exemplified the intersection of news, politics and entertainment. The brilliant covers of *George* and provocative articles illustrated how much the entertainment industry and political processes had come together during late 20th century America. JFK, Jr. was probably the least observer of political culture to be surprised that a former president of the Screen Actors Guild, Ronald Reagan, had become a successful two-term president. Neither would JFK, Jr. be surprised by the successful gubernatorial campaigns of former WWF wrestler Jesse Ventura and former body builder and film action star, Arnold Schwarzenegger. Like Bill Clinton, JFK, Jr. understood the critical role that the media's attention on celebrities had on the political process.

In addition to magazines like *George*, *People*, *Entertainment Weekly*, and others, a number of political science scholars have traced the increased influence of celebrities who have been elected to political office, even the Presidency, during the past fifty years.[19] Famous actors, athletes and other celebrities in addition to Reagan, Schwarzenegger, and Ventura have won a variety of political offices. It is now common for former professional athletes, movie stars, musicians and singers, and other entertainment professionals to use their fame to help them win offices in regional, state and national elections.

In addition to running for political office, a number of celebrities seek to influence public policy as lobbyists and spokespersons. In the following chapter we will consider many of the social causes of celebrities, but many of these causes also have political dimensions. For example, consider the ongoing political debate about gun ownership and gun violence in the U.S. The U.S. is one of the most violent societies among western nations in the world, with much of the violence involving the use of a firearm. The entertainment industry is right in the center of this debate, with television programs and films regularly depicting gun violence, rap music featuring gun violence, a host of celebrities calling for stronger laws to restrict gun ownership, and other celebrities such as Charlton Heston and Tom Selleck strongly supporting second Amendment rights to keep and bear arms.

Another good example of a politically charged issue that has generated important political activism among entertainers is stem cell research. The popular term "stem cell research" is actually a generalized description of multiple kinds of research involving the use of different kinds of stem cells. Only one type of stem cell research uses human embryos; yet the American public is generally unaware of these distinctions. When the average American hears that a political candidate "opposes stem cell research," the person does not distinguish between the different kinds of stem cells and assumes the candidate opposes all research with stem cells. Thus, it is very easy to misrepresent the positions of political candidates on this moral issue.

Two celebrities have had a powerful public influence on the stem cell research debate: Christopher Reeve (and his wife Dana) and Michael J. Fox. Both Reeve and Fox were tragically affected by neurological conditions, Reeve through paralysis that resulted from a horse-riding accident and Fox through Parkinson's Disease, conditions that might be improved or even completely overcome through stem cell research. Before their premature deaths, the Reeves campaigned tirelessly to promote every kind of stem cell research, with and without human embryos, even speaking before the U.S. Congress to get all restrictions lifted. Michael J. Fox has done the same, also speaking before the U.S. Senate.

During the 2006 congressional campaigns, Fox campaigned for several candidates of the Democrat Party in states where the Republican candidate opposed the use of live human embryos for stem cell research. Two of these political campaigns involved tight races for a Senate seat, one in Virginia and one in Missouri. Fox even made campaign commercials in which the effects of Parkinson's disease on his physical body was powerfully apparent. Whether by accident or design, the campaign commercials featuring Fox failed to mention that both Republican candidates generally supported stem cell research but only opposed on religious and moral grounds the use of human embryos for research. In both states the elections were extremely close, within a single percentage point of the total vote. In both cases the Democrat candidate won, changing control of the Senate from the Republicans to the Democrats.

No social scientific study has been able to document the effects of Michael J. Fox's campaign ads on these two Senate races. However, given Michael J. Fox's popularity and likeable personality, it is easy to see how his influence could have swayed a very small percentage of voters and changed the outcomes of these elections if he had not been involved. Everyone I know likes Michael J. Fox and wants to see him healed from Parkinson's Disease, just like everyone I know wanted to see Christopher Reeve walk again and his wife Dana overcome breast cancer. The research that I reviewed in an earlier chapter shows that we can develop such a close relationship with the actors we like that they become like close friends or family members to us. Again, the 2006 U.S. Senate victory for the Democrats illustrates the confluence of our entertainment culture and news with our political processes.

Entertainment culture also affects the way in which the news media cover politics in the U.S. Consider the reporting of sex scandals among political candidates. The political campaign of presidential hopeful Gary Hart was virtually destroyed by media reports of his infidelity, which Hart brought on himself by challenging reporters to follow him. As to whether Hart's personal romantic relationships were legitimate campaign news is still debated. However, those reporters who broke the story sold a lot of newspapers and news magazines, not because of the information appeal but because of the entertainment appeal. The same questions were debated regarding the allegations of Jennifer Flowers against Bill Clinton during his campaign. Again, the entertainment value of the Flowers allegations was high. The added entertainment value of such political spectacles brings increase the commercial value of news stories but not necessarily their political value.[20]

When celebrities enter politics and the news media become a part of the entertainment industry, the public image of political leaders becomes more and more susceptible to manipulation. Like celebrities, political figures can cultivate their public image through image handlers and engineered media campaigns that treat voters like fans.[21] Timothy Weiskel refers to the construction of mediated political personas as "the politics of distraction" because important political issues are not receiving the type of scrutiny and media attention that is being devoted to less important characteristics of our political leaders.[22]

One of the results of this distraction is what the news media focus less time on. William Hachtenhas observed that television news in the U.S. has provided less coverage of world affairs while simultaneously exporting increasing amounts of American culture through the worldwide distribution of our entertainment media products.[23] Thus, the American population is becoming more ignorant of world events in comparison to what the world perceives about life in the United States. Hachten also notes that the domestic television networks and news services have devoted less news coverage to the White House, Congress and the Supreme Court in recent years.[24]

Entertainment and Political Commentary

The politics of distraction not only affects our knowledge of the world but also our ability to evaluate the advantages and disadvantages of opposing courses of action that result from political decision making. As an example, let's consider the work of filmmaker and political activist Michael Moore, considered to be one of America's most prominent political leftists. Moore has reached a large number of people through his political documentaries, frequent interviews on prime-time television programs, and bestselling books. Kevin Mattson describes Moore's modus operandi as follows:

> Donning his signature baseball cap and scruffy clothes, Moore plays up his working-class persona as he shuffles into the citadels of power-while the cameras roll-in order to expose the darker side of the American dream. Moore's techniques are not new. He draws on a rich tradition of left-leaning political criticism. Think of Charlie Chaplin's tramp. Chaplin too was born poor, immersed himself in the cultural left of his time (Max Eastman was a close friend), and played the "forgotten man." Closer to Moore's own time, the New Left embraced "guerrilla theater" as a means of confronting power. Consider Abbie Hoffman and his Yippie brethren trying to levitate the Pentagon or throwing dollar bills onto the floor of the New York Stock Exchange to mock capitalist greed. Add to Chaplin and Hoffman the news magazine tradition of Edward R. Murrow and 60 Minutes (muckraking brought to television), mix in a heavy dose of postmodern irony, and you've pretty much got Michael Moore.[25]

What Michael Moore has excelled at is his ability to make political criticism entertaining. Coupled with the trend for young people to get their news from entertainment programs, Moore provides a powerful means for political influence that functions well within our entertainment culture. It is not so important as to whether Moore has his facts right, as long as it is entertaining.

Of course, Michael Moore is not the only one who provides political commentary as he entertains. *Comedy Central* has a plethora of political commentators to join Rosie O'Donnell, Jon Stewart, and others who made it an art form to slice and dice the political leaders and government administrations that they disliked. Not to be outflanked by the political left, Bill O'Reilly teamed up with comedian Dennis Miller, who regularly appeared on O'Reilly's former number one rated cable news program (for more than a decade now), *The O'Reilly Factor*, to provide humorous commentary from a libertarian and more conservative perspective. In a similar vein, comedian Ben Stein has grown into an influential political and social commentator that has challenged the liberal ideological beliefs commonly espoused by the media elite.

Selling Political Candidates through Entertainment

In 1968, Joe MgGinnis wrote a best-selling book about selling political candidates.[26] In his book he suggests that you can sell a presidential candidate using the same methods that you can sell any other product. As I noted earlier with Bob Dole and Bill Clinton, it is fascinating to see how entertainment functions in political campaigns. If there is any one political leader who knew much about the entertainment business it was Ronald Reagan. Reagan entered the world of entertainment as a sports announcer in 1933, a year after he graduated from Eureka College with a BA in economics and sociology. During that time, he learned how to broadcast Chicago Cubs home games based on telegraph reports from Wrigley Field. While attending the Chicago Cubs' spring training camp on Catalina Island in the spring of 1937, he made a screen test for Warner Brothers. The producers liked what they saw and signed Reagan as a contract player on April 20th.

Early that summer, Reagan participated in his first Warner Brothers film, *Love is on the Air*. In February of 1938, his second film, *Sergeant Murphy*, was released. Two years later Reagan starred in what was probably his greatest film, *Knute Rockne – All American*, in which he played the role of football legend George Gipp. If you have not seen that great classic you then watch this short trailer. Late in August of 1945 Reagan signed a multi-million-dollar contract with Warner Brothers and two years later, was elected to his first of five consecutive one-year terms as President of the Screen Actors Guild. In addition to making films, Reagan also appeared on television with the *Nash Airflyte Theatre* and then with the *General Electric Theatre*, amassing 60 television credits.[27]

Reagan's ability to take what he learned in Hollywood and apply it to the world of politics was a key to his political success. Stephen Vaughn explored how Reagan applied his Hollywood experiences to his political life, concluding that Reagan recognized that the Hollywood film industry provided a media base for using movies to influence attitudes about patriotism, national defense, communism, the welfare state, race, sex, and civil liberties.[28]

Ronald Reagan thrived in this environment. During his years in Hollywood from 1937 to 1952, he formed many of the ideas which were later carried into his presidency. Not merely a star, Reagan also became an articulate industry spokesperson and skilled propagandist, playing an important role in the battle to 'capture the minds' of humanity in the struggle against communism. By the time he left Warner Bros. in 1952, Reagan had abandoned his New Deal liberalism and had become a militant anti-communist. Based on hundreds of interviews (including some with Reagan himself), former secret FBI files, and material from more than 150 archival collections, Vaugh's book is among the most comprehensive works on this subject to date, providing incisive analysis of Reagan's formative years in Hollywood.[29]

Although Ronald Reagan exemplifies one of the most influential political leaders in world history who arose out of the entertainment industry, other celebrities in the United States also have used their celebrity appeal to be elected to a variety of public offices. These include actor Fred Thompson, a distinguished U.S. Senator; Academy-award winning actor and director Clint Eastwood, who served as the mayor of Carmel, California; New York Knick's NBA stars Bill Bradley and Jim Bunning, who both served as U.S. Senators, and NBA star Kevin Johnson, who became the Mayor of Sacramento; NFL players Jack Kemp, Jim Ryan, J.C. Watts, and Steve Largent, who all were elected to the U.S. House of Representatives; performing artist and television star Sonny Bono, who also was elected to the U.S. House of Representatives; astronaut John Glenn, who served many terms in the U.S. Senate, and professional wrestler Jesse Ventura, who served as a popular governor in Minnesota. These are only some of the many examples of entertainment professionals who established themselves as influential political leaders. It is no longer unusual for former professional athletes, movie stars, musicians and singers, and other entertainment professionals to run for office in state and national elections. Ironically, Senator Fred Thompson of Tennessee, a professional actor who played the President of the United States twice on film, ran as a presidential candidate in the Republican primaries of 2008.

Turning Celebrity Capital into Political Influence

In order to better understand how celebrity capital is turned into political influence, I will discuss two important case studies: Arnold Schwarzenegger and Lynn Swann. How did an Austrian-born unknown body builder and immigrant to the U.S. become one of the most influential political power brokers in American politics? That question intrigued me when I decided to study the California gubernatorial race that Schwarzenegger won, leading to two terms as governor of the most politically influential state in the U.S.

The November 19th issue of *US News & World Report* in 2007 featured Schwarzenegger on the cover under the title, "America's Best Leaders 2007."[30] It was no small favor when presidential hopeful John McCain received Schwarzenegger's endorsement for the Presidency in January of 2008. Although Schwarzenegger's political influence substantially waned as California's fiscal crisis deepened during his final years in office, Schwarzenegger's rise to political power provides great insight into the characteristics of celebrity influence.

Short-term voter anger cannot explain Schwarzenegger's initial success and rise to become one of the most popular political leaders in the U.S. Not only did Schwarzenegger win the recall election in late 2003 as a novice Republican candidate against several experienced candidates of the Democrat Party, but he also won re-election in November 2006 convincingly, gaining 56% of the vote in a state that votes heavily for Democrats. Since Schwarzenegger had never been elected to public office prior to his run for governor, other factors not directly related to his political experience must have accounted for his dramatic ascension into one of the most powerful governor's seats in the U.S.

Based on two of the theories of involvement discussed earlier, I developed a theoretical framework for assessing Schwarzenegger's political influence. First, I determined the degree to which people became involved with Schwarzenegger through parasocial interaction and identification. This led us to my first research question, which explored to what extent people formed a parasocial relationship with Arnold Schwarzenegger and if that relationship predicted identification with him. My second research question explored the political consequences of involvement with Schwarzenegger. In particular, I predicted that two specific effects of Schwarzenegger's celebrity appeal would help explain the outcome of the California recall election. These two effects were seeking out information about Schwarzenegger's political beliefs and practices and accessing websites to learn more about him.

To conduct this study, I developed and administered a survey questionnaire with one of my colleagues via the Internet, beginning three days before the California recall election on October 7, 2003. The survey was posted as an advertisement on Google's website and was activated when users of Google's search engine entered any of the following words or phrases: Arnold, California election, and Schwarzenegger. All study participants were self-selected and none were paid any remuneration for completing the survey. All participants were anonymous and no names or email addresses were attached to the questionnaires. A total of 497 demographically diverse sample completed the survey during the three-day period. Details concerning our research instrument, measured variables and scales, statistical analysis procedures, and sample characteristics are provided in a research paper that I presented with my colleague Ben Fraser at the National Communication Association's annual conference in New Orleans in 2004.[31]

Results of our study indicated the overall sample was not deeply involved with Schwarzenegger through parasocial interaction and identification.

The research results from our study indicate that although most of the respondents did not become strongly involved with Schwarzenegger through parasocial interaction and identification, those who did wanted to learn more about him, felt that he was politically appealing, believed his celebrity status would win him votes, and were more likely to search the web for stories about him. A subsequent regression analysis confirmed our prediction that those who did exhibit stronger parasocial relationships with Schwarzenegger would more strongly identify with him.

The second part of our study explored the extent to which involvement with Schwarzenegger through parasocial interaction and identification might be associated with political influence. Results of several correlation analyses show that both measures of involvement were positively associated with: (1) learning more about Schwarzenegger's beliefs and political practices, (2) belief in Schwarzenegger's strong political appeal, (3) belief that Schwarzenegger's celebrity status would win him votes, and (4) accessing websites on the Internet to learn more about Schwarzenegger.

Finally, we wanted to know if the political influence that resulted from Schwarzenegger's celebrity appeal would result in actually voting for him. Casting a vote for a celebrity to attain political office is one of the strongest measures of celebrity influence. We predicted that those people in our study with stronger involvement with Schwarzenegger through parasocial interaction and identification would more likely vote for him to become Governor of California. Results from two T-tests supported our prediction. Those with stronger parasocial interaction and stronger identification with Schwarzenegger were more likely to vote for him.

Analysis of Open-Ended Responses

Our final analysis involved an evaluation of an open-ended question on our survey regarding Schwarzenegger's values and beliefs. This question asked respondents to "briefly describe the values and beliefs that they think Arnold Schwarzenegger lives by and to explain how these values and beliefs influenced their life."

The most often mentioned qualities or values associated with Schwarzenegger was that he is a hardworking, disciplined, organized and highly motivated individual. As one person wrote, "Arnold believes in and exemplifies the ideal of living up to one's full potential. He got to his current position in life by virtue of hard work, period. What he has – what he is – he earned. He is a good man who believes in doing what is right." Another respondent stated, "Arnold lives by the values of hard work, popular success, and brute charisma." Another respondent indicated that he believes Arnold is "driven by personal success and status." This respondent indicated that to his way of thinking Schwarzenegger "strongly believes in the value and strength of American freedoms and opportunities" and that Schwarzenegger would work to give other people the same opportunities he had. What many people may be responding to here is the image of a common man who through his own hard work and discipline was able to realize his dreams of wealth and success. On one level Schwarzenegger is another version of a "rags to riches" story of a man who was a poor immigrant who through self-discipline acquired popularity and wealth. Much like Elvis Presley, who rose from poverty to stardom and success, Schwarzenegger has built his own financial empire on his acquired celebrity status.

As a celebrity, Schwarzenegger was able to turn his athletic ability and self-determination into political capital as he ran for governor of California. Many respondents admired him for his self-discipline in athletics. As one respondent stated, "I most admire his incredible self-discipline in the areas of health and fitness." Another respondent stated, "He displays self-discipline — that is the most important quality. He can control himself and his "destiny" (if you will). He shows me that ANYTHING is possible- you can't help but admire the man." Typically, people responded to this question by stating that they were not fully informed of Arnold's values but were impressed with his work ethic and with the way he has handled money in his personal life. One respondent stated, "I don't know enough about Arnold to describe his values and beliefs. I do know that he has worked hard to get where he is and he obviously handles money fairly well because he is well off but he has also married well."

Schwarzenegger was a lightning rod for media attention and this had both positive and negative consequences on his gubernatorial campaign. Many people who believe that he is powerful and hard-working are less than enamored with his other values. For example, one respondent wrote, "I think Arnold worked hard (with the help of some influential friends) to become a rich man." However, the respondent went on to state that, "He is beholden to them and now he hopes to pay them back by becoming governor of California and doing whatever they tell him to do." Schwarzenegger's image of being hard working, powerful and in control was not always helpful to his gubernatorial candidacy. One respondent complained, "I think he believes in power and control (i.e. his admiration for Hitler and his misogynistic behavior) and would lie, cheat and steal to have both. When he goes to prison, I'll visit."

What begins to emerge from our understanding of both the quantitative and qualitative data that we collected is that one of the advantages that Schwarzenegger brought to this political election was his ability to communicate strength through both his verbal and nonverbal behavior. As one respondent stated, "I think he is serious about bringing California back. He exhibits strength and power through his nonverbal and verbal gestures/communication." The respondent went on to suggest that his lack of political experience is seen by some to be a positive attribute. "The fact that he has no political background experience makes him a more appealing candidate." In summary, Schwarzenegger presented a public image of a powerful, hardworking, and successful businessman, athlete and actor, who is a good communicator but who lacked political experience. The fact that he was seen as an outsider who lacked political experience was not necessarily harmful to his image or his gubernatorial campaign.

Clearly Schwarzenegger's ability to communicate was helpful to his campaign. Many respondents in our study indicated that his presence communicates power and that both those who like him and his ideals and those who do not like him or his ideas see him as a powerful figure. Again, one respondent who admired Schwarzenegger described him as having a "strong sense of purpose, very strong will power. He knows how to influence people to get things done. Charisma. [I have a] sense of appreciation for what our state and our country have allowed him to achieve."

A negative picture of Schwarzenegger by some respondents also emerged from our study. Some respondents perceived him as egotistical, opportunistic, narcissistic, and ambitious. People who saw him in this light were generally negative toward his gubernatorial election. Those who identified the values that they believed Schwarzenegger represented as being hard working and self-disciplined, could possess either a positive or negative attitude toward him. Many respondents viewed Schwarzenegger as a person who achieved the "American dream." One respondent stated, "Arnold Schwarzenegger seems to have the ambition needed in this country to achieve his ends, and to many, this is what the 'American dream' is all about." If Schwarzenegger embodied the "American dream" for some he was seen as a nightmare for others. One respondent stated, "Arnold Schwarzenegger lives by the principles of obtaining power, and constantly striving to consolidate more power. I view him as incredibly narcissistic and interested in being worshipped by as large a body of people as possible, which makes him dangerous, because the vague, amorphous ideologies he touts come second to his thirst for power. I think he's a prime example of everything that's wrong with our celebrity obsessed culture, and he displays a large dose of disrespect for people culturally or 'underneath' his social status." Another respondent stated, "Arnold has values dejour. He does not have a strong moral code. He lives an egocentric life fueled by his ego and desire. This man is used to bullying his way around and using his influence to get what he wants."

As these responses indicate, not everyone was enamored with Schwarzenegger's celebrity status or his strong "can do" attitude. One respondent stated, "He is an egocentric male chauvinist. He is inconsiderate to women, people of color, the lower class, and the environment. Having him as governor of California would be extremely detrimental since he is the least qualified candidate with no real prior experience in politics. He has not influenced my life in any way, except he has helped me understand how easily people can be manipulated by celebrities." Here, we see a negative reaction to Schwarzenegger's celebrity status. Many respondents were skeptical of people like Schwarzenegger who run for public office whose only qualification is their celebrity status.

A number of respondents were concerned with Schwarzenegger's attitude toward women. As one woman stated, "As a working woman, I have had to deal with sexual predators like Arnold. They do not act like that around their wives or 'equals.' As a parent of two daughters, I am afraid of his kind hurting them. Condoning him condoned his behavior and it gets worse. The Republican party should think about what they are showing the world." One respondent represents a number of attitudes when he stated, "Apparently he believes that he is God's gift to women and that he can treat them like possessions." Another respondent stated, "He is a steroid-using womanizer who seeks to have all men behave as though they never passed the 12- to 13-year-old development stage. How Maria Shriver ever got mixed up with him was clearly a Faustian bargain. Now, she has descended to the gutter that he espouses and lives by. Very sad." The image of Arnold as a womanizer clearly emerged from many respondent comments. Although it was occasionally excused as a sin of the past, it is still a very real and negative image that has emerged from the study results.

There are many other values that were attributed to Schwarzenegger. For example, there were about the same number of people who saw Arnold as honest as those who saw him as a liar. This is possibly one of the clearest indications of a candidate's ability to polarize an electorate. Also, quite a few respondents were not aware (or not fully aware) of Arnold's political values and apart from his celebrity status, which he achieved through his athletic, and movie career were not fully informed as to his political beliefs. This may have worked in his favor, in that given the negative environment of the gubernatorial campaign in which people were so upset with the current governor, they wanted to vote for anyone who they felt could change the current situation, even if they weren't sure of his values and beliefs. They may have felt that they had nothing to lose. If no clear values were communicated, they were left to vote on the image they had of the candidate. This may be a clear example of a political election in which most people voted for an image rather than on the substance of candidates' beliefs and positions on issues. Although voting on image may seem superficial, it is one of the most important dimensions a political candidates' overall appeal, and no doubt played a large role in Presidential and Congressional elections of 2012.

The results of our study demonstrate that Schwarzenegger was able to turn his celebrity capital into political influence. People's involvement with him promoted seeking more information about him, particularly his political beliefs and practices. Our results suggest that even those who did not like Schwarzenegger, about two thirds of our sample, still recognized his political influence. However, we must realize that Schwarzenegger's ability to cash in on his celebrity capital is not easy to do. Many other celebrities have failed politically as we shall see in my next example.

The Political Campaign of Lynn Swann

One of the most famous unelected celebrities of the 2006 Congressional elections was Pittsburgh Steeler great Lynn Swann. Swann was born in Alcoa, Tennessee, a greatly segregated factory town at the foot of the Great Smoky Mountains. The working-class town was named after an aluminum corporation. During Swann's teenage years, his family moved to California, where he received an academic scholarship to attend Junipero Serra High School in San Mateo, a Catholic boys' school. Swann became one of the first minority students to enroll in the school. Distinguishing himself with his athletic abilities, Swann became a high school All-American football player and received a scholarship to attend the University of Southern California (USC). At USC, he became a team captain, helping lead the Trojans to two Rose Bowl and the1972 National Championship. The following year he was named a collegiate All-American. Twenty years later, his college achievements were memorialized with his election to the College Football Hall of Fame.[32]

Swann was drafted by the Pittsburgh Steelers as their number one choice and the 21st player drafted overall. His storybook career continued as he became an integral member of the Steelers' dynasty during the 1970s in which the team won an unprecedented four Superbowls during a six-year period. Swann played in all four Super Bowl championships and in three pro-bowls. In 2001 he was elected to the Pro-Football Hall of Fame. In addition, he was named to the NFL 1970s All-Decade Team by Hall of Fame voters.[33]

Seven years before retiring from his distinguished NFL career, Swann began a second career in broadcasting, debuting as a sports analyst for ABC in 1976. Swann hosted a number of different sporting events, including the 1984 Summer Olympics, the Winter

Olympic Games in 1988, International Diving Championships, NCAA sports events, college and Monday Night Football, the Kentucky Derby, the Preakness and Belmont Stakes, the Irish Derby, the Iditarod dog sled race, and Wide World of Sports.

Swann distinguished himself not only in his professional careers as an athlete and on-air television commentator, but also in his private life.[34] In 1980, he began serving as the National Spokesman for Big Brothers Big Sisters of America. At the time of this writing, he is a member on their National Board of Directors, and he served as board president board from 1993 to 1995. In this capacity, he traveled across the country, testified before Congress, and visited the White House on behalf of the nation's premiere one-to-one mentoring organization. Swann also was appointed Chairman of the President's Council on Physical Fitness and Sports, a role, once held by California Governor Arnold Schwarzenegger. He also is a board member for H.J. Heinz Co. and Hershey Entertainment and Resorts.

Swann also became a minor actor and polished speaker. He has numerous acting credits, having appeared on episodes of *Family Matters* and *The Paper Chase*. He also hosted TV shows *Battle of the Network Stars* and *To Tell the Truth*, and played himself in the movie, *The Waterboy*, with Adam Sandler.[35] Swann also made a cameo appearance in ballet tights on *Mister Rogers' Neighborhood*. His name appears on eight Trivial Pursuit game cards and his online biography readily admits that he used his celebrity status to raise money to provide scholarships for the Pittsburgh Ballet.

In summary, a review of Swann's extensive achievements provides evidence of his high degree of celebrity status. Born in poverty-stricken Appalachia, he rose to fame through hard work and perseverance. He humbly attributes his sense of balance that distinguished his football feats as a wide receiver to the dance lessons that his mother enrolled him when he was only eight years old. He became well-known not through self-promotion but by athletic achievements and community service.

Despite being raised in a family of Democrats, Swann gravitated toward the Republican Party because, he explained, "conservative values was more the way I lived."[36] Since Swann clearly is a positive role model, the reason why his celebrity status fail to propel him into the Pennsylvania's Governor's mansion in 2006 is not easy to discern.

In order to assess the gubernatorial election of Lynn Swann, one of my former doctoral students, Dr. Douglass Campbell, conducted a study of statements by political pundits published in newspapers. These statements were gathered from political science professors at Pennsylvania universities, opinion pieces from editorials, comments from reporters thought worthy of quoting from ordinary persons, and reports and interpretations by journalists of political polling. In addition, Campbell emailed a 10-question, Likert-type survey to three categories of persons. One category comprised journalists who included their email address when they wrote a story about the campaign.

These journalists were selected on the assumption that those who write about a campaign are better able to analyze the campaign that those who do not. Another category comprised the pollsters whose polls included the Swann-Rendell contest. The third group was comprised of selective political science professors at Pennsylvania universities; these political scientists were identified by accessing a variety of public and private Pennsylvania university web pages.

The first phase of Campbell's study, he rhetorically analyzed the newspaper texts, focusing on the three kinds of content: statements from political scientists, editorial opinions, and comments from ordinary persons. In the second phase of the study, he analyzed the results of the 10-question survey.

Campbell ironically discovered that most pundits believed Swann was the victim of the very celebrity status that won him the Republican primary. When Swann announced his candidacy, Ed Rendell, Swann's opponent, was mired in voter backlash against a widely loathed pay raise bill he signed into law for legislators, judges, and the executive branch. Although Rendell did not accept his raise, he initially was attacked by constituents for signing the bill.

In contrast to Rendell's problems, Swann's celebrity status gave him the appearance of an extremely strong challenger. The Republican Party in Pennsylvania recognized Swann's ability to successfully speak and fund-raise during his assistance in 2004 with President Bush's campaign. Allegheny County Councilwoman Jan Rea observed, "'I saw the way crowds reacted to him. There was an instant response. He had that charisma.'"[37] Another observer, Renee Amoore, the deputy state chair of the Pennsylvania Republican Party, noticed when Swann was on the scene "there was a lot of buzz."[38] The president of the State Senate told the Pittsburgh Post-Gazette that Swann was "Ed Rendell's worst nightmare."[39] When Swann appeared before a crowd estimated at 250,000 celebrating the Pittsburgh Steeler's 2006 Super Bowl victory, the crowd shouted "governor, governor."[40]

USA Today reported that Swann's "strong suit is his presence–jokes and charm on top of a storied athletic career that makes him the center of attention in any room. Standing ovations and autograph requests are routine."[41] George Will, in his syndicated column for the Washington Post, wrote that he "hopes his celebrity will get voters' attention, and that he then can persuade them that a change in Harrisburg is required."[42] Christopher Borick, professor of political science at Muhlenberg College, thought that the Republican party "saw the potential for Swann to really energize voters with his celebrity and his personable characteristics, and that he would be someone much more competitive at this point."[43]

The three other Republican candidates who had planned on entering the Republican primary race were so impressed with Swann that they aptly withdrew their candidacies after the party endorsed Swann. One of these candidates, Former Lt. Gov. Bill Scranton, the son a very popular former governor, expressed his admiration of Swann, stating that

"Everyone focuses on his celebrity. What they don't focus on is what it took to achieve that. You don't achieve what he has without a lot of grit and determination."[44]

Swann's endorsement by the Republican Party was criticized by several political leaders who worried that Swann, a celebrity handpicked by the state's Republican establishment, would be unable to maintain an independent voice against a legislature under his party's control. Swann strongly refuted this charge, explaining that his position as his party's candidate was the result of his own making and not of any Republican effort to force out contenders. Nevertheless, many other potential candidates and their supporters held the perception that it was Swann's celebrity status that garnered the Republican Party endorsement and not his qualifications as a candidate.

Ironically, Swann's strong candidacy and lack of challenges became his undoing. Swann had few opportunities to debate the critical issues of voters with other candidates. Professor Jack Treadway, chair of the political-science department at Kutztown University of Pennsylvania , observed that "Swann didn't get even an iota of in-the-trenches experience and so made all his mistakes in the general election."[45] Treadway said a primary contest would have given Swann the chance to work out the early miscues from his campaign.[46] One editorial in the Pottstown Mercury noted another weakness in Swann's candidacy, stating "The paradox of Lynn Swann's candidacy for governor is that everyone knows who he is, but nobody knows much about him."[47] Ray Wrabley, a political science professor at the University of Pittsburgh at Johnstown, noted that "Sometimes a bruising primary can be helpful. Swann might have been able to hone better skills and come out looking like a winner."[48] According to most of the political scientists quoted in Pennsylvania newspapers, Swann's celebrity status constituted the single most important reason Swann won the endorsement of his party also was the origin of his failure to produce a winning campaign. First, it elicited resentment from the very persons possessing the most influence to support and fund his campaign (i.e., his former inter-party rivals), and, second, it precluded an opportunity for him to use his attention-getting celebrity status as a forum for presenting his platform and his qualifications.

Despite Governor Rendell's problems, overall, he was still a popular governor, and Pennsylvanians had never failed to re-elect a governor since a second term was made possible by a 1968 change in the commonwealth's constitution. Also, opinion polls revealed a high favorable rating for Rendell. Without a large body of discontent voters, a great advantage Schwarzenegger had in his race in California, Swann could not gain the critical impetus to convince voters that a change was needed.

Swann's late campaign proposals to reduce the corporate income tax, roll back the personal income tax, and phase out the inheritance tax, did not gain traction. Swann promised to reduce the size of the state government and lower spending, but he could not articulate how he would do so. Rendell supporters began to question Swann's ability to lead the state government. One editorial in the *State College Centre Daily Times* noted, "Republican businessman Lynn Swann has shown a gracious manner and a classy aversion to gutter politics. But Swann's lack of command of the basics of state issues has been embarrassing."[49] Well respected political commentators Madonna and Young concluded that "Swann was, for much of the campaign, unconvincing as a reformer."[50] Political scientists wondered if Swan had been forced to win voter approval in a primary instead of being handed the endorsement without a fight, he might have been more highly motivated to more clearly and specifically outline his positions on the issues most important to voters.

Most political commentators concluded that Swann lost his single most important political advantage when he failed to capitalize on the overwhelming voter antagonism against the pay-raise bill Governor Rendell had signed. Rendell used the millions of dollars he had raised before Swann had entered the campaign to define himself and blame the State legislature for the pay raise, so by the time Swann began blaming the governor, "people weren't buying it."[51]

One polling group who tracked the race closely suggested that the decline in Swann's initial overwhelming support among Pittsburgh Steeler fans "may be an indicator of Swann's inability to convince voters of his credentials for the office beyond his fame as a gridiron star."[52] Although Swann was the first African-American to be nominated for governor by a major political party in Pennsylvania, Rendell's support among non-white voters actually increased during the campaign, reaching a 7 to 1 margin over Swann. Shortly before the election, Rendell was endorsed by a group of African American clergy.[53] Swann ultimately won only 13% of the African-American vote.[54]

Few would question the critical role of money in a political campaign's success. Rendell took the lead early in a fund-raising effort supporting a massive advertising campaign and never relinquished it. He raised more than $30 million, while Swann was able to raise only $10 million. One consequence of this differential was that Rendell was able to run television advertisements long before Swann. "'One of the linchpins in this race is the ability to raise money to get on TV,'" Madonna said. "'Rendell took a very close election and blew it open, in part because he could spend $5 million on TV commercials . . . to remind voters of what he's done for them and to dispel this myth that he's the governor of Philadelphia.'"[55] Swann, in contrast, was not able to launch an aggressive television campaign until well into September. He had so little money left a week before election day ($318,777) that he was forced to choose between spending it all on either an advertisements blitz or a get-out-the-vote effort. Borick opined, "'That's beyond a shoestring budget; If I am rolling the dice and that's as much money as I have left, I am putting it all into the famed 72-hour Republican 'get out the vote' blitz.'"[56] Here again, Swann's celebrity status appeared to hurt more than it helped. As a celebrity, he did not have to raise a great deal of money to get his voice heard. Easy access to the media, however, is not identical to running television advertisements.

Finally, at times his celebrity status drew attention away from his qualifications to be governor and concentrated them on his fame as an outstanding football player. The Harrisburg Bureau Chief for the Scranton Times-Tribune said, "His celebrity status gives him a level of name recognition most politicians would envy, but it also can prove a distraction. At many campaign events, people flock not to hear a stump speech, but in the hopes of getting his autograph. He typically rejects autograph requests, which has left some would-be supporters upset."[57]

Given this context of both positive and negative influences on Lynn Swann's campaign, that is why my student, Doug Campbell, wanted to assess why Swann was not able to cash in on his celebrity appeal into political capital. His study provided enough data to offer some insights from persons who would generally be considered as opinion leaders.

Results showed that 80 percent of the respondents felt that Swann related very well his celebrity status to his campaign, and half of them felt at least four out of five voters recognized Swann as a celebrity. However, 80 percent of the respondents also felt that Swann conducted his campaign poorly. All of the respondents agreed that his status as a hall-of-fame football player for the Pittsburgh Steelers affected his campaign positively, but most of them did not feel his football and broadcasting careers actually translated into votes in the Philadelphia area. The respondents unanimously agreed that Swann's career as a Pittsburgh Steeler accounted most significantly for his celebrity status, even more than did his career as a national television journalist. The problem with Swann's geographically centered celebrity appeal is that Pittsburgh's population of a little more than 300,000 is only 17 percent of Philadelphia's 1.8 million at the time of the election. Thus, celebrity status as a Steeler may have helped Swann in Pittsburgh but likely had little influence in his opponent's home base of Philadelphia.

Campbell's study reaffirmed that celebrityhood does not guarantee success in the political world. When Swann told stories during the campaign, his narratives were favorably received; but his appeal began to wane "when his lengthy explanation of property tax reform dulled some of his celebrity sheen."[58] Swann seemed to be unaware of the potential power of his narratives about his own life story. In contrast, the most often mentioned quality or value associated with Arnold Schwarzenegger during his campaign for governor of California was that he is a hardworking, disciplined, organized, and highly motivated person. Schwarzenegger voters responded favorably to what they perceived as a common man who, through his own hard work and discipline, was able–as was Swann–to achieve success. By failing to continually tell voters the story of his rise from rural Appalachia to football stardom, sports journalism, and public service, Campbell concluded that Swann missed a valuable opportunity to convince voters he indeed does have the experience or at least the capacity to serve as governor.[59]

Campbell developed several theoretical explanations for Swann's failure to win the governorship. These three theories are known as priming, framing, and agenda-setting.

Priming relates to the salience of a message to audiences and the accessibility of memory tags. Framing relates to how news stories are positioned in media, telling audiences what to think about regarding an issue. Agenda-setting relates to how the importance of a news story is portrayed, telling audiences which issues are most important and which ones can be ignored. All three of these theoretical approaches provide a basis for assessing the failure of the Swann's campaign.

First, by not focusing early on a limited number of issues and raising enough funds to repeat his viewpoints in a never-ending mantra-like succession, Swan was unable to prime voters because he provided no memory tags for them to access. In contrast, Rendell's supporters "use[d] every opportunity to characterize Mr. Swann as unqualified because he has never held or run for public office before."[60]

Second, by not providing enough specific information to satisfy his audiences (whether journalists, attendees at rallies, or simply crowds at campaign stops), Swan was unable to frame the issues of the campaign in a way that would bias them towards his viewpoints. Rendell, for example, supported a lucid proposal limiting gun purchases to one a month. Swann's official policy statement said he had been an avid outdoorsman his entire adult life and that he would serve as a strong coalition of men and women who believe that we must preserve and support a sportsman's philosophy in the Commonwealth of Pennsylvania, but he did not explain his philosophy specifically. In his third debate with Rendell, Swann simply asserted without detail or relevant facts that he believed a more aggressive enforcement of current laws was the best response to rising gun violence.

Failure to fully understand the issues is another reason Swann was unable to frame them. When asked about abortion by George Stephanopoulos of ABC, for example, he gave an answer showing he did not understand Roe v. Wade. "'Should the court overturn that ruling, he said, abortion would be illegal. Not so, Mr. Stephanopoulos had to point out. Roe v. Wade merely limited what restrictions states could put on abortions. If it were overturned, individual states would still have to pass laws outlawing abortion.'"[61] When asked about stem cell research, Swann responded "I am not an expert on stem cell research at this particular time."[62]

Because one important consequence of the media attention given to celebrities is their influence on the public agenda, Swann's celebrity status at least should have given him some power to set his agenda. Yet, by indecisively circumventing the pay-raise issue early in the campaign and by a last-minute desperate thrust at a corruption charge related to Rendell's staff's use of government airplanes, Swann failed to proffer a consistent campaign agenda, allowing Rendell to focus attention instead on Swann's inexperience. Moreover, as a well-liked mayor of Philadelphia, Rendell also enjoyed name recognition, especially in southeastern Pennsylvania, giving him some celebrity status to help promote his agenda.

Parasocial interaction theory also can account for some of his poor showing. From the very first, theorists attributed the strongest parasocial effect emanating from persons who appear to be speaking directly to an audience, such as newscasters or talk show hosts. Swann's football broadcast career was launched from the sidelines as an intermittent fifteen-second interviewer, not from the booth where celebrities enjoyed nearly incessant airtime, thus limiting the effect of his parasocial interaction. Ironically, Rendell, whose law degree was earned at an Ivy League university, projected an image that identified him more with the average person than did Swann's, even though Swann rose from humble beginning by dint of effort. Rendell often wore wrinkled suits, made no secret of his love for fast food (especially donuts), and felt at ease joking in casual conversation. Swann, in contrast, dressed impeccably, preferred healthy food at upscale restaurants, and, although he exhibited a friendly smile and a warm personality, became almost somber when discussing issues on the campaign trail. Consider, for example, this anecdote that Rendell related when campaigning, "'He said that a friend of his . . . got into a political discussion with the cabbie. 'Who are you going to vote for?' the businessman asked. 'Lynn Swann?' 'No,' the cabbie said, 'he's too pretty. I'm voting for the ugly one.' Mr. Rendell laughed and said, 'In politics you take your support where you find it.'"[63]

Campbell identified one additional theoretical explanation for Swann's failure to capitalize on his celebrityhood – the tendency of human automation or fixed action pattern responses.[64] One such automatic response occurs when we ask someone to do us a favor. If we also provide a reason for the favor, we will be more successful. Psychology scholar Robert Cialdini notes people simply like to have reasons for what they do.[65] Yet, when a man shaking Swann's hand at 15th Street and Snyder Avenue in Philadelphia said, "'You were a hell of a ballplayer,'" Swann replied, "'And I'll be a hell of a governor too.'"[66] Instead of explaining how his football achievements also qualify him for governor, Swann simply refocused attention on the fact that he is campaigning for the governorship, not engaging in an autograph tour. By deliberately refocusing only the purpose for his appearance, Swann lost an opportunity to give an admirer reasons for why he deserved election, or, said differently, to state his qualifications for serving as governor.

In summary, Swann's celebrity status granted him instant entrée into the primary campaign and provided him with widespread name recognition and significantly high favorability ratings, but his political inexperience resulted in early awkward responses to media interview questions, to the formation of cursory policy statements, and to the neglect of fundraising and advertising. Because Swann didn't tell his story, didn't relate his experience to the governorship, didn't focus consistently on a clear message, failed to be specific, and failed to raise money and so fell behind in TV advertisements, he couldn't turn his celebrity status into political capital. Nevertheless, although his gubernatorial campaign was a failure, his campaign to become a political force very well may have been a success.

The Future of Celebrity Politics

In conclusion, whether it's Bono flying to Africa with America's Treasury secretary, Sean Penn visiting Iraq to protest the then-impending war, Bruce Springsteen stumping and strumming for John Kerry, or Sarah Jessica Parker hosting President Obama and his wealthy supporters in her Manhattan home, celebrities increasingly are communicating their political and social views into the political realm in an effort to effect social change. These efforts are believed to pay political dividends; and evidence supports this belief in some cases. Pease and Brewer found that Oprah Winfrey's endorsement of Barak Obama affected her audience members views of Obama's viability as a candidate.[67] An experimental study by Anthony Nownes showed that when study participants who disliked Jennifer Aniston were exposed to information about her support for Democrats, they report liking the Democratic Party less; and when participants who liked Peyton Manning were exposed to information about Manning's support for Republicans, they reported liking the Republican Party more.[68]

These studies suggest that meaning is transferred from the socially mediated world into the political world. Given the overwhelming support that President Obama enjoyed strong support from Hollywood celebrities, this may have been an important factor in his 2012 re-election victory. In contrast, Donald Trump received very little support from Hollywood celebrities, with a few notable exceptions. It is not surprising that more than 90 percent of the broadcast media coverage of President Trump has been negative, according to a large study of ABC, CBS, and NBC evening newscasts.[xii] There has been very little coverage of Trumps many accomplishments such as criminal justice reform, lowering unemployment among minorities and women to historic levels, leading an unprecedented economic recovery, creating new business development initiatives for minority business ventures in urban areas, decreasing subscription drug abuse and overdoses, fixing the recurring problems at veteran's hospitals, leading the U.S. into energy independence for the first time in its history, and brokering new peace agreements in the U.S. between Israel and several Arab nations and between Servia and Kosovo, garnering multiple Nobel Peace Prize nominations.

Consider the visual comparison of major news magazine covers of President Obama and President Trump published by the Washington Free Beacon.[xiii] Try and find any popular women's magazines like *People* or *Vanity Fair* or *Cosmopolitan* or *Elle* with Melania Trump on the cover as compared to the dozens of magazines with Michelle Obama on the cover,

---

[xii] Go to https://www.newsbusters.org/blogs/nb/rich-noyes/2019/01/15/networks-trashed-trump-90-negative-spin-2018-did-it-matter

[xiii] Go to https://freebeacon.com/politics/comparing-media-portrays-trump-obama-magazine-covers/

despite the fact that Melania was the professional model. There is a clear disadvantage of being on the wrong side of the media elite that control celebrity politics.

In the future, celebrity politics will continue to be an important area of news media research and the study of popular culture. The conglomeration of the entertainment industry has brought about a convergence of news media, entertainment and politics. Political processes in western cultures should not be studied in isolation without also considering the news media and the entertainment industry. Entertainment companies oversee news media operations that encourage involvement with celebrities because they can generate revenues. When given a great deal of social capital, many celebrities spend their capital by exchanging it for political influence. Thus, political processes in entertainment cultures like the U.S. are greatly influenced by the entertainment industry. This trend in the U.S. should also become an important international trend.

In the next chapter, we will consider the strategic use of celebrity appeal to market social causes. Focusing on the lives of public figures, professional athletes and entertainers, I will review how celebrity influence is rallying people to support important social needs.

Discussion Questions

1. Do entertainment values have an important influence in the places where you obtain much of your news?
2. What role does celebrity politics play in the creation and consumption of major news stories?
3. Are you concerned about the control of news media multi-billionaires with clear political agendas; and if so, how should this situation be remedied?
4. What celebrities most powerfully influence the political views that you hold?

Chapter 12 Marketing Social Causes through Entertainment

One of the most exciting opportunities for professional athletes and entertainers is the potential they have to use their fame and public good will in order to promote worthy social causes and improve the quality of life of people around the world. I refer to the influence of celebrities as an effect that comes through "entertainment" because our relationship with celebrities is formed by the way in which our entertainment culture functions. More than fifty years ago, Wiebe posed the question, "why can't you sell brotherhood like you sell soap?"[1] In other words, Wiebe wanted to know if marketing concepts and techniques could be effectively applied to the promotion of social objectives such as brotherhood, safe driving, and family planning. He said out to explore this question by studying four social campaigns to determine what made them successful or not. His results showed that the more these social campaigns were like product marketing campaigns, the more successful they were.

Social marketing, which began to take hold during the 1970s, involves the application of product marketing concepts to social causes. It has been practiced and examined extensively during the past several decades.[2] Recently, a number of academic books have been written on the subject and now social media is integrated within many social marketing campagins.[3] In this chapter, I want to focus on one important application of the social marketing strategy – using entertainment and particularly, celebrities, to advance social causes. I'll begin with discussing one of the most influential celebrity spokespersons for social change, Princess Diana.

Princess Diana as Celebrity Humanitarian

As we remember the anniversary of Princess Diana's tragic death on August 31st of 1997, we should particularly remember the social causes she carried close to her heart. I want to focus on several of those causes and explain why Princess Diana was a powerful force for positive social change. Of course no one would refer to Diana as an entertainer, however, with her office she became a celebrated persona, a public celebrity, which serves the entertainment needs of the public who seek to build parasocial relationships with famous people, especially those who are well liked and respected. There is no doubt that Princess Diana was both an international celebrity and an international humanitarian.

Humanitarian work played an important role in the life of Princess Diana. She was involved in dozens of humanitarian efforts both in the U.K. and abroad. Her interests were reflected in the organizations of which she was Patron or President, including the Great Ormond

Street for Sick Children in London, the Royal Marsden Hospital, which specializes in treating cancer, Centerpoint, an organization assisting the homeless, The National Aids Trust and The Leprosy Mission. In addition to these major involvements, Diana served as a patron during periods of her short lifetime for an additional 100 charities.[4]

Princess Diana traveled extensively abroad for humanitarian work. She made many trips to North America to visit hospices, schools, charities and to attend fundraising galas. Other major overseas travel included visits to Angola, Australia, Bosnia, Egypt, India, Pakistan, and many European countries. During these trips, Diana publicly addressed a wide range of social issues and used her high profile and celebrity appeal to raise awareness of social needs and promote generous giving toward charitable causes. Diana touched the lives of thousands of people personally, establishing her reputation as one of the most respected humanitarians during her life. Those who traveled with Diana and who observed her interactions with people said she communicated a warmth and genuine interest in the situations and difficult circumstances of those she met, devoting thousands of hours to listening to their individual stories and problems. Others observed that Diana had a natural empathy with people who had lost loved ones or who were close to death.[5] On August 31, 2012, the 15th anniversary of her death, Princess Diana was once again in the news as millions around the world turned their attention to her death and great accomplishments for others in her life.

Although there is some debate about the contrasting lifestyles of Mother Teresa of Calcutta and Princess Diana and the role models they provided for others, both women remarkably modeled compassion.[6] In fact, Princess Diana visited Mother Teresa in Calcutta in February 1992 and might have learned by observing the master of compassion. During that visit to Mother Teresa's Hospice for the Sick and Dying in Kolkata, India, Diana visited every one of the 50 patients who were close to death. Mother Teresa no doubt witnessed a kindred spirit. In Rome shortly afterwards, then later in London and at another time in New York, Diana and Mother Teresa spend time together and formed a strong personal friendship.

Commenting on her work with the Royal Brompton Hospital in London, Diana, sounding very much like Mother Teresa, described her experiences as follows:

> "I make the trips at least three times a week and spend up to four hours at a time with patients holding their hands and talking to them. Some of them will live and some will die, but they all need to be loved while they are here. I try to be there for them."[7]

Those who worked with Diana believe she understood the power of her role in the public spotlight and used the attention focused on her to change attitudes toward important social issues and needs. In particular, three social causes received her strong devotion: those suffering from HIV/AIDS, those afflicted by Leprosy and those whose lives had been devastated by landmines. She continually addressed these three issues publicly and urged others to support those who had been marginalized by society.

Diana was aware of the powerful communicative force of images. She recognized that the image of her standing in a minefield in Angola in January 1997 would put the issue of landmines in the headlines throughout the world. She knew that when she was photographed shaking hands with an AIDS patient at Middlesex Hospital in London, a compassionate gesture her advisers had tried to dissuade her from doing, that she would help to reduce the stigma of HIV/AIDS and promote a compassionate response to those afflicted by the disease. She embraced people with AIDS on a regular basis, not just for show, as she did at Harlem Hospital in New York when she held a baby with AIDS in 1989; or when she visited a home for orphaned children with AIDS in Sao Paulo, Brazil, two years later.

Visits to the poor, sick, homeless and dying in Indonesia, Cameroon, Pakistan, India, Zimbabwe, Argentina, Angola, and Bosnia during the 1990s followed, each one designed to bring genuine love, compassion, and aid; and to raise awareness and solicit similar responses from millions of people who followed her life. In 1994, The Princess of Wales was awarded the title of 'International Humanitarian of the Year' in the United States, and in 1997, she received a similar humanitarian award in Italy from the Pio Manzu Center.

What Diana seemed to intrinsically understand that many other celebrities do not fully grasp is the power of celebrity appeal to motivate others to produce positive social change. It is this power of celebrity appeal that enables celebrities to pull millions of people into involvement with social causes like a powerful gravitational force pulls celestial bodies. Her sensitivity to her celebrity influence is revealed in her own words below:

> "Being constantly in the public eye gives me a special responsibility, particularly that of using the impact of photographs to transmit a message, to sensitize the world to an important cause, to defend certain values."[8]

Land Mines

Princess Diana devoted much of her life campaigning for the ban of land mines. On January 15, 1997, during her visit to Angola, she called for an international ban on land mines. Some government ministers were unhappy with her call but others praised her such as Shadow defense spokesman, David Clark. Clark remarked: "I think we should all welcome the fact she has gone to Angola and she has tried to warn the world of the dangers of these terrible weapons. I think we should be applauding what she's doing."[9] Diana made the following statement:

> "The world is too little aware of the waste of life, limb and land which anti-personnel landmines are causing among some of the poorest people on earth."[10]

A year after Princess Diana's death, Prime Minister Tony Blair signed the international Ottawa convention on banning landmines. The convention came into force on March 1,

1999, but several key countries have still not signed the agreement as of the time of this writing, including the United States, Russia and China, along with 29 other nations. Land mines today still kill and main innocent civilians, including thousands of children[xiv].

National AIDS Trust

The National AIDS Trust is the United Kingdom's leading independent policy and campaigning voice on HIV and AIDS. A registered charity, the trust develops policies and campaigns to reduce the spread of HIV and improve the quality of life of people affected by HIV and AIDS, both in the UK and internationally. Diana made substantial contributions to the National AIDS Trust during her role as a patron from 1991 until the time of her death. The Trust has pledged to continue Diana's legacy to reduce HIV/AIDS around the world and to remove the stigma of those affected by the disease. In honor of the Princess, the National AIDS Trust has established a lecture series called "The Diana, Princess of Wales lecture on AIDS."

In December of 2001, President Bill Clinton, the chosen lecturer for that year, summarized Princess Diana's international influence on public opinion, stating:

> "In 1987, when so many still believed that AIDS could be contracted through casual contact, Princess Diana sat on the sickbed of a man with AIDS and held his hand. She showed the world that people with AIDS deserve no isolation, but compassion and kindness. It helped change world opinion and gave hope to people with AIDS."[11]

The National AIDS Trust has permanently integrated Princess Diana's life work to halt the spread of HIV/AIDS, to assist those with the disease into its programs and campaigns, and to eradication the stigma and discrimination against those infected.

Cerebral Palsy

One of the important social causes high on Princess Diana's list of social concerns was Cerebral Palsy. Diana visited children afflicted by the disease and actively raised funds for those fighting the disease and treating its victims. In 1989, Princess Diana presented the Women of the World Award to Mildred Robbins Leet, one of the founders of United Cerebral Palsy of New York City. The organization presented Diana with the Cerebral Palsy's Humanitarian Award on December 11, 2005, in New York.[12] At that annual banquet,

---

xiv *UN News.* (12 Nov. 2020). Landmine toll still high amid concerns over COVID-19 impact on clearance efforts. Retrieved from https://news.un.org/en/story/2020/11/1077502

Diana helped to raise $2 million dollars, twice the amount raised at the previous year's banquet. Summarizing Diana's lasting contribution to fight cerebral palsy the year after her death, Edward Matthews, the executive director of United Cerebral Palsy, stated:

> "Usually when a celebrity dies, within six months you hear very little of them. We're just about at the point now [of raising another $2 million], and you see no diminishing."[13]

Princess of Wales Memorial Fund

Within hours of the Princess Diana's death, people began arriving at Kensington Palace with flowers and with envelopes containing notes and monetary donations. Finding the right home for the money was a challenging task, but by the following day the decision was made to create the "Diana, Princess of Wales Memorial Fund" as a charity in the Princess's memory. Charitable status for the fund was officially granted on September 4, 1997, under the leadership of three Founder Trustees: Lady Sarah McCorquodale, Michael Gibbins and Anthony Julius. Small sums of money from the public rapidly built up. Within days, the fund received a huge donation from Sir Elton John and Polygram's *Candle in the Wind '97,* a generous long-term gift that assured the fund's future viability. In the first nine years of its existence, the fund distributed some £70 million in grants to over 350 organizations around the world.[14]

Memorial Concert for Princess Diana

Prince William and Prince Harry marked the 10th anniversary of their mother's death with a special concert to celebrate her life. The "Concert for Diana" was held in the new Wembley Stadium on July 1, 2007, which would have been Diana's 46th birthday.[15] Ticket proceeds from the concert went to the charities supported by the late Princess and to charities of which the Princes are Patrons.

The Princess of Wales Memorial Fund welcomed the announcement of the concert celebrating the life of Diana, Princess of Wales in 2007, the 10th anniversary of her death and of the Fund's establishment. The following announcement was made on December 12, 2006, by Dr. Astrid Honeyman, Chief Executive of the fund:

> "We are delighted that Princes William and Harry have invited the Fund to be among the beneficiaries of the concert."[16]

For those unable to attend the concert in person, the event was shown live on television and on the Internet.

Both of Diana's sons immediately carried on the charity work to which their mother was dedicated. Prince William is Patron of Centerpoint, the UK's leading youth homelessness charity. As a child, the Prince visited homelessness charities in London with his mother. He also visited a homelessness charity in Newport, Wales with his father just before his 21st birthday. In 2005, William spent a few days volunteering at Centerpoint working with young people.

In April 2006, Prince Harry and Lesotho's Prince Seeiso founded a new charity called Sentebale (which means, "forget me not") to help vulnerable children and young people in Lesotho, particularly those orphaned as a result of AIDS.[17] This new organization is a fulfillment of Prince Harry's pledge to continue his mother's work with disadvantaged children. He co-founded the charity with Lesotho's Prince Seeiso, whose own mother Queen Mamohato, a much-loved figure in the country, died in 2003. The two princes chose the name Sentebale as a memorial to the charity work of our own mothers and to remind others not to forget Lesotho or its children.

In summary, Princess Diana has had and continues to have an enormous influence on a number of social causes to which people who have admired her have given themselves. Although it is not possible to quantify the total effects of Diana's celebrity influence, we can clearly see that hundreds of thousands of lives have been changed for the better because she understood how to wield that influence for the good of others.

The Social Causes of Celebrities

There are literally hundreds of social causes that are linked to hundreds of celebrities. Like Princess Diana, many celebrities have multiple social causes while others focus on a single cause. Celebrities have a long history of involvement in political and social issues. Humphrey Bogart led a group to protest the U.S. government's probe of communism in Hollywood in 1947. Danny Kaye worked with UNICEF for 30 years, starting in the 1950s. Audrey Hepburn worked with the United Nations International Children's Emergency Fund from 1988 until her death in 1993. However, the last few years have seen a marked increase in the scope of involvement of celebrities in both political and social issues.

Whether the involvement of celebrities in social causes is a welcomed development depends on your perspective. Non-profit organizations that work closely with celebrities have greatly benefited, receiving millions of dollars of media coverage that they otherwise could not afford. Some segments of the public are skeptical and question the motives of celebrities and their degree of knowledge of the issues they promote. Celebrities who are ill-informed of issues they insert themselves into can do more harm than good.[18]

Some celebrities know their social cause extremely well and are single focused on a need. There is probably no greater example of a focused celebrity effort than Jerry Lewis and his fight against muscular dystrophy. On September 2-3, 2007, Lewis broadcast his 41st Labor Day telethon to fight muscular dystrophy from the South Point hotel-casino south of the Las Vegas Strip. Lewis was age 81 at that time and was delighted to be back in Las Vegas.

The 2008 telecast raised a record $65 million,[19] bringing the total raised by Lewis for the Muscular Dystrophy Association (MDA) to an estimated $2.45 billion in his lifetime.[20] Jerry Lewis began hosting telethons to benefit MDA in 1952 after a plea from a staff member who worked on Dean and Jerry's *Colgate Comedy Hour* show. Lewis's name is now completely identified with MDA, which works to defeat more than 40 neuromuscular diseases through research programs and professional and public health education. Lewis' telethon featured dozens of well-known celebrities who use their celebrity appeal to motivate television viewers to donate funds to MDA. Although Lewis is no longer hosting the MDA telethon, his legacy lives on.

Other celebrities such as Bono and Angelina Jolie have multiple causes. Paul Hewson, more commonly known as Bono, has become one of the world's most influential activists on behalf of the poor. Gaining fame during the 1980s and 1990s as lead singer for the successful rock band U2, Bono has used his celebrity influence to raise awareness of world hunger and HIV/AIDS and to promote African debt relief and poverty alleviation. In 2005, Bono shared Time magazine's Person(s) of the Year award with Bill and Melinda Gates for their collective humanitarian efforts.[21] The following year, he was awarded an honorary knighthood by Queen Elizabeth II, receiving the award in March of 2007. Bono has been a key participant of Band Aid, Live Aid, Amnesty International's Conspiracy of Hope tour, Net Aid, and the One campaign to end world poverty.

Jolie, who served as the United Nations refugee agency Goodwill Ambassador, has been actively involved in refugee relief, adoption, and caring for AIDS orphans. She also has lobbied the U.S. Congress and other political representatives of other countries for funding for these critical needs. The Academy Award-winning actress, who has worked with UNHCR as a Goodwill Ambassador since 2001, used her acceptance speech to draw attention to the plight of refugees and the work of the UN refugee agency. She said that apart from her children, spending time with refugees was "the greatest gift – the greatest life lesson I could ever receive;" and she also paid special tribute to all those working with refugees." In any UNHCR office, in any one of the many areas around the world, you will find an amazing mix of hard-working and often very tired people. What is beautiful to me is that the men and women are always a mix of nationalities who have come together with the common goal – to help others. That is the UN at its best."[22]

In his congratulatory message, the UN High Commissioner for Refugees, António Guterres, pointed out that "Ms. Jolie had given an entirely new meaning to the words global humanitarian action. The depth of your dedication and commitment inspires many others, especially the legions of young people who admire you, to think about how they too can help to make the world a better place," he added.[23]

Celebrities like Bono and Jolie have a broad appeal both domestically and internationally. Celebrities who express a strong passion for a social cause are able to influence a great number of people. Sahar Moridani, Director of Media Relations of the Elizabeth Glaser

Pediatric AIDS Foundation, said in an interview with the Washington File, "The importance of this kind of broad appeal is that it causes people who may not have known about your issue to think about the issue, look at your Website, maybe attend an event and "Hometown fans get a chance to honor their hero."[24]

Many celebrities like Angelina Jolie use their influences to draw attention to social and political causes or special health issues, like Jolie's promotion of breast cancer awareness and prevention. Other notable celebrities in addition to Jolie and Bono are communicating with government officials. During the past two decades, Congress has heard from many different celebrities on a broad spectrum of social issues. Celebrities advocating social causes include Ashley Judd, the global ambassador for Youth AIDS, George Lucas, who testified before Congress about the Coalition called Digital Promise, actor Pierce Brosnan's support for the environmental group, the Natural Resources Defense Council, actress Kyra Sedgwick and her work for the Children's Hope Foundation, actress Selma Hayek's advocacy against domestic violence, Grammy music award winner Mary J. Blige funding for the Minority AIDS Project, actress Calista Flockhart's work as the national spokeswoman for the Los Angeles Commission on Assaults Against Women, actor Ben Affleck's work on behalf of ataxia-telangiectasia (AT), a rare, recessive genetic childhood disorder characterized by neurologic problems, game show host and animal rights activist Bob Barker and his campaign to raise awareness about the importance of spaying and neutering pets, news anchor Katie Couric's testimony on colon cancer, and George Clooney and the genocide in Sudan.[25]

The globalization of media personae and their ability to induce public involvement in political and social issues is an important social influence process that needs to be more fully understood by social scientists and media scholars. The potential power of celebrities with social causes is enormous. There are numerous social needs and international problems in which celebrities could help by using their social influence for good. Every society is going to have its celebrities and heroes. Those whose influence is global should be encouraged to use their celebrity currency to build bridges across the cultural divides that often keep us from finding solutions to critical problems. As has been demonstrated by Bono and bin Laden, celebrity heroes can use their fame to be powerfully constructive or powerfully destructive. As new communication media continue to break time, space, and cultural barriers, media personae have become influential factors of change in the global post-modern society. Thus, future research should address the international influence of media personae across cultural boundaries.

In the next chapter I will focus on two specific genres of new media and their potential for entertainment-education—videogames and interactive websites.

Chapter 13
Learning through Interactive Video Games and Websites

One of the fastest growing sources of learning today is through interactive games and websites. If you have teenagers in your home or family life, you know that interacting over the computer is like second nature to them—they don't even have to think about it. Social networking websites such as Instagram, YouTube, Tik Tok and Facebook have grown phenomenally. Social media platforms change rapidly too. In 2006, My Space was adding 300,000 new users every day.[1] When Rupert Murdoch, CEO of News Corp, bought My Space for $580 million in 2005, he thought it was of the best buys of his life until he had to sell it for $35 million in 2011.[2] Murdoch believed the website would be worth a lot more money in years to come once he had collected all kinds of personal information from teenagers. However, My Space was rapidly eclipsed by Facebook in 2008, which left it in the dust and became the most popular social networking site, having 845 million active users worldwide by 2012.[3] Today, in 2020, Instagram is the most popular social media platform, with more than one billion monthly users.[xv]

Despite Murdoch's miscue by underestimating the competition, he correctly assessed that marketing companies are salivating to gain access to the wealth of information on social networking sites. What many teenagers don't realize is that none of the information on their "personal pages" is private information. They don't own or control the website where their information is, and it can be sold to the highest bidder. However, teens love sharing information, music, pictures, videos, etc., so social networking sites will continue to grow and be a primary source of social learning throughout the world.

Like the web, video games are extremely popular among teenagers and young adults. Many baby boomers and their parents know little about *Halo 3*, *The Sims*, or *The Legend of Zelda*, games their children have played; and thus, feel out of the loop on video games. On the first day of its release in 2007, *Halo 3* made $170 million, making it the highest grossing entertainment product in history at the time; then the first day sales of *Halo: Reach* exceeded $200 million in 2010.[4] More people are familiar with *Mario* and *Pokémon*, the two all-time most popular video games in history. Some 195 million people have purchased *Mario*, launched in 1983, and another 164 million units of *Pokémon* have been sold since its release in 1996. Those who recognize the name Zelda, the wife of F. Scott Fitzgerald, as connected to a videogame, are more exposed to these games than most adults. Even those

---

[xv] Robinson, R. (28 Dec. 2020). The 7 top social media sites you need to care about in 2020). *Adobe Spark*. Retrieved from https://spark.adobe.com/make/learn/top-social-media-sites/

in the large group who know about video games have likely played *Tetris*, the great distracter of office work created by Russian computer programmer Alexey Pajintov. Those with very old computers probably have a copy of *Tetris* on it — 70 million copies have been sold.

In addition to video games, there are other ways to explore virtual worlds. If you have visited interactive websites you may have heard of *Another Life* and *MapleStory*, or if you are among the pre-teens, now called "tweens," you may be waddling around the world of *Club Penguin*. If you have no idea what I am referring to, let me explain. *Club Penguin* is one of many Internet clubs. It was launched in October of 2005 by three fathers in British Columbia who were trying to safe their fledgling media company. *Club Penguin* is a virtual world where you take on the identity of a very sophisticated penguin – after all, have many penguins do you know who give each other flowers, go out on dates, buy furniture for their igloos, dance and fly? In January of 2007, there were 4 million visitors to the *Club Penguin* website, most of them in the 8-14-year-old age range, and the website traffic grew by 329 percent from June 2006 to June 2007.[5] Suppose you don't want to be a penguin? There are many other on-line virtual worlds you can go to in order to create a new identity. A virtual character, commonly referred to as an "avatar," has many options. In *MapleStory*, an online game where players hunt cartoon monsters and text message each other, North American players purchased 600,000 avatar items in February of 2007 for $1.6 million.[6] Why? If you want to meet your spouse on an online site and then get married on the site, as Frank and Cyndi Lester did, you must have a good-looking avatar. Cyndi, a homemaker from West Virginia, says she spends about $100 a month purchasing new clothes and hairstyles for her avatar on *MapleStory*.[7] So why should you care that some homemaker from West Virginia spends several hours a day in a virtual world? Or why should you care that nearly 2 million children a month have fun in an on-line world of penguins?

I think you know already, but to reiterate the central thesis of this book – because it's not just entertainment! Video games and online websites are places of learning because we learn through entertainment. Let me quote the three fathers who created Club Penquin when asked about the online romances of children on their website: "In real-world sandboxes, kids flirt. Why shouldn't they be able to flirt in this virtual sandbox, too?"[8]

I don't know about you, but when I played in parks and playgrounds in the late 1950s and early 1960s, I didn't flirt with anyone. I don't want someone with a totally different set of values than my family tradition setting up online romance centers to attract 8 to12 year-olds into "romantic relationships" when they should be enjoying their childhoods instead of awaking sexual feelings. This clash of values illustrates the importance of understanding video games, websites, and virtual worlds, and to see them as places of learning, not just places of entertainment.

Children and teens now spend an enormous amount of time using new media such as computers, cell phones, and video games. In 2005, the Kaiser Family Foundation published a study of the media use of 8 to 18-year-olds based on the interviews of more than 2000 school children and teenagers. The study results showed that the average school-aged child or teen was exposed to 8.5 hours a day of media and directly used media outside of school an average of 6.5 hours a day and 44.5 hours a week.[9] Because kids are multi-tasking as was discussed earlier, they use multiple media at the same time and therefore have increased their use of cell phones and the Internet without really decreasing their television consumption. The foundation report is full of all kinds of fascinating information, like more than two-thirds of all 8-18-year-olds have a television set in their bedrooms (68% to be exact), 54% have their own VCR or DVD player, 37% have satellite or cable TV, 31% have a computer, and 20% have Internet access – all in the privacy of their bedrooms away from the overseeing eyes of parents or any other adults who are supposed to monitor their media content.[10]

In case you think I'm picking on children, adults are multi-tasking as well, especially women. According to BIG Research, women are significantly more likely than men to use multiple forms of media simulataneously.[11] Most women have the television on as background noise while they are doing other activities liking surfing the Internet or reading. Another study shows heavy media consumers occasionally or regularly use two or three mediums at the same time.[12] This study confirmed many others that show television viewing and Internet use tend to go hand in hand.

The multi-media tasking of most people today in the home environment are central in facilitating or hindering social interaction – talking to each other. If everyone in a family is watching a different television set or on a different computer, it's difficult to have interaction. One study found that families tend to exchange time spent in real relationships for mediated or virtual relationships (interacting with real or fictitious characters through media).[13] The popular use of television program websites has also contributed to the close relationship of television and internet use. One study found that more than 78% of web users have visited a television website in the past year.[14]

Television programs commonly feature websites in order to keep existing viewers and attract new viewers. One of the ways in which they do this is through providing more information about actors, storylines, etc. Another way is by allowing program viewers to network with each other through online discussion boards and web blogs. In this way, regular viewers of specific television programs can form online communities around the programs. Thus, the Internet has actually enhanced the ability of television networks to create and build audiences for specific television programs. By daily consuming television while using the Internet, cell phones, and other mobile communication devices, the interactive media environment of the 21st century has created a new dynamic for learning that we are only beginning to comprehend.

Interactive Learning Environments

Interactive communication technology has changed our understanding of learning. The new definition of learning proposed by scholars and educators describes learning as "participation in a learning environment or community where learners work together and support each other as they use information resources and tools to pursue their learning goals and solve problems."[15] The idea of a learning environment being inside a fixed "place of learning" such as a school or college is becoming obsolete. Learning environments can spring up anywhere where communication technology exists and learning communities can span across geopolitical, socioeconomic and cultural boundaries.

The diffusion of new communication technologies throughout the world is changing the way in which communication and learning take places. No longer is the concept of "mass communication" an accurate description of how people create and exchange messages. Digital technologies and the Internet make communication multi-directional and interactive, not one-way and passive. We can no longer view communication as either "interpersonal" or "mass mediated," because it is both.[16] The information superhighway is a two-way street that creates the potential for every person to be both a student and a teacher. On the Internet, there are no passive learners; every person is an active seeker of information, educational experiences, and entertainment.

In the new digital media environment, the temporal and spatial limitations of traditional mass media no longer apply. People do not have to show up at a certain time on a certain day to access the media they want, as they did with traditional broadcast television before the age of video recorders and TIVO. Communication scholars refer to this type of communication in which a person interacts with one or more people through unlimited media access at any time as "asynchronous communication." Today, most distance education programs, including the communication program in which I teach, utilize asynchronous communication. I go to a website and post my reading assignments and discussion questions, and my students, who live in many different time zones around the world, access their assignments whenever they want, complete their readings, and then post answers to my discussion questions on a discussion board. Other students do the same and then we have a discussion, not all at the same time, but asynchronously. This provides a tremendously flexible learning environment for students who have full-time jobs, family responsibilities, and who live far from my university. The COVID-19 pandemic exploded the use of online educational programs.[xvi]

---

xvi Dhawan, S. (June 2020). Online learning: A panacea in the time of COVID-19 crisis. *Journal of Educational Technology Systems.* Retrieved from https://www.ncbi.nlm.nih.gov/pmc/articles/PMC7308790/

Accessing the media whenever you want puts learning in the hands of each person. My students can learn a great deal or very little, depending upon how much they access and interact with the resources I provide for them, with me, and with their classmates. Jane Singer refers to this characteristic of the Internet as the "ultimate in individualism" because it has the capability to "empower the individual in terms of both the information he or she seeks and the information he or she creates."[17] This empowerment effect of the Internet and wireless communication channels is what attracts millions of people to interactive games and websites. People now have the ability to play games and interact with websites when they want and sometimes with whom they want. In addition to group activities that are enhanced through personal websites, web blogs, and pod-casting, as noted earlier, people can also interact with each other through internet-based interpersonal communication channels such as e-mail, instant messenger, cell phones and PDAs. One of the most popular forms of interactivity over the Internet is through the use of interactive games.

Learning through Games

Interactive games provide a powerful means of learning and have been used to teach children for many decades. In fact, just go to any on-line search engine and conduct a website search with the words, "learning through games." When I first tried this on google.com the search engine produced more than 600,000 web links in 2013. There are hundreds of companies now that specialize in making interactive games through which both children and adults can learn. When I pursued the academic literature by conducting the same search on google scholar, I found 811 related articles and books. Several decades ago, researchers at Johns Hopkins University conducted a seven-year study to show how people learn through playing games.[18] The use of interactive games, both face-to-face and computer-mediated, can greatly enhance learning. Medical students can now use computer game models as a tool for surgical education.[19] Post-graduate business students can learn management principles and decision-making through entertaining online computer simulations.[20] Students can learn health care information through online games.[21] Educators are even building web-based learning communities so virtually anything can be taught through interactive games.[22]

The use of interactive games for learning is not restricted to developed countries. A number of health-related needs are being met through interact games. In Malawi, for example, the Malawi Institute of Education published a report in 1991 that assessed the efficacy of an interactive board game increased students' accurate knowledge about HIV/AIDS.[23] At the time of the study, an appalling amount of inaccurate information existing among students, perpetuating misconceptions and myths which allowed HIV/AIDS to run rampant among the young and old.

Research results indicated that the board games facilitated both learning and enjoyment, and that the entertainment value of the game was an important contributor to students' inclination to learn about HIV/AIDS. In this study, the game players showed significant improvement in scores each time the game was played. In addition, the control group in the study (those who did not play the game) became positively influenced through discussions with the game-playing students.

One of the advantages of interactive computer programs is that the programs can be designed to address individual needs, concerns, and questions. Hawkins and colleagues tested the effectiveness of a drug abuse prevention computer game designed to help young people learn how to act when approached with drugs, stop using drugs, or how to get a friend to stop using drugs.[24] The computer game was taught to teachers and students by the Body Awareness Resource Network (BARN), which involved 5500 students ages 12-18. The researchers found that the game was effective in answering questions the adolescents had about drugs they had not tried, which could prove as a powerful tool in prevention.

Learning through Interactive Websites

Interactive websites are increasingly being used as centers for learning for both adults and children. The number of children accessing websites at school and home continues to skyrocket. By 2010, almost six out of ten children ages three to 17 used the Internet at home (57 percent) in the U.S.[25] Today, most American children are online. The overall buying power of the U.S. youth market is growing rapidly, attracting billions of online advertising dollars evidenced by the increasing number of ads aimed at children on the Internet. The Kaiser Family Foundation reported that more than 500 branded online games for food products, also called advergames, targeted children.[26] The combination of children spending more time online and additional advertising messages targeted to children makes media literacy one of the most important learning areas for children.

Online Media Literacy Learning

One of the most popular websites for children is Neopets.com. The website has more than 100 million accounts and more than 30 million total users, making Neopets one of the most influential children's websites on the Internet.[27] The website is translated into 10 languages and has a global audience, the largest concentrations being in the U.S.A., Canada and Australia. Neopets' press kit states the site is the ninth most visited site on the Internet based on a company-sponsored study by Media Matrix, which estimates that 39 percent of its users are under 13-years-old, 40 percent 13-17-years-old, and the remaining 21 percent are adult users.[28] The site attracts slightly more females than males with 57 percent female users.

Neopets.com was launched in 1999 by two British college students, Adam Powell and Donna Williams, who no longer own Neopets but continue to work with the company. Powell and Williams sold the company to Doug Dohring in April 2000. Dohring, who became the company's CEO, turned a profit in only four months after taking over the company. In 2005, Viacom's MTV Networks, which also owns Nickelodeon children's television network, purchased Neopets for $160 million.[29] The purchase of Neopets in conjunction with other Viacom holdings gave the company more than half of the children's online market share in 2006.

Because of Neopets.com faithful users, the site has been dubbed "the stickiest kids' site on earth."[30] Marketers use the term "sticky" in reference to the amount of time spent on any given website. The longer a user is on a website, the more opportunity that user will have to view advertising. In July of 2006, Media Matrix, an Internet ratings service, estimated that the average time spent per person per month on the Neopets website is 5 hours and 24 minutes.[31] Because Neopets.com has been so successful, many similar sites now exist such as Webkinz and *Club Penguin*. Both sites also are based on pets, as Webkinz has real-world plush pets while *Club Penguin* is completely virtual.

Dr. Eileen Wollslager, one of my doctoral students, conducted research to see if children could be taught media literacy skills through their interactions on the Neopets' website.[32] Her study specifically explored the ability of 4th and 5th graders to identify online advertising on the website after being given one media literacy training session. The goal of the training session was to teach children how to identify embedded online advertising. Only 23 percent of children were initially able to identify the purpose of branded games as advertising. Results of her study showed that after the training session, children's recognition of embedded ads increased 33 percent and recognition of branded advertising increased 26 percent. Initially, older children were able to recognize online advertising more readily than younger ones, but that difference disappeared after both groups were exposed to media literacy training. Thus, children can be taught how to recognize the persuasion techniques commonly employed by online advertisers.

Online Health Information

One of the most popular uses of the Internet is to access online health information. Some health-oriented websites mix entertainment with health knowledge to create a greater appeal. In general, more interactive design features provide a higher entertainment value to these websites. Those health-related websites with greater accessibility, usability, credibility and currency are the one that are the most popular, especially when combined with high degrees of interactivity.

For example, one of the uses of interactive HIV/AIDS prevention websites is to provide survivor stories from those who have received treatment for HIV infection and other serious diseases.[33] Use of the Internet has made these stories accessible to a great number of people. One group of researchers examined the quality of "transformation perspective" is a group of stories posted on a website.[34] This quality is defined as a "self-communicative experience that changes an individual's life so that priorities and self-identity are refocused."[35] The trigger event that alters the individual's life might be a diagnosis with cancer, HIV, diabetes, or some other serious illness; divorce; financial tragedy; unemployment; or retirement. The entertainment value of these stories is contingent on the dramatic elements of each story.

Learning through Weblogs

Although research on weblogs is still relatively new, studies have examined the motivations of people who both create their own blogs and who read blogs of others.[36] In the following section I will explain what blogs are, how they function, and why they can be a form of learning.

Blogs are most simply understood as online journals with archived entries presented in a chronological order. To read a blog is akin to reading a person's personal journal or diary. However, communication technology allows a blogger to greatly expand the form, content, structure, and functions of blogs. A typical blog, also called a weblog, not only provides Internet users with access to a series of archived Internet posts typically consisting of brief texts entered in reverse chronological order, but also provides hypertext links to other sites recommended by the author.[37] Although blogs are similar to a personal journal or diary, the web postings in a blog are intended for public consumption. Blogs are usually produced using special software. Some people use blogs as a Content Management System (CMS) or knowledge management tool to collect and post information for future reference that can be retrieved online anywhere and anytime a person has access to the Internet.

Blogs are products of blogging tools or platforms which automate the process of publishing online. The aid of blogging tools makes updating a blog a relatively simple process accomplished through a few clicks of a mouse. By opening a webpage, logging into an account, typing text into a text box, and clicking "submit," a blogger can update his or her blog. Even people with rudimentary computer skills can produce a blog.

The social influence of bloggers is found in the subculture they are creating in cyberspace. Famous bloggers are becoming celebrities on the Internet and in real life. Both journalists and academics have been attracted to blogs. It is difficult to estimate the total number of all the active blogs because blogs are still in the early stage of adoption. New blogs are being created every day while old ones are being abandoned as well; but overall, the number of blogs is constantly growing and blogging is becoming a trend in Internet community. More and more people are becoming involved in blogging, using their creative abilities to provide text, pictures, audio and video clips, and links to online resources. Talented bloggers have the ability to create entertainment content on their blogs, but also to educate and persuade others who view their blogs.

To date, most of the social influence of blogs has been political in nature.[38] However, consider the potential impact of the blogs produced by health professionals such as medical doctors, health nutritionists, and psychiatrists; or the blogs of celebrities such as actors, performing artists, and famous athletes. What about a weblog created by a famous terrorist such like Osama bin Laden? There is virtually no limit to the potential for promoting good and potential for promoting destructive behavior through weblogs. Just like radio, television, and film, the entertainment value of blogs will attract people and the informational content, values, and beliefs promoted will produce social change.

Children on the Internet

Children are fast becoming the Internet experts of the 21st century. Although many households contain one or more computer-literate parents, children are generally more expert in using the Internet than most adults and thus gain status through their internet skills. Children and young adults are especially attracted to the flexibility of the Internet, enabling them to educate themselves, complete their school work, communicate with friends and relatives using email, instant messaging and chat rooms, play games alone or with others, download music, visit fan sites, create their own website, and produce a weblog. By creating and exchanging information on the Internet, children and young adults are acquiring new technical skills and learning styles, replacing didactic learning and rule-bound knowledge acquisition with 'learning by doing.'[39]

The interactive characteristics of the Internet make it an ideal medium for entertainment-education. As internet literacy increases, children and young adults will find new opportunities of learning online through involvement in communication networks, role playing, online games, and consumption of entertainment. Current research shows that internet use appears to foster, rather than undermine, existing social contacts, connecting children into local, rather than global, networks.[40]

Bulletin Boards

Several producers of entertainment have used electronic bulletin boards to enhance the overall effects of entertainment-education productions. Electronic bulletin boards provide a means for media consumers to post feedback to entertainment messages. In a study of an entertainment-education drama on divorce on Korean television, researchers found that by providing a bulletin board for the program, program viewers increased their involvement with the program characters, which facilitated learning from the characters.[41] Numerous entertainment programs and fan websites use bulletin boards to facilitate discussion, thus creating online learning environments.

Interactive Games

Like many other forms of entertainment, video games and interactive websites were initially relegated to the realm of pure entertainment, with the exception of militaries around the world that soon discovered video games were great training laboratories, or what Tom Peters, co-author of *In Search of Excellence*, refers to as "skunk works."[42] Peters appropriated the name from Lockheed Aircraft's secret research lab where they designed the jet fighter for the U.S. Army Air Corps during World War II. The term originally came from the Al Capp cartoon strip, 'Lil Abner. The Skunk Works (or, alternatively Skonk Works) were where Lonesome Polecat and Hairless Joe brewed their 'Kickapoo Joy Juice.' Often the military are the most innovative in finding new ways to train and help people to learn quickly or create some special "juice" as Al Capp would say, especially during times of national crisis.

Thanks to many dozens of recent studies, we now understand that interactive games have much more learning potential than only for military applications. Video games and gaming websites have the potential to teach us all kinds of things, including biology, chemistry, medical science, health care, social relations, life-saving techniques, and communication skills. Twenty years from now, interactive video games and websites may be standard modes of learning in homes, classrooms, and universities throughout the world. Thus, it is very short-sighted to view interactive games through new communication technology as wasteful entertainment.

There are several important characteristics of interactive video games and websites that make them a powerful means of learning. Like all forms of communication, video games and gaming websites have both positive and negative effects. Like much of the media effects research, more studies have been conducted on the negative effects of video games. Unfortunately, the focus on study of the effects of violent video games has overshadowed the beneficial effects of video games for learning. Numerous scholars who contributed to an edited book by Peter Vorderer and Jennings Bryant provide evidence that learning through video games has enormous potential because of the way in which video games and websites draw and keep our involvement.[43]

More than 25 years ago, Thomas Malone identified three important factors that intrinsically motivate people to play video games: challenge, fantasy and curiosity.[44] These three motivational factors also draw people into interactive websites. Not knowing the outcome of a game provides a challenge, as do other players and time constraints. Also, knowing the outcome of previous games, such as "your wife's solitary record is 124 seconds," can provide part of the challenge. If you win the game by beating other players or even by beating a computer, as in a computer chess game, or perform better than others before you, the satisfaction you feel motivates you to play again. If you lose the game or like me, can't beat your wife's solitary record, you are also motivated to play again.

When a game player becomes cognitively and emotionally involved in the game, often through identification with the virtual player, the game player engages in what Malone called fantasy.[45] By identifying with the virtual player in a game a person can overcome the natural boundaries and limitations of real life. Fantasy is a great draw to get involved in an interactive game. Malone described curiosity as attraction to the technical aspects of a game that engage the player's sensory perception and intellect, such as the game's narrative or scenario, the control mechanisms to move players and navigate, and the sound cues that direct action. The combination of these three factors creates an intrinsically motivating high involvement experience for the interactive game player.

In addition to the challenge, fantasy and curiosity of interactive games, video game play also has four important characteristics that make them the most appealing of all media – they have a narrativity, they involve simulation, they are highly interactive, and they feature intelligence.[46] No other medium has all four of these characteristics. Narrativity simply means the telling of a story. Books, television programs and video games all have a narrative structure with a beginning, middle and some kind of climax leads to an end. Simulation—the ability to represent and mimic reality—is a strength of both television and video games. The tremendous advances in computer and animation technology have made digital simulation life-like. Interactivity, the ability for the media consumer to respond to the video game characters and vice versa, is not an attribute of television. Neither is intelligence, the ability of the game system to gather information from the media user and modify responses based on that information. Video games have two big advantages over traditional media systems: they are highly interactive and intelligent. These four characteristics all enhance learning through video games by creating the highest levels of motivation and involvement. You can't play a video game passively like you can watch television or listen to the radio. You have to be fully engaged. You must think, respond and interact and you can't go into an automatic response mode because the game can also be responding to you. Once you become deeply involved in a video game the potential for learning is maximized.

Christine Javid's research summarizes some of the important ways in which video games help people learn.[47] First, they use previous knowledge and learning as a currency to purchase highest levels of play and challenge, which leads to more learning. Second, video games provide immediate visual and audio feedback, directing players to learn quickly how to modify their learning strategies to become more effective. Third, the skills gained by video games are applicable to real life situations requiring the rapid processes of visual stimuli and quick decision making. Finally, video games motivate people to learn new ideas or tasks.

Examples of Learning through Games

Video games are increasingly being used around the world for educational purposes. In 2006, there was a gathering of educators, communication scholars, video game developers, and media professionals in Washington, DC for a serious games summit.[48] The purpose of the summit was to discuss the educational uses and effects of video games. Presenters from around the world shared many of the entertainment-education video games that have been developed and new gatherings of series games developers are taking place throughout the world.

Singapore's Nanyang Technological University created the Virtual Orchestra project in order to provide a realistic virtual orchestral experience to its players.[49] The project's objective is to develop a new and flexible tool that can be used both as an entertaining computer game and to introduce children to music, and a basic training tool for music students. The project incorporates multiple technological features, including 3D graphics, gesture recognition, real-time music score processing, and audience modeling. Children are able to receive a fully interactive and original orchestra experience.

In Washington, D. C., Jeff Kelsey, a game development teacher, from McKinley Technology High School, and Heidi Taylor, Director of Training for the Office of Disaster Preparedness of The American Red Cross, presented a video game that teaches fire prevention with two high school students.[50] Through the collaborative efforts of the High School with the Red Cross, Kelsey introduced an innovative curriculum by including educational game playing and game development.

Another way video games are being used is for science education. A video game called *Uncharted Depths* teaches ecology, zoology and oceanography through the simulation of a submarine.[51] Students can experience deep ocean exploration through the game and must learn to think like scientists while playing. The goal of *Uncharted Depths* is to turn the classroom into a miniature scientific community in which students learn to both procedurally and cognitively internalize the practices by which scientists answer questions about the world. Another science game, *Quest Atlantis*, is a water quality simulation that utilizes a 3D virtual, multi-user environment. Funded by National Science Foundation, *Quest Atlantis* combines strategies used in the commercial gaming environment with lessons from educational research on learning and motivation.[52] The game has been used by more than 5000 children located all over the world.[53] The game creates a virtual park called Taiga, and presents to students the serious ecological problems in the park which they have to study and help solve as field investigators.

If you would like to learn about the ancient civilizations on the Tigris and Euphrates Rivers, you can do so through *Discover Babylon*, an educational game that seeks to broaden and enhance public understanding and appreciation of Mesopotamian culture.[54] Or perhaps you want to learn how to speak Arabic but don't have a lot of time for language school. The U.S. military funded a video game called *Tactical Iraqi*, developed at the University of Southern California, to accelerate a learner's acquisition of spoken Arabic to assist in the rapid deployment of soldiers into volatile tactical situations.[55] One of the unique aspects of the *Tactical Iraqi* mission game is that it analyzes how "trust" is constituted in both virtual and experimental worlds, how digital experiences of the "self" of language learning are constructed as complex amalgams of "identity," "role," "subjectivity," and "voice." Sometimes problematic ideologies of language learning and literacy inform the design philosophy of the game.

Improving Athletic Performance

Athletes have been using video games for many years to learn all kinds of sports. The University of Memphis and University of Kentucky basketball teams play complex computer games in order to make them better on the basketball court by developing their visual and decision-making skills. One of the games they play, *IntelliGym*, originally was developed by an Israeli company and used to train Israeli fighter pilots.[56] Marc Prensky explains in his book, Digital Game-Based Learning, that video games are being used for so many different things that involve high levels of eye-to-hand coordination such as flying airplanes, using military weapons, and conducting surgery.[57] Those who play video games develop better visual skills as compared to those who don't. *IntelliGym* works by moving two sets of abstract figures across a dark screen. One set is larger and egg-shaped, while the other looks like small video-game spaceships. A player tries to attach one of the smaller figures to a larger one to steal its "energy." The player also must "shoot" to transfer power from one small figure to another as openings appear. The game gets progressively more difficult as it's played and is individually adjusted depending on a player's strengths or weaknesses.

University of Memphis basketball coaches expect to judge the game's success by turnover rates, shooting percentages and other statistics. If a player starts picking better shots or getting more assists, it might be due, in part, to the computer game. Mark Galloway, Head Coach of Carmel High School in Indiana, credits the *IntelliGym* for a record-breaking season in 2008 with a 22-3 record, including MIC Conference Champions and Sectional Champions.[58] One of the Memphis coaches speculates that video game training may one day become as common as weight rooms and strength coaches.

Games for Health, Physical Therapy and Rehabilitation

Interactive video games are increasingly being used by the medical community and by health educators. Some games facilitate physical therapy and rehabilitation. Others promote exercise and help people to learn about important health issues. One of the growing epidemics in the U.S. is obesity. Although overuse of video games can certainly contribute to obesity, video games can also be used to help prevent obesity. One such video game is *Dance Dance Revolution*, first introduced as an arcade game in Japan. Jason Enos, product manager at Konami Digital Entertainment America in Redwood City, California, reported that 2.5 million copies of the game were sold in North America in its first four years of distribution in the U.S., which began in 2001.[59] *Dance Dance Revolution*, abbreviated *DDR*, is being used not only by individuals, but also by a number of organizations seeking to improve the health of its employees and their families.

One such organization is the West Virginia Public Employees Insurance Agency (PEIA) as part of a health program. PEIA has 215,000 public employees, including teachers and their dependents. The agency believes it is the first insurance provider to use the game to cut costs. Konami Digital Entertainment America distributes the Japanese game in the United States. Nidia Henderson, the health promotions manager of PEIA, estimated that obesity claims in 2004 cost the company $77 million.[60] In partnership with researchers at West Virginia University, *DDR* was made available to at-risk children in twenty West Virginia schools. In that state, nearly 43% of children screened in the Coronary Artery Risk Detection in Appalachian Communities project were considered overweight and more than 25% were obese.[61]

Playing *DDR* improves cardiovascular health as well as eye-hand coordination. Players stand on a three-foot-square metal mat with an arrow on each side pointing in an up, down, right or left direction. Arrows scroll up the video screen to the beat of more than 100 tunes chosen by the player. As an arrow moves across the video screen, the player steps on the corresponding arrow on the dance platform. As players improve their speed and scores, hidden songs are uncovered. The speed of the game increases as players skill level increases, resulting in a vigorous aerobic workout. New players of the game can easily become winded after two or three songs.

Researchers at Syracuse University in New York have been investigating the game's potential to improve cardiovascular and physiological effects of children. Penn State University scholars also are studying how much energy children use playing *DDR* and similar games.[62] At Morgantown High School, one of the 20 pilot sites, curiosity about the flashing lights and upbeat music drew students inside health classes, attracting the sedentary and the seasoned athlete alike.[63] Several studies by researchers in the U.S. and Finland report weight loss and other health benefits of *DDR*.[64]

The home version of *DDR* includes a workout mode that counts how many calories the user burns while playing. As Jason Enos says, "The fitness and workout aspect of *Dance Dance Revolution* is hidden behind a layer of fun and entertainment — that is what is motivating kids who are overweight to get them up on the dance pad and move their bodies."[65] Other video games are on the market today that teach and promote fitness by skillfully combining entertainment and exercise instruction.[66]

One of the innovative games developed by Warhol, Realtime Associates, Inc. for teenagers and young adults dealing with cancer is *Re-Mission* and *Re-Mission 2*.[67] Another company, Forterra Systems, Inc., has developed a multiplayer online simulation (MOS) to teach high school students CPR (cardio-pulmonary resuscitation) and other medical emergency actions. In a similar vein, a team from the University of Illinois at Chicago (UIC) have developed two innovative technologies–a 2D simulation and a mobile application, both designed to train public health workers to effectively respond to a bioterrorism attack or natural outbreak, such as pandemic flu. Whereas the game is ideal for pre-event training, the session will show how cell phone technologies can be leveraged for just-in-time training for first responders and the general public in bioterrorism response planning. The company has developed the mobile Panflu-prep (www.publichealthgames.com) to help the general public prepare for a pandemic flu epidemic.

Another important use of video games is for physical therapy and rehabilitation. One of the most difficult treatment challenges of doctors is to alleviate the pain experienced by burn patients during surgery and physical therapy. The pain endured by burn victims can be unbearable and patients commonly report experiencing excessive pain during medical procedures, especially during severe burn wound care.[68] The opioid analgesics now used by doctors to manage pain during burn wound care have many side effects, including nausea, constipation, interference with appetite, and disruption of sleep cycles. Patients treated for severe burn trauma typically undergo daily care to clean wounds and to monitor the healing progress, which requires taking off bandages and putting new ones on, causing severe to excruciating pain.[69]

One of the innovative approaches to pain treatment is through video games. The functions of the brain employed while enjoying entertainment reduces the transmission of pain messages to the brain. In other words, while the brain is engaged in entertainment it has less capacity to process pain. One of the video games being used by doctors and burn patients to lessen pain is called *SnowWorld*, the first virtual world custom-designed for burn patients.[70] Patients who play this game are able to escape mentally into an immersive virtual world can help reduce their pain experience.[71] By wearing a virtual reality (VR) helmet, instead of patients seeing their burn wounds during treatment and therapy, they see themselves floating through an icy 3-D canyon. In this ice canyon they can shoot snowballs at snowmen, igloos, and robots which explode with 3-D animations and sound effects; or they can shoot at penguins which turn upside down with a quack.

Clinical studies show that playing *SnowWorld* can reduce patient's pain ratings during severe burn wound care by 30–50 percent.[72] Patients who played *SnowWorld* during physical therapy also reported large reductions in the amount of time they spent thinking about pain.[73] In one case study, a patient engrossed in *SnowWorld* experienced an amazing 90 percent reduction in feeling pain during staple removals from a severe burn as compared to pain ratings while playing a Nintendo video game control condition during the same wound care session.[74]

Consistent with the attentional hypothesis of how virtual reality reduces pain, a recent double-blind, laboratory-controlled, thermal-pain study found significantly greater pain reduction in a group that engaged in a high-tech virtual reality experience as compared to a group that received a low-tech virtual reality experience.[75] It seems the higher the quality of entertainment of the video game the more it reduces sensations of pain.

Another video game being used to help children overcome pain during medical procedures is *Free Dive*, a virtual reality-based, 3D undersea exploration adventure that invites players to swim with sea turtles and tropical fish as they hunt for hidden treasure. The virtual reality entertainment, created by BreakAway ltd., is being studied by medical researchers at University of Maryland Medical Center and the non-profit foundation Believe in Tomorrow.[76] *Free Dive* enables children to experience a rich undersea world of adventure where they can swim with sea turtles and tropical fish while they search for hidden treasure. Research shows that therapeutic power of *Free Dive* enabled children to better tolerate painful medical procedures.[77]

Smoking and Substance Abuse Prevention

As well as promoting healthy lifestyles, video games are also being used to curtail destructive health behaviors such as smoking, drug and alcohol abuse. Researchers at the Center for Health Communication and Marketing at the University of Connecticut are designing and testing two entertainment-education approaches to reduce substance abuse and risky sexual behaviors, which are often related. One video game they have developed with hip-hop artists is called *Xperience*, which addresses the risks of club drug use (including alcohol, marijuana, ecstasy, and angel dust). Players interact with critical components of urban youth culture, showing that substance-free events can be just as fun and fulfilling as alternative events but without the risk of substance abuse. The *Xperience* game tag line is "for those who choose not to use." Initial research indicates that youth in the 14-20 age group accept drug-free entertainment and are receptive to persuasive drug resistance messaging in video games.[78]

Darion Rapoza and William Urquhart patented a drug abuse prevention program that uses computer-based role-playing games enable players to experience simulated effects of substance abuse on the individual, family, friends, and community.[79] Players learn about drug use by experiencing the adverse consequences of drug abuse and the rewards of avoiding drugs. Each player takes the role of a character in the story, which could be a positive or negative role model. To avoid risky behavior, players must practice social resistance skills and are rewarded for avoiding drugs as well as for helping other characters avoid drug use. The game creates a social learning environment to teach players to avoid substance abuse as they learn by experience about the negative effects of drugs and teaches them how to resist pressures to use drugs.

One of the popular smoking prevention video games is *Rex Ronan: Experimental Surgeon*. Rex Ronan, the star character in the game, is an experimental surgeon who shrinks to near-microscopic size, enters the body of his patient, and uses his laser scalpel to blast away the tar, phlegm, plaque, debris, and precancerous cells caused by years of smoking. Players move Rex Ronan through nine areas of the body and answer questions about the effects of tobacco. When players see realistic images such as arteries clogged with plaque and tar deposits in the lungs, they learn about the harmful effects of tobacco use and are repulsed by the vivid visual imagery showing the destruction of the human body from smoking. Research shows that children and teens who use the *Rex Ronan* video game are more likely to decide to not start smoking.[80]

In summary, interactive video games and interactive websites are increasingly being used to promote health and facilitate learning in many different areas. These forms of entertainment are extremely popular and represent the new frontier of entertainment-education for social change. The next chapter will explore the use of entertainment to promote intellectual and spiritual growth.

Chapter 14
Entertainment for Spiritual Growth

One of the areas of greatest potential for entertainment is the promotion of socially beneficial values and beliefs that stimulate intellectual and spiritual growth. In Metta Spencer's ground-breaking book, *Two Aspirins and a Comedy*,[1] she devotes a considerable amount of time discussing the ability of television to create transcendence, that is, to help people to think beyond themselves and their material needs and wants and focus instead on the most important things in life – family, friendships, moral development, and spiritual fulfillment. Spencer argues that good entertainment does not simply help people to relax and pass the time diverting attention from the demands of life, but also nourishes the soul.

Most entertainment has some philosophical or religious worldview embedded in its content. Spencer notes that the important question is not whether a certain television program or film is saying something about transcendent values and beliefs, but rather what it is teaching. As was discussed in earlier chapters, it is naïve for us to be satisfied with the cliché, "it's only entertainment," which is often uttered by writers and producers when asked to be accountable for the content they create. The academic research presents overwhelming evidence showing that people learn from entertainment and role model what they see and hear. Violent entertainment content will promote violent behavior in some consumers;[2] media depictions of irresponsible sexual behavior will promote sexual irresponsibility;[3] and even stories of suicide will encourage suicide among some people suffering severe depression.[4] Thus Spencer is correct in framing the important question as not whether we learn about transcendence, but rather, what do we learn. Entertainment teaches us something about the origin, nature and existence of man, the nature and existence of God, life beyond this material world, and life after death.

Although it's clear that some entertainment programs on American television have promoted prosocial values and beliefs, very few entertainment programs are specifically designed to enhance intellectual and spiritual development. The television programs that have addressed important social values and beliefs have produced mixed results. Egalitarianism, a worldview which regards of equal value all men and women irrespective of race, creed, age, or social practices, is rooted in the transcendent belief that "all men are created equal." Hurr and Robinson assessed the impact of *Roots,* a television miniseries, acclaimed as a prosocial program that was intended to encourage positive attitudes of Whites toward Blacks in the United States.[5] Results of their study indicated that the program did not produce substantial changes in racial attitudes. Three other communication scholars, Ball-Rokeach, Grube, and Rokeach[6] analyzed the effects of *Roots II*, a follow-up miniseries to *Roots*, on television viewers' belief in egalitarianism. They found no evidence to support that *Roots II* positively influenced viewers to value egalitarianism to a greater degree.

Shogun was a third miniseries that was analyzed in terms of its prosocial effects. Although exposure to *Shogun* did not change stereotypical views of Japanese, the program did increase viewers' knowledge of the Japanese language, history, and customs; and slightly affected attitudes by increasing viewers' desire for closer social ties with the Japanese.[7] Prosocial content in situational comedies has also received some attention by media scholars. Viewers have learned a variety of prosocial behaviors from entertainment-oriented serials.[8] Amato and Malatesta demonstrated that family situational comedies enabled viewers to learn a wide variety of skills related to coping, facilitating, and assertive behaviors.[9]

I briefly discussed in an earlier chapter how a group of researchers at the University of Washington in Seattle created an experiment to determine if a single television program could effectively promote two important social values—egalitarianism and environmentalism. As predicted, I reported how viewers of the program donated significantly more money to pro-environmental and pro-egalitarian organizations than did non-viewers.[10] Program viewers also increased the degree to which they valued equality and a clean environment.

The researchers attribute their results by explaining the "self-reflection" and "self-education" effect of the program.[11] Viewers were able to assess their own values in comparison to the values of others, and then made changes based on these comparisons. Viewers who discovered areas of prejudice, sexism, or irresponsible environmental behavior in their lives were motivated to eliminate those antisocial beliefs and behavior. Many scholars were surprised by the powerful prosocial effects of a single 30-minute television program. What the researchers demonstrated through their innovative experiment is that by discussing important values and comparing them through an entertainment program people can be motivated to make changes in their lives.

Attraction to Spiritual Themes

It should not be surprising that people want prosocial entertainment and are interested in content that promotes positive values and addresses spiritual issues. Entertainment television programs in the U.S. which depict or convey shared values, moral guidelines and spiritual or religious concepts and messages have attracted sizable viewing audiences. The United States not only has a strong Judeo-Christian heritage but there is considerable evidence that it is still largely a religious nation whose current beliefs are rooted in its past. Studies by The Barna Research Group indicate 90 percent of Americans have some kind of religious faith and 69% believe in God when described as the all-powerful, all-knowing, perfect creator of the universe who rules the world today.[12] In addition, three quarters of the sample strongly agreed there is only one true God who created the world and still reigns over it. In 2008, approximately 101 million people in the U.S. identified themselves as born-again Christians.[13]

Three out of five adults indicated they had made a "personal commitment to Jesus Christ." Also, prayer and to a lesser extent, organized religion play a significant part in the lives of many. Barna's assessment is similar to the research findings from national Gallop polls, which indicate 86-90 percent of American adults believe in God, 81 percent believe in heaven, 70 percent believe there is a devil and that hell exists, and 75 percent believe in angels.[14] The vast majority of Americans also believe in the divinity of Jesus Christ, the Bible as the literal or inspired word of God, life after death, and miracles performed by the power of God. In summarizing the results of numerous studies on the state of religion in the united States in more recent years, George Gallup Jr. has identified several underlying themes: (1) widespread, continuing appeal of religion, (2) a high percentage of people attesting to orthodox Judeo-Christian beliefs and doctrines, (3) people's limited acknowledgment of the Bible, doctrines, and traditions of their own church, (4) inconsistent and overlapping beliefs, (5) superficiality of faith or not knowing what one believes, and (6) eager searching for meaning in life, hunger to know God, and belief in prayer and present-day miracles.[15]

Although these statistics change each year, Barna's 20-year project of measuring the Christian faith among Americans still shows that the U.S. is predominantly Christian with regards to its religious preference, with one in four Americans actively involved in Christian practices.[xvii]

In addition to the commonly held faith in God expressed by many Americans, there also is a growing interest in angels, miracles, and supernatural stories that emerged in Hollywood during the 1990s, as evidenced by the number of films released in recent years with spiritual plots, often featuring angelic beings. These films include the *Lord of the Rings* trilogy based on the works of JRR Tolkien, the *Chronicles of Narnia* series based on the works of C.S. Lewis, and the following films: *Dear God and Life Less Ordinary* in 1996, *The Preacher's Wife*, Michael, *The Apostle*, and *Bogus* in 1997, *What Dreams May Come*, *Meet Joe Black*, *Prince of Egypt*, and *Simon Birch* in 1998, *Sixth Sense*, *End of the Age*, *Revelation*, *Lost Souls*, the *Omega Code*, *Stigmata* and *Dogma* in 1999, *Johan: A Veggie Tales Movie*, *Signs* in 2002, *The Passion of the Christ* in 2004, and *The Diary of a Mad Black Woman* in 2005, and *Facing the Giants*, *One Night with the King*, and *The DaVinci Code* in 2006, and *The Nativity Story* and *Amazing Grace* in 2007. While religious themes have always been popular, the current level of popularity seems to have a different nature. A *USA Today* article observed that "while there is not a new intersection,... ,there is a new celebratory take on it [religion] all. These [faith and spiritual the E-1 me] films explore and embrace a higher authority in a more humanistic way."[16]

While one might suggest the resurgence of spiritual themes to be motivated by the bottom-line revenue potential or by public concern over the quality of films and television

---

[xvii] Barna. (4 March 2020). *Barna: State of the Church.* Retrieved from https://www.barna.com/research/changing-state-of-the-church/

programs, the increased interest in spirituality may be a larger societal social change. According to Michael Medved, "it [increase in films with faith] clearly is a response that's going on in the larger culture."[17] If the growth in the number of films and television programs with spiritual themes is a result of a cultural change, one might also assume a difference in the manner in which viewers interact with the programs. Further interest in angelic themes is evident in the growing number of special interest sites on the Internet. There are more than 150 homepage sites on the Internet catering to the consumer interested in angelic themes. Themes range from meeting your guardian angel to personal testimonies of encounter with angels. At the height of its popularity, the unofficial *Touched by an Angel* website had attracted nearly 7000 visitors per month.[18]

The relationship between religion and television has been explored by a number of communication scholars. Buddenbaum and Stout's edited book on media and religion indicates viewers of religious television programming seek many of the same benefits from viewing as most television viewers but also use religious programs to support their belief systems and fulfill a need to know themselves better.[19] Abelman discovered that disenchantment with secular television, in conjunction with religiosity, motivated some religious television viewers to seek out purely religious television content.[20] However, George Gerbner and his colleagues discovered that viewers of religious television programming basically had similar viewing tastes as non-viewers of religious programming.[21] In the first chapter I mentioned that religious talk show viewers also enjoy quasi-spiritual talk shows like those of *Oprah Winfrey*.[22]

These studies indicate that there is probably more in common with religious and non-religious television viewers that what many people might assume. Both groups like good drama, they like good talk show hosts that are concerned about spiritual issues, and they like programming content that deals with transcendent themes like angels, miracles, and life after death. The surge that began during the 1990s of books, articles, television programs, films, websites and other forms of communication that promote Christian beliefs and practices has not really been that unusual. Moll points out that these recent manifestations of the life of Jesus in popular culture are not a recent phenomenon, since "Jesus has been a regular feature since moving pictures were invented in the 1890s."[23]

CBS Television and Spiritual Themes

Since *The Great American Values Test* showed how a single 30-minute television program could influence beliefs, many wondered if long-running television series focused on spiritual themes could have a strong influence. This was a natural question that Ken Wales and Martha Williamson, producers of the CBS television series *Christy* and *Touched by an Angel* respectively, wondered. However, they had a lot of convincing to do. CBS executives did not give strong support both series, letting one of them die and nearly killing the second one too. Nevertheless, both series are some of the best examples of popular prosocial programming that have aired on network television in the U.S. *Christy*, which lasted 20 episodes, was aired for two seasons in 1994 and 1995. Based on the bestseller by Catherine Marshall, *Christy* told the story of an idealistic nineteen-year-old who leaves the comforts of her home in Asheville, Tennessee, in 1912, to teach school in the impoverished Appalachian community of Cutter Gap. Armed only with an inner strength, unwavering faith, and endurance, the inexperienced *Christy* Huddleston encounters and overcomes unexpected challenges and wins the love and respect of the local community, including the close friendship and love of two men. Due to changes in CBS's corporate structure and executive leadership, *Christy* was discontinued after two years despite its loyal following and growing audience. However, the audience it built gravitated to the second family-oriented program launched by CBS in 1994, *Touched by an Angel.*

Touched by an Angel addressed contemporary problems of society through its positive portrayal of God and angels. The program attracted a highly loyal viewer following, generated considerable fan mail, and encouraged viewers to participate through unofficial websites where they can acquire information on their favorite angel, read synopses on upcoming shows, and even get "angelic" counsel. The success of the program was reflected in the Nielsen ratings which consistently placed the program in the top 10 of all prime-time programs from 1996 through its last season in 2002-2003. The program, which ended after 212 episodes, successfully entered syndication and in 1999 was broadcast every weekday on PAX-NET that year to as faraway places as Ulaan Bataar, Mongolia.[24] Although there were no academic research on how the spiritual themes in *Christy* affected television viewers, a major study was conducted on assessing the influence of *Touched by an Angel.*

There are several reasons why *Touched by an Angel* is an interesting focal point for media research. First, the dramatic series is both a reflection of and response to a growing interest in angels which has permeated the American culture in the 1990s. This has taken place both inside and outside traditional religious circles and institutions and is evidenced by the prevalence of books, articles, seminars, Internet sites and other materials devoted to the subject.[25] Second, although occasionally there have been popular television programs in the past which have dealt with angels and other religious concepts and themes, the television and film industry has been criticized for ignoring religion and spiritual matters and even producing anti-religious content in the recent past.[26] *Touched by an Angel* contradicted the criticism that the American television industry was reluctant to provide family programming because of its focus on the advertising potential of a younger demographic. Third, the apparent intensity of fan interest in *Touched by an Angel* gave it a cult-like following and status that successful television programs and films sometimes achieve. Thus, the influence of *Touched by an Angel* is expected to be more powerful and long-term that most television programs.

Touched by an Angel is a prosocial television series that presents an alternative answer to the problems faced by society. The issues addressed in the series are not necessarily unique but the solution to the issues is one of the differentiating characteristics of the series. The intent of each episode is to present God as the solution to the problem through the intervention of angels. The angelic characters encourage the human characters to discover that God loves you, forgiveness is healing, and the truth will set you free.[27] Wendy Kaminer describes the program as a "blend of new age optimism, liberal social attitudes, and old-time religion."[28] According to *Touched by an Angel* executive producer Martha Williamson, "every successful [television] show has a point-of-view and ours is: God exists, He has a plan, He knows what he is doing, and he doesn't make mistakes."[29]

The existence of a set of well-defined production rules is not a unique quality of the program. The practice of creating a "production bible" is widely used within the industry. The bible sets forth certain rules of the production that should be followed and not broken. The spiritual dimension of the rules for the production of *Touched by an Angel* establish the program as a unique resource for testing religious and spiritual dimensions and the degree to which the audience identify these elements.

The popularity among viewers of the program is clearly evidenced by the ratings history and audience feedback since the program's inception in 1994. Although *Touched by an Angel* was given a less than enthusiastic endorsement from CBS, who ordered only 6 programs rather than the general practice of 13 programs, the audience ratings were high. In spite of the high ratings, CBS made plans to cancel the program after the first season. They later reversed their plans after receiving more than 30,000 phone calls and letters requesting continuation of the series.[30] The popularity of *Touched by an Angel* was consistently high for many years, making it CBS's most popular prime-time drama of the 1990s. *Touched by an Angel* began its sixth season in the top 10 of all prime time television programs.

According to Betsy Sharley of MediaWeek , "While it [*Touched by an Angel*] does well in the heartland, Angel is also extremely strong in urban markets, including New York, Chicago and Los Angeles. Its viewers cut across demographic, economic, religious and racial lines. Letters come by the thousands, ..."[31] The program has received over 2000 letters from fans each week. An analysis of a sample of letters provided by the program producers indicates significant interaction between the viewers and the cast of the program. The letters include comments like "I had planned to kill myself ... but I would like to thank you for giving me back my life," as well as viewers who felt compelled to ask others for forgiveness, and reports of reconciled marriages.[32] Both the producers and cast of *Touched by an Angel* have acknowledged that the program has touched their own lives. According to Williamson, people are deeply affected by the primary message, "God loves you."[33] Audience accounts of the program's influence have spawned such episodes as "More True Tales from *Touched by an Angel*."[34]

Research of *Touched by an Angel* indicates that television audiences are looking for spiritual uses of dramatic television programming.[35] *Touched by an Angel* viewers were often attracted to the program because it dealt with spiritual issues, stimulated their spiritual awareness, and caused them to think about and evaluate their own life experiences, beliefs and the world around them in spiritual terms. They were less likely to use the program to form new beliefs, make decisions and take relevant actions such as become more involved in organized religious institutions or activities.

Dramatic programming represented by *Touched by an Angel* can draw audiences who seek to explore or reinforce their spirituality and encourage them to think more deeply and feel good about spiritual matters. For some viewers, including many who participated in the study by Piper and colleagues, viewing dramatic television programming containing spiritual content may cause substantial changes in beliefs and behavior.[36]

The effects of watching *Touched by an Angel* also spilled over into peoples' interpersonal relationships. Viewers of the program encouraged an average of 9.4 people to watch the program and discussed episodes of *Touched by an Angel* with an average of 11.4 people.[37] This suggests that programs of this nature may stimulate interpersonal communication and that interaction between programming containing spiritual content and audiences seeking it for various reasons may, in turn, prompt audience growth in some special way.

Research also confirms a great deal of previous research which indicates that audience members form strong parasocial relationships with television characters, including fictional ones. The results further suggest that some television viewers may develop unusually strong parasocial attachments to spiritual characters. Viewers of *Touched by an Angel* were very consistently "involved" with the program's three angel characters as indicated by their responses to all parasocial scale items which were included in the study. These research findings suggest that parasocial relationships with spiritual characters and the spiritual uses and gratifications audiences seek from dramatic programming containing spiritual content may be closely associated.

In summary, the success of *Christy* and *Touched by an Angel* during the 1990s opened the door to more religious-oriented television drama. One spinoff program, the television drama *Promised Land*, was developed from one of the story themes in the *Touched by an Angel* series. In the past two decades there have been many different television dramas that have addressed transcendent values and beliefs. These programs are a source of learning about religious values and beliefs and promote dialogue about spirituality.

Spirituality in Film

As noted earlier, theatrical films in the U.S. have a long history of portraying biblical stories from both the old and new testaments of the Bible. It is important to note that the depictions of Jesus in popular film can vary greatly and have been explored by several film scholars. While trying to place *The Passion of the Christ* within the context of the "Jesus film" genre, Hartenstein discovered in the Internet Movie Database that there were more than a hundred significant interpretations of Jesus in films.[38] These depictions range from "costume-dramas" to stylized contemporary updates and imaginative efforts to capture spirit more than letter. Kinnard and Davis chronicle the life of Jesus on film from 1897 to 1992, reviewing 46 of the more notable films in this genre.[39] These reviews provide a glimpse of the broad scope of popular films, predominantly produced in Hollywood, that touch on the life of Jesus. Ivan Butler's *Religion in the Cinema* presents a broad overview of how religious figures and themes have been portrayed in films, beginning with a review of the silent film era.[40] His work incorporates film treatments of all sorts of religious characters, including priests, ministers, evangelists, missionaries, churches, saints, nuns and witches. In Larry May's work on mass culture and the motion picture industry, he devoted a considerable time to discussing religious influences in film.[41] May's attention to the religious aspects of popular film history sparked Terry Lindvall's fascinating work on the church's relationship to moving pictures during the silent era, which revealed the popular use of film by churches as a means of providing educational content for church attendees.[42]

A number of scholars have discussed the role of religion in shaping the cultural environment in which American films were created. A strong alliance between entertainment entrepreneurs and churchgoers created a bridge for the use of films in churches.[43] For example Musser spent a considerable amount of time studying *The Passion Play* on stage and on screen, showing the popular appeal of the dramatic story of Jesus.[44] In a similar vein of scholarship conducted in Great Britain, Burrows showed the symbiotic relationship between the British theatre of the late Victorian and Edwardian era and the early British silent film industry. Both British theatre and early film have dealt with spiritual values and religious faith.[45]

In their study of the American silent film era, both Sloan[46] and Ross[47] acknowledge the important role of religious faith and church practices in the shaping of early American film culture. In a study of Hilltown, Indiana, Waller[48] explored the intersection of race, religion and movie viewing from 1896 to 1930. Focusing in on movie fans in small American towns, Fuller examined the influence of the church and cinema on morality during the silent film era.[49] All these studies showed a good deal of desire for transcendent themes in popular films.

Moving beyond the boundaries of American culture, Holloway contributed a groundbreaking international perspective to the history of film and religion. His broad survey presents a theological perspective for the study of film and provides useful guidelines for understanding religious films. Holloway's critical reflections helped film scholars to view cinema within the context of the intellectual history of ideas such as transcendentalism and existentialism. For example, Holloway[50] shows how cinema reflects the human predicament, provides political commentary, and invites religious dialogue; he casts filmmakers like Carl Dreyer, Ingmar Bergman, Robert Bresson, and Charlie Chaplin as theologians of a visual twentieth century.

In addition to Holloway's work, another valuable international perspective of film and religion was generated by group of film historians who attended the 1990 Domitor Conference, resulting in a voluminous work titled *Une Invention du Diable? Cinema des Premiers Temps et Religion* (*An Invention of the Devil? Religion and Early Cinema*). The participants discussed both the stylistic and historiographic aspects of early film and organized religion. Contrary to some perceptions that people of religious faith generally resisted films as evil, there is much evidence to show that many religious people believed film could be a powerful medium to promote religious faith.[51] The power of film to show not only biblical history, but also the lives of modern day believers, was not lost on the Church.

Learning Spiritual Beliefs through Film

One framework for analyzing religious faith and popular film within the cultural milieu is to view film going as a dialogic encounter in which, in the traditional of Martin Buber and Mikhail Bakhtin, "the spectator allows the images to suggest their own meaning" without "sacrificing one's own religious faith and convictions.[52] One of the important ways in which people engage films is to explore their own faith and religious beliefs and to help them to communicate their faith and religious beliefs to others. Certainly, Hollywood's epic biblical films and films that promote other religious faiths such as *Gandhi* (Hinduism), *Little Buddha* (Buddhism), *Seven Years in Tibet* and *Kundun* (Tibetan Buddhism), *The Message* and *Malcolm X* (Islam, Nation of Islam), to name a few, are great sources of learning about religious beliefs. Beginning in the 1930s evangelical churches launched a sustained effort to communicate through film, or what Terry Lindvall and Andrew Quicke refer to as "celluloid sermons."[53]

Jesus films are modern day parables that communicate the gospel through narratives embedded in contemporary culture.[54] Konzelman theorizes that films are processed by people like parables of Christ and can both create dialogue about Christianity and promote Christian education.[55] Others scholars like Williams,[56] Ostwalt[57] and Johnston[58] focus on the broad influence of film on religion and culture, recognizing that the movie theater is the new pulpit from which religious beliefs are addressed. More people today will receive spiritual messages in a movie theater than will receive them in a church. People are spiritually influenced by films, regardless of whether they are perceived to be religious or not. In an edited volume on film portrayals of elusive connections to Scriptural texts, for example, Aiechele and Walsh extend the imagination by mining all kinds of biblical themes in contemporary cinema.[59] Coates also provides creative space for bridging contemporary films with biblical themes.[60]

There are so many Hollywood films with biblical content that one must read several books to develop a good understanding of the extensiveness of spiritual themes in popular cinema. Kreistzer tediously traced the transference of biblical texts and concepts onto the big screen.[61] Two other scholars, Campbell and Pitts, created an exhaustive catalog of films and television programs that dealt with biblical subjects during the time span of 1893 through 1980.[62] In his study of religious and biblical spectaculars, Forshey sees a close connection between popular films, historical context and religion, noting that many of the religious scenarios in popular biblical narratives addressed national crises such as wars, threats, racism, and sexual violence.[63] He argued that in every generation Jesus is contextualized on film as a savior of that time period.

In his study of Christ characters and anti-Christ characters in film, Malone focused attention on the ways in which Jesus has been depicted in popular cinema.[64] Babington and Evans focused their research on Hollywood epic films such as Hebrew Bible films, Christ films, and Roman-Christian epic films.[65] Their review highlights the political subtexts of religious films and their commentary on American religious culture. In 1997, W. Barnes Tatum published his review of films dealing with the life of Jesus, reflecting on the cultural histories in which the films were received.[66] Focusing on the modes of storytelling and mythmaking in a narrative tradition, Walsh identified specific scriptural texts with specific depictions of Jesus on film.[67]

Some scholars speculate that movie viewers see Jesus films as visual gospels.[68] A Jesus film is defined as a film which dramatizes a historical biography of Jesus based on the New Testament. Mikkelson and Gregg's research focused attention on the narrative fidelity of the portrayals of Jesus based on historical records and biblical texts.[69] But again, their vantage point has been that of the scholar. Though conceptions of narrative fidelity and historicity of Jesus films are often discussed by academics, movie viewers have their own perspectives. Having discussed some of the important scholarly contributions of religion and film with a focus on the life of Jesus, I now will discuss one of the most powerful Jesus films, *The Passion of the Christ*.

The Passion of the Christ

One of the most widely viewed and profitable films in the history of American cinema is *The Passion of the Christ*, produced and directed by Mel Gibson. The film, released just prior to the Easter season of 2004, portrays the last twelve hours of the life of Jesus Christ. It is the most recent in a long line of dramatic films dealing with the life of Jesus Christ in some way. Many of these films, including Gibson's epic, have been designed to both entertain audiences, thus reaping large profits, and to educate them about the life of Christ and His teachings. The Passion of the Christ is unique within the genre of films dealing with the life of Christ for several reasons. First, the sheer scope of its audiences and related commercial success is unprecedented for films about the life of Christ. From its release on Ash Wednesday, 2004 through July 2004, the 30 million dollar film earned nearly $612 million in theater revenue worldwide.[70] Nearly one in three Americans (31 percent) reportedly watched the film in a random survey conducted by Barna.[71] In the first week of its subsequent release on DVD and VHS, nearly nine million copies were sold, topping such popular films as *The Lord of the Rings*.[72]

Second, *The Passion of the Christ* has unique aesthetic and technical qualities. Gibson focused almost exclusively on the suffering of Christ through the brutal treatment by the Romans. The language spoken during the time period of the film, Aramaic, is the spoken language of the film. Gibson allowed the film to be subtitled in English partly due to feedback from audiences who reviewed the film in the U.S. prior to its release.[73]

A third distinctive is that the film was promoted through a creative, contemporary, and multi-faceted $25 million dollar marketing strategy.[74] The film was financed and promoted by one filmmaker, Mel Gibson, and not a large entertainment conglomerate like most commercial feature films. Gibson was unable to broker a typical financing and distribution plan, and thus directly partnered with large churches and Christian organizations. The magnitude of Mel Gibson's celebrity status and his ability to fund the project personally were important variables contributing to the film's influence.

Finally, *The Passion of the Christ* is unique because it stirred a great deal of controversy prior its release. Although other biblical epics and films about Jesus, for example, *The Last Temptation of Christ*, have stirred controversy. However, the controversy produced by *The Passion of the Christ* was multifaceted. It included the film's very graphic and violent content, its historical and biblical accuracy, fears that anti-Semitism would be stimulated by the story of Jesus Christ's final hours, and claims that media coverage of the film was unfairly critical and lacked objectivity.

These four characteristics of *The Passion of the Christ* gave it a unique entertainment appeal. Even those not drawn to religious films went to watch it to see what all the fuss was about. I conducted a study with two colleagues to assess how viewers responded to the film by posting a 70-item survey questionnaire on the Internet for those who had seen the film. The responses to my survey were extraordinary as I collected more than 1800 completed surveys in about a week. Although the survey respondents represented a non-probability sample, web-based survey designs are rapidly growing in the social sciences and are one of the most efficient means for gathering a large amount of data from a heterogeneous population in a short period of time time.[75] Statistical controls can be used to determine meaningful relationships among variables when collecting data in this manner, so the study produced some interesting results.

Before discussing the results, let me describe the sample of survey respondents. A total of 1832 respondents completed the entire survey. The sample was quite diverse in many respects but was generally more educated and with higher incomes than the average American and was about three-fifths female.

The first research objective of the study examined reasons why respondents went to see the film. The first reason why people said they went to see *The Passion of the Christ* was "for personal spiritual growth" and the second reason was that they had an "interest in the story." Nearly 77 percent of the respondents said these were the two primary reasons that drew them to the film.[76] Although other reasons were given such as being "curious about the controversy," or the film was "recommended by others," or they "liked the director," most people wanted to know more about the last hours of Christ's life before His crucifixion. I also found out most of the respondents rated the film as "capturing my complete attention."

Through my study, I also wanted to find out if the film would reinforce the faith of those who considered themselves to be practicing Christians. The survey results strongly indicate that viewers perceived that the film reinforced their Christian beliefs. This finding was no surprise, but it did show that the supposed "controversy" was exaggerated as few film viewers found anything in the film to be controversial or contrary to the account given in the Bible. When asked directly about whether they saw the film as controversial, the great majority of viewers said no. In fact, most of the viewers said, "the controversy of the film was greatly exaggerated by the news media."

Although I did find that non-Christians were slightly more critical of the film than Christians, both groups had very low criticism of Gibson's epic. The great majority of viewers, irrespective of their religious convictions, reported that the film spiritually influenced their lives. Likewise, both self-identified Christians and non-Christians rated the quality of the film very high and found it to be educational.

These research findings demonstrate how a single film can influence religious beliefs and perspectives. *The Passion of the Christ* generated a tremendous amount of media attention, which in turn inspired public discussion about the life of Christ. Both Christians and non-Christians assessed the film as educational and captivating. Both groups also indicated that the film had a spiritual influence on them. These findings are consistent with Barna's study, which found that one out of every ten viewers of *The Passion* indicated that they had changed some aspect of both their religious beliefs and practices in response to the movie and one out of every six viewers said the film affected their religious beliefs.[77] Two open-ended essay questions at the end of the survey produced many reams of paper filled with explanations and personal accounts from viewers of how the film had influenced their lives.

Gibson's film was clearly a successful form of entertainment-education. The film had a clear educational goal—to enable viewers to understand the suffering Jesus endured during the last 12 hours of his life. The film was clearly entertaining and rated highly by most viewers, regardless of their religious faith. Interviews with Gibson highlight that he purposefully intended the film to have an educational and persuasive effect on audiences.

The tremendous box office success of *The Passion of the Christ* can be explained in part by its strong emotional and spiritual appeal. The public wanted to talk about this film, especially news commentators and film critics. Although Gibson worked hard to promote the film, it was the nature of the film's content that drew viewers. Other historical film epics released shortly after *The Passion of the Christ* such as *Alexander* and *Troy* generated less than half the domestic revenue combined as compared to *The Passion of the Christ*, which generated $371 million in the U.S.[78]

The success of *The Passion of the Christ* will no doubt continue the long history of theatrical film productions that feature religious content and themes, providing new opportunities for film viewers to gain knowledge of religious beliefs and practices and to grow spiritually. The general commercial success of *The Passion of the Christ* and audience responses to the film shows that widely distributed "blockbuster" feature films can be used as a vehicle for intentionally integrating artistic entertainment and significant educational messages.

Evidence that religion, entertainment, and education can compatibly mix and touch audiences through one of the most popular and powerful communication vehicles (feature films) of our day is a highly significant revelation with implications for religious organizations, the film and entertainment industries, and communication, religious studies and other scholars. As pollster George Barna noted, "Don't lose sight of the fact that about 13 million adults changed some aspect of their typical religious behavior because of the movie and about 11 million people altered some pre-existing religious beliefs because of the content of that film. That's enormous influence."[79]

One of the most intriguing implications of *The Passion of the Christ* and its influence is whether or not religious films are replacing organized churches as authorities for religious beliefs. Johnston claims that dramatic films increasingly are displacing organized churches as the place people go to gain greater understanding of who they are, who God is, and other profound questions about their lives.[80] If this is true, then perhaps the long line of Jesus films, including the evangelistic film produced by Campus Crusade and reportedly seen in 228 countries by more than five billion people,[81] have a much greater cultural influence over time than social scientists and media scholars can assess. Even more effective are culturally relevant Jesus films like India's *Daya Sagar*, written and produced within the cultural context where it is viewed. The rich cultural history of religious films beckons for more focused attention by media scholars intrigued by these religious and cultural artifacts.

Learning about Faith from *Rocky Balboa*

Few people expected box office phenomenon Sylvester Stallone to make a film about faith. From the very first shot of *Rocky Balboa*, a painting of Jesus overlooks the determined but worn boxer. He's sparring in a converted church-turned-gym and the viewer notes that these smartly placed spiritual references demonstrate the Hand of Providence throughout his life. Writer, Director and Actor Sylvester Stallone says, "The character of Rocky was built on the idea that he was chosen to do something. That's why the first image in Rocky is the picture of Christ." But what does a movie about a boxer have to do with Christianity? "This is a story of faith, integrity and victory. Jesus is the inspiration for anyone to go the distance," Stallone explained in a television interview. "You could compare his courage to that of David, who as the epic underdog, defeated the giant Goliath in battle or look at his integrity in comparison to Esther, whose uncle asked, And who knows but that you have come to royal position for such a time as this? No matter which way you look at it, it is easy to find similar themes between the Rocky movies and stories throughout the Bible."[82]

Rocky Balboa, the popular boxing character created by Sylvester Stallone, returns to the ring in the latest *Rocky* film for the fight of his life! Against incredible odds, and with courage, integrity and faith, Rocky gives a powerful example of faith. *Rocky Balboa* is likely the last installment in MGM's *Rocky* film series. In this last story, Rocky now owns Adrian's, an Italian restaurant named for his beloved wife who has passed away. His grief heavy, the retired boxer struggles to connect with his son, Robert, and fills his lonely hours with his brother-in-law, reminiscing about the glory days. When ESPN broadcasts a computer-simulated fight and declares Rocky the victor over the current heavyweight champion, his passion re-ignites and the aging Rocky is eager to return to the ring.

Stallone says that in the past, his ego and worldly temptations took over in his life and he went spiraling out of control. Rather than living like Rocky with some sense of ideal, he didn't. "I thought I was entitled to things. You're not entitled to anything," Stallone says. "You are what you leave behind."[83] Stallone says the more he goes to church, and the more he turns himself over to the process of believing in Jesus and listening to his Word and helping him guide his hand, he feels as though the pressure is off himself.

A detailed Bible study based on the film was made available online through the *Rocky Balboa* website. The materials encourage young people to adopt the values of courage, integrity, faith and victory. In addition, discussion and training materials are available for free on the website for youth leaders who wish to use the film to teach young people about good character and integrity. A leader's guide can be downloaded from the site as a pdf file. The guide includes discussion starters, scriptural references, fun trivia, tools, and recommended actions, which could include hosting an interfaith event, distributing or reprinting information to your group or organization, or utilizing the materials for a small group.

C. S. Lewis and J. R.R. Tolkien

The fictional works of C.S. Lewis and J.R.R. Tolkien have generated many billions of dollars in media revenues, likely eclipsing the global impact of their many excellent scholarly non-fiction works. Lewis and Tolkien's popular narratives have generated two of the most lucrative transmedia enterprises of the 21st century.[84] Lewis became well known as a great apologist for the Christian faith. He led the Oxford debate society for many years. Lewis discovered that a powerful way of "stealing past those watchful dragons" of the mind that can resist truth due to existing prejudices is to tell compelling stories.[85] Lewis and Tolkien both understood the potency of indirectly communicating truth through story or myth, a strategy that was powerfully presented through the works of Soren Kierkegaard powerfully in the mid-1800s.[86] They embraced the understanding that great stories could be both universal and redemptive by engaging the imagination, thus preparing the way for the true myth. Both Lewis and Tolkien especially identified fairy tales as the most powerful genre for creating a condition for truth to emerge through experience and imagination.[87]

Interactive Visual Media

During the 1990s, the rise of multimedia productions and increased use of the Internet by Christian organizations provided many new opportunities for Christian ministries to expand their audience in the 21st century. In 1990, the American Bible Society (ABS) launched a major effort to produce visual translations of the Bible for distribution on video and CD-ROM. By 1995, the ABS had created three visual translations: *Out of the Tombs* (Mark 5:1-20), *The Visit* (Luke 1:39-56), and A Father and Two Sons (Matthew 15:11-32). A South African company released the first visual Bible products with the book of Matthew and the book of Acts. Both video series also were marketed by the *Readers Digest* Association.

Another Christian CD-ROM publisher, Jubilee Tech International, began worldwide distribution of their interactive CD-ROM Bible in four languages: Japanese, Korea, Mandarin, and English in the mid-1990s. The company became one of the major software localization companies in the U.S. during the 1990s, translating popular computer software programs into foreign languages for distribution worldwide.

Ark Multimedia Publishing, another Christian software developer, began distributing an interactive CD-ROM Bible and entertainment-education software programs in the early 1990s. The company, which focuses its development on making products for children and pre-teens, employs NASA-trained computer scientists to develop high-quality graphics and highly interactive games. The computer games industry is one of the fastest growing software markets in the world and provides innovative opportunities for Christians to communicate biblical truths to large numbers of people.

Project Light, a Christian ministry focusing on the literacy needs of lower-income families in major urban areas of the U.S., has been distributing a language and phonics learning program on compact digital disks since the early 1990s. The program has been used to advance literacy in the English language throughout the world.[88] Project Light distributes several programs that use the Bible to teach reading, language, and phonics. The interactive nature of the programs gives them a moderate entertainment value are they are ideal for people who wish to learn English as a second language and for children who have difficulties learning how to read.

Most major Christian media organizations now have their own sights on the Internet. Yahoo! Internet Life reported finding 9500 Christian-related internet sites by 1998 and within ten years, that number had doubled to more than 20,000 sites.[89] There are several sites, such as http://www.crosswalk.com, that serve as a central repository of Christian internet addresses. When the Vatican's home page was revised shortly after it came on-line on Christmas Day in 1995, the site received 2.9 million visitors in three days (see www.vatican.va). Other sites focus on specific areas of religious faith and media, such as Common Sense Media (https://www.commonsensemedia.org/movie-reviews/), which provides film reviews. Other media ministries have provided short film clips that pastors can use to help illustrate sermons.[90]

Almost all religious organizations use the Internet extensively. The Internet provides educational and evangelistic opportunities for religious groups throughout the world. Unlike other forms of devotional content such as film, video, radio, television, and print media, the Internet enables direct communication with others across time and space boundaries. Coded electrical impulses can move through fiberoptic cable at the speed of light or through coaxial cable at slower speeds but fast enough to provide instant communication across the other side of the world. Once a country develops public access to a telecommunication network, it is difficult for governments to completely control the flow of messages, although many countries like China and North Korea block religious websites. The digital revolution in communication technology in the 21st century is providing unparalleled opportunities for people of religious faith to communicate their beliefs across political, economic, and cultural boundaries.

Chapter 15
Prosocial Entertainment for Life-Long Learning

The most powerful means of learning through entertainment in the 2lst century will not be through the print or broadcast media. Print publications, radio and television as we know them today are radically changing. The media of tomorrow, if we still call them "media," will be completely digital and interactive. The very idea of "broadcasting" is already obsolete because mediated communication through digital channels does not so much come to people as people come to them. The practice of one-to-many communication, such as one media enterprise, say NBC, which can communicate the same message to masses of people, is phasing out. Mass communication as we know it today is being replaced by one-to-one and many-to-many communication. Media consumers can no longer be viewed as passive receivers of media messages nor as blocks of consumers, but rather, as active individual seekers of information, education and entertainment.

The world's digital information network, what we used to call "new" media, is rapidly becoming the "information highway" that we theorized about 35 years ago, but now with many "country roads," "side streets," and "jogging paths." On the world's interconnected digital network, everyone can make their own roads and rest stops. What the media conglomerates will be doing in the future is amazing large data bases of information, educational materials, and entertainment (films, television programs, music, videos, and pictures), that people will be seeking out and accessing from around the world according to each person's individual needs and desires. National governments also will be amassing such information, creating legal, political and social conflicts such as the NSA and IRS controversies that took place in the U.S. in 2013. In addition, individuals, affinity groups, and private organizations will be amassing their own data bases (think of these as rest stops and sites to see along the road) and regularly selling those databases to big media companies. These sales transactions are taking place almost daily; although many people never intend to sell their databases and not all digital materials that people collect have commercial value.

These monumental changes in the way we interact and communicate in our world will radically change the ways in which we learn. Everyone will need to be an active learner, to purposefully seek out information and educational experiences, and entertainment will be everywhere. It will be mixed with information and it will be an important part of our education, both formal and informal. In the 20th century, people learned primarily through didactic educational methods. In the 21st century, people will learn a great deal through entertainment media.

The opportunities for life-long learning through new entertainment ventures are virtually unlimited. The world is rapidly moving toward one interconnected global network in which every individual will have the opportunity to both create and disseminate their own media, including news, information, and of course, entertainment. There is already an unprecedented level of video production taking place throughout the world. In Nigeria, Africa's most populous nation, for example, hundreds of movies are being produced each week by entrepreneurial videographers and budding filmmakers. The rave in Nigeria now is making your own film for your family and friends. Children in the developed countries are growing up with communication technology that their parents never even dreamed about when they were children. Producing your own film and making it available on the Internet will be as common in the 21st century as was making a yearbook at the end of the school year in the 20th century. Web portfolios will be much more sophisticated than what we see on Instagram or FaceBook today. We have only touched the tip of the iceberg of the learning potential of the Internet.

The Moral Education of Children

The moral education of children has long been discussed, debated, and analyzed. In the ancient world, Plato declared that the education of youth should be paramount in society in his oft-quoted Republic, stating:

> "Do you not know, then, that the beginning in every task is the chief thing, especially for any creature that is young and tender. For it is then that it is best molded and takes the impression that one wishes to stamp upon it." "Quite so." "Shall we, then, thus lightly suffer our children to listen to any chance stories fashioned by any chance teachers and so to take into their minds opinions for the most part contrary to those that we shall think it desirable for them to hold when they are grown up?" "By no manner of means will we allow it."[1]

Plato goes on to explain how children learn through allegory:

> A child cannot distinguish the allegorical sense from the literal, and the ideas he takes in at that age are likely to become indelibly fixed; hence the great importance of seeing that the first stories he hears shall be designed to produce the best possible effect on his character.[2]

Parents throughout history have searched for quality methods and means to educate their children in positive character traits in hopes of developing them into productive, moral, ethical human beings. Indeed, many parents and guardians today follow the instruction of Solomon in the book of wisdom when he says to, "Train up a child in the way he should go and when he is old, he will not depart from it."[3] Today, with the pervasiveness of media in every area of daily life, this search has become more arduous. While media are not wholly to blame for the moral problems of societies, the content of media, which many times seems devoid of moral values or virtues, has caused much concern among parents and educators.

Historically, cultural values were passed down through the home, the religious institution, the school and one's elders or community leaders. Today our culture has become a mediated culture with the dominant cultural ideology and values passed down through movies, television, and music.[4,5] Media also reflect culture as well. The relative extent to which they either shape or reflect culture is one of the questions media scholars address.

While the idea of a media culture passing on values to youth might be a bit unsettling, Crane recognizes today that media transmit the dominant cultural ideology. This means that whatever children, or even adults, choose to watch, becomes what they believe the world to be like as well as what they will assume people believe. As Stanton states, "The mass media believe in the broad dissemination of as much as can be comprehended by as many as possible. They (the media) employ techniques to arrest attention, to recruit interest, to lead their audiences into new fields"[6]

Stories are at the basis of most media offerings today. Stories perform a needed function for children by providing familiarity as well as a coherent way to understand what is being presented.[7] Stories are told and disseminated today with the help of media channels such as movies, television, and radio. Some scholars contend that television has taken the place of organized religion and other cultural organizations, such as the family, school, and religious organizations, as the great common storyteller and social teacher.[8,9]

Children especially like stories; they learn from them, imitate them, and widen their imaginations through them. Children's programming today follows a somewhat formulaic approach in its presentation; familiar storylines, or narratives, and characters can be combined in a myriad of ways to attract and hold children's attention; what has changed, according to some media researchers, is the way that parents and others are using television and media to educate and entertain children.[10]

Children's Media Use

I will conclude this book where I began, talking about children. By the beginning of this century, the average American child was growing up in a home with two televisions, three tape players, three radios, two VCRs, two CD players and one computer.[11] Television has been a primary media source of learning for children.[12] However, in one study it was found that if given a choice of using only one medium, 33% of children aged 8-17 would choose the Internet with boys (38%) choosing it more often than girls (28%).[13] As far as weekly use of media, especially television, children continue to use a lot of media, but television viewing drops as children enter the pre-adolescent and adolescent years. According to the Kaiser Family Foundation study cited earlier of 3,000 children and their media use, children aged 2-18 use media an average of five and a half hours per day with two and a half hours spent watching television.[14]

Children are captivated by television, its stories, its format, its movement. Consider that children spend more time watching television than they spend in any other activity; the medium is a primary teacher of children.[15] Children actively process what they view on television; they are not passive participants in their watching. They will react to auditory and visual content cues as well as deciding whether or not to watch a particular program. According to Huston and colleagues, children seek entertainment from television, but they also use it for learning.[16]

Children become actively involved in television programs when they become meaningful to them. Some children's programming has been developed and tested with the intent of not only entertaining them but also teaching them prosocial concepts, values or behaviors through their involvement. Excellent examples of this active engagement are such shows as *Sesame Street*, *Blue's Clues*, and *Dora the Explorer*. The schema, or storyline of these programs, invites and engages children in recognizing clues and solving the problems presented. Children become accustomed to schema and the more accustomed they become to it, the more active they will be in viewing.[17]

Children also learn more about watching television as they grow older. For example, studies have shown that older children remember plot lines more readily than younger children do. Also, children ages eight and older are more cognitively aware of what is central to the plot than are younger children.[18] Children also pay more attention to the form of the television show as they age. Many times, these are referred to as formal features such as the grammar and syntax of the television show. Changes in scenes, content areas and other formal features are used to move the story along within the television production. Huston and Wright found that perceptually salient features like special visual effects, fast pace, and sound effects will influence how much attention children pay to particular shows.[19] These formal cues have also been found to influence children's determination of the difference between fantasy and reality.[20] According to Perloff , "children become more 'media wise' with increasing age; that is they become increasingly adept at recognizing that certain types of features signal certain types of content, and they view television more strategically and critically."[21] Also important to this discussion is the symbol system used to transmit the message within programming.

Salomon found that media provide symbolic systems for processing, explaining:

> Media transmit not only contents. Their contents have shape and structure. Even more generic to media, each medium cultivates its own blend of symbol systems and then—through its developing technology—generates additional unique forms of expression.[22]

Children also learn from the media they experience; they learn how to think and act. They learn how to decipher media, its form and format and its characters and storylines. Children learn early that certain features signal certain types of content. Animation, peculiar voices, and sound effects are commonly used with child-oriented content that is designed with children in mind.[23]

These devices are not only more evident in the media offerings for our children, but as Strasburger and Wilson have found, most media offerings for children that rely repetitive, obnoxious, marketing tie-ins which want the younger set to nag their parents to spend money on merchandise associated with the programming.[24] Values are seldom espoused that children would do well to emulate; few narratives teach young minds anything of value.[25] A 2002 *Newsweek* article exemplified this idea when it devoted an entire issue to "Why TV is good for kids and why it is not."[26] Notable examples of "good" television were the national icons *Sesame Street* and *Mister Roger's Neighborhood*. More recent examples included *Dora the Explorer*, *Bear in the Big Blue House*, *Blue's Clues*, and *Doug*.

Warren notes what is needed most is for parents to be cultural agents, viewing visual material with children and engaging in an active dialogue about the images and narratives seen. In this way, parents consciously shape children's tastes and become a part of cultural agency in the development of children's hearts, souls and minds.[27] The benefits of programs designed to encourage parents and children viewing together is supported by scholarly studies that have found that children learn and understand more from programming when it is co-viewed.[28]

In summary, entertainment media are the most powerful source of learning for children, who spend more time-consuming entertainment then they do in the classroom or in teaching scenarios with their parents. If as Condoleezza Rice recently said, that education (and the current failure of public schools) is the "civil rights issue of our day," then we must take on as a cultural mandate the need to reform and strategically use media to teach children knowledge, skills and moral behavior.[29] Learning through entertainment is a life-long process – it is a part of human nature. Dr. Walter Fisher, Professor Emeritus at the University of Southern California, was correct when he shared with his doctoral students in class that when God created man he man him homonarran (storyteller), which he explains in his ground-breaking book.[30] I was fortunate enough to be in Dr. Fisher's class at the Annenberg School for Communication when he taught on human narration. It was in that class and others like it that the early seeds of my thinking on entertainment-education were formed.

I conclude with this thought – if we really want to change our world into a more kind, peaceful, and loving place, then we must change the stories we tell our children and grandchildren through the media. Whatever country you may live in, this is a human task that should engage all of us. Whether you are an academic scholar, teacher, media professional, community leader, government representative, educator, or concerned parent, I hope that you will join me in this great quest.

Notes to Chapter 1

1 Experian Simmons. (2009, July 14). New media study discovers Americans need 38hours per day to complete their tasks. Earth Times, http://www.earthtimes.org/articles/show/new-media-study-discovers-americans, 891148.shtml (accessed 11 August 2009).

2 Gitlin, T. (2002). Media unlimited. New York, NY: Henry Holt and Company.

3 Gabler, N. (2000). Life: The movie: How entertainment conquered reality. New York, NY: Vintage Books, Random House.

4 Potter, J. (2010). Media literacy (fifth ed.). Thousand Oaks, CA: Sage Publications.

5 University of San Francisco (2010, August). Internet usage statistics: The Internet big picture, http://www.internetworldstats.com/stats.htm (accessed 11August 2010).

6 Kaiser Family Foundation. (2010). Generation M2: Media in the lives of 8-18 year olds, http://www.kff.org/entmedia/upload/mh012010presentL.pdf (accessed 11August 2010).

7 Ibid, charts 1 and 2.

8 Ibid, charts 3 and 28.

9 Ibid, charts 13 and 15.

10 Ibid, charts 5 and 9.

11 Graft, K. (2009, August 7). Study: 40 Percent of US homes have gaming console, as HDTV adoption rises. Gamasutra, http://www.gamasutra.com/php-bin/news_index.php?story=24757 (accessed 10August 2009)

12 Hendrick, B. (2009, January 6). Online game lets kids do good works in cyberspace. The Journal-Constitution, http://www.ajc.com/ business/content/metro/stories/2009/01/06/elf_island.html (accessed 11August 2009).

13 Kaiser Family Foundation, 2010, chart 18.

14 Negroponte, N. P. (1996). Being digital. New York, NY: Random House, Inc.

15 Zheng, L. (2009, February 28). Microsoft Office Labs vision 2019 (montage + video), http://www.istartedsomething.com/20090228/microsoft-office-labs-vision-2019-video/ (accessed 7 August 2009).

16 Young, D. G., & Tisinger, R. M. (2006). Dispelling late-night myths: News consumption among late-night comedy viewers and the predictors of exposure to various late-night shows. International Journal of Press/Politics, 11, 113-134.

17 Hollander, B. A. (2005). Late-night learning: Do entertainment programs increase political campaign knowledge for young viewers? Journal of Broadcasting & Electronic Media, 49, 402-415.

18 Singhal, A., & Rogers, E. M. (2002). India's information revolution. New Delhi: Sage Publications.

19 Blakely, J. (2001). Entertainment goes global: Mass culture in a transforming world. Los Angeles, CA: Norman Lear Center, University of Southern California.

[All Notes]

Notes to Chapter 2

1 Curry, J. C., Brannon, D. K., & Geis, P. A. (2006). History of cosmetic microbiology. In Philip A. Geis (Ed.), Cosmetic microbiology: A practical approach (second edition) (pp. 3-18). New York: Taylor & Francis Group.

2 Box Office Mojo. (2009). All time box office: Worldwide grosses, http://www.boxofficemojo.com/alltime/world/ (accessed 12 August 2009).

3 Brown, W. J., & Singhal, A. (1999). Entertainment-education strategies for social change. In D. P. Demers & K. Viswanath (Eds.), Mass media, social control and social change (263-280). Ames, Iowa: Iowa State University Press; Piotrow, P. T., & de Fossard, E. (2004). Entertainment-education as a public health intervention. In A. Singhal, M. J. Cody, E. M. Rogers, & M. Sabido (Eds.), Entertainment-education and social change: History, research, and practice (pp. 39-60). Mahwah, NJ: Lawrence Erlbaum Assoc, Inc.

4 Blumler, J. G. (1979). The role of theory in uses and gratification studies. Communication Research, 6, 9-36.

5 Katz, E., Blumler, J. G., & Gurevitch, M. (1974). Utilization of mass communication by the individual. In J. G. Blumler & E. Katz (Eds.), The Uses of Mass Communication (pp. 19-31). Beverly Hills, CA: Sage Publications.

6 Gurevitch, M., Bennett, T., Curran, J., & Woollacot, J. (Eds.) (1982). Culture, society and the media. New York, NY: Methuen & Company, Taylor & Francis.

7 McQuail, D. (1984). With the benefit of hindsight: Reflections on uses and gratifications research. Critical Studies in Media Communication, 1, 177-193.

8 Rosengren, E. (1974). Uses and gratifications: A paradigm outlined. In J. G. Blumler & E. Katz (Eds.), The uses of mass communication: Current perspectives on gratifications research (pp. 269-286). Beverly Hills, CA: Sage Publications.

9 Rubin, A. M. (2002). The uses and gratifications perspective of media effects. In J. Bryant & D. Zillman (Eds.), Media effects: Advances in theory and research (2nd edition). (pp. 525-548). Mahwah, NJ: Lawrence Erlbaum.

10 Windahl, S. (1981). Uses and gratifications at the crossroads. In G. C. Wilhoit & H. de Bock (Eds.), Mass communication review yearbook. Beverly Hill, CA: Sage Publications.

11 Swanson, D. L. (1987). Gratification seeking, media exposure, and audience interpretations: Some directions for research. Journal of Broadcasting and Electronic Media, 31, 237-254.

12 Rubin, A. M. (1986). Uses, gratifications, and media effects research. In J. Bryant & D. Zillman (Eds.), Perspectives on media effects(pp. 281-302). Hillsdale, NJ: Lawrence Erlbaum.

13 Lull, J. (1980). The social uses of television. Human Communication Research, 6, 197-209.

14 Abelman, R., & Hoover, S. M. (Eds.). (1990). Religious television: Controversies and conclusions. Norwood, NJ: Ablex.

15 Stout, D. A., & Buddenbaum, J. M. (Eds.). (1996). Religion and mass media: Audiences and adaptations. Thousand Oaks, CA: Sage Publications.

16 Buddenbaum, J. M. (1981). Characteristics and media-related needs of the audience for religious TV. Journalism Quarterly, 58, 266-272.

17 Abelman, Robert (1989). PTL Club viewer uses and gratifications. Communication Quarterly, 37, 54-66.

18 Gerbner, G., Gross, L., Hoover, S., et al. (1984). Religion and television. Philadelphia, PA: The Annenberg School for Communication, University of Pennsylvania.

19 Brown, W. J., & Fraser, B. P. (1993). A comparative analysis of audience involvement with "The 700 Club" and other daytime television talk shows. Paper presented to the 3rd Christianity and Communication Conference, June 2-4, Virginia Beach, VA.

20 Hamilton, N., & Rubin, A. (1992). The influence of religiosity on television viewing. Journalism Quarterly, 69, 667-678.

21 Ball-Rokeach, S. J. (1998).A theory of media power and a theory of media use: Different stories, questions, and ways of thinking. Mass Communication and Society, 1, 5-40.

22 Ball-Rokeach, S. J., & Loges, W. E. (1996). Making choices: Media roles in the construction of value choices. In C. Seligman, J. M. Olson, & M. P. Zanna (Eds.), The psychology of values: The Ontario symposium (pp. 277-298). Mahwah, NJ: Erlbaum.

23 Bineham, J. L. (1988). A historical account of the hypodermic model in mass communication. Communication Monographs, 55, 230 – 246.

24 Katz, E., Lazarsfeld, P. (1955). Personal influence: The part played by people in the flow of mass communications. New York, NY: The Free Press.

25 Weimann, G. (1982). On the importance of marginality: One more step in the two-step flow of communication. American Sociological Review, 47, 64-773.

26 Holbert, R. L., & Stephenson, M. T. (2003). The importance of indirect effects in media effects research: Testing for mediation in structural equation modeling. Journal of Broadcasting & Electronic Media, 47, 556–572.

27 Singhal, A., Papa, M. J., Sharma, D., Pant, S., Worrell, T., Muthuswamy, N., & Witte, K. (2006). Entertainment-education and social change: The communicative dynamics of social capital, Journal of Creative Communications, 1, 1-18.

28 Singhal, A., & Rogers, E. M. (1999). Entertainment-education: A communication strategy for social change. Mahwah, NJ: Lawrence Erlbaum, pp. 1-7.

29 Singhal, A., Obregon, F., & Rogers, E. M., (1994). Reconstructing the story of "Simplemente Marìa, the most popular telenovela in Latin America of all time. Gazette, 54(1), 1-15.

30 Brown, W. J. (1992). The use of entertainment television programs for promoting prosocial messages. The Howard Journal of Communications, 3, 253-266.

31 Alexander, A., & Stewart, J. (1989, September 19). Detective Sonny Crockett: Leader in fashion weaponry. The Honolulu Star-Bulletin, p. B-1.

32 Brown, W. J., & Singhal, A. (1990). Ethical dilemmas of prosocial television. Communication Quarterly, 38(3), 268-280.

33 Singhal & Rogers, 1999, p. 100; Brown, W. J. (1990). Prosocial effects of "Hum Log," India's first long-running television soap opera. Asian Journal of Communication, 1, 113-135.

[All Notes]

Notes to Chapter 3

1 Hunt, D. (1998). O.J. Simpson facts & fictions: New rituals in the construction of reality, http://www.usc.edu/dept/LAS/SC2/pdf/hunt.pdf (accessed 12 August 2009).

2 Feldman, C. (2004). Feldman: Strange scene for Jackson appearance, http://www.cnn.com/2004/LAW/01/16/otsc.feldman/ index.html (Accessed 18 January 2004).

3 Postman, N. (1985). Amusing ourselves to death: Public discourse in the age of showbusiness. New York, Viking.

4 UPI. (1975, July 29). Elvis buys woman a car. Boca Raton News, p. 5, http:/news/google.com/ newspapers?nid=129&dat=19750729&id=tsPAAAAIBA&sjid=7owDAAAAIBAJ&pg=5301, 3356187 (accessed 20 July 2008).

5 Taraborrelli, J. R. (2009). Michael Jackson: The magic, the madness, the whole story, 1958-2009. Boston, MA: Hachette Book Group.

6 Gelman, D., Springen, K., & Raghavan, S. (1993, June 28). I'm not a role model. Newsweek, 56-57.

7 Smith, V. E., & Boeth, J. (1993, May 24). Who are you calling hero? Newsweek, 64-65.

8 Wren, C. S. (2001, March 10). 14-year-old gets life sentence for murder. The Virginian Pilot, p. A-2.

9 Donaldson-Evans, C. (2005). 'Love child' the latest celeb must-have." Fox News, http://www.foxnews.com/story/0,2933,175126,00.html (accessed 13 August 2008).

10 Duke University. (2008). Brief history of World War II advertising campaigns: War loans and bonds, http://library.duke.edu/digitalcollections/adaccess/warbonds.html (accessed 13 August 2009).

11 Prial, F. J. (1986, June 18). Kate Smith, all American singer, dies at 79. New York Times Magazine, http://www.nytimes.com/specials/magazine4/articles/smith1.html (accessed 13 August 2009).

12 Merton, R. (1946). Mass persuasion. New York, NY: Harper.

13 Ibid, p. 52.

14 Ibid, p. 55.

15 Ibid, p. 65.

16 Kate Smith Commemorative Society. (2008). Kate Smith's biography, http://katesmith.org/katebio.html (accessed 13 August 2009).

17 Merton, 1946.

18 Ibid.

19 Ibid.

20 Kate Smith Commemorative Society, 2008.

21 Smith, J. K. A. 2006. Who's afraid of post-modernism. Grand Rapids, MI: Baker Academic.

[All Notes]

Notes to Chapter 4

1 Kittleson, M. L. (1998). The soul of popular culture. Peru, IL: Open Court Publishing, pp. 6-7.

2 Boorstin, D. J. (1961). The image: A guide to pseudo-events in America. New York: Harper and Row.

3 Campbell, J. (1988). The power of myth. New York: Doubleday.

4 Ibid, p. xv.

5 Vogler, C. (1998). The writer's journey: Mythic structure for writers. Los Angeles, CA: Michael Wise Productions, p 35.

6 Boorstin, 1961, op. cit.

7 Campbell, J. (1973). The hero with a thousand faces. Princeton, NJ: Princeton University Press.

8 Gamson, J. (1994). Claims to fame: Celebrity in contemporary America. Berkeley, CA: University of California Press.

9 Lippmann, W. (1960). Blazing publicity: Why we know so much about "Peaches" Browning, Valentino, Lindbergh and Queen Marie. In C. Amory and F. Bradlee (Eds.), Vanity Fair (pp. 121-122). New York: Viking Press. [Original work published 1927].

10 Boorstin, 1961, p. 61.

11 Dyer, R. (1991). A star is born and the construction of authenticity. In C. Glendale (Ed.), Stardom: Industry of desire (pp. 136-144). London: Routledge.

12 Meyer, D. S., & Gamson, Joshua (1995). The challenge of cultural elites: Celebrities and social movements. Sociological Inquiry, 65, 181-206.

13 Alberoni, F. (1972). The powerless 'elite': Theory and sociological research on the phenomenon of the stars. In Dennis McQuail (Ed.), Sociology of mass communications (pp. 75-89). Harmondsworth: Penguin.

14 Gamson, J. (1992). The assembly line of greatness: Celebrity in twentieth century America. Critical Studies in Mass Communication, 9, 1-24.

15 Boorstin, 1961, op. cit.

16 Strate, L. (1994). Heroes: A Communication Perspective. In S. J. Drucker & R. S. Cathcart (Eds.), American heroes in a media age (pp. 15-23). Cresskill, NJ: Hampton Press, Inc.

17 Balio, T. T. (Ed.). 1985. The American film industry. Madison, WI: University of Wisconsin Press, p. 266.

18 Lippman, 1960, p. 121.

19 Campbell, 1988, p. 134.

20 Edelstein, A. (1996). Everybody is sitting on the curb. Westport, CT: Praeger Publishers, p. 8; Loftus, M. (1995, May). The other side of fame. Psychology Today, 28(3), 48-53, 70-80.

21 Cowen, T. (2000, May). The new heroes and role models: Why separating celebrity from merit is good. Reason, 32, 30-36.

22 Ibid.

23 Ewen, S. (1988). All consuming images. New York: Basic Books, Harper Collins, p. 13.

24 Brown, W. J., Duane, J. J., & Fraser, B. P. (1997). Media coverage and public opinion of the O. J. Simpson trial: Implications for the criminal justice system. Communication Law & Policy, 2, 261-287.

25 Adel, D. (2000, September 1). One for the money. Entertainment Weekly, pp. 30-37.

26 Bonko, L. (2000, August 29). Rudy has eye on space. The Virginian-Pilot, pp. E1-E2.

27 Hall, K. (2000, September 9). Rudy's a hero, but not for "Survivor." The Virginian- Pilot, p. B6; Sinha, V. (2000, August 30). "Rudypalooza!" draws crowd of thousands for homecoming. The Virginian-Pilot, pp. A1, A9.

28 Bandura, A. (1977). Social learning theory. Englewood Cliffs, NJ: Prentice-Hall; Bandura, A. (1986). Social foundations of thought and action: A social cognitive theory; Englewood Cliffs, NJ: Prentice-Hall; Bandura, A., Ross, D., & Sheila, A. (1963). Vicarious reinforcement and imitative learning. Journal of Abnormal and Social Psychology, 67, 601-607; Carroll, W. R., & Bandura, A. (1982). The role of visual monitoring in observational learning of action patterns: Making the unobservable observable. Journal of Motor Behavior, 14, 153-167.

29 Bandura, 1977, p. vii.

30 Canedy, D. (2001, January 26). Boy convicted of murder in wrestling death. New York Times, http://www.nytimes.com/2001/01/26/us/boy-convicted-of-murder-in-wrestling-death.html (accessed 10 August 2008).

31 Bernthal, M. J., & Medway, F. J. (2005). An initial exploration into the psychological implications of adolescents' involvement with professional wrestling. School Psychology International, 26(2), 224-242.

32 Smith, T. A. (2009). Athletes as role models: Is it a good idea?" Regal Magazine, http://www.regalmag.com/athletes-role-models-good-idea-a-371.html (Accessed 17 August 2009).

33 City-Data.com. (2009). Memphis: Recreation – Sightseeing, http://www.city-data.com/us -cities/The-South/Memphis-Recreation.html (Accessed 17 August 2009).

34 Hoy, P. (2008). Elvis still the king of dead celebs. Forbes.com, http://articles.moneycentral.msn.com/Investing/Forbes/ TopEarningDeadCelebrities.aspx (accessed 17 August 2009).

35 Polston, B. (1996, October 15). Personal interview. Williamsburg, VA.

36 Gampell, J. (2000, January). Isn't that Elvis? Sawadee, pp. 47-52.

37 Fraser, B. P., & Brown, W. J. (2002). Media, celebrities, and social influence: Identification with Elvis Presley. Mass Communication & Society, 5, 185-208.

38 Wise, D. (1995, June 3). Personal interview. Virginia Beach, VA.

39 Giddens, C. (1995, June 2). Personal interview.

40 Riggs, S. (1996). Personal interview.

41 Cunida, J. (1996, June 1). Personal interview.

42 Tom, L. (1996, December 7). Personal interview.

43 Ibid.

44 Wise, 1995.

45 Ibid

46 Ibid.

47 Lopez, R. (1995, June 4). Personal interview.

48 Ibid.

49 Ibid.

50 Ibid.

51 Giddens, 1995, op. cit.

52 Miller, C. (1996, August 13). Personal interview.

53 Fritz, R. (1996, June 24). Personal interview.

54 Brickle, J. (1995, June 3). Personal interview.

55 Minnery, J. (1997, June 1). Personal interview.

56 Tom, 1996, op. cit.

57 Lopez, 1995, op. cit.

58 Ibid.

59 Minnery, 1997, op. cit.

60 Spigel, L. (1991). Communicating with the dead: Elvis as medium. Camera Obscura, 23, 176-205.

61 Brown, W. J., & Basil, M. D. (1995). Media celebrities and public health: Responses to "Magic" Johnson's HIV disclosure and its impact on AIDS risk and high-risk behaviors. Health Communication, 7, 345-371; Hoffner, C., & Cantor, J. (1991). Perceiving and responding to mass media characters. In Jennings Bryant & Dolf Zillman (Eds.), Responding to the screen: Reception and reaction process (pp. 63-102). Hillsdale, NJ: Lawrence Erlbaum Associates, Publishers; McGwire, W. J. (1974). Psychological motives and communication gratification. In Jay Blumler & Elihu Katz (Eds.), The uses of mass communications: Currents perspectives on gratifications research (pp. 167-196). Beverly Hills, CA: Sage Publications.

62 Albert, R. S. (1957). The role of mass media and the effect of aggressive film content upon children's aggressive responses and identification choices. Genetic Psychology Monographs, 55, 221-285; Noble, G. (1975). Children in front of the small screen. Beverly Hills, CA: Sage Publications.

63 MTV News Online. (1997, October 2). Elton "amazed" by the success of "Candle," http://www.mtv.com/news/articles/1430664/19971002/john_elton.jhtml?paid=984 (accessed 16 September 2001).

64 The Associated Press (1997, October 22). 'White Christmas' at No. 2, http://www.ardmoreite.com/stories/102397/fun/fun03.html (accessed 16 September 2001).

65 Kantrowitz, B., Pedersen, Daniel, & McGuire, Stryker. (1997, September 15). The day England cried. Newsweek, 80(11), 30-36.

66 Blowen, M. (1997). With grace and depth, ABC ruled. The Boston Globe, September 7, p. A32; Payne, J. G. (2000). Preface to an era of celebrity and spectacle. In G. Payne (Ed.), An era of celebrity and spectacle: The global rhetorical phenomenon of the death of Diana, Princess of Wales (p. x). Boston, MA: Center for Ethics in Political and Health Communication, Emerson College.

67 Shales, T. (1997, September 7). Live television coverage unites the world in a good cry. Washington Post, p. A23.

68 Brown, W. J., Basil, M. D., & Bocarnea, M. C. (2003). Social influence of an international celebrity: Responses to the death of Princess Diana. Journal of Communication, 53, 587-605.

69 Boorstin, 1961, pp. 8, 57.

70 Jun, Suk-ho., & Dayan, D. (1986). An interactive media event: South Korea's televised "family reunion." Journal of Communication, 36, 73-82.

71 Brown, W. J., Fraser, B. P., & Bocarnea, M. C. (1994, February). The agenda-setting effects of celebrities: Audience responses to the O.J. Simpson case. Paper presented to the Western States Communication Association, Portland, Oregon.

72 McCombs, M. E., & Shaw, D. L. (1972). The agenda-setting function of the mass media. Public Opinion Quarterly, 36, 176-185.

73 McCombs, M. E., & Shaw, D. L. (1993). The evolution of agenda-setting research: 25 years in the marketplace of ideas. Journal of Communication, 43, 58-67.

74 Ibid.

75 Basil, M. D., & Brown, W. J. (1994). Interpersonal communication in news diffusion: Effects of "Magic" Johnson's HIV announcement. Journalism Quarterly, 71, 305-320.

76 Brown, Fraser, & Bocarnea, 1994, op. cit.

77 Shenk, J. W. (1996, June). Star struck. The Washington Monthly, pp. 12-18.

78 Boorstin, 1961, op. cit.

79 Shenk, 1996, op. cit.

80 Neimark, J. (1995, May). The culture of celebrities. Psychology Today, 28(3), 57.

81 Ibid, p. 57.

82 Graeff, T. R. (1996). Using promotional messages to manage the effects of brand and self-image on brand evaluations. Journal of Consumer Marketing, 13(3), 4-18.

83 Brown, W. J. (2010). Steve Irwin's Influence on Wildlife Conservation. Journal of Communication, 60, 73-93.

84 Friedman, H. H., Termini, S., & Washington, R. (1977). The effectiveness of advertisements using four types of endorsers. Journal of Advertising, 6, 22-24.

85 Kamins, M. A., Brand, J. J., Hoeke, S. A., & Moe, J. C. (1989). Two-sided versus one-sided celebrity endorsements: The impact on advertising effectiveness and credibility. Journal of Advertising, 18, 4-10.

86 Friedman, H. H., & Friedman, L. (1979). Endorser effectiveness by product type. Journal of Advertising Research, 18, 63-71.

87 Erdogan, B. F., Baker, M. J., & Tagg, S. (2001). Selecting celebrity endorsers: The practitioner's perspective. Journal of Advertising Research, 41, 39-48; Hsu, C. K., & McDonald, D. (2002). An examination of multiple celebrity endorsers in advertising. Journal of Product & Brand Marketing, 11(1), 19-29.

88 Agrawal, J., & Kamakura, W. A. (1995). The economic worth of celebrity endorsers. Journal of Advertising Research, 23, 57-61; Mathur, L. K., Mathur, I., & Rangan, N. (1997). The wealth effects associated with a celebrity endorser. Journal of Advertising Research, 37, 67-73.

89 Stephens, A., & Rice, A. (1998). Spicing up the message. Finance Week, 76(26), 46-47.

90 Kilburn, D. (1998). Star power. Adweek, 39(2), 20-21.

91 Atkin, C., & Block, M. (1983). Effectiveness of celebrity endorsers. Journal of Advertising Research, 23, 57-61

92 Goldman, K. (1994, January 7). Dead celebrities are resurrected pitchmen. The Wall Street Journal, p. B-1; Miller, C. (1993, March 29). Some celebs just now reaching their potential–and they're dead. Marketing News, 27(7), pp. 2-4.

93 Rose, L. (2006, October 24). Top-earning dead celebrities. Forbes, http://www.forbes.com/ 2006/10/23/celebrities-earnings-fame-tech-media-06deadcelebs-cx 1r topearnint. (accessed 26 October 2006).

94 Jacobs, A. J. (1998, June 5). Leo ads up. Entertainment Weekly, p. 17.

[All Notes]

Notes to Chapter 5

1 Brown, W. J. (2010). Steve Irwin's Influence on Wildlife Conservation. Journal of Communication, 60, 73-93.

2 Rubin, A. M. (1996, November). Personal involvement with the media. Paper presented to the 82nd Annual Convention of the Speech Communication Association, Nov. 23-26, San Diego, CA.

3 Rubin, R. B. & McHugh, M. P. (1987). Development of parasocial relationships. Journal of Broadcasting and Electronic Media, 31, 279-292.

4 Brown, W. J., & Cody, M. J. (1991). Effects of an Indian television soap opera in promoting women's status. Human Communication Research, 18(1), 114-142; Shefner-Rogers, C. L., Rogers, E. M., & Singhal, A. (1998). Parasocial interaction with the television soap operas 'Simplemente Maria' and 'Oshin.' Keio CommunicationReview, 20, 3-18; Singhal, A., Obregon, R., & Rogers, E. M. (1994). Reconstructing the story of "Simplemente Maria" The most popular telenovela in Latin America of all time. Gazette, 54, 1-15.

5 Petty, R. E., & Cacioppo, J. T. (1979). Issue involvement can increase or decrease persuasion by enhancing message-relevant cognitive responses. Journal of Personality and Social Psychology, 37, 1915-1926.

6 Sigelman L. (1986). Basking in reflected glory revisited: An attempt at replication. Social Psychology Quarterly, 49, 90-92.

7 Cialdini, R. B., Borden, R. J., Thorne, A., Walker, M. R., Freeman, S., & Sloan, L. R. (1976). Basking in reflected glory: Three (football) field studies. Journal of Personality and Social Psychology, 34, 366-375.

8 Snyder, C. R., Lassegard, M., & Ford, C.E. (1986). Distancing after group success and failure: Basking in reflected glory and cutting off reflected failure. Journal of Personality and Social Psychology, 51, 382-388.

9 Wann, D. L., & Branscombe, N. R. (1990). Die-hard and fair-weather fans: Effects of identification on BIRGing and CORFing tendencies. Journal of Sport and Social Issues, 14, 103-117.

10 Fowles, J. (1992). Star struck: Celebrity performers and the American public. Washington, DC: Smithsonian Institution Press.

11 Horton, D., & Wohl, R. R. (1956). Mass communication and parasocial interaction: Observations on intimacy at a distance. Psychiatry, 19, 215-229.

12 Levy, M. (1979). Watching television news as parasocial interaction. Journal of Broadcasting, 23, 69-80.

13 Fraser, B. P., & Brown, W. J. (1995). An analysis of daytime television talk shows. Paper presented at the World Communication Association's 13th biennial conference, July 23-27, Vancouver, B.C.

14 Rubin, A. M., & Perse, E. M. (1987). Audience activity and soap opera involvement: A uses and gratifications investigation. Human Communication Research, 14, 246-268.

15 Babb, V., & Brown, W. J. (1994). Adolescents' development of parasocial relationships through popular television situation comedies. Competitive paper presented to the 44th Annual Conference of the International Communication Association, Sydney, July 11-15.

16 Brown, W. J., & Basil, M. D. (1995). Media celebrities and public health: Responses to "Magic" Johnson's HIV disclosure and its impact on AIDS risk and high-risk behaviors. Health Communication, 7, 345-371; Brown, W. J., Basil, M. D., & Bocarnea, M. C. (2003). Social influence of an international celebrity: Responses to the death of Princess Diana. Journal of Communication, 53, 587-605.

17 Brown, W. J., Basil, M.D., & Bocarnea, M. C. (2003). The influence of famous athletes on health beliefs and practices: Mark McGwire, child abuse prevention, and androstenedione. Journal of Health Communication, 8, 41-57; Brown, W. J., Duane, J. J., & Fraser, B. P. (1997). Media coverage and public opinion of the O.J. Simpson trial: Implications for the criminal justice system. Communication Law and Policy, 2(2), 261-287.

18 Brown, W. J., Barker, G., & Presnell, K. K. (2008). The social impact of mediate celebrities: Cognitive and emotional responses to the death of Dale Earnhardt. Paper presented to the National Communication Association's Annual Conference, San Diego, California.

19 Bechtel, M. (2001, February 26). Dale Earnhardt knew life wasn't fair. Sports Illustrated, 94 (9), p. 38.

20 Singhal, A., Obregon, R., & Rogers, E. M. (1994). Reconstructing the story of "Simplemente Maria," The most popular telenovela in Latin America of all time. Gazette, 54, 1-15.

21 Green, M. C., Brock, T. C., & Kaufman, G. F. (2004). Understanding media enjoyment: The role of transportation into narrative worlds. Communication Theory, 14, 311-327.

22 Biocca, F., Harms, C., & Burgoon, J. (2003). Toward a more robust theory and measure of social presence: Review and suggested criteria. Presence, 12, 456-480; Nowak, K. (2001). Defining and differentiating copresence, social presence, and presence as transportation,

http://www.temple.edu/ispr/prev_conferences/proceedings/2001/Nowak1.pdf (accessed 24 March 2008).

23 Green, Melanie C., Brock, T. C. (2000). The role of transportation in the persuasiveness of public narratives. Journal of Personality and Social Psychology, 79, 701.

24 Fraser, B. P., & Brown, W. J. (2002). Media, celebrities, and social influence: Identification >with Elvis Presley. Mass Communication & Society, 5, 185-208.

25 Green, M. C., Kass, S., Carrey, J., Herzig, B., Feeney, R., & Sabini, J. (2009). Transportation across media: Repeated exposure to print and film. Media Psychology, 11, 512-539.

26 Green, M. C., Brock, T. C., & Kaufman, G. F. (2004). Understanding media enjoyment: The role of transportation into narrative worlds. Communication Theory, 14, 311-327.

27 Cohen, J. (2001). Defining identification: A theoretical look at the identification of audiences with media characters. Mass Communication & Society, 2001, 245-264.

28 Green et al., 2004, op. cit.

29 Freud, S. (1922). Group psychology and the analysis of ego. New York: Norton; Freud, S. 1989). An outline of psychoanalysis (J. Strachey, Trans.). New York, NY: Norton. (original work published 1940).

30 Lasswell, H. D. (1931). The measurement of public opinion. American Political Science Review, 25, 311-326; Lasswell, H. D. (1965). World politics and personal insecurity. New York: Free Press. (original work published in 1935).

31 Cohen, 2001, op. cit.

32 Wollheim, R. (1974). Identification and imagination. In Richard Wollheim (Ed.), Freud: A collection of critical essays (pp. 172-195). New York, NY: Anchor/Doubleday.

33 Kelman, H. (1958). Compliance, identification, and internalization: Three processes of attitude change. Journal of Conflict Resolution, 2, 51-60.

34 Kelman, H. (1961). Process of opinion change. Public Opinion Quarterly, 25, 57-78.

35 Bettelheim, B. (1943). Individual and mass behavior in extreme situations. Journal of Abnormal and Social Psychology, 38, 417-452.

36 Kelman, 1958, op. cit.

37 Kelman, 1958, p. 63.

38 Kelman, 1961, p. 64.

39 Kelman, 1961, pp. 63-64.

40 Brown, Duane & Fraser, 1997, op. cit.; Brown, W. J., & deMatviuk, M. A. C. (2010). Sports celebrities and public health: Diego Maradona's influence on drug use prevention. Journal of Health Communication, 15, 358-373.

41 Maltby, J. (2004). Celebrity and religious worship: A refinement. The Journal of Psychology, 138, 286-288; Maltby, J., Day, L., McCutcheon, L. E., Gillett, R., Houran, J., & Ashe, D. D. (2004). Personality and coping: A context for examining celebrity worship and mental health. British Journal of Psychology, 95, 411-428; Maltby, J., Day, L., McCutcheon, L. E., Martin, M. M., & Cayanus, J. L. (2004b). Celebrity worship, cognitive flexibility, and social complexity. Personality and Individual Differences, 37, 1475-1482; Maltby, J, Houran, J., Lange, R,. Ashe, D. & McCutcheon, L.E. (2002). Thou shalt worship no other gods – unless they are celebrities: The relationship between celebrity worship and religious orientation. Personality and Individual Differences, 32, 1157-1172; Maltby, J., Giles, D. C., Barber, L., & McCutcheon, L. E. (2005). Intense-personal celebrity worship and body image: Evidence of a link among female adolescents. British Journal of Health Psychology, 10, 17-32; Maltby, J., Houran, J., & McCutcheon, L. E. (2003). A clinical interpretation of attitudes and behaviors associated with celebrity worship. Journal of Nervous and Mental Disease, 191(1), 25-29.

42 Giles, D. C. (2000). Illusions of immortality: A psychology of fame and celebrity. Basingstoke, UK: MacMillan Publishers.

43 Jindra, M. (1994). Star Trek fandom as a religious phenomenon. *Sociology of Religion*, 55(1), 27-51.

44 Maltby et al., 2002, op. cit.

45 Maltby, Houran, & McCutcheon, 2003, op. cit.

46 McCutheon, L. E., Ashe, D., Houran, J. & Maltby, J. (2003). A cognitive profile of individuals who tend to worship celebrities. The Journal of Psychology: Interdisciplinary and Applied, 137, 309.

47 Giles, 2000, op. cit.

48 Maltby, Houran, Lange, Ashe, & McCutcheon, 2002, op. cit.

49 Maltby, Giles, Barber, & McCutcheon, 2005, op. cit.

50 Ibid.

51 Fraser & Brown, 2005, op. cit.

52 Maltby, Houran, & McCutcheon, 2003, op. cit.

[All Notes]

Notes to Chapter 6

1 Hazzard, M. L., & Cambridge, V. C. (1990). Specialized content and narrative structure in the radio dramas of Elaine Perkins of Jamaica. In J. A. Lent (Ed.), Caribbean popular culture (pp. 106-119). Bowling Green, OH: Bowling Green State University Popular Press.

2 Perkins, E. (2000, September). Proceedings from the 4th Entertainment-Education for Social Change conference, The Netherlands, pp. 34-35.

3 Cambridge, V. (1992). Radio soap operas: The Jamaican experience 1958-1989. Studies in Latin American Popular Culture (Volume II), 93-109; Stone, C. (1986). First national survey on "Naseberry Street" programme. Unpublished manuscript. Mona.: University of West Indies; Tichenor, P. J., Donohue, G. A., & Olien, C. N. (1973). Mass communication research: Evolution of a structural model. Journalism Quarterly, 50, 419-425.

4 Donohue, G. A., Tichenor, P. J., & Olien, C. N. (1975). Mass media and the knowledge gap: A hypothesis reconsidered. Communication Research, 2, 3-23.

5 Rosin, H. (2006, June 5). Annals of broadcasting: Life's lessons. The New Yorker, 40-45.

6 LaPastina, A. C., Rego, C. M, & Straubhaar, J. D. (2003). The centrality of telenovelas in Latin America's everyday life: Past tendencies, current knowledge, and future research. Global Media Journal, 2(2), http://lass.calumet.purdue.edu/cca/gmj/ (accessed 10 August 2011).

7 Law, G., & Morita, N. (2003). Japan and the internationalization of the serial fiction market. Book History (volume 6), pp. 109-125, http://www.jstor.org/stable/30227344 (accessed 10 August 2011). Baltimore, MD: Johns Hopkins University Press.

8 Garrels, E. (1988). El Facundo como folletín. In B. Sarlo (Ed.), Revista Iberoamericana, LIV (143), 419-448. Special issue dedicated to D. F. Sarmiento.

9 Singhal, A., Obregon, R., & Rogers, E. M. (1994). Reconstructing the story of "Simplemente Maria," the most popular telenovela in Latin America of all time. Gazette, 54, 1-16.

10 Singhal, A. & Rogers, E. M. (1999). Entertainment-education: A communication strategy for social change. Mahwah, NJ: Lawrence Erlbaum Associates.

11 Rosin, 2006, p. 42.

12 Singhal & Rogers (1999).

13 Nariman, H. N. (1993). Soap operas for social change: Toward a methodology for entertainment-education television. Westport, CT: Praeger Press.

14 Sabido, M. (2004). The origins of entertainment-education. In A. Singhal, M. J. Cody, E. M. Rogers, & M. Sabido (eds.), Entertainment-Education and Social Change: History, Research, and Practice (pp. 61-74). Mahwah, NJ: Lawrence Erlbaum Associates.

15 Brown, W. J., Singhal, A., & Rogers, E. M. (1989) . Pro-development soap operas: A novel approach to development communication. Media Development, 4, 43-47.

16 Ryerson, W. (2001, November). About PMC – Sabido method. Shelburne, Vermont: Population Media Center.

17 Poindexter, D. (2004). A history of entertainment-education: 1958-2000. In A. Singhal, M. J. Cody, E.M. Rogers, & M. Sabido (eds.), Entertainment-Education and Social Change: History, Research, and Practice (pp. 21-26). Mahwah, NJ: Lawrence Erlbaum Associates.

18 Singhal, A. (1990). Entertainment-education communication strategies for development. Doctoral dissertation. Los Angeles, CA: University of Southern California, Annenberg School of Communications.

19 Singhal & Rogers (1999).

20 Brown, W. J., & Cody, M. J. (1991). Effects of a prosocial television soap opera in promoting women's status. Human Communication Research, 17, 114-142.

21 Singhal, A., & Rogers, E. M. (1989). Prosocial television for development in India. In R. E. Rice & C. K. Atkin (Eds.), Public communication campaigns (2nd ed). (pp. 331-350). Newbury Park, CA: Sage.

22 Brown, W. J. (1990). Prosocial effects of "Hum Log," India's first long-running television soap opera. Asian Journal of Communication, 1(1), 113-135.

23 Brown & Cody, 1991, op. cit.

24 Singhal & Rogers, 1989.

25 Law, S., & Singhal, A. (1999). Efficacy in letter writing to an entertainment-education radio serial. Gazette, 61, 355-372.

26 Rosin, 2006, p. 43.

27 Singhal & Rogers, 1999.

28 Law & Singhal, 1999, op. cit.

29 Rosin, 2006, p. 44.

30 Singhal, A., Rogers, E. M., & Brown, W. J. (1993). Harnessing the potential of entertainment-education telenovelas. Gazette, 51, 1-18.

31 Mazrui, A. & Kitsao, J. (1988, June). A formative survey of Ushikwapo Shikimana. Nairobi, Kenya: National Council for Population and Development.

32 Singhal & Rogers, 1999, pp. 130-131.

33 Kincaid, D. L., Yun, S. H., Piotrow, P. T., Yaser, Y. (1993). Turkey's mass media family planning campaign. In T. E. Backer, E. M. Rogers, & R. Denniston (Eds.), Impact of organizations on mass media health behavior campaigns (pp. 68-92). Newbury Park, CA: Sage.

34 Singhl, A., & Udornpim, K. (1997). Cultural shareability, archetypes and television soaps: “Oshindrome” in Thailand. Gazette, 59, 171-188.

35 Jung, C. G. (1936/1969). The concept of the collective unconscious. In R. F. C. Hull (Trans.), Collected works: Vol. 9. The archetypes and the collective unconscious (2nd ed., pp. 42-53). Princeton, NJ: Princeton University Press. In Understanding dreams (pp. 99-104).

36 Jung, C. G. (1968). The archetypes and the collective unconscious (3rd ed.). Princeton, NJ: Princeton University Press.

37 Jung, C. G. (1958). Psychology and religion, trans. R. F. C. Hall. New York, NY: Pantheon Books, p. 130.

38 Lozano, E., & Singhal, A. (1993). Melodramtic television serials: Mythical narratives for education. Communications: The European Journal of Communication, 18, 115-127.

39 Mowlana, H., & Rad, M. H. (1992). International flow of Japanese television programs: The "Oshin" phenomenon. Keio Communication Review, 14, 51-68.

40 Tehranian, M. (1993). Islamic fundamentalism in Iran and the discourse of development. In M. E. Marty & R. S. Appleby (Eds.), Fundamentalisms and society (vol. 2). Chicago, IL: University of Chicago Press.

41 Mowlana & Rad, 1992), op. cit.

42 Ibid.

43 Ito, Y. (1990). The trade winds change: Japan's shift from an information importer to an information exporter, 1965-1985. In J. A. Anderson (Ed.), Communication Yearbook 13 (pp. 430-465). Newbury Park, CA: Sage.

44 Singhal & Rogers,1989, op. cit.

45 Wang, M., & Singhal, A. (1992). Ke Wang, a Chinese television soap opera with a message. Gazette, 49, 177-192.

46 Ram, A. (1993). Women as sign: A semiotic analysis of gender portrayal in Hum Raahi. Unpublished Master's Thesis. Athens, OH: Ohio University, School of Interpersonal Communication.

47 De-Goshie, J. (1986). Mass media and national development: A content analysis of a Nigerian developmental television drama series -- "Cock Crow at Dawn". Ph.D. Thesis. Athens, Ohio: Ohio University, College of Communication.

48 Muroki, F. (1989, May 25). 'Tushauriane': Now actor speaks out. Standard (Nairobi, Kenya), p. 3E.

49 Kincaid, D. L., Yun, S. H., Piotrow, P. T., Yaser, Y. (1993). Turkey's mass media family planning campaign. In T. E. Backer, E. M. Rogers, & R. Denniston (Eds.), Impact of organizations on mass media health behavior campaigns (pp. 68-92). Newbury Park, CA: Sage.

[All Notes]

Notes to Chapter 7

1 Cleland, J., Bernsten, S. Ezeh, A. Faundes, A., Glasier, A., & Innnis, J. (2006). Family planning: The unfinished agenda. The Lancet, 368(9549), 1810-1827.

2 Eastwood R., &Lipton, M. (1999). The impact of changes in human fertility on poverty. Journal of Development Studies, 36, 1–30; Eastwood, R., & Lipton, M. (2001). Demographic transition and poverty: Effects via economic growth, distribution, and conversion. In N. Birdsall, A. C.Kelley, & S. W. Sinding (Eds.), Population matters: demographic change, economic growth, and poverty in the developing world (pp. 213-259). Oxford: Oxford University Press.

3 Population Reports (1986, Sept.-Oct.). Radio spreading the word in family planning, 32, J853-886.

4 Risopatron, F., & Spain, P. L. (1980). Reaching the poor: Human sexuality education in Costa Rica. Journal of Communication, 30, 81-89.

5 Cleland, et al., 2006, op. cit.

6 Singhal, A., & Rogers, E. M. (1989). Educating through television. Populi, 16(2): 39-47.

7 Church, C.A., & Geller, J. (1989). Lights! camera! action! Promoting family planning with TV, video, and film. Population Reports, J-38. Baltimore, MD: Johns Hopkins University, Population Information Program.

8 Singhal, A., Rogers, E. M., & Brown, W. J., (1993). Harnessing entertainment for education. In Anamaria Fadul (ed.), Serial Fiction in TV: The Latin American Telenovelas, Sao Paulo, Brasil: Escola de Communicacoess e Artes, Universidade de Sao Paulo.

9 Nariman, H. (1993). Soap operas for social change. Westport, CT: Praegar.

10 Sabido, M. (1981). Towards the social use of soap operas. Mexico City, Mexico: Institute for Communication Research.

11 Piotrow, P. T., Rimon, J. G., Winnard, K., Kincaid, D. L., Huntington, D. & Convisser, J. (1990). Mass media family planning promotion in three Nigerian cities. Studies in Family Planning, 21, pp. 265-274.

12 Singhal & Rogers, 1989, p. 41.

13 Mazrui, A. & Kitsao, J. (1988, June). A formative survey of Ushikwapo Shikimana. Nairobi, Kenya: National Council for Population and Development.

14 Advocates for Youth. (1998). The use of mainstream media to encourage social responsibility: The international experience. Menlo Park CA: Kaiser Family Foundation.

15 Population Communication International (2005). Kenya - Ushikwapo Shikamana, http://www.population.org/programs_ushikwapo_kenya.shtml (accessed 10 August 2010); Ligaga, D. (2005). Narrativising development in radio drama: Tradition and realism in the Kenyan radio play Ushikwapo Shikamama. Social Identities, 11, 131-145.

16 Advocates for Youth, 1998, op. cit.

17 Yaser, Y. (2004). The Turkish family Health and Planning Foundation's entertainment-education campaign. In A. Singhal, M. Cody, E. Rogers, & M. Sabido (Eds.), Entertainment-Education and Social Change: History, research and practice. London: Lawrence Erlbaum Associates.

18 Singhal & Rogers, 1989, p. 41.

19 Ibid.

20 Yaser, 2004, op.cit.

21 Lane, S. D. (1997). Television minidramas: Social marketing and evaluation in Egypt. Medical Anthropology Quarterly, 11, 164 – 182.

22 Singhal & Rogers, 1989, p. 41.

23 Lettenmaier, C., Krenn, S., Morgan, W., Koles, A. & Piotrow, P. (1993). Africa: Using radio soap operas to promote family planning. Hygie. 12, 1, 5-10.

24 Valente, T. W., Kim, Y. M., Lettenmaier, C., Glass, W., & Dibba, Y. (1994). Radio promotion of family planning in the Gambia. International Family Planning Perspectives, 20(3), 96-100.

25 Andere, A. (1987, May 17). 'Tushauriane' takes off tonight. Standard (Nairobi, Kenya), p. 4; Muchiri, F. (1989, May 18). They must return 'Tushauriane' to us. Kenya Times, p. 3A. Muroki, F. (1989, May 25). 'Tushauriane': Now actor speaks out. Standard (Nairobi, Kenya), p. 3E; Odindo, J. (1987, May 11). Local soap opera sets new standards. Daily Nation (Kenya), p. A1.

26 World Health Organization (2010). UNAIDS global facts and figures, http://data.unaids.org/pub/FactSheet/2009/20091124_FS_global_en.pdf (accessed 12 April 2011).

27 Ibid.

28 Singhal, A. (2005). Entertainment-education: A communication strategy for HIV prevention. University of Western Cape's Papers in Education, 3, 40-49.

29 Lyons, M. (2004). Mobile populations and HIV/AIDS in East Africa. In E. Kapipeni, S. Craddock, J. R. Oppong, & J. Ghosh (Eds.), HIV and AIDS in Africa: Beyond epidemiology (pp. 175-203). Malden, MA: Blackwell Publishing.

30 Vaughan, P. W., Rogers, E. M., Singhal, A., & Swalehe, R. M. (2000). Entertainment-education and HIV/AIDS prevention: A field experiment in Tanzania. Journal of Health Communication, 5, 81-100.

31 Rogers, E. M., Vaughan, P. W., Swalehe, R. A., Rao, N., Svenkerud, P., & Sood, S. (1999). Effects of an entertainment-education radio soap opera on family planning behavior in Tanzania. Studies in Family Planning, 30(3), 193-211.

32 Vaugh et al., 2000, op. cit.

33 Vaugh et al. 2000, op. cit.

34 Poindexter, D. (2004). A History of entertainment-education, 1958-2000. In A. Singhal, M. Cody, E. Rogers, & M. Sabido (Eds.), Entertainment-Education and Social Change: History, research and practice (pp. 30-??). London: Lawrence Erlbaum Associates.

35 Populations Communications International, 2005, 2000, op. cit.

36 Sawyer, J. (2002, December 1). Soap operas are proving helpful in informing public. St. Louis Post-Dispatch, p. B-1, 34.

37 Human Sciences Research Council. (2005). HIV risk exposure among young children: A study of 2–9-year-olds served by public health facilities in the Free State, South Africa. Cape Town, South Africa: HSRC Press.

38 Clacherty, G., & Kushlick, A. (2004). Meeting the challenge of research with very young children: A practical outline of methodologies used in the formative research and pre-testing of the Takalani Sesame HIV and AIDS television and radio programmes. Paper presented to the Fourth International Entertainment-Education Conference, Sept. 26–30, Cape Town, http://www.comminit.com/africa/edutainment/edutainmentEE4/edutainment-30.html (accessed 10 May 2011).

39 Dagan, E. A. 1990. Emotions in motion: Theatrical puppets and masks from Black Africa. Montreal: Galerie Amrad African Arts.

40 Leyser, Y., & Wood, J. (1980). An evaluation of puppet intervention in a second-grade classroom. Education, 100, 292 - 296.

41 Kruger, M. S. (2004, September). Puppets in entertainment-education: Universal principles and African performance traditions as a model for interaction. Paper presented to the Fourth International Entertainment-Education Conference, Cape Town.

42 Ibid.

43 Den Otter, E. 1995. Verre Vrienden van Jan Klaasen. Amsterdam: Koninklijke Instituut van de Tropen.

44 Kruger, 2004, op. cit.

45 Menon, K. (2004, September). Thandi breaks her silence! An evaluation of the power of the comic as an element of an HIV/AIDS communication strategy. Paper presented to the Fourth International Entertainment-Education Conference, Cape Town, http://www.ee4.org/Papers/ EE4_Menon.pdf (accessed 10 August 2010).

46 Ibid.

47 Elvgren, G. (2005). HIV/AIDS prevention play for Nepal. Virginia Beach, VA: Regent University.

48 Singhal, A., & Rogers, E. M. (2003). Combating AIDS: Communication strategies in action. Thousand Oaks, CA: Sage Publications.

49 DramAidE (2001). Annual Report, 2000-2001. Kwadlangezwa, South Africa: Office of DramAidE, University of Zululand.

50 Sutherland, I. (2002). DramAidE RMB project: Evaluation report. Durban, South Africa: Office of DramAidE, University of Natal.

51 Ibid.

52 Singhal, A. (2004). Entertainment-education through participatory theater: Freirean Strategies for empowering the oppressed. In A. Singhal, M. Cody, E. Rogers, & M. Sabido (Eds.), Entertainment-Education and Social Change: History, research and practice. London: Lawrence Erlbaum Associates, p. 396.

53 Singhal, 2004, p. 394.

54 Ibid.

55 Valente, T. W., & Bharath, U. (1999). An evaluation of the use of drama to communicate HIV/AIDS information. AIDS Education and Prevention, 11, 203-211.

56 Vidmar, N., & Rokeach, M. (1974). Archie Bunker's bigotry: A study in selection perception and exposure. Journal of Communication, 24, 36-47.

57 Sharf, B. F., & Freimuth, V. S. (1993). The construction of illness on entertainment television: Coping with cancer on thirtysomething. Health Communication, 5, 141-160.

58 Beck, V. (2004). Working with daytime and prime-time television shows in the United States to promote health. In Singhal, A., Cody, M. J., Rogers, E. M., and Sabido, M. (Eds.), Entertainment-education and social change: History, research, and practice (pp. 207-224), Mahwah, NJ: Lawrence Erlbaum Associates.

59 Winsten, J. A. (1994). Promoting designated drivers: The Harvard alcohol project. American Journal of Preventive Medicine, 10 (supplement 1), 11-14.

60 Dejong, W., & Winsten, J. A. (1990). The Harvard alcohol project: A demonstration project to promote the use of the "designated driver." Cambridge, MA: Harvard School of Public Health, Harvard University.

61 Winsten, J. A., & DeJong, W. (2001). The designated driver campaign. In R. E. Rice & C. Atkin (Eds.), Public communication campaigns (3rd ed.) (pp. 290-294). Newbury Park, CA: Sage Publications.

62 Dejong & Winsten, 1990, op. cit.

63 Wallack, L., Grube, J. W., Madden, P. A., & Breed, W. (1990). Portrayals of alcohol on prime- time television. Journal of Studies on Alcohol, 51, 428-437.

64 Kean, L. G., & Albada, K. F. (2003). The relationship between college students' schema regarding alcohol use, their television viewing patterns, and their previous experience with alcohol. Health Communication, 15, 277-298.

65 Winsten & DeJong, 2001, op. cit.

66 Calvert, S. L., Kotler, J., Murray, W., Gonzales, E., Savoye, K., Hammack, P., Weigert, S., Shockey, E., Paces, C., Friedman, M., & Hammar, M. (2002). Children's online reports about educational and informational television programs. In S. L. Calvert, A. B. Jordan, & R. R. Cocking (Eds.), Children in the digital age: Influences of electronic media on development (pp. 165–182). Westport, CT: Praeger.

67 Singhal, A. & Rogers, E. M., (1988). Television soap operas for development in India. Gazette, 41(3), 109-126.

68 Brown, W. J., Kiruswa, S., & Fraser, B. P., (2003). Promoting HIV/AIDS prevention through soap operas: Tanzania's experience with "Maisha." Communicare, 22, 90-111.

69 London, A. J. (2005) Justice and the human development approach to international research. Hastings Center Report, 35, 24-37.

70 Abdulla, R.A. (2004). Entertainment-education in the Middle East: Lessons from the Egyptian oral rehydration therapy campaign. In Singhal, A., Cody, M.J., Rogers, E.N. and Sabido, M. (Eds.), Entertainment-Education and Social Change (pp 301-320). Mahwah, New Jersey: Lawrence Erlbaum Publishers.

71 White, 1991

72 Ball-Rokeach, S., Rokeach, M., & Grube, J. (1984). The great American value test. New York: Free Press.

73 Stevenson, 1990, op. cit.

74 Boyce, W., & Paterson, J. (2002). Community based rehabilitation for children in Nepal, http://www.aifo.it/old_sito/english/apdrj/January%202002%20Selected%20Readings%20CBR%20II.pdf#page=58 (accessed 13 February 2008).

75 Ibid.

76 Parisammy, K. (2007, August 12). Personal interview. Virginia Beach, VA.

77 Strong, D. A., & Brown, W. J. (2011). Promoting prosocial beliefs and behavior toward people with disabilities in Nepal through a children's entertainment-education program. Disability, CBR, and Inclusive Development, 22(2), 22-37.

78 Moutrey, D. (2007). Exploring opportunities for research: Collaborations between media centres and HEIs. Journal of Media Practice, 8, 71-78.

79 Sood, S., Menard, T., & Witte, K. (2004). The theory behind entertainment-education. In A. Singhal, M. J. Cody, E. M. Rogers & M. Sabido (Eds.), Entertainment-education and social change: History, research, and practice (pp. 117-149). Mahwah, NJ: Erlbaum.

80 Johns Hopkins University Center for Communication Programs (2010). International projects, http://www.jhuccp.org/ (accessed 21 September 2011).

81 USAID (2009, November 4). USAID Awards NetWorks Malaria Prevention Grant to Johns Hopkins, the Malaria Consortium and Catholic Relief Services, http://www.usaid.gov/press/releases/2009/pr091104_1.html (accessed 21 September 2011).

82 Netherlands Entertainment-Education Foundation (NEEF), and Johns Hopkins University Center for Communication Programs (JHU/CCP). (2001, September),

Proceedings from the Third Entertainment-Education Conference for Social Change, Arnhem and Amsterdam, The Netherlands.

83 Bouman, M. P. A. (2009). Assessment of Go Out Plug In campaign. Gouda, the Netherlands: Centre for Media and Health and the Netherlands Entertainment-Education Foundation.

84 Population Media Center (2009). 2008 Annual Report, http://www.populationmedia.org/wp-content/uploads/2009/07/POP-MEDIA-FOR-WEB.pdf (accessed 27 March 2010).

85 Population Services International (2010). At a glance, http://www.psi.org/about-psi/psi-at-a-glance (accessed 12 March 2011).

86 Soul City Institute for Health & Development Communication (2010). http://www.soulcity.org.za/ (accessed 12 March 2011).

87 World Health Organization. (1986, Nov. 21). Ottawa Charter for health promotion. First International Conference on Health Promotion. Ottawa, Canada, http://www.who.int/hpr/NPH/docs/ottawa_charter_hp.pdf (accessed 12 March 2011).

88 Singhal, A. (2003). The entertainment-education strategy in development communication. In C. C. Okigbo & F. Eribo (Eds.), Development and communication in Africa (chapter 12). Boston, MA: Rowan & Littlefield Publishers.

89 Usdin, S., Singhal, A., Shongwe, T., Goldstein, S., & Shabalala, A. (2004). No short cuts in entertainment-education: Designing soul city step-by-step. In A. Singhal, M. J. Cody, E. M. Rogers, & M. Sabido (eds.), Entertainment-education and social change: History, research, and practice (pp. 153-176). Mahwah, NJ: Lawrence Erlbaum Associates.

90 Japhet, G., & Goldstein, S. (1997). Soul City experience. Integration, 53, 10-11.

91 Soul City Institute for Health & Development Communication. (2010). Soul City Series 4, http://www.soulcity.org.za/projects/soul-city-series/soul-city-series-4 (accessed 12 March 2011).

92 Usdin et al., 2004, op. cit.

93 Ibid.

94 BBC News (2002, Aug. 15). UN Aids drama not realistic enough, http://news.bbc.co.uk/2/hi/africa/2195252.stm (accessed 12 March 2011).

95 The Norman Lear Center. (2001). TV viewing habits and effects, http://www.learcenter.org/html/projects/?cm=hhs/research#porter (accessed 22 March 2011).

96 The Norman Lear Center. (2010). University of Southern California Annenberg School for Communication. http://www.learcenter.org/html/about/?cm=about (accessed 22 March 2011).

[All Notes]

Notes to Chapter 8

1 Baker, J. A., Lepley, C. J., Krishnan, S., Victory, K. S. (1992). Celebrities as health educators: media advocacy guidelines. Journal of School Health, 62, 433-436.Fumento, M. (1992). Do you believe in Magic? The American Spectator, 25 (2), 16-23.

2 Fumento, M. (1992). Do you believe in Magic? The American Spectator, 25 (2), 16-23.

3 Brown, W. J. (1991). An AIDS prevention campaign: Effects on attitudes, beliefs, and communication behavior. American Behavioral Scientist, 34, 666-687.

4 Leerhsen, C. (1991, November 18). National AIDS hotline. Newsweek, 58-62.

5 Brown, W. J., & Basil, M. D. (1995). Media Celebrities and Public Health: Responses to "Magic" Johnson's HIV disclosure and its impact on AIDS risk and high-risk behaviors. Health Communication, 7, 45-371.

6 Basil, M. D. (1996). Identification as a mediator of celebrity effects. Journal of Broadcasting & Electronic Media, 40, 478-495.

7 Basil, M. D., & Brown, W. J. (1997). Marketing AIDS prevention: Examining impact hypothesis and identification effects on concern about AIDS. Journal of the differential Consumer Psychology, 6, 389-411.

8 Schwartz, L. (2007). Before trial, Simpson charmed America. Available at http://espn.go.com/sportscentury/features/00016472.html

9 Ibid.

10 Pro Football Hall of Fame (2000). O. J. Simpson. Available at http://www.profootballhof.com/hof/member.aspx?player_id=195

11 Schwartz (2007), op. cit.

12 Ibid.

13 Ibid.

14 PBS Newshour (1994). Available at http://www.pbs.org/newshour/generationnext/demographic/timeline_media.html

15 Rogers, E. M., Dearing, J. W., & Bregman D. (1993). The anatomy of agenda setting research. Journal of Communication, 43, 68–84.

16 Brosius, H. B., & Kepplinger, H. M. (1992). Beyond agenda-setting: The influence of partisanship and television reporting on the electorate's voting intentions. Journalism Quarterly, 69, 894-901.

17 McCombs, M. E., & Shaw, D. L. (1972). The agenda-setting function of the mass media. Public Opinion Quarterly, 36, 176-187.

18 McCombs, M. E., & Shaw, D. L. (1993). The evolution of agenda-setting research: Twenty-five years in the marketplace of ideas. Journal of Communication, 43, 58-67.

19 Fan, D. P., Brosius, H. B., & Kepplinger, H. M. (1994). Predictions of the public agenda from television coverage. Journal of Broadcasting & Electronic Media, 38, 163-178.

20 Brown, W. J., & Facciola, P. C. (1991). Effects of media coverage on public attitudes and beliefs of the Persian Gulf War. Competitive paper presented at the seventy-seventh Annual Conference of the Speech Communication Association, Oct. 31-Nov. 3, Atlanta. Vincent, R. C. (1992). CNN: Elites talking to elites. In H. Mowlana, G. Gerbner & H. I. Schiller (Eds.), Triumph of the image: The media's war in the Persian Gulf—A global perspective (pp. 181-201). Boulder, CO: Westview Press.

21 Rogers, E. M., Dearing, J. W., & Chang, S. (1991). AIDS in the 1980's: The agenda-setting process for a public issue. Journalism Monographs, No. 126.

22 Brown & Basil (1995), op. cit.

23 Kalichman, S.C., & Hunter, T. L. (1992). The disclosure of celebrity HIV-infection: Its effect on public attitudes. American Journal of Public Health, 82, 1374-1376.

24 Brown, W. J., Fraser, B. P., & Bocarnea, M. C. (1994). The agenda-setting effects of media coverage of the O.J. Simpson trial. Competitive paper presented to the Western States Communication Association, February 11-14, Portland.

25 Ibid.

26 Ibid.

27 Brown, W. J., Duane, J. J., & Fraser, B. P. (1997). Media coverage and public opinion of the O.J. Simpson trial: Implications for the criminal justice system. Communication Law and Policy, 2, 261-287.

28 Ibid.

29 Verducci, T. (1998, September 14). Making his mark. Sports Illustrated, 28-33.

30 McGregor, E. J. (1998). Mark McGwire is a hero for more than his homers. Sports Illustrated, 89(12), 22.

31 Levine, S. (2001, April 9). The price of child abuse. U.S. News & World Report, 130(14), p. 58.

32 Peddle, N., & Wang, C. T. (2001). Current trends in child abuse, prevention, reporting, and fatalities. Chicago, IL: Prevent Child Abuse America.

33 Mark McGwire Foundation for Children (2010). Available athttp://www.mcgwire.com/charity.html

34 National Kidney Foundation. (1999, October 22). Mark McGwire teams up with the National Kidney Foundation for public service campaign on bed-wetting. [On-line]. Available: www.kidney.org. St. Louis Post Dispatch. (1998, September 10). McGwire tapes commercials for child abuse prevention. [On-line]. Available: www.pnnonline.org/people/bigmac0910.cfm.

35 Puget Sound Business Journal (1999, July 12). Starbucks, Mark McGwire raise $140,000 to help kids read. Seattle, WA: American City Business Journals Inc.

36 Yesalis, Charles E. III (1999). Medical, legal and societal implications of androstenedione use. Journal of the American Medical Association, 281, 2043-2044.

37 Finkelstein, J., Susman, E., & Chinchilli, V. (1997). Estrogen or testosterone increases self-reported aggressive behaviors in hypogonadal adolescents. Journal of Clinical Endocrinology Metabolism, 82, 2433-2438. King, D. S., Sharp, R. L., & Vukovich, M. D. (1999). Effect of oral androstenedione on serum testosterone and adaptations to resistance training in young men: A randomized controlled trial. Journal of the American Medical Association, 281, 2020-2028. Zorpette, G. (1998, December). Andro angst. Scientific American, 279(6), 22, 26.

38 Brown, W. J., Basil, M.D., & Bocarnea, M. C. (2003). The influence of famous athletes on health beliefs and practices: Mark McGwire, child abuse prevention, and androstenedione. Journal of Health Communication, 8, 41-57.

39 Ibid.

40 Ibid.

41 Ibid.

42 Schrof, J. M. (1998, September 7). McGwire hits the pills. U.S. News & World Report, 53-54.

43 Turner, M. J. (1998, September 28). McGwire and steroids. U.S. News & World Report, p.5.

44 National Call to Action (2000, July 19). Working to eliminate child abuse and neglect. [On-line]. Available: www.nationalcalltoaction.com. Prevent Child Abuse America. (2001, April). An important message from our President and Chairman of our Board. [On-line]. Available: www.preventchildabuse.org.

45 Dickey, C. Helmstaedt, K., Nordland, R., & Hayden, T. (1999, February 15). The real scandal. Newsweek, 48-54.

46 Lefavi, R. (1999, May). Andro: The Harvard study. Muscular Development, 144-147.Horovitz, B. (1998, August 27). Sales of nutrition supplement out of ballpark. USA Today, p. B-1.

47 Hewitt, B., & Sider, D. (2001). A hero's last lap: Legendary NASCAR driver Dale Earnhardt died as he had lived, running his car flat out and never backing off. People Magazine, 55(9), 101-106.

48 Sullivan, R., et al. (2001, March 5). The Last Lap, Dale Earnhardt: 1951-2001. Time Magazine. Available at http://www.time.com/time/magazine/article/0,9171,999359,00.html

49 Saward, J. (2001, Feb. 20). Obituary: Dale Earnhardt. The Independent, p. 6.

50 Miller, E. (2001, Feb. 20). Earnhardt fans grieve - stunned followers buy memorabilia, struggle to cope with loss of racing superstar. The Virginian-Pilot, February 20. Available at http://www.highbeam.com/doc/1G1-70684288.html.

51 Marquand, I. (2001, September 1) Covering America's heroes. The Quill, p. 8.

52 Hewitt & Sider (2001), op. cit.

53 Miller, E. (2001), op. cit.

54 Brown, W. J., Barker, G., & Presnell, K. K. (2008). The social impact of mediated celebrities: Cognitive and emotional responses to the death of Dale Earnhardt. Paper presented to the National Communication Association's Annual Conference, San Diego, California.

55 Ibid.

56 Sobel, R. S., & Nesbitt, T. M. (2007). Automobile safety regulation and the incentive to drive recklessly: Evidence from NASCAR. Southern Economic Journal, 74, 71-84.

57 Maradona, D. (2000). Yo Soy el Diego de la Gente. Buenos Aires, Planeta., p. 13.

58 Gamon, C. (1986, July 7). The king of soccer: Diego Maradona and Argentina win the World Cup. Sports Illustrated, 65(1), 14.

59 de Matviuk, M. A. C. (2005). The social influence of sports celebrities: The case of Diego Maradona. Doctoral Dissertation. Virginia Beach, VA: Regent University.

60 BBC News (2004). Maradona in intensive care. Article retrieved on June 15, 2005, fromhttp://news.bbc.co.uk/sport1/hi/football/3666357.htm.

61 Reuters. (2010). Tumultuous life of a flawed genius. The Peninsula, 15(4679), p. 27.Available at www.thepeninsulaqatar.com

62 Brown, W. J., & deMatviuk, M. A. C. (2010). Sports celebrities and public health: Diego Maradona's influence on drug use prevention. Journal of Health Communication, 15, 358-373.

63 Alabarces, P., & Rodríguez, M. G. (1996). Cuestion de Pelotas. Buenos Aires. Editorial Atuel.

64 Grech, D. (2004). Argentina ties its pride, pain to gravely ill Diego Maradona. Available at www.latinamericanstudies.org/argentina/maradona.htm.

65 Brown, Basil, and Bocarnea (2003), op. cit.

66 Cialdini, R. B., Borden, R. J., Thorne, A., Walker, M. R., Freeman, S., & Sloan, L. R. 1976). Basking in reflected glory: Three (football) field studies. Journal of Personality and Social Psychology, 34, 366-375.

67 Ibid.

68 Wann, D. L., & Branscombe, N. R. (1990). Die-hard and fair-weather fans: Effects of identification on BIRGing and CORFing tendencies. Journal of Sport and Social Issues, 14, 103-117.

69 Branscombe, N. R., & Wann, D. L. (1991). The positive social and self-concept consequences of sports team identification. Journal of Sport and Social Issues, 15, 115-127.

70 McCracken, G. (1989). Who is the celebrity endorser? Cultural foundations of the endorsement process. Journal of Consumer Research,16, 310-321.

71 Fowles, J. (1992). Star struck: Celebrity performers and the American public. Washington, DC: Smithsonian Institution Press.

72 Zillmann, D., & P.B. Paulus. (1993). Spectators: Reactions to sports events and effects on athletic performance. In R. N. Singer, M. Murphey, & L. K. Tennant (Eds.), Handbook of Research on Sport Psychology (pp. 600-619). New York: Macmillan.

73 Zurawick, D. (2010, July 9). ESPN gets big ratings for LeBron James hype-o-rama. The Baltimore Sun. Available at http://weblogs.baltimoresun.com/entertainment/zontv/2010/07_espn_lebron_james_ratings.html. ESPN (2010, July 9). Letter from Cavs owner Dan Gilbert. Available at http://sports.espn.go.com/nba/news/story?id=5365704

74 National Institute of Statistics and Census of Argentina (2004). Available at http://www.mundoandino.com/Argentina/National-Institute-of-Statistics-and-Census-of-Argentina.

75 AVERT (2005). Latin America HIV & AIDS statistics. Available at http://www.avert.org/southamerica.htm

76 de Matviuk (2005), op. cit., p. 104.

77 Stack, S. (2000). Media Impacts on Suicide: A quantitative review of 293 findings. Social Science Quarterly, 81, 957-971.

78 Benoit, W. (2006). Image repair in President Bush's April 2004 news conference. Public Relations Review, 32, 137-143.

79 Youth in Philanthropy (2010). Famous and celebrity philanthropists. Available athttp://youth.foundationcenter.org/

80 Knepp, S., Kresovich, A., Parker, E., & Ray, S. (2012, March). We may never meet, but we tweet: Examining the effect of Twitter on parasocial relationships. Paper presented at AEJMC Midwinter Conference, Norman, OK.

[All Notes]

Notes to Chapter 9

1 Kolb, G. R. (1996). Read with a beat: Developing literacy through music and song. The Reading Teacher, 50, 76-77.

2 Kujawa, A. (2006, April 6). Culturally specific content key to Sesame Street's success.America.gov. Available at http://www.america.gov/st/washfileenglish/2006/April/20060406104915aawajuk0.4600336.html

3 The Ozone Hole Inc. (2010). Music changes the world: 1960's and 1970's-A time of change. Available at http://www.solcomhouse.com/music6070.htm

4 UNICEF. (2010). The Concert for Bangladesh. Available athttp://www.concertforbangladesh.com/home.html

5 Inglis, I. (2003). George Harrison 1943-2001. Popular music and society, 26, 225 – 226.

6 Decurtis, A. (2010). George Harrison: Concert for Bangladesh reissue. Rolling Stone Magazine. Available at http://www.rollingstone.com/music/reviews/album/7733/38837

7 Fricke, D. (2005, Oct. 25). Harrison show revisited/Rolling Stone CFN article. Available at http://board.georgeharrison.com/viewtopic.php?f=3&t=7259

8 Carter, R. B. (2006, Aug. 6). George Harrison honoured on 35th anniversary of 'Concert for Bangladesh.' UNICEF. Available at http://www.unicef.org/infobycountry/bangladesh_35176.html

9 Fricke (2005), op. cit.

10 Landau, J. (1972, Feb. 3). George Harrison: Concert for Bangladesh. Rolling StoneReviews. Available at http://www.rollingstone.com/music/albumreviews/concert-for-bangladesh-19720203

11 Nehring, N. (2011). Evolution of the political benefit rock album. In I. Peddie (Ed.),Polular music and human rights, Vol. 1: British and American music (pp. 91-100). Farnham, UK: Ashgate Publishing Limited.

12 Nkosi, J., & Nkosi, M. (2010). Reflections on International humanitarian interventions inAfrica. Conference proceedings. Sponsored and organized by USA for Africa in Collaboration with Trust Africa and Africa Humanitarian Action and Hosted by the United Nations Economic Commission on Africa. Available at http://www.usaforafrica.org/pdf/completereport.pdf

13 Nehring, N. (2011), op. cit.

14 Weiss, T. G., & Thakur, R. (2010). Protecting against pandemics. Global governance and the UN: An unfinished journey (pp. 286-308). Bloomington, IN: Indiana University Press.

15 McDougal, D. (1986, Nov. 2). Hands across American, May 25, 1986: Hands' bills paid in full, but homeless still waiting. Los Angeles Times. Available at http://articles.latimes.com/1986-11-02/entertainment/ca-15476_1_expenses

16 Farm Aid (2011). 26 years of amazing concerts. Available at http://www.farmaid.org/site/c.qlI5IhNVJsE/b.2739785/apps/s/content.asp?ct=3851529

17 Garofalo, R., Bragg, B., Cheng, T., Fast, S., Frith, S., George-Warren, H., et al. (2005) Who is the world? Reflections on music and politics twenty years after live aid. Journal of Popular Music Studies, 17, (3), 324-344.

18 Earthly Issues (2008). Music changes the world. Available at http://www.earthlyissues.com/music.htm

19 Ibid.

20 George, N. (1998). Hip Hop America, p. viii. New York: Viking.

21 Fernando, S.H. Jr. (1999). Back in the day:1975-79. In A. Light (Ed.), The Vibe history of hip hop (pp. 13-22). New York, NY: Three Rivers Press.

22 Flash, G. (1999). Foreword. In A. Light (Ed.), The Vibe history of hip hop, p. vii. New York: Three Rivers Press.

23 Rose, T. (1994). Black Noise: Rap music and Black culture in contemporary America. New England: Wesleyan University Press.

24 Ibid, p. 31.

25 Toop, D. (1991). Rap Attack 2: African rap to global hip hop. New York: Serpent's Tail.

26 Fernando, S.H. Jr. (1999), op cit, p. 14.

27 Ibid, pp. 14-20.

28 Perkins, W.E. (1996) The rap attack: An introduction. In W. Perkins (Ed.), Droppin' science: Critical essays on rap music and hip-hop culture (pp. 5-6). Philadelphia, PA: Temple University Press.

29 George, N. (1998), op. cit., p. 19.

30 Anderson, R. (2003). Black beats for one people: Causes and effects of identification with hip-hop culture. Virginia Beach, VA: Unpublished doctoral dissertation; McLeod, K. (1999). Authenticity within hip-hop and other cultures threatened with assimilation. Journal of Communication, 49, 134-150.

31 Ibid, pp. 138 –139.

32 Ibid, p. 143.

33 Ibid, p. 144.

34 Earthly Issues (2006). Students reach and teach the world. Available at http://www.earthlyissues.com/rap.htm

35 Rule, S. (1992, July 29). 'Cop Killer' to be cut from Ice-T album. The New York Times. Available at http://www.nytimes.com/1992/07/29/arts/cop-killer-to-be-cut-from-ice-t-album.html

36 Rose, T. (1994), op cit, pp. 63 –64.

37 Ibid, p. 64.

38 Ibid, p. 67.

39 Ibid, p. 69

40 Snead, J.A. (1981). On repetition in Black culture. Black American Literature Forum, 14, 146-154.

41 Rose, T. (1994), op cit, p. 70.

42 Ibid, p. 125.

43 Samuels, A., Croal, N., & Gates, D. (2000, October 9). Battle for the soul of hip-hop. Newsweek, 36(15), 58-65.

44 Considine, J.D. (1999). The big willies. In A. Light (Ed.), The vibe history of hip hop (pp. 153-155). New York: Three Rivers Press.

45 Grossberg, J. (2001, June 30). Hip-hop summit: It's makeover time. E! Online. Available at www.eonline.com/News/Items/0,1,8405,00.html

46 Jennings, J. T. (1992). Voting and registration in the election of November 1992.Publication No. P20-466. Washington, DC: Bureau of the Census.

47 Cassel, C. A., & Hill, D. B. (1981). Explanation of turnout decline: A multivariate test American Politics Quarterly, 9, 181-195.

48 Jennings (1992), op cit.

49 Tindell, J. H., & Medhurst, M. J. (1998): Rhetorical reduplication in MTV'S rock the vote Campaign. Communication Studies, 49(1), 18-28.

50 Jennings (1992), op cit.

51 Bono (2001, June 12). My name is Bono, and I am a rock star. Harvard Magazine. Available at http://harvardmagazine.com/2001/07/bono-speeches-commencement-2001

52 Bono (2006, February 2). Transcript: Bono remarks at the National Prayer Breakfast. USA Today. Available at http://www.usatoday.com/news/washington/2006-02-02-bono-transcript_x.htm

53 Bono (2005, July 2). The St. Petersburg G-8 Summit 2006. Available at http://www.live8live.com/

54 Youngs, I. (2006, July 2). Did Live 8 make a difference? BBC News. Available at http://news.bbc.co.uk/2/hi/entertainment/5128344.stm

55 Ibid.

56 TXL Films (2004). United. Available at http://txlfilms.com/films/docs_worldtour2004.html

57 PRWEB (2004, December 17). Presented in Brussels a brand-new educational tool for human rights to celebrate the United Nations International Human Rights Day. Available at http://www.prweb.com/releases/2004/12/prweb189184.htm

58 A Better World (2004, November 20). Music video release. Available at http://towardspeace.blogspot.com/2004_12_02_archive.html

59 Church, C.A., & Geller, J. (1989). Lights! camera! action! Promoting family planning with TV, video, and film. Population Reports, J-38. Baltimore, MD: Johns Hopkins University, Population Information Program.

60 Coleman, P. L., & Meyer, R. C. (Eds.) (1990). Proceedings from the 1997 entertainment-education conference: Entertainment for social change. Baltimore, MD: Johns Hopkins University, Center for Communication Programs.

61 Kincaid, D. L., Jara, R., Coleman, P., & Segura, F. (1988). Getting the message: The Communication for young people project. Washington, DC: U.S. Agency for International Development, AID Evaluation Special Study 56.

62 Rimon, J. G. II (1989, December). Leveraging messages and corporations: The Philippine experience. Integration, 22, 37-44.

63 Kincaid, D. L., Rimon, J. G., Piotrow, P. T., & Coleman, P. L. (1992, April). The enter-educate approach: Using entertainment to change health behavior. Paper presented to the Population Association of America, Denver.

64 UNAIDS (2010). Outlook Report, Al-Vida, p.29. Available at http://data.unaids.org/pub/outlook/2010/20100713_outlook_report_web_en.pdf

65 UNAIDS (2012). India AIDS information. Available at http://www.unaids.org/en/regionscountries/countries/india/

66 Jain, S. (2005, November 27). Bringing home the virus. The Hindu. Available at http://www.hindu.com/mag/2005/11/27/stories/2005112700190400.htm

67 Ibid.

68 Ibid.

69 Ibid.

70 Ibid.

71 Johns Hopkins School of Public Health (1997, January). Center for Communication Programs, Working Paper No 3, Reaching Men Worldwide: Lessons Learned from Family Planning and Communication Projects, 1986-1996. Baltimore, MD: JHCCP.

72 AVERT International HIV & AIDS Charity (2011). HIV and AIDS in Uganda. Available at http://www.avert.org/aids-uganda.htm

73 UNAIDS (2006). Uganda AIDS information. Available at http://www.unaids.org/en/regionscountries/countries/uganda/

74 Center for Communication Programs (2012, May). HPC Uganda: Final report. Available at http://www.jhuccp.org/sites/all/files/HCP%20Uganda%202007-2012%20Final%20Project%20Report.pdf

75 Media Diversity Institute. (2011). Media for social change: Kafunda stage scripts. Available at http://www.media-diversity.org/mdi/index.php?option=com_content&view=article&id=305: media-for-social-change-kafunda-stage-scripts-

76 Media Materials Clearinghouse (1995). Hits for hope. Available at http://www.mmc.org/mmc_search.php?sp=&ref_crmb=&ref_id=&step=results&view=detail&detail_id=VT_UGA_8&adv=mat

77 Ibid.

[All Notes]

Notes to Chapter 10

1 Wartella, E., & Reeves, B. (1985). Historical trends in research on children and the media: 1900-1960. Journal of Communication, 35, 118-133.

2 Cressey, P. G. (1938). The motion picture experience as modified by social background and personality. American Sociological Review, 3, 516-525.

3 U.S. Department of Justice (1934). The Communications Act of 1934. Available at http://www.it.ojp.gov/default.aspx?area=privacy&page=1288

4 National Film Board of Canada (2012). NFB profiles: John Grierson. Available at http://www.onf-nfb.gc.ca/eng/portraits/john_grierson/

5 Baird, J. W. (1983). From Berlin to Neubabelsberg: Nazi film propaganda and Hitler youth quex. Journal of Contemporary History, 18, 495-515.

6 Gunston, D. (1960). Leni Riefenstahl. Film Quarterly, 14, 4-19.

7 Hinton, D. B. (2000). The films of Leni Riefenstahl (3rd ed.). Lanham, MD: Scarecrow Press. Available at http://www.brynmawr.edu/archaeology/CSem/Hinton.pdf

8 Barsam, R. M. (1992). Non-fiction film: A critical history (pp. 122-133). Bloomington, IN: Indiana University Press.

9 Hinton (2000), op. cit., p. 58.

10 Watersprite-Gale (2007, July 27). For the ages: Leni Riefenstahl. Available at http://watersprite-gale.blogspot.com/2011/07/for-ages-leni-riefenstahl.html

11 Olympia won a gold medal in Paris in 1937, recognition in Venice a year later as the world's best film, the Olympic Award (a gold medal and diploma) by the International Olympic Committee in 1939, and in 1956 its recognition as one of the world's best ten films.

12 Carney, R. (1986). The films of Frank Capra. Cambridge, UK: Cambridge University Press.

13 RTBOT (2012). Prelude to War. Available at http://www.rtbot.net/prelude_to_war

14 The number is closer to 260 German planes shot down.

15 Gallup (1999, Dec. 6). The most important events of the century from the viewpoint of the people. Available at http://www.gallup.com/poll/3427/ most-important-events-century-from-viewpoint-people.aspx

16 McGuire, W. J. (1996). The Yale communication and attitude-change program in the 1950s. In E. E. Dennis & E. Wartella (Eds.), American communication research: The remembered history (pp. 39-60). Mahwah, NJ: Lawrence Erlbaum Associates, Inc.

17 Fairhaven College (2010). John Riber, visiting faculty. Available at http://www.wwu.edu/fairhaven/about/faculty/visiting/riber.shtml

18 Riber, J. (1992). Synopsis of the film Sonamoni (Golden Pearl). Columbia, MD: Development Through Self-Reliance.

19 Brown, W. J. (1991). An AIDS prevention campaign: Effects on attitudes, beliefs, and communication behavior. American Behavioral Scientist, 34, 666-687.

20 Coleman, P. L., & Meyer, R. C. (Eds.) (1990). Proceedings from the entertainment-educate conference: Entertainment for social change. Baltimore, MD: Johns Hopkins University, Center for Communication Programs. (pp. 37-39)

21 Rogers, E. M., Aikat, S., Soonbum, C., Poppe, P., & Sopory, P. (1989, April 1). Proceedings from the conference on entertainment-education for social change. Los Angeles, CA: Annenberg School of Communications, University of Southern California, p. 19.

22 Ibid, p. 21.

23 Medved, M. (1992). Hollywood vs. America: Popular culture and the war on traditional values. New York: HarperCollins.

24 Hungwe, K. (1991). Southern Rhodesian propaganda and education films for peasant farmers, 1948-1955. Historical Journal of Film, Radio and Television, 11, 229-241.

25 Hungwe, K. (2005). Narrative and ideology: 50 years of filmmaking in Zimbabwe. Media, Culture & Society, 27, 83-99.

26 Brown, W. J., & Singhal, A. (1993). Ethical considerations of promoting prosocial messages through the popular media. Journal of Popular Film & Television, 21(3), 92-99.

27 Tomaselli, K. G., Shepperson, A., & Eke, M. (1995). Towards a theory of orality in African Cinema. Research in African Literatures, 3 (26), 18-35.

28 Hill, H. (1993). The widow's revenge. Africa Report, 38(2), 64-66.

29 Wray, R. (1991). Taking stock of "Consequences". MA Thesis. Ithaca, NY: Cornell University, Department of Communication.

30 Buenting, D. (2007). Audience involvement with Yellow Card, an entertainment-education initiative promoting safe-sex behavior among African youth. Doctoral dissertation. Virginia Beach, Virginia: Regent University.

31 Smith, S. C. (1991). Social message video production and distribution in Sub-Saharan Africa: A suggested approach. New York: National Video Resources.

32 Buenting, D. K., & Brown, W. J. (2009). Exploring audience involvement with Yellow Card and its promotion of sexual responsibility among African youth. Paper presented to the International and Intercultural Communication Division of the National Communication Association for presentation at the 95th annual convention, Nov. 12-15, Chicago.

33 Ngenge, T. (2003, January). Sex, AIDS and videotape: Video as a tool in informing about HIV/AIDS among young people in rural Mozambique. Unpublished Manuscript, Malmo University: Unpublished manuscript available from: http://www.mfdi.

34 Buenting, D. (2003). Computer mediated communication as a means of assessing entertainment education in Africa: A case study of Yellow Card. Unpublished article available from: http://www.mfdi.net.

35 Ngenge, T. (2003, January). Sex, AIDS and videotape: Video as a tool in informing about HIV/AIDS among young people in rural Mozambique. Unpublished Manuscript, Malmo University: Unpublished manuscript available from: http://www.mfdi.

36 Ibid, p. 46.

37 Ibid, p. 50.

38 Soul Beat Africa – HIV/AIDS (2001). Impact data: It's not Easy film/video project. Available at http://comminit.com/hiv-aids-africa/node/298915

39 Kaiser Family Foundation (1995, September 1). The use of mainstream media to Encourage social responsibility: The international experience - Inventory of project – Advocates for Youth (pp. 125-127). Washington, DC: Henry J. Kaiser Family Foundation. Available at http://www.comminit.com/experiences/ pdsmay15/experiences-1740.html

40 Ibid, pp. 125-127.

41 Brown, W. J., Kiruswa, S. K, & Fraser, B. P. (2005). Promoting HIV/AIDS prevention through dramatic film: Responses from Eastern Africa. Eastern Africa Journal of Humanities and Sciences, 5(1), 1-20.

42 Englehard, L. (2003). Media activism in the screening room: The significance of viewing locations, facilitation and audience dynamics in the reception of HIV/AIDS films in South Africa. Visual Anthropology Review, 19, 73-85.

43 Ibid.

44 Ibid.

45 Malone, T. (1981). Toward a theory of intrinsically motivating instruction. Cognitive Science, 4, 333-369. Mahwah, NJ: Lawrence Erlbaum Associates.

46 Ibid.

47 Ibid.

48 Brown, W. J., & Meeks, J. D. (1998). Experimenting with the entertainment-education strategy in film and video: Prosocial media f Regent University. Journal of Film and Video, 49, 30-43.

49 Ibid.

50 Johns Hopkins University Center for Communication Programs. (2008). Projects. Available at http://www.jhuccp.org/programs.

51 Health Communication Partnership. (2006). South African HIV/AIDS serial drama helps decrease stigma and improve prevention behaviors among youth. Communication Impact, 20, pp. 1-2.

52 Center for Communication Programs (2012, August). Where we work, http://www.jhuccp.org/ (accessed 22 March 2011).

[All Notes]

Notes to Chapter 11

1 Wolf, M. J. (1999). The entertainment economy. New York, NY: Times Books.

2 Rogers, E. M. (1986). Communication technology: The New Media in Society. New York, NY: The Free Press, p. 10.

3 Dyer, R. (2002). Only entertainment (second edition). London, UK: Routledge, p 2.

4 Shefrin, E. (2004). Lord of the Rings, Star Wars, and participatory fandom: Mapping new congruencies between the internet and media entertainment culture. Critical Studies of Media Communication, 21(3), 261-281.

5 Gelm, R. J. (2008). How American politics works: Philosophy, pragmatism, personality and profit. Newcastle, UK: Cambridge Scholars Publishing, p. 93.

6 The Hollywood Reporter (2011, June 6). It's official: Katie Couric will host syndicated talk show at ABC. Available at http://www.hollywoodreporter.com/news/official-katie-couric-will-host-195032

7 Winch, S. P. (1997). Mapping the cultural space of journalism: How journalists distinguish news from entertainment. Westport, CT: Praeger.

8 Guskin, E., & Rosenstiel, T. (2012). The state of news media 2012. Pew Research Center. Available at http://stateofthemedia.org/2012/network-news-the-pace-of-change-accelerates/

9 NBC Universal (2011, December 31). NBC Universal Media LLC, 2011 Form 10-K, submitted to the U.S. Security and Exchange Commission. Available at http://apps.shareholder.com/sec/viewerContent.aspx?companyid=cmcsa&docid=8430852

10 Yalof, D., & Dautrich, K. (2005, January). Future of the First Amendment: What America's high school students think about their freedoms. Miami, FL: John S. and James L. Knight Foundation.

11 Feldman L., & Goldthwaite-Young, D. (2008). Late-night comedy as a gateway to traditional news. Political Communication, 25, 401–422.

12 Yadamsuren, B., & Erdelez, S. (2011). Online news reading behavior: From habitual reading to stumbling upon news. Proceedings of the American Society for Information Science and Technology, 48(1), 1-10.

13 Shenk, J. W. (1996, June). Star Struck. The Washington Monthly, pp. 12-18.

14 Boorstin, D. J. (1961). The image: A guide to pseudo-events in America. New York: Atheneum, p. 15.

15 Shenk (1996), op cit, p. 13.

16 Neimark, J. (1995, May). The culture of celebrities. Psychology Today, 28(3), pp. 54-57, 84, 87, 90.

17 Ibid, p. 57.

18 Wenger, D. H., & MacManus, S. A. (2009). Watching history: TV coverage of the 2008 campaign. Journalism Studies, 10, 427-435.

19 West, D. M., & Orman, J. M. (2003). Celebrity politics. New York, NY: Prentice-Hall, pp. 10-11.

20 Compton, J. (2004). The integrated news spectacle: A political economy of cultural performance. New York, NY: Peter Lang, pp. 15-15.

21 Weiskel, T. C. (2005). From sidekick to sideshow— Celebrity, entertainment, and the politics of distraction. American Behavioral Scientist, 49, 393-409.

22 Ibid.

23 Hachten, W. A. (2005). The troubles of journalism: A critical look at what's right and wrong with the press (3rd ed.) Mahwah, NJ: Lawrence Erlbaum, p. 176.

24 Ibid, pp. 14-29.

25 Mattson, K. (2003, Spring). The perils of Michael Moore. Dissent. Available at http://www.dissentmagazine.org/article/?article=510

26 McGinniss, Joe (1969). The selling of the president 1968. New York: Simon & Schuster.

27 Reagan Foundation. (2007). Ronald Reagan's biography. Available at http://www.reaganfoundation.org/reagan/biography/default.asp

28 Vaughn, S. (1994). Ronald Reagan in Hollywood: Movies and politics. Cambridge, UK: Cambridge University Press, p. xi.

29 Ibid.

30 US News & World Report (2007, November 19). America's best leaders – 2007. Available at http://www.usnews.com/usnews/pr/fact_sheets/07-abl_honoreebios.htm

31 Brown, W. J., & Fraser, B. P. (2004). Turning celebrity capital into political influence: Lessons from Schwarzenegger's gubernatorial election in California. Competitive paper presented to the Political Communication Division at the 54th Annual Conference of the International Communication Association, May 27-31, New Orleans.

32 College Football Hall of Fame. (1993). Lynn Swann. Available at http://www.collegefootball.org/famer_selected.php?id=70012

33 Pro Football Hall of Fame. (2001). Lynn Swann. Available at http://www.profootballhof.com/hof/member.aspx?PlayerId=208

34 Lynn Swann (2001). Biographical information. Available at http://www.lynnswann.com/BiographicalInformation.htm

35 TV Guide (2012). Lynn Swann: Credits. Available at: http://www.tvguide.com/celebrities/lynn-swann/credits/254208

36 Worden, A. (October 29, 2006). Lynn Swann: With star power and a storied life of successes, he makes first electoral bid. Philly.com. Available at: http://www.philly.com/mld/ inquirer/news/special_packages/pa_voters/15873264.htm, par. 7.

37 Barnes, T. (2006 August 17). Poll shows Rendell holding big lead in race for governor. [Electronic Version]. Pittsburgh Post Gazette, p. B1.

38 Ibid.

39 Ibid.

40 O'Neill, B. (2006, February 9). Can Swann be a big-play governor? [Electronic Version] The Pittsburgh Post-Gazette, p. A2.

41 Swann: NFL hall of famer charms crowds. (2006, June 8). USA Today, p. A7.

42 Will, G. F. (2006 June 24). Swann's uphill battle in the Pennsylvania governor's race, celebrity intensity may not be enough [Electronic version]. The Pittsburgh Post Gazette, p. B7.

43 Mauriello, T. (2006, October 17). Ad watch: Swann's campaign ad doesn't quite do opponent justice. Pittsburgh Post-Gazette. Available at: http://www.postgazette.com/pg/06293/ 731649293.stm

44 Ibid, p. A14.

45 Barnes (2006), p. A1.

46 Ibid.

47 Brandt, E. (2006, October 15). Swann: A new face everybody recognizes. Pottstown Mercury. Available from: http://www.pottstownmercury.com/site/index.cfm?newsid=17329592&BRD=1674&PAG=461&dept_id=18041&rfi=8, par. 4.

48 Griffith, R. (2006 November 3). Former Steelers star Swann an underdog in Pa. governor's race. The Johnston Tribune-Democrat. Available from: http://www.sapulpadailyherald.com/sports/cnhinsprosports_story_307103714.html?keyword=topstory,par. 7.

49 2006 Inquirer Endorsements. (2006 November 5). Centre Daily Times. Available at: http://www.centredaily.com/mld/centredaily/news/opinion/15930387.htm, par. 9.

50 Ibid, p. 3.

51 Race, M. (2006 November 5). Teflon ed' connects with state's voters. The Times-Tribune. Available from http://www.thetimes-tribune.com/site/news.cfm?newsid=17424251&BRD=2185&PAG=461&dept_id=416046&rfi=6, par. 22.

52 Micek, J. L. (2006 November 9). For Lynn Swann, it was 4th and long from the get-go. Morning Call Online. Available from http://www.mcall.com/sports/football/all-a3_5swannnov09,0,2369886.story?coll=all-sportsmorefootball-hed, par.7.

53 Brown, N. (2006 October 30). Rendell, Swann campaign in Philadelphia. CBS3. Available from http://cbs3.com/topstories/local_story_303162756.html, par. 2.

54 Hanif, C. B. (2006 November 12). 2006 not year of the Black Republican. Palm Beach Post. Available from: http://www.palmbeachpost.com/opinion/content/opinion/epaper/2006/11/12/a2e_hanifcol_1112.html, par. 5.

55 Barnes, T. (2006, August 17). Poll shows Rendell holding big lead in race for governor [Electronic Version]. Pittsburgh Post Gazette, p. B1.

56 Smith, S. (2006, October 28). Will Swann bank on ads or put stock in turnout? The Patriot-News. Available from http://www.pennlive.com/news/patriotnews/index.ssf?/base/news/1162004119322430.xml&coll=1, par. 12.

57 Race, M. (2006, November 5). Swann wants chance to get things done. Scranton Times-Tribune. Available from http://www.thetimes-tribune.com/site/news.cfm?newsid=17424252&BRD=2185&PAG=461&dept_id=416046&rfi=6, par. 9.

58 Ruibal, S. (October 31, 2006). EX-NFL players Swann, Shuler seek comebacks as political stars. USA Today. Available from http://www.usatoday.com/sports/football/nfl/2006-10-31-election-cover_x.htm?POE=SPOISVA, par. 11.

59 Campbell, D. (2007). Celebrityhood by achievement: An assessment of Lynn Swann's 2006 gubernatorial campaign. Unpublished paper. Virginia Beach, VA: Regent University.

60 Mauriello (2006), par. 12.

61 Roddy, D. B. (2006 November 8). Why speedy Swann slowed down so fast. Pittsburgh Post-Gazette. Available from http://www.post-gazette.com/pg/06312/736514-178.stm, par. 27.

62 Ibid, par. 29.

63 Casey's lead slim in region. (2006 October 20). The Tribune-Democrat. Available from: http://www.tribune-democrat.com/local/local_story_293231559.html, par. 16.

64 Langer, E. J., Blank, A., & Chanowitz, B. (1978). The mindlessness of ostensibly thoughtful action: The role of "placebic" information in interpersonal interaction. Journal of Personality and Social Psychology, 36, 635-642.

65 Cialdini, R. A. (2001). Influence: Science and practice. (4th). Boston: Allyn and Bacon, p. 7.

66 Warner, B. (November 7, 2006). Today the voters will have their say: Governor, senate, house & local races wind up. Philly.com. Available from http://www.philly.com/mld/dailynews/news/local/15947702.htm, par. 14.

67 Pease, A., & Brewer, P. R. (2008). The Oprah factor: The effects of a celebrity endorsement in a presidential primary campaign. Harvard International Journal of Press/Politics, 13, 386-400.

68 Nownes, A. J. (2012). An experimental investigation of the effects of celebrity support for political parties in the United States. American Politics Research, 40, 476-500.

[All Notes]

Notes to Chapter 12

1 Wiebe, G. D. (1952). Merchandizing commodities and citizenship on television. Public Opinion Quarterly, 15, 679-691.

2 Kotler, P., & Zaltman, G. (1971). Social marketing: An approach to planned social change. Journal of Marketing, 35(3), 3-12.

3 see Goldberg, M. E., Middlestadt, S. E., & Fishbein, M (1997). Social marketing: Theoretical and practical perspectives. Mahweh, NJ: Lawrence Erlbaum Associates; Ewing, M. T. (Ed) (2001). Social marketing. New York: The Haworth Press, Inc.; and Kotler, P., Lee, N. R., & Roberto, N. L. (2002). Social Marketing: Improving the quality of life (second edition). Thousand Oaks, CA: Sage Publications, Inc.

4 The Diana, Princess of Wales Memorial Fund. (2007). The work continues, http://www.theworkcontinues. org/about.shtml (accessed 17 May 2007).

5 Ibid.

6 Evanski, J., Bocarnea, M. C., Rowe, J. B., & Fraser, B. P. (1998). Responding to the death of Mother Teresa: Involvement across cross-cultural boundaries. Paper presented to the National Communication Association and the International Communication Association joint summer conference, July 15-18, Consiglio Nazionale delle Ricerche, Rome, Italy.

7 Diana forever (1997). The humanitarian princess, http://www.dianaforever.com/ human.htm (accessed 23 August 2012).

8 The Diana, Princess of Wales Memorial Fund, op. cit.

9 Ibid.

10 The Speech Site. (1997, June 12). Responding to landmines: A modern tragedy and its consequences, http://thespeechsite.com/en/famous/Diana-1.shtml (accessed 23 August 2012).

11 National AIDS Trust (2007). How you can help, http://www.nat.org.uk/How-You-Can-Help/Events/Diana-Princess-of-Wales-Lecture (accessed 17 May 2007).

12 Obits Tribute: Princess Diana (2007). Princess Diana, http://obits.eons.com/tribute/gallery/2459?section=princess-diana-section&category=princess-diana (accessed 17 May 2007).

13 Time (1998, February 2). Touched by Diana, http://www.time.com/time/daily/special/diana/readingroom/sept9798/9.html (accessed 17May 2007).

14 The Diana, Princess of Wales Memorial Fund, op. cit.

15 Concert for Diana (2007, July 1). http://www.concertfordiana.com/home/ (accessed 17May 2007).

16 Honeyman, A. (2006, December 12). The Diana, Princess of Wales Memorial Fund, op. cit.

17 Prince Harry (2006). Charities and patronages: Centebale, http://www.princeofwales.gov.uk/personalprofiles/princeharry/atwork/charitiesandpatronages/ (accessed 23 August 2012).

18 Curiel, J. (2005, June 5). Star power: When celebrities support causes, who really winds upbenefiting? San Francisco Chronicle, http://www.sfgate.com/cgi-bin/article.cgi?f=/c/a/2005/06/05/ING9QD1FIE1.DTL (accessed 10 June 2006).

19 Associated Press (2008, September 2). Jerry Lewis Telethon Raises Record $65 Million for Muscular Dystrophy Association. FOX News.com, http://www.foxnews.com/story/0,2933,414781,00.html#ixzz24OuiBacE (accessed 23 August 2012).

20 Lee, C. (2010, September 3). Lighting it up. Los Angeles Times, http://articles.latimes.com/2010/sep/03/entertainment/la-et-0903-jerry-lewis-20100903 (accessed 23 August 2012).

21 Time Specials (2005). Persons of the year 2005: Bill Gates, Melinda Gates and Bono: Three people on a global mission to end poverty, disease — and indifference, http://www.time.com/time/specials/packages/article/0,28804,2016788_2016757,00.html (accessed 20 August 2012).

22 UNHCR (2005, October 13). Goodwill ambassador Angelina Jolie accepts global humanitarian award, http://www.unhcr.org/cgi-bin/texis/vtx/search?page=search&docid=434e17b84&query=jolie (accessed 10 June 2012).

23 Ibid.

24 Walker, C. (2005, November 22). U.S. entertainment industry notables work for social causes. Washington File, http://news.findlaw.com/wash/s/20051122/20051122134618.html (accessed 23 August 2012).

25 Bell, D. (2012, August). Celebrities who have testified to Congress. U.S. News& World Report, http://www.usnews.com/news/slideshows/celebrities-who-have-testified-to-congress (accessed 23 August 2012).

[All Notes]

Notes to Chapter 13

1 Owyang, J. (2008, January 9). Social network stats: Facebook, My Space, Reunion,http://www.web-strategist.com/blog/2008/01/09/social-network-stats-facebook-myspace-reunion-jan-2008/ (accessed 22 August 2012).

2 Nakashima, R. (2011, August 11). News Corp stock up after earnings report. USA Today,http://searchenginewatch.com/article/2167518/Worldwide-Social-Media-Usage-Trends-in-2012.

3 Arno, C. (2012, April 13). Worldwide social media usage trends in 2012. Search Engine Watch, http://searchenginewatch.com/article/2167518/Worldwide-Social-Media-Usage-Trends-in-2012 (accessed 23 August 2012).

4 McDaniel, T. (2010, September 16). First day sales for Halo Reach beyond $210 million. Javid, C. (2004, August 2). Video games as effective health-care training. Paper presented at the Games for Health Conference, Wisconsin.

5 MC Marketing Charts (2007, June). Club Penguin, snatched by Disney, grew 329 percent in past year, http://www.marketingcharts.com/interactive/club-penguin-snatched-by-disney-grew-329-in-past-year-1178/hitwise-club-penguin-share-virtual-world-visitsjpg/ (accessed 1 September 2012).

6 Bloomberg Businessweek Magazine. (2007, March 25). The new avatar in town, http://bwads.businessweek.com/stories/2007-03-25/the-new-avatar-in-town (accessed 1 September 2012).

7 Ibid.

8 Virtual World News. (2007, August 1). Disney acquires Club Penguin for $700 million. Retrieved August 14, 2008, from http://www.virtualworldsnews.com/2007/08/disney-acquires.html. (accessed 25August 2007).

9 Moore, E. S. (2006). It's child's play: Advergaming and the online marketing of food to children. Menlo Park, CA: Kaiser Family Foundation, http://www.kff.org/entmedia/upload/ 7536.pdf. (accessed 17 April 2007).

10 Ibid.

11 Schultz, D. E., Block, M., & Raman, K. (2009). Media synergy comes of age — Part I Journal of Direct, Data and Digital Marketing Practice,11, 3-19. doi:10.1057/dddmp.2009.13

12 Pilotta, J. J., Schultz, D. E., Drenik, G. & Rist, P. (2004). Simultaneous media usage: A critical consumer orientation to media planning. Journal of Consumer Behaviour, 3, 285-292.

13 Barnes, S. B. (2002, June). Media ecology and symbolic interactionism. Paper presented at the annual convention of the Media Ecology Association, Marymount Manhattan College, New York, NY.

14 Wang, A. (2007). Branding over mobile and internet advertising: the cross-media effect. International Journal of Mobile Marketing, 2, 34-42.

15 Looi, C. K. (2001). Enhancing learning ecology on the Internet. Journal of Computer Assisted Learning, 17 (1), 13–20.

16 Reardon, K. K., & Rogers, E. M. (1988). Interpersonal versus mass media communication: A false dichotomy. Human Communication Research, 15, 284-303.

17 Singer, J. B. (1998). Online journalists: Foundations for research into their changing roles. Journal of Computer Mediated Communication, 4 (1), http://onlinelibrary.wiley.com/doi/ 10.1111/j.1083-6101.1998.tb00088.x/full (accessed 1 September 2012).

18 Coleman, J. S., Livingston, S. A., Fennessey, G. M., Edwards, K. J., & Kidder, S. J. (1973). The Hopkins games program: Conclusions from seven years of research. Educational Researcher, 2, (8), 3-7.

19 Mann, B. D, Eidelsonb, B. M., Fukuchi, S. G., Nissman, S. A., Robertson, S., & Jardines, L. (2002). The development of an interactive game-based tool for learning surgical management algorithms via computer. The American Journal of Surgery, 183, 305–308.

20 Tonks, S. A. (1997). A framework for understanding learning from management simulations. Journal of Computer Assisted Learning, 13 (1), 48–58

21 Braithwaite, J., & Westbrook, J. I. (2001). The health care game: An evaluation of a heuristic, web-based simulation. Journal of Interactive Learning Research, 12, 89-104.

22 Antonellis, I., Bouras, C., Kapoulas, V., & Poulopoulos, V. (2005). Design and implementation of a game-based learning-related community. IADIS International Conference Web Based Communities, Algarve, Portugal, http://www.iadis.net/dl/final_uploads/200502L024.pdf (accessed 1 September 2012).

23 MacLachlan, M., Chimombo, M., & Mpemba, N. (1997). AIDS education for youth through active learning: A school-based approach from Malawi. International Journal of Educational Development, 17(1), 41-50.

24 Hawkins, R. P., Gustafson, D. H., Chewning, K. B., & Day, P. M. (1987). Reaching hard-to-reach populations: interactive computer programs as public information campaigns for adolescents. Journal of Communication, 3, 8-28.

25 Child Trends Data Bank (2012, July). Home computer access and internet use, http://www.childtrendsdatabank.org/?q=node/105 (accessed 1 September 2012).

26 Moore, E. S. (2006, July). It's child's play: Advergaming and the online marketing of food to children. Menlo Park, CA: The Henry J. Kaiser Foundation, http://www.kff.org/entmedia/upload/7536.pdf. (accessed 1 September 2012).

27 Wollslager, M. E. (2007). Children's awareness of online advertising on Neopets: The effect of media literacy training on recall. Unpublished paper. Virginia Beach, VA: Regent University.

28 NeoPets, I. (2006). Neopets' press kit, http://info.neopets.com/presskit (accessed 15 April 2007).

29 Oser, K., & Klaassen, A. (2005). MTV networks' pet project likely to pay off. Advertising Age, 76(26), 52.

30 Wollslager, M. E. (2009). Children's awareness of online advertising on Neopets: The effect of media literacy training on recall. Studies in Media & Information Literacy Education 9(2), 31-53.

31 Ibid

32 Wollslager, 2007, op. cit.

33 Keller, S. N., Labelle, H., Karimi, N., & Gupta, S. (2004). Talking about STD/HIV prevention: a look at communication online. AIDS Care, 16(8), 977-992.

34 Mohammed, S. N., & Thombre, A. (2005). HIV/AIDS stories on the world wide web and transformation perspective. Journal of Health Communication, 10, 347 – 360.

35 Ibid

36 Nardi, B. A., Schiano, D. J., Gumbrecht, M., & Swartz, L. (2004, December). The blogosphere. Communications of the ACM, 47(12), 41-46.

37 Li, D. (2005). Why do you blog: A uses and gratifications inquiry into bloggers' motivations? Unpublished master's thesis. Milwaukee, WI: Marquette University.

38 Ibid

39 Livingstone, S., & Bober, M. (2003). UK children go online: Listening to young people's experiences [online]. London: LSE Research Online, http://eprints.lse.ac.uk/archive/0000388 (accessed 10 June 2011).

40 Ibid

41 Bae, H. S., & Lee, B. (2004). Audience involvement and its antecedents: An analysis of the electronic bulletin board messages about an entertainment-education drama on divorce in Korea. Asian Journal of Communication, 14, 6-21.

42 Peters, T. J. (1997). A skunkworks tale. In R. Katz (Ed.), The human side of managing technological innovation (pp. 347-355). New York: Oxford University Press.

43 Vorderer, P., Bryant, J. (eds). (2006). Playing video games: Motives, responsibilities, and consequences. Mahwah, NJ: Erlbaum.

44 Malone, T. (1981). Toward a theory of intrinsically motivating instruction. Cognitive Science, 4, 333-369.

45 Ibid

46 Ibid

47 Javid, C. (2004, September 24). Video games promoted as effective health-care training. Games for Health Conference. Wisconsin Technology Network, http://wistechnology.com/printarticle.php?id=1193. (accessed 16 October 2011).

48 See http://www.seriousgamesummit.com

49 See http://www.virtualorchestra.com/Pages/Education.html

50 Kelsey, J., Taylor, H., Bell, C., Davis, D., & Stewart, K. II (2006, October 30). Presentation to the Serious Games Summit, Washington, DC.

51 White, D. (2006, October 31). Charting the depths: Building a next generation science game. Presentation to the Serious Games Summit, Washington, DC.

52 Barab, S. (2006, October 31). Designing and re-designing academic play spaces to support science learning. Presentation to the Serious Games Summit, Washington, DC.

53 Ibid

54 Roper, M. (2006, October 31). Discover Babylon: What works (and doesn't!) for informal learning. Presentation to the Serious Games Summit, Washington, DC.

55 Losh, E. (2006, October 31). On the Ground with Tactical Iraqi. Presentation to the Serious Games Summit, Washington, DC.

56 Baird, W. (2004, November 7). Seeking edge, college hoop teams try a video game. USA Today, http://www.usatoday.com/tech/products/games/2004-11-07-training-tech_x.htm (accessed 10 August 2008).

57 Prensky, M. (2004). Digital game-based learning. New York, NY: McGraw-Hill Pub. Co.

58 Drotman, Doug. (2008). Fighter Pilot Training Helps Four Indiana High School Basketball Teams Have Historic Seasons. Reuters, http://www.reuters. com/article/press Release/idUS102643+01-May-2008+ PRN20080501?sp =true (accessed 10 August 2008).

59 Lieberman, D. A. (1997). Interactive video games for health promotion: Effects on knowledge, self-efficacy, social support and health. In R. L. Street, W. R. Gold, & T. Manning (Eds.), Health promotion and interactive technology: Theoretical applications and future directions (pp. 103-120). Mahwah, NJ: Lawrence Erlbaum Associates.

60 Barker, A. (2005, April 4). Study uses video games to fight obesity. USA Today, http://www.usatoday.com/news/nation/2005-04-02-obesity-video-game_x.htm (accessed 12 August 2008).

61 Ibid

62 Brown, Damon. (2006). Playing to win: Video games and the fight against obesity. Journal of the American Dietetic Association, 106(2), 188-189.

63 Ibid

64 Unnithan, V. B., Houser, W., & Rernhall, B. (2005). Evaluation of the energy cost of playing a dance simulation video game in overweight and non-overweight children and adolescents. International Journal of Sports Medicine, 26, 1-11.

65 Lieberman, 1997, op. cit.; Tan, B., Aziz, A. R., Chua, K., & The, K. C. (2002). Aerobic demands of the dance simulation game. International Journal of Sports Medicine, 23, 125-129.

66 Schott, G., & Hodgetts, D. (2006). Health and digital gaming. Journal of Health Psychology, 11, 309-316.

67 Gordon, D. (2005). Virtual reality pain distraction. American Pain Society Bulletin, 15(2) [online], http://www.ampainsoc.org/pub/bulletin/spr05/index.htm (accessed 10 August 2008); Dahlquist, L. A., Weiss, K. E., Clendaniel, L. D., Law, E. F, Ackerman, C. S., & McKenna, K. D. (2008, March 26). Effects of videogame distraction using a virtual reality type head-

mounted display helmet on cold pressor pain in children. Journal of Pediatric Psychology, 34, 574-584, doi:10.1093/jpepsy/jsn023

68 Melzack, R. (1990). The tragedy of needless pain. Scientific American, 262(2), 27–33.

69 Carrougher, G. J., Ptacek, J. T., Sharar, S. R, Wiechman, S., Honari, S., Patterson, D. R., et al. (2003). Comparison of patient satisfaction and self-reports of pain in adult burn-injured patients. Journal of Burn Care and Rehabilitation, 24(1), 1–8.

70 Cohen, L. L., MacLaren, J. E., & Lira, C. S. (2008). Pain and pain management. In R. G. Steele, T. D. Elkin, & M. C. Roberts (Eds.), Handbook of evidence-based therapies for children and adolescents: Bridging science and practice (pp. 283-295). New York, NY: Springer Science and Business Media.

71 Hoffman, H. G., Doctor, J. N., Patterson, D. R., Carrougher G. J., & Furness T. A., III. (2000). Use of virtual reality for adjunctive treatment of adolescent burn pain during wound care: A case report. Pain, 85(1–2), 305–309.

72 Das, D. A., Grimmer, K. A., Sparnon, A. L., McRae, S. E., & Thomas B. H. (2005, March 3). The efficacy of playing a virtual reality game in modulating pain for children with acute burn injuries: A randomized controlled trial. BMC Pediatrics, 5(1), http://www.biomedcentral.com/1471-2431/5/1 (accessed 10 August 2008); Hoffman, H. G., Patterson, D. R., Magula, J., Carrougher, G. J., Zeltzer, K., Dagadakis, S., et al. (2004). Water-friendly virtual reality pain control during wound care. Journal of Clinical Psychology, 60(2), 189–195; Hoffman, H. G., Patterson, D. R., Carrougher, G. J. (2000). Use of virtual reality for adjunctive treatment of adult burn pain during physical therapy: A controlled study. The Clinical Journal of Pain, 16(3), 244–250.

73 Hoffman, H. G., Garcia-Palacios, A., Patterson, D. R., Jensen, M., Furness, T. A., III, & Ammons, W. F., Jr. (2001). The effectiveness of virtual reality for dental pain control: A case study. Cyberpsychological Behavior, 4, 527–535.

74 Hoffman, H. G., Patterson, D. R., Carrougher, G. J., & Sharar, S. (2001, September). The effectiveness of virtual reality-based pain control with multiple treatments. The Clinical Journal of Pain, 17(3), 229–235.

75 Hoffman, H. G., Sharar, S. R., Coda, B., Everett, J. J., Ciol, M., Richards, T. L., et al. (2004). Manipulating presence influences the magnitude of virtual reality analgesia. Pain, 111(1–2), 162–168.

76 Dahlquist et al., 2008, op. cit.

77 Ibid

78 University of Connecticut (2008). Place-based marketing to prevent urban youth party drug use. Center for Health Communication and Marketing Projects, http://www.chcm.uconn.edu/research.html#proj2 (accessed 22August 2008).

79 Rapoza, D., & Urquhart, William E. (2003). US Patent 6561811 - Drug abuse prevention computer game. Entertainment Science, Inc, http://www.patentstorm.us/patents/6561811/description.html (accessed 22 August 2008).

80 Lieberman, 1997, op. cit.

[All Notes]

Notes to Chapter 14

1 Spencer, M. (2006). Two aspirins and a comedy: How television can enhance health and society. Boulder, Colorado: Paradigm Publishers.

2 Brown, K. D., & Hamilton-Giachritsis, C. (2005). The influence of violent media on children and adolescents: a public-health approach. The Lancet, 365(9460), 702-710 [online], http://dx.doi.org/10.1016/j.bbr.2011.03.031(accessed 3 September 2012).

3 Stack, S. (2000). Media Impacts on Suicide: A quantitative review of 293 findings. Social Science Quarterly, 81, 957-971.

4 Hurr, K. K., & Robinson, J. P. (1978) The social impact of "Roots." Journalism Quarterly, 55(1), 19-24, 83.

5 Ball-Rokeach, S., Grube, J. W., & Rokeach, M. (1981). “Roots: The Next Generation” – Who watched and with what effect? Public Opinion Quarterly, 45, 58-68. doi: 10.1086/268634

6 Shatzerab, M. J., Korzenny, F., & Griffis-Korzenny, B. A. (1985). Adolescents viewing Shogun: Cognitive and attitudinal effects. Journal of Broadcasting & Electronic Media, 29, 341-346.

7 Gunter, B. (1984). Television as a facilitator of good behavior amongst children. Journal of Moral Education, 13, 152-159, DOI: 10.1080/0305724840130302.

8 Lovelace, V., & Huston, A. C. (1983). Can television teach prosocial behaviour? In J. N. Sprafkin, C. Swift, & R. Hess (Eds.), Rx television: Enhancing the preventive impact of TV (pp. 93-106). New York: The Haworth Press.

9 Amato, P. P., & Malatesta. A. (1987). Effects of prosocial elements in family situation comedies. Paper presented to the 37th Annual Conference of the International Communication Association, Montreal.

10 Ball-Rokeach, S. J., Rokeach, M., & Grube, J. W. (1984). The great American values test: Influencing behavior and belief through television. New York: Free Press.

11 Perry, David K. (2002). Theory and research in mass communication: Contexts and consequences. Mahwah, NJ: Lawrence Erlbaum Associates, pp. 70-92.

12 Barna, G. (2007). Beliefs: General religious, http://www.barna.org/ FlexPage.aspx?Page=Topic&TopicID=2 (accessed 24 August 2008).

13 Barna, G. (2006). Born again Christians, http://www.barna.org/FlexPage.aspx?Page=Topic&TopicID=8 (accessed 24 August 2008).

14 PollingReport.com (2008). Religion, http://www.pollingreport.com/religion.htm (accessed 24August 2008).

15 Gallup, G. Jr., & Jones, T. (2000). The next American spirituality: Finding God in the twenty-first century. Colorado Springs: Cook.

16 Oldenburg, A. (1986, November 1). Hollywood immersed in a spiritual rebirth. USA Today, p. E-1.

17 Ibid.

18 Piper, D. P., Keeler, J., & Brown, W. J. (1997, April). Audience involvement with Touched by an Angel. Competitive paper presented to the 42nd annual convention of the Broadcast Education Association, Las Vegas.

19 Buddenbaum, J. M., & Stout, D. A. (Eds.). (1996). Religion and mass media. Thousand Oaks, CA: Sage Publications.

20 Abelman, R. (1987). Religious television uses and gratifications. Communication Quarterly, 31, 293-307.

21 Gerbner, G., Gross, L., Hoover, S., Morgan, M., & Signorielli, N. (1984). Religion and television. Philadelphia: University of Pennsylvania Press.

22 Brown, W. J., & Fraser, B. P. (1993, October). A comparative analysis of the uses and impact of daytime television talk shows on religious television viewers. Competitive paper presented to the Annual Conference of the Society for the Scientific Study of Religion, Raleigh, N.C.

23 Moll. R. (2004). Jesus is back in style. Christianity Today Library, http://www.ctlibrary.com (accessed 16 September 2004), p. 2.

24 Piper et al., 1997, op.cit.

25 Shalit, R. (1998, July 27). Quality wings: Angels on television, angels in America. New Republic, 24-31.

26 Billingsley, K. L. (1989). The seductive image: A Christian critique of the world of film. Westchester, IL: Crossway Books; Rothman, S., & Lichter, R. S. (1984). What are moviemakers made of? Public Opinion Quarterly, 48, 14-18.

27 Smith, S. (1996, April). Heaven-sent. Aspire, 27-32.

28 Kaminer, W. (1997, Winter). Touched in the head by an angel. Free Inquiry, 7-9.

29 Smith, 1996, op. cit.

30 Brill, S. (1995, November 13). Touched by an Angel. Christianity Today, 65.

31 Sharley, B. (1995, December 11). 'Angel' earns its wings. Mediaweek, 5, 20.

32 Smith, 1996, op. cit.

33 Rice, L. (1997, February 24). Heaven Can't Wait. Broadcasting & Cable, 26-31.

34 Lipton, M. A. (1999, February 22). Heaven help us! Lifting hearts, saving Lives. People Magazine, 51(7), 86-92.

35 Piper et al., 1997, op. cit.

36 Ibid.

37 Ibid.

38 Hartenstein, M. (2004, September 16). Epic survey of Jesus movies. Cornerstone Festival Newsletter, http://www.flickerings.com/2004/films/jesusmovies/index.htm (accessed 16 September 2004).

39 Kinnard, R., & Davis, T. (1992). Divine images: A history of Jesus on the screen. New York: Citadel.

40 Butler, I. (1969). Religion in the Cinema. New York: A. S. Barnes.

41 May, L. (1980). Screening out the past: The birth of mass culture and the motion picture industry. New York: Oxford University Press.

42 Lindvall, T. R. (2004). Religion and film: Part 1: History and criticism. Communication Research Trends, 23(4), 3-43.

43 Musser, C., & Nelson, C. (1991). High-class moving pictures: Lyman H. Howe and the forgotten era of traveling exhibition, 1880-1920. Princeton, NJ: Princeton University Press.

44 Musser, C. (1993). Passions and the Passion Play: The theatre, film and religion in America, 1880-1900. Film History, 5, 419-456.

45 Burrows, J. (2003). Legitimate cinema. Exeter, UK: University of Exeter Press.

46 Sloan, K. (1988). The loud silents: Origins of the social problem film. Urbana, IL: University of Illinois Press.

47 Ross, S. J. (1998). Working class Hollywood: Silent film and the shaping of class in America. Princeton: Princeton University Press.

48 Waller, G. A. (1995). Main street amusements: Movies and commercial entertainment in a Southern City, 1896-1930. Washington, DC: Smithsonian Institute Press.

49 Fuller, K. H. (1996). At the picture show: Small-town audiences and the creation of movie fan culture. Washington D. C.: Smithsonian Institution Press.

50 Holloway, R. (1977). Beyond the image. Geneva: World Council of Churches.

51 Lindvall, T., & Quicke, A. (2011). Celluloid sermons: The emergence of the Christian film industry, 1930-1986. New York, NY: New York University Press.

52 Lindvall, 2004, p. 5.

53 Lindvall and Quicke, 2011, p. xi.

54 Kahle, R., & Lee, R. E. A. (1971). Popcorn and parable: A new look at the movies. Minneapolis: Augsburg.

55 Konzelman, R. G. (1972). Marquee ministry: The movie theater as church and community forum. New York: Harper and Row.

56 Williams, P. W. (1980). Popular religion in America: Symbolic change and the modernization process in historical perspective. Englewood Cliffs: Prentice Hall.

57 Ostwalt, C. E. Jr. (1995). Conclusion: Religion, film, and cultural analysis. In J. W. Martin & C. E. Ostwalt, Jr. (Eds.), Screening the Sacred: Religio, myth, and ideology in popular American film (pp. 152-159). Boulder, CO: Westview.

58 Johnston, R.K. (2000). Reel Spirituality: Theology and Film in Dialogue. Grand Rapids, MI: Baker Book House.

59 Aichele, G., & Walsh, R. (2002). Screening Scripture: Intertextual connections between Scripture and film. Harrisburg, PA: Trinity Press.

60 Coates, P. (2002). Cinema, religion and the romantic legacy: Through a glass darkly. Aldershot, UK: Ashgate Publishing.

61 Kreitzer, L. J. (1993). The New Testament in fiction and film. Sheffield, UK: Sheffield Academic Press; Kreitzer, L. J. (1994). The Old Testament in fiction and film. Sheffield, UK: Sheffield Academic Press; Kreitzer, L. J. (1999). Pauline images in fiction and film. Sheffield, UK: Sheffield Academic Press.

62 Campbell, M. H., & Pitts, M. R. (1981). The Bible on film: A Checklist, 1897-1980. Metuchen, NJ: Scarecrow Press.

63 Forshey, G. (1992). American religious and Biblical spectaculars. Westport, CT: Praeger; Forshey, G. (1980, April 30). Popular religion, film and the American psyche. Christian Century, 30, 489-493.

64 Malone, P. (1990). Movie Christs and antichrists. New York: Crossroad.

65 Babington, B., & Evans, P. W. (1993). Biblical epics: Sacred narrative in the Hollywood cinema. New York: Manchester University Press.

66 Tatum, W. B. (1997). Jesus at the movies: A Guide to the first hundred years. Santa Rosa, CA: Polebridge.

67 Walsh, R. (2003). Reading the Gospels in the Dark: Portrayals of Jesus in Films. Trinity Press International.

68 Mikkelson, D. K., & Gregg, A. C. (2001). King of kings: A silver screen Gospel. New York: University Press of America.

69 Ibid.

70 Box Office Mojo (2004, August). The Passion of the Christ daily box office, http://www.boxofficemojo.com/movies/?page=main&id= passionofthechrist.htm (accessed 29 November 2005).

71 Barna, G. (2004, July 10). New survey examines the impact of Gibson's "Passion" movie, http://www.barna.org/FlexPage.aspx?Page=BarnaUpdateNarrow&BarnaUpdateID =167 (accessed 29 November 2005).

72 Hollywood Reporter (2004, March 17). Hollywood Reporter's box office.

73 Schihl, R. (2004, August 24). Personal communication. Virginia Beach, VA: Regent University.

74 Brown, W. J., Keeler, J. D., Lindvall, T. R. (2007). Audience responses to the Passion of the Christ. Journal of Media & Religion, 6, 87-107.

75 Ibid.

76 Ibid.

77 Barna, 2004, op. cit.

78 Box Office Mojo, 2004, op. cit.

79 Barna, 2004, op. cit.

80 Johnston, 2000, op. cit.

81 The Jesus Film Project. (2005, October 1), http://www.jesusfilm.org/progress/statistics.html (accessed 11October 2004).

82 CBN (2008). Sylvester Stallone on faith, integrity, and Rocky Balboa. The 700 Club, http://www.cbn.com/700club/guests/bios/ Sylvester_Stallone121906.aspx (accessed 18 September 2008).

83 Ibid.

84 Hurtado, D., & Brown, W. J. (2012). Exploring audience involvement in a transmedia enterprise: Lewis' Chronicles of Narnia. Paper presented to the National Communication Association, November 14-17. Orlando, Florida.

85 Lewis, C. S. (2000). Sometimes fairy stories may say best what's to be said. In L. Walmsley (Ed.), Essay collection and other short pieces (pp. 526-528).London: Harper Collins; Hooper, W. (2007). Past watchful dragons: The origin, interpretation, and appreciation of the Chronicles of Narnia. Eugene, OR: Wipf and Stock Publishers, p. 527.

86 Fraser, B. P., & Brown, W. J. (2011). C. S. Lewis and Flannery O'Connor's contribution to the art of indirect communication. Paper presented to the Annual Meeting of the Religious Communication Association, November 14-15, New Orleans.

87 Starr, C. W. (2010). Aesthetics vs. anesthesia: C.S. Lewis on the purpose of art. Inklings Forever, Volume VII: A Collection of Essays Presented at the Seventh Frances White Colloquium on C.S. Lewis & Friends. Upland, IN: Taylor University. Retrieved from http://library.taylor.edu/dotAsset/e0530ce0-be3c-4980-ba6a-c3ed39e810b3.pdf

88 Project Light (2008), http://www.projectlight.org/ (accessed 10 October 2008).

89 The Christian Arsenal (2008), http://www.christianarsenal.com/Christian_Arsenal/Home.html (accessed 3 September 2012).

90 Movie Ministry (2012), http://www.movieministry.com/ (accessed 3 September 2012).

[All Notes]

Notes to Chapter 15

1 Plato (380 B.C.). The Republic, Book 2, 377, http://nlp.perseus.tufts.edu/hopper/text?doc=Perseus%3Atext%3A1999.01.0168%3Abook%3D2%3Apage%3D377 (accessed 3 September 2012).

2 Plato (380 B.C.). Extracts from Plato, Republic, trans. Francis Cornford (Oxford: Oxford University Press, 1941, pp. 68–72, 74–80, 324–40), http://www.blackwellpublishing.com/content/BPL_Images/Content_store/Sample_chapter/9781405112086/John_001.pdf (accessed 3 September 2012).

3 Bible Gateway.com (2011). Proverbs, chapter 12, verse 7, http://www.biblegateway.com/ (accessed 10 October 2010).

4 Poe, H. L. (2001). Christian witness in a postmodern world. Nashville: Abingdon, p. 48.

5 Crane, D. (1992). The production of culture: Media and the urban arts. Newbury Park: Sage, pp. 19-22.

6 Stanton, F. (1961). Parallel paths. In N. Jacobs (Ed.), Culture for the millions: Mass media in modern society (pp. 85-91). Princeton: D. Van Nostrand Co.

7 Cawelti, J. G. (1976). Adventure, mystery and romance. Chicago: University of Chicago Press, pp 1-6.

8 Gerbner, G., Gross, L., Morgan, M., & Signorelli, N. (1994). Growing up with television: The cultivation prospective. In J. Bryant & D. Zillman (Eds.), Media effects: Advances in theory and research (pp. 17-41). Hillsdale, NJ: Erlbaum.

9 Cawelti, 1976, p.1.

10 McGuinn, D. (2002, November 11). Guilt free TV. Newsweek, 140, 52-59.

11 Kaiser Family Foundation (2000, March 2). Media use, http://www.mediaandthefamily.org/facts_mediause.shtml (Accessed 14 October 2002).

12 Weitz, A. (1999, November 17). New study finds kids spend equivalent of full work week using media, http://www.kff.org/content/1999/1535/pressreleasefinal.doc.html (accessed 14 October 2002).

13 US kids choose Internet over other media (April 2002), http://www.nua.ie/surveys/index.dgi?f=VS&art_id=905357821&rel=true (accessed 21 October 2002).

14 Kaiser Family Foundation, 2000, op. cit.

15 Perloff, R. M. (1997). Social effects: Children and the mass media. In L.W. Jeffres R.M. Perloff (Eds.), Mass media effects (pp. 175-204). (2nd ed.). Prospect Heights, IL: Waveland.

16 Huston, A.C., Donnerstein, E., Fairchild, H., Feshbach, N.D., Katz, P.A., Murray, J.P., Rubinstein, E.A., Wilcox, B.L., and Zuckerman, D. (1992). Big world, small screen: The role of television in American society. Lincoln, NE: University of Nebraska Press.

17 Perloff, 1997, p. 177.

18 Ibid, pp. 178-180.

19 Huston, A.C. & Wright, J.C. (1983). Children's processing of television: The informative functions of formal features. In J. Bryant & D.R. Anderson (Eds.), Children's understanding of television: Research on attention and comprehension (pp. 35-68). New York: Academic Press.

20 Wright, J.C., Kunkel, D., Pinon, M., and Huston, A.C. (1989). Children's affective and cognitive reactions to televised coverage of the space shuttle disaster. Journal of Communication, 39(2), 27-45.

21 Perloff, 1997, p. 181.

22 Salomon, G. (1983). Television watching and mental effort: A social psychological view. In J. Bryant and D.R. Anderson (Eds), Children's understanding of television: Research on attention and comprehension (pp. 99-110). New York: Academic Press.

23 Huston et al., 1992, p. 94.

24 Strasburger, V.C. & Wilson, B.J. (2002). Children, adolescents, and the media. Thousand Oaks, CA: Sage.

25 Strasburger & Wilson, 2002, pp. 34-61.

26 McGuinn, D. (2002, November 11). Guilt free TV. Newsweek, 140, 52-59.

27 Warren, M. (1997). Seeing through the media: A religious view of communications and cultural analysis. Harrisburg, PA: Trinity, pp. 18-21.

28 Strasburger, V.C. & Donnerstein, E. (1999). Children, adolescents and the media: Issues and solutions. Pediatrics, 103(1), 129; Nathanson, A.I. (2001). Parent and child perspectives on the presence and meaning of parental television mediation. Journal of Broadcasting & Electronic Media, 45(2), 260-275.

29 Jones, S. (2012, August 30). Condoleezza Rice: Failing schools are 'the civil rights struggle of our day.' CNSNews.com [online], http://cnsnews.com/news/article/condoleezza-rice-failing-schools-are-civil-rights-struggle-our-day (accessed 3 September 2012).

30 Fisher, W. (1987). Human communication as narration: Toward a philosophy of reason, value and action. Columbia, SC: University of South Carolina Press, p. 6.

[All Notes]

Sweeter than Honey Index

Skip to [A] [B] [C] [D] [E] [F] [G] [H] [I] [J] [K] [L] [M] [N] [O] [P] [Q] [R] [S] [T] [U] [V] [W] [X] [Y] [Z]

A

[Back to Index Navigation]

B

[Back to Index Navigation]

C

[Back to Index Navigation]

D

[Back to Index Navigation]

E

F

G

[Back to Index Navigation]

H

I

J

K

L

[Back to Index Navigation]

M

N

O

P

[Back to Index Navigation]

Q

[Back to Index Navigation]

R

[Back to Index Navigation]

S

[Back to Index Navigation]

T

[Back to Index Navigation]

U

[Back to Index Navigation]

V

W

X

[Back to Index Navigation]

Y

[Back to Index Navigation]

Z

[Back to Index Navigation]

www.ingramcontent.com/pod-product-compliance
Lightning Source LLC
LaVergne TN
LVHW061202120826
845149LV00011B/1877
9780986049552